Ge

Creative Deviations

How you can infuse your storytelling, fundraising and direct response with more creativity.

John Lepp

civil sector press

Creative Deviations: How you can infuse your storytelling, fundraising and direct response with more creativity

Library and Archives Canada Cataloguing in Publication
Title: Creative Deviations: How you can infuse your storytelling, fundraising and direct response with more creativity / John Lepp.

Names: Lepp, John, author.

Identifiers: Canadiana (print) 20220188505 | Canadiana (ebook) 20220188599 |
ISBN 9781927375815

(softcover) | ISBN 9781927375822 (HTML)

Subjects: LCSH: Fund raising—Handbooks, manuals, etc. | LCSH: Creative ability in business.

Classification: LCC HV41.2 .L47 2022 | DDC 361.7068/1—dc23

Publisher: Civil Sector Press
Canada
Box 86, Station C, Toronto, Ontario, M6J 3M7 Canada
Telephone: 416.267.1287
www.charityinfo.ca
United States of America
2626 Glenway Ave, Cincinnati, OH 45204 USA
Telephone: 513.471.6622

Editor: Lisa MacDonald and Rachel Zant
Book design and production: John Lepp and Lindsey Jacobs

We acknowledge that the land where we live and work is the traditional territory of many nations from across Turtle Island, and is covered by the *Dish With One Spoon Wampum Belt Covenant*, an agreement between the Haudenosaunee and the Ojibway and allied nations, including the Mississaugas, the Anishnabeg, the Chippewa, and the Wendat peoples to peaceably share and care for the lands around the Great Lakes. This land today is home to many diverse First Nations, Inuit, and Métis peoples. We honor and thank them for their stewardship of these lands, and stand committed to be partners in truth-seeking, healing, reconciliation, and justice for all.

This paper consists of 100% post-consumer fibres. It was manufactured using Biogas renewable energy and was processed chlorine-free in Canada. This paper is both FSC and Ancient Forest Friendly™ certified.

Dedication

Tara, Evan and Julia who have loved and supported me my whole life and career,

Jen for being the best business partner, creative collaborator and friend you could ever hope for

&

Rachel for giving me the love, courage, guidance and support I needed to bring this book to life.

Acclaim for Creative Deviations

Creative Deviations is a how-to guide for helping you, the fundraiser responsible for storytelling and donor communications, become more creative — and more effective.

Within the pages of this book, you'll discover:

- What really works when it comes to envelopes — and why should you care?
- What's the coffee ring trick?
- Why do you want to forget about the logo?
- How do you create donor engagement pieces — and what can you learn from them?
- What is your organization's URG?
- How and why should you strive to delight and inspire your donors?

An enchanting read loaded with examples, I predict you'll be returning over and over again to *Creative Deviations*. A must for every direct response fundraiser's bookshelf.

Pamela Grow, Founder, Basics & More Fundraising

If you want to raise your fundraising communications to the next level, *Creative Deviations* should be your next read. Real-life examples of fundraising pieces, down-to-earth advice on how to step into new territory, and bursting with ways to delight your donors. It's all there!

Sarah Lundberg, CFRE, The Better Fundraising Co.

"The beginning of success is to be different, the beginning of failure is to be the same". Yet so much charity communication is copycat. So, creative deviation — the subject and the book — will quickly repay study by all fundraisers, experienced or new. More than 20 campaigns from the 25-year experience of one of our sector's leading creatives — whether you read it all from the top or dip in to find something specific, where else could you find such a productive tutorial?

Ken Burnett, Author, Relationship Fundraising and other books.

Have you ever dreamed of a book to guide you through creative donor communications?

One that gives you an inside look at how it's done — and why?

One full of examples — not just theory, but practice?

You'll want John Lepp's *Creative Deviations*. And you'll keep it close at hand, I'm sure.

I've been writing fundraising copy for a long time. Agents of Good has always been an example I work to live up to. In this book, John takes you inside… thought processes, creative processes, all that he's learned over the years.

From design to language to tactics… this book gives you all of it. Most of all, it urges you to approach the work with all your creativity — and that's the part that makes this work a joy.

I've read John's book… and I'm still going to buy it. Because I want it above my desk, where I can reach for it whenever I need inspiration. You should, too.

Mary Cahalane, Hands-On Fundraising

My promise to you: This book is revolutionary. My promise to you: It's a "*once in a generation*" book. It will rewire your brain. My promise to you: It will explain exactly why your charity's communications now, currently, in your latest giving season, might have under-performed (because you can't BORE people into giving you $$$, to adapt wisdom from David Ogilvy). And... it will lay before your mind a feast of new ideas worth trying!

Tom Ahern, Ahern Communications

Foreword

Dear Reader,

Archbishop Desmond Tutu, of blessed memory called the fundraising profession noble. I believe we're a community of people who give a damn — who want to apply their skills and knowledge to make the world better through justice, equity, kindness and with purpose. Unfortunately, it's often assumed that these values do not lend themselves to a deep understanding of marketing principles and practice, but I would suggest the opposite.

Jeff Bezos once said "*We're not competitor obsessed, we're customer obsessed. We start with the customer and we work backwards.*" To the social sector practitioner, the "customer" wears many faces: beneficiary, donor, volunteer and board member. Ultimately, it's our job to balance the right message to the right customer at all times. We must provide clear, compelling reasons for our communications (whether to give time, talent or treasure) to drive our mission impact forward.

As you embark on this reading journey come prepared to learn, think, grow and change. Your practice won't be the same.

I've had a good fortune to work with John as a client and have always relished the opportunity to see the creativity that Agents of Good (AOG) bring to their projects.

I recall meeting John for the first time. He can make you feel like you're the only person in the room and that your discussion is profoundly important. Over the years, I've realized that his attentiveness, and orientation towards listening are significant strengths as both a person and a consultant.

What makes AOG and John exceptional in their field is that the notional idea of donor "centredness" or "love" isn't a theoretical construct existing in the ether. As practitioners, AOG lives within this framework, ensuring that donors feel deeply connected to the mission.

Creative Deviations is an extension of this belief system. It offers an opportunity to learn and understand, in concrete terms, the ways that we can use our communications to bring donors inside the journey of our organizations. As I read this book, I recognized fundraising stories that as a client, I helped to create. I also revisited moving stories that inspired me to make a gift.

Creative Deviations is for people who want to be better fundraisers. It's for those who see the art and the science of philanthropic work and who recognize the need for intention in how we bring that vision to life. As John points out, connection is in the details. It's also about seeing donors as partners, helping to make our communities and world a little kinder and more just.

This book is a feast for the eyes as much as it is for the mind. If you're open to it, it may even touch your soul. *Creative Deviations* will become a go-to resource, with its pages earmarked and sticky noted. It's practical and real, written from a spirit of generosity to help all of us grow and be more successful at sharing stories that create meaningful philanthropic engagement with our donors.

So, get out your sticky notes, pencil, and highlighter. While you're at it, put on the kettle too. Then, settle in to explore the new paths you can take to better your practice. Enjoy.

Tania Little, CFRE, CSR-P, GCB.D

Acknowledgements

I could probably write ten pages listing all of the people who have helped me along the way so I could be in a position to write a book like this. I am grateful to all of you who have supported me, cheered me, and guided me. Thank you so much.

Thanks also goes to donors everywhere & **all of you**, our tireless and passionate peers, colleagues and friends.

Also, Tom Ahern, Liz Attfield, Daniel Banko, Ashley Barron, Lynne Boardman, Jeff Brooks, Ken Burnett, Gwen Chapman, your donor Dale, Veronica Davies, Shanon Doolittle, Leah Eustace, Jessica Rae Gordon, Jono Grapsas, Rory Green, Pamela Grow, Lindsey Jacobs, Lorraine Hebert, Marnie Helmy, Stephanie Highfield, Dean Hughes, Derek Humphries, *the late and forever great* Simone Joyaux, Lacey Kempinski, Emma Lewzey, Tania Little, Ashlee Livingstone, Beth Ann Locke, David Love, Sarah Lundberg, Kimberley MacKenzie, Harvey McKinnon, Heather Nelson, Damian O'Broin, Holly Paulin, Gail Perry, Mark Phillips, Ann Rosenfield, Steven Screen, Simon Scriver, Dana Segal, Steven Shattuck, Melissa Smith, Beate Sørum, Steve Thomas, Sean Triner, Sabrina Turcotte & Brock Warner.

Special thanks to my editor and friend, Lisa MacDonald. I asked Lisa to edit this book for me because she knows who I am and how I got here. I also knew she would move through her work with love, thoughtfulness, gentleness and not remove my voice from my words.

Author's Note

I mention this a few times in the pages to follow, but I am a big nerd for direct response, direct marketing, direct mail, design and storytelling. That being said, I often forget that there is a lot of inside baseball that goes on when you are talking with other nerds or nerds in training.

Sometimes I forget that not everyone obsesses over all of this as much as I do.

Both of my editors, Lisa MacDonald and Rachel Zant suggested that I add this quick note about assumptions and jargon. I try to acknowledge it as I go through the book but for a quick reference, when I say:

- Pack — I am usually talking about a direct mail pack, at the very least a typical mail pack will consist of an outer envelope, a letter, a reply device (donation form) and a business reply envelope
- OE — outer envelope, the delivery vehicle for your pack, can be addressed or unaddressed
- BRE — postage paid, business reply envelope
- RE — postage paid or no postage, reply envelope
- Coupon, reply form, reply device, donation form — the part your donor sends back (hopefully) with a donation
- Letter — typically the piece that states your case for support
- Lift, insert, enclosure — basically any other piece that will go into your direct mail pack.

Trail Guide

Introduction

"The merest act of pioneering, the smallest deviation, can lead to much greater impact."
– George Smith, Asking Properly, White Lion Press, 1995

A number of years ago, while sitting on a dock in northern Ontario with a glass of rose, I flipped open a book I hadn't opened for a long time.

The book was called *Asking Properly* by George Smith. Even if you have never heard of George, I guarantee you have been inspired by his creative thinking.

In my early fundraising days, George's thinking was impressed upon me almost every day by the people I learned from.

- Good fundraising sounds like someone talking.
- Ask for one thing and only one thing.
- Every appeal should be special.

As I poured a second glass of wine, I was struck by two things. First, how much of George's thinking about creativity in fundraising still wasn't being honoured, and second, how much of my fundamental inspiration and creative thinking comes from this one fellow.

Something else that has stuck with me through the years is Ken Burnett telling me that *"80% of all fundraising really is just common sense."*

Isn't it true?
If we would only take a moment to ask ourselves if the letter in front of us makes sense. Is it clear and simple? How would I write it if I was sending it to my grandmother? Would the words make her feel seen and appreciated, understanding where she is at in her life? Does it address what she cares about? What did I send to her last? What am I hoping she will do? How can I make it as easy as possible for her to help? How do I hope she feels when she reads this letter? Why should she care about this problem? And so on.

If we put down "the data" that we look at and listen to in order to make decisions, and instead, pick up that photo of a favourite donor and remind ourselves of the beautiful privilege we have in having conversations with her, I think our sector would be in a different place.

Creative Deviations is an anecdotal and thoughtful how-to guide to help you become more creative. It's *part* graphic design, *part* design thinking, *part* storytelling, *part* strategic thinking and *part* love note to you amazing humans who work so hard for your causes, your donors, your mission and your desire to contribute and make positive change in our world. **Thank you.**

This book will not be filled with tons of stats, data, ROIs, results, percentages and dollar signs, since these things change over time and by client. However, almost everything I reference and talk about is based on standard best practice that's been developed out of testing and experience through the years, by myself, here at Agents of Good and by my friends and colleagues from charities and agencies around the world.

To do direct response and individual giving appropriately, just as in our real life relationships, you have to acknowledge where you (your organization) and your donor have come from, where you and your donor and our world, is at right now and where you and your donors are going — together and separately.

If we stop thinking about donors as detached from the everyday work we are churning out and instead, think of them as our moms or grandmothers, we might slow down and think about **what we are doing, what we are asking for** and **how we are going about those things.**

Love isn't a check box.
The relationships we form with other humans — on any level — can't be whittled down to a simple "10-step process." You cannot form deep human connections through statistics and one-directional talking.

There is no magic bullet or new big idea.
Direct response and fundraising is only successful when you obsess over the 1,000 small things you need to be thoughtful about.

You need to do your work with love every day. And I beg you, if you aren't able to help your organization be authentic and vulnerable to those you are asking for help from, then move on.

But back to this book of deviations.

Every day for the past 12 years, I have had the privilege to be a part of Agents of Good alongside my business partner Jen Love (aka Jen, Agent Jen, JLo) and her dad, the legendary David Love (aka David, The Godfather of Good). So much of the creativity and ideas that are gathered in this book reflect our combined knowledge and nerdiness about our craft.

To that point, I have been peering into the mailbox of your donor and examining the fundraising that she gets every day for more than 25 years. Here's what I've learned:

- It continues to be automated, created by cold computers and digital presses.
- It looks perfect and is overly branded leaving very little space for the donor to be a part of the story.
- It tells stories without asking for anything.
- It is maintaining status quo.

This book will show you how taking small steps off the trailblazed path will lead to interesting and successful results.

At times the direction I am taking you in will seem counter-intuitive, scary and downright wrong. Just like being a human. Nonetheless, we know that if we take a deviation from the norm, a better future may be the reward.

Design isn't about how something looks.
It about how the damn thing works. How it all comes together — in one pack and

over time.

Good design should be seen, should be understood, should be acted upon and most importantly needs to get results… everything else is garbage.

This isn't a book full of check boxes. I know we are looking for them but I've found there are very few definitives in the art form of direct response. As in, next to none.

That's what makes relationships and individual giving difficult and challenging. This is why we cannot automate it, or teach it in a single course.

It's made up of a thousand small moving pieces at any given time. You need to thoughtfully be aware of them, acknowledge them, manipulate them and study them. This craft of direct response is an art and a science, and requires a level of obsession to do it well.

Being creative means getting messy.
It means making mistakes. It means starting over. It means you say sorry once in a while. It means you do hard things that make you afraid and that you will be judged for. It means there will be crying, and there will be laughing.

My hope is that *Creative Deviations* will help you feel more freedom to do your work every day and not worry too much about 'breaking something' by making a mistake or trying something new. Donors are a forgiving bunch. They often give more when you mess up.

My hope is that by adopting some of the deviations in this book — you will feel more engaged with your work. Through perfecting your craft, I hope that you will care for your donors a little more while having pride in yourself and the good you bring to our world.

I have the beautiful privilege of connecting with many fundraisers every single day. I see, and acknowledge, all of the love and passion you put into your work and into learning more about this strange art form that is direct response.

I am honoured and appreciate your time and attention for picking this book up, moving your way through it and thoughtfully considering how you can adopt and adapt some of these ideas into your day-to-day work.

From the depths of my heart, thank you.

John Lepp
July 2021

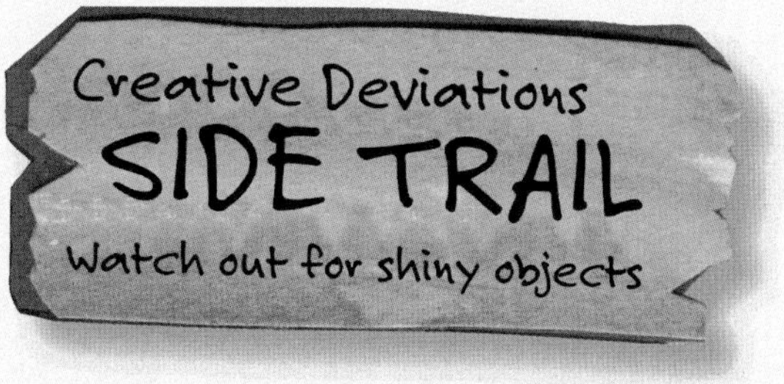

THE SYMPHONY OF DIRECT RESPONSE

We often talk about the "symphony" of amazing direct response.

The concept of the symphony is that every — note — is played as perfectly as possible so that the collective noise of it creates a beautiful, musical story.

In fundraising terms, that means you focus on *every* appeal, *every* tweet, *every* thank you call, *every* exchange with your donor, **every "note"**.

If you ensure that **every "note"** is sent at the right time, with the right ask, coated in love and appreciation for your donors… if you ensure it gets noticed and looked at… then, you will have a fundraising program that others will envy.

Here is something to consider.

Sometimes, your donor will only give to you once a year. Or maybe something in her life has changed and she won't give to you at all this year.

Your donor might give you a small regular gift when you call and ask, or she might not. She might give a single cash gift to your direct mail pack or she might not be interested in what you need that day. She might "like" your post on Facebook and give to you online. Or maybe not.

My point is, just because one of your "notes" isn't pitch perfect to her does not indicate failure. It is the totality of the sounds you create for her that matters.

If your direct mail appeal results are low, that doesn't mean it's a failure — especially if you have worked hard on the things mentioned.

You can never gauge your program on the success or failure of one appeal, or one channel. Or even on one donor for that matter.

It's the totality of the notes that matter.

Deviation One — Forget about your logo

This deviation will respectfully ask how your brand can leave space for your donor to be a part of your story. At the end of the day, effective fundraising has very little to do with your logo or brand story. In fact, your branding could be working against you and pushing donors away.

Sorry, not sorry.

Throughout my career, I have seen too many great ideas dismissed with a swoop of the hand and someone saying, *"I'm sorry. This doesn't adhere to our brand guidelines."*

#cries

Every director or fundraiser I have worked with will tell you that I've tried to skirt around their "guidelines."

That's because guidelines are often created by branding agencies or by people who do not have donors at the front and center of their mind. They are getting in the way of your ability to tell great stories and create effective fundraising that your donor will love and cherish.

There. I said it.

Branding is a commercial idea, acting as a sort of professional bubble wrap, that tends to get in the way of emotive, vulnerable fundraising conversations with our loving donors.

In the context of effective fundraising, your branding guidelines and your logo really aren't that important.

In fact, I've seen instances where including your logo on the outer envelope lowers the response rate.

That said, branding and your logo probably are *not* the deal breaker between getting a gift vs. not getting a gift.

Your brand should be about how your donors *experience* you in the stories you tell them and about the problems you solve together. It is the way the donor *feels* when they give to you. It is the promises you make to them and the values you and they share together.

All branding, all marketing, all communications, are part of fundraising. They serve the same master, which ultimately is your ability to raise funds and meet the needs of your mission.

Factors influencing a donor's decision to give following a rebrand

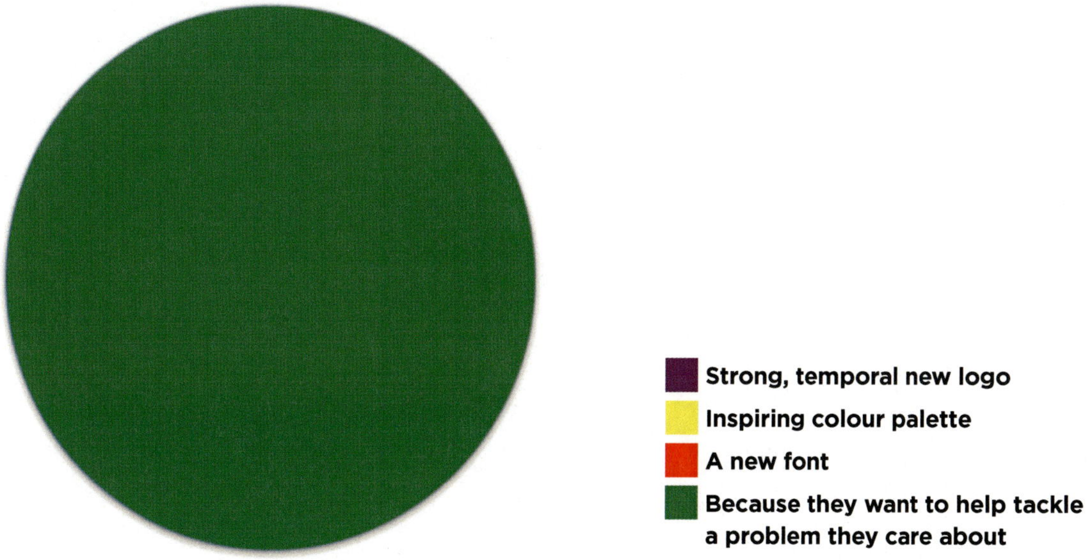

source: Mark Phillips: BlueFrog UK

Your donor doesn't know, nor do they care:

- what your font is
- what PMS colour your logo uses
- that it's your 10th Anniversary
- about your latest "awareness" campaign
- when they are scheduled to get your next e-blast or piece of mail
- about all the amazing things you do
- about your brand story
- what your mission statement is.

Your donor wants to:

- know how you used their last gift
- feel like they are important to meeting the needs of your mission
- know what problem they can help solve today and why they should care
- know what the problem is
- feel needed, like a part of the team
- feel appreciated for their efforts
- be remembered
- make the world a better place
- help you **WIN**.

Design for donors

What does "design for donors" mean?

It means that the donor's needs are placed ahead of the needs of your boss, your designer, and the marketing and communications team with all of their subjective opinions about design.

As a "designer," I need to meet my donor where she is, not where I want to be.

I may not like certain fonts or that when I remove myself from "design," something becomes more effective but... here we are.

Two envelopes (Figure. 1.1).

In a test, which do you think would be more effective?

The more your mail or email, whatever it may be, looks like a human made it, touched it, wrote on it, the more effective it likely will be (i.e., it will raise more money).

Often in presentations, I will stop and ask the room if they can guess what my favourite font is.

Figure 1.1: In a test, which do you think would do better?

It's rare that people guess correctly.

It's:

`Courier.`

Do you know why?

It's my favourite because when I use it in appeals, I often raise more money.

(In fact, I am partial to san-serif fonts. Gotham and Franklin Gothic being two of my current favorites.)

Using Courier type in your appeal does a few things.

`When your beloved donor pulls out your letter they see something that reminds them of a gentler time. A time long ~~ago~~ past. Perhaps, they hear the far-off clackity-clack of metal type on a long arm smashing against the paper, leaving the mark of the letter behind. Then the next letter, and the next, until they hear that DING and have to pull the`

arm and push the platen back to the right to start the next line.

This is a powerful moment.

Nostalgia involves remembering. It's emotionally more complex than just feeling happy or sad or angry.

These are things I need to acknowledge as a designer, yet I have never seen Courier discussed in branding or design guidelines. **Donors are never mentioned either.**

By the way, I would have given you bonus points if you said:

Prestige (instead of Courier).

Design for donors is what is appropriate for the donor.
For example, if you are designing anything you want your donor to read, do not set the type size to anything smaller than 12 point. I don't give a crap about graphic standards. If you can go bigger than 12 point, please do. Your donors will appreciate it, and thank you by hopefully giving or responding.

Design for donors is methodical.
Think through every element. What do I want the donor to look at first? Which font might work best for this piece and why am I using it instead of another? How do I want the donor to feel as they read this lift note? Does this need to be four-colour or will black and white do? Does this letter need to be four pages or will two pages and an insert do better?

Design for donors is concise.
Get to the point. Communicate and ask for one thing (AND get out of the way!!!). Do it as simply and quickly as possible. Do not mess with your donor's attention span.

Design for donors can be cheesy.
Goofy. Fun. Light. Have you ever had a donor call you up laughing at the latest piece you sent them and happily make a gift? Have you ever asked yourself how you can surprise and delight your donor?

Design for donors can be ugly. (It's not ugly to me obviously.)
Most graphic designers and creatives cannot stand direct mail. Why? Because a boring 9″ x 6″ envelope with a logo on it will beat almost anything else most of the time. Because Courier will make the letter more interesting and more effective than that latest font that they are drooling over.

I remember being dismissed as a designer because "I design mail for old people."

It's HARD to be this good. I have spent years untraining designers from making things look pretty to making them *effective*.

Design and branding for donors only works when we have them in mind.
I wanted to share this example of how sometimes, your brand can get in the way of good storytelling.

It's not that your logo and graphic standards should be ignored or pushed aside, but as a storyteller, I always let the story dictate the format.

STORY OF COLINA

This is a gratitude report Agents of Good worked on for the Alzheimer Society of Nova Scotia. It told the story of Colina and her family.

After Jen Love interviewed David, Colina's husband and her family, I knew that the gratitude report should feel as personal as their story. It had to represent their life together; something sticky, tactile and vibrant. Something like a photo album that our parents had kicking around on a shelf in the basement.

The cover of the 2017 Alzheimer Society of Nova Scotia Gratitude Report.

The best examples of direct response, of #donorlove, of conversations with donors, feel like they were created with someone's hands and heart.

Any other solution would have felt detached from the personal nature of Colina and David's story.

There are a lot of senses and emotions involved with this sort of treatment.

Nostalgia is one of them.

Your donors have photo albums like these tucked away in boxes and bookshelves filled with moments of their lives: growing up, long-gone family members, Christmas' past, picnics...

You recognize the puffy, squishy cover and remember the faux plastic leather smell, the etched-in type and what it feels like as you run your fingers across the stitching at the edges.

This report was designed to unlock a different response than that you would get with just a nice shiny photo and logo with "2017 Annual Report" typeset on it.

Most donors would be familiar with the sticky, tearing noise these pages would make as you pull back the acetate page to place your photo. These pages were all computer generated, but I didn't want it to look like that at all.

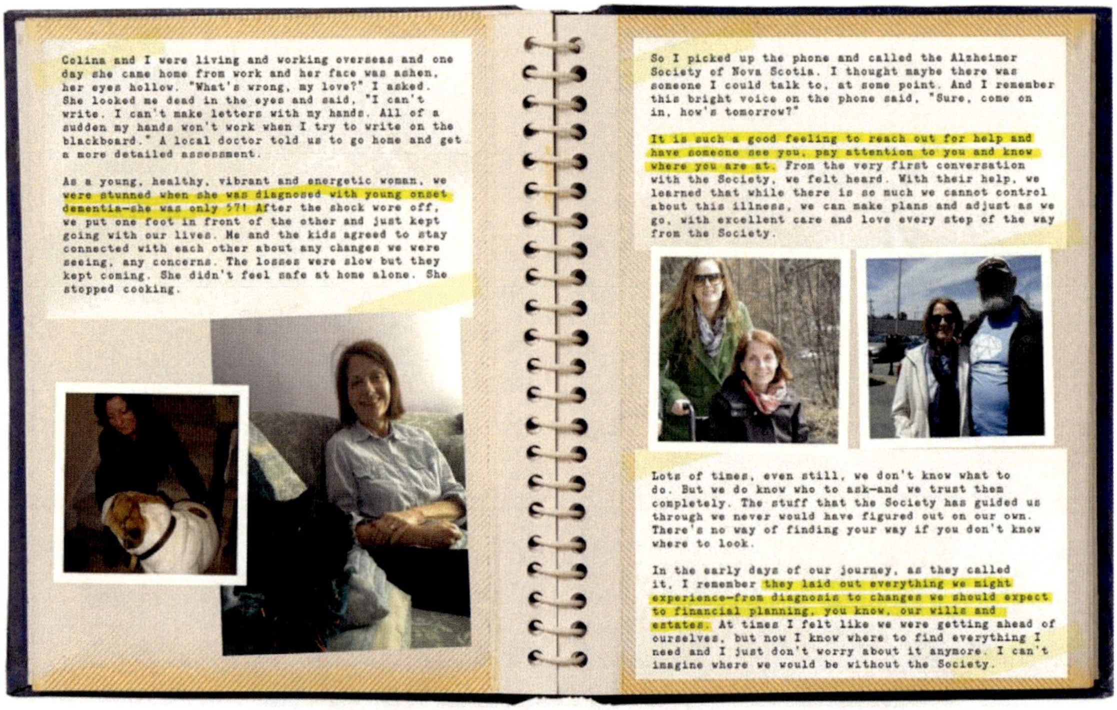

Other elements included the taped edges, staining the paper beneath, highlighted, imperfect copy, and glossy 4″ x 6″ images or older square format.

Even the financials reflect the period. They were designed, printed, hand-coloured, photographed and filtered to achieve this effect.

This report was built with the donor in mind. It told a moving story in a way that would have the most impact.

The best brands should leave space for the donor to be a part of the story and help you win.

In actuality, very few do.

Thanks to Sarah Lyon of the Alzheimer Society of Nova Scotia for all of her trust and help with this passion project.

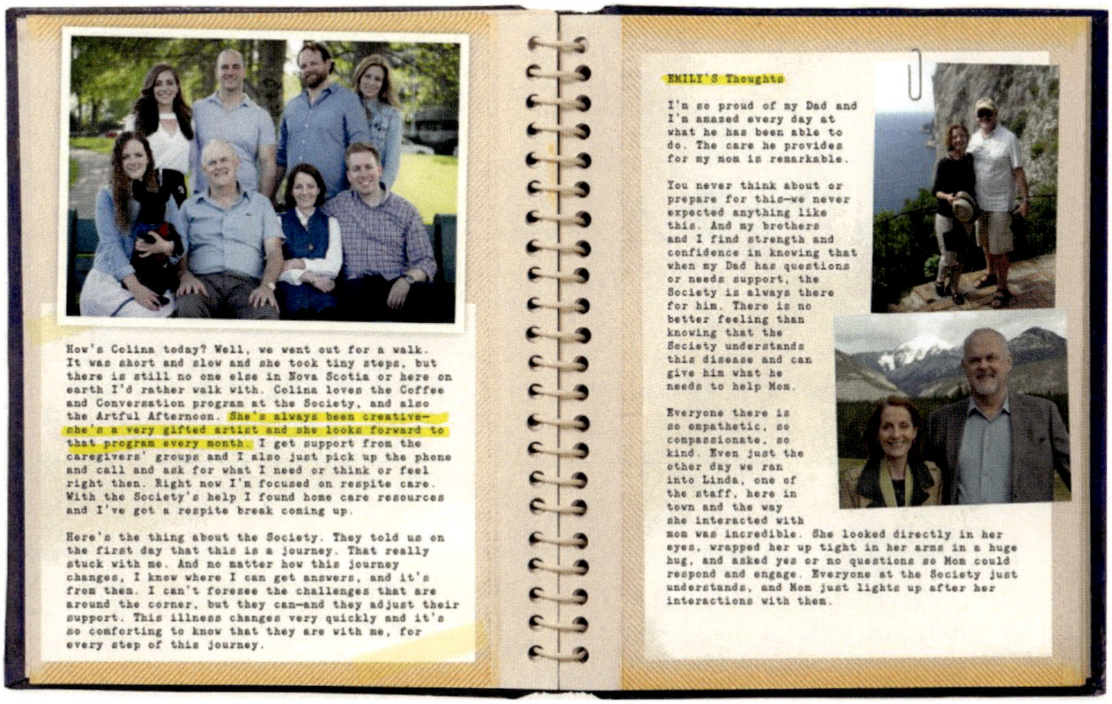

How's Colina today? Well, we went out for a walk. It was short and slow and she took tiny steps, but there is still no one else in Nova Scotia or here on earth I'd rather walk with. Colina loves the Coffee and Conversation program at the Society, and also the Artful Afternoon. She's always been creative–she's a very gifted artist and she looks forward to that program every month. I get support from the caregivers' groups and I also just pick up the phone and call and ask for what I need or think or feel right then. Right now I'm focused on respite care. With the Society's help I found home care resources and I've got a respite break coming up.

Here's the thing about the Society. They told us on the first day that this is a journey. That really stuck with me. And no matter how this journey changes, I know where I can get answers, and it's from them. I can't foresee the challenges that are around the corner, but they can–and they adjust their support. This illness changes very quickly and it's so comforting to know that they are with me, for every step of this journey.

EMILY'S Thoughts

I'm so proud of my Dad and I'm amazed every day at what he has been able to do. The care he provides for my mom is remarkable.

You never think about or prepare for this–we never expected anything like this. And my brothers and I find strength and confidence in knowing that when my Dad has questions or needs support, the Society is always there for him. There is no better feeling than knowing that the Society understands this disease and can give him what he needs to help Mom.

Everyone there is so empathetic, so compassionate, so kind. Even just the other day we ran into Linda, one of the staff, here in town and the way she interacted with mom was incredible. She looked directly in her eyes, wrapped her up tight in her arms in a huge hug, and asked yes or no questions so Mom could respond and engage. Everyone at the Society just understands, and Mom just lights up after her interactions with them.

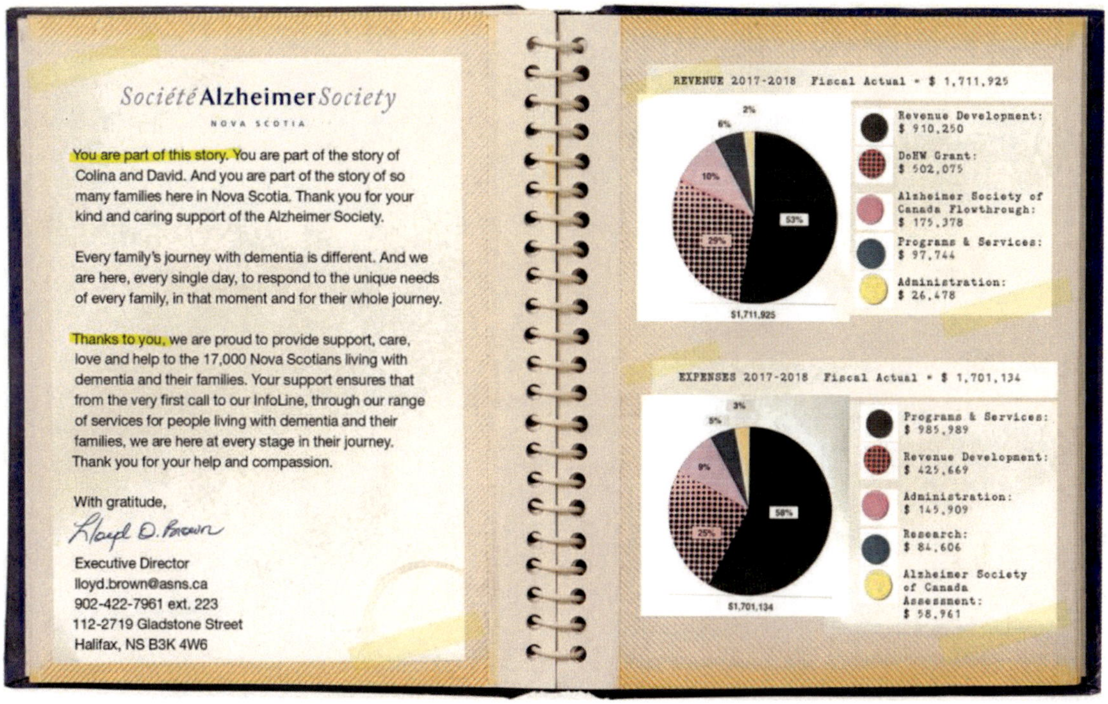

Société **Alzheimer** *Society*

NOVA SCOTIA

You are part of this story. You are part of the story of Colina and David. And you are part of the story of so many families here in Nova Scotia. Thank you for your kind and caring support of the Alzheimer Society.

Every family's journey with dementia is different. And we are here, every single day, to respond to the unique needs of every family, in that moment and for their whole journey.

Thanks to you, we are proud to provide support, care, love and help to the 17,000 Nova Scotians living with dementia and their families. Your support ensures that from the very first call to our InfoLine, through our range of services for people living with dementia and their families, we are here at every stage in their journey. Thank you for your help and compassion.

With gratitude,

Lloyd D. Brown

Executive Director
lloyd.brown@asns.ca
902-422-7961 ext. 223
112-2719 Gladstone Street
Halifax, NS B3K 4W6

REVENUE 2017-2018 Fiscal Actual • $ 1,711,925

Revenue Development: $ 910,250
DoHW Grant: $ 502,075
Alzheimer Society of Canada Flowthrough: $ 175,378
Programs & Services: $ 97,744
Administration: $ 26,478

EXPENSES 2017-2018 Fiscal Actual • $ 1,701,134

Programs & Services: $ 985,989
Revenue Development: $ 425,669
Administration: $ 145,909
Research: $ 84,606
Alzheimer Society of Canada Assessment: $ 58,961

ST. PATRICK'S HOME

St. Pat's of Ottawa, Ontario is a lovely long-term home and very much an important part of the community.

As a "brand," they have always understood that they serve their residents and their families in the most loving and supportive way they can, and that donors are an important part of that being able to happen.

St. Patrick's Home of Ottawa abides by a vision to provide residents with the highest quality of care, within a welcoming home, where everyone feels supported and cared for.

The Foundation is honoured to work alongside the Home, and with the community, to support this vision.

They have always understood that it isn't about **what they** (the Foundation) does, it's about **what you** (the donor) make possible. They live and breathe that.

There are so many way to support St. Pat's

Give in the manner that works best for you

Your support enhances care and daily life at St. Pat's

At St. Pat's, we work with volunteers, and with feedback from residents and their families to ensure excellent, personal care and the delivery of quality programs that support residents and enhance Home life. Your donation today helps to make this possible.

The following appeal focused on the importance of the music program.

The outer envelope featured the tagline, "*All it takes is 1 song to bring back 1,000 memories…*"

The donor is instantly thinking of, and hearing, a tune.

St. Patrick's Home of Ottawa **Foundation**

Date

<Addressee>
<Address>
<City> <PR> <POSTAL>

Sometimes, it's not the song that makes you emotional, it's the people and things that come to your mind when you hear it. -Unknown

Dear <Salutation>,

Can you relate to this inspiring quote?

I certainly do! I think music is an important part of our lives, from the moment we hear our first lullaby. It's about sharing happiness, sorrow, and memories—it's something we are all touched by, and has the power to heal us.

Here at St. Patrick's Home, we see first-hand just how much our music therapy program enriches the lives of our residents. The ladies and gentlemen in our home absolutely love music. It fills our home—and hearts—with joy.

And I hope it warms your heart to know that your gifts to St. Pat's made it possible for us to start this vital and vibrant program. Thank you for your kind support!

Today, we have an exciting opportunity to expand and grow our music therapy program, and I'm writing to ask you to consider making a special gift to St. Pat's. And to add your voice to our chorus!

Your gift today will provide crucial support to our music therapy initiatives, including purchasing equipment and resources to enhance our home choir, bringing professional musicians to our Home for performances, and taking our residents on outings to musicals, orchestras and other arts events in our city.

Please turn over...

2865 Riverside Drive, Ottawa, Ontario K1V 8N5 www.stpats.ca

Charitable Registration #88897 0399 RR0001

The two-page letter:

1. **Focuses on what the problem is**

> I certainly do! I think music is an important part of our lives, from the moment we hear our first lullaby. It's about sharing happiness, sorrow, and memories—it's something we are all touched by, and has the power to heal us.
>
> Here at St. Patrick's Home, we see first-hand just how much our music therapy program enriches the lives of our residents. The ladies and gentlemen in our home absolutely love music. It fills our home—and hearts—with joy.

2. **Articulates the solution and how donors can be a part of that**

> And I hope it warms your heart to know that your gifts to St. Pat's made it possible for us to start this vital and vibrant program. Thank you for your kind support!
>
> Today, we have an exciting opportunity to expand and grow our music therapy program, and I'm writing to ask you to consider making a special gift to St. Pat's. And to add your voice to our chorus!

3. **States what the donor can do and why they should do it right now**

> Your gift today will provide crucial support to our music therapy initiatives, including purchasing equipment and resources to enhance our home choir, bringing professional musicians to our Home for performances, and taking our residents on outings to musicals, orchestras and other arts events in our city.

I recently spent a delightful afternoon gathering some details for you to write this letter. I spoke with Elsa, our Choir Coordinator, and she told me a few amazing things I wanted to share with you.

Did you know that music therapy stimulates and improves cognitive function? Even in later stages of Alzheimer's and dementia, residents feel calmed and soothed by music. Our residents are able to reconnect with music they enjoyed long before their memories began to decline. And it stimulates interaction with others, just like old friends sharing their love of song.

I also sat in on a choir practice, and I joined the singing, tapping our feet, clapping our hands and even slapping our knees! I chatted with a few of our residents, Patricia who is a devoted and proud choir member because it reminds her of when she would sing to her children. She loves it so much she never misses a practice.

Along with you can hear a few more voices on the enclosed note. And you can see Elsa's music therapy wish list! As you read, I hope you can see just how profoundly important and joyful our music therapy program is. And I hope it inspires you to give today!

You'll find enclosed a reply form you can use to choose your gift. And I would love if you would add your voice to our chorus and share a song that makes you feel emotional or brings back a memory you cherish. I promise we'll try our best to share your favourite melodies with our residents in the music room!

Thank you for your continued support of St. Pat's!

Yours truly,

Ruth Catana, Executive Director

P.S. **Together, we urgently need to raise $20,000 to fund our Music Wish List and expand our delightful and critical music therapy program. Please, give today! And add your voice to our chorus!**

Page 2 (back) of the letter:

4. **Reiterates the problem**

> Did you know that music therapy stimulates and improves cognitive function? Even in later stages of Alzheimer's and dementia, residents feel calmed and soothed by music. Our residents are able to reconnect with music they enjoyed long before their memories began to decline. And it stimulates interaction with others, just like old friends sharing their love of song.

5. **Specifies how donors can be a part of the solution**

> Along with you can hear a few more voices on the enclosed note. And you can see Elsa's music therapy wish list! As you read, I hope you can see just how profoundly important and joyful our music therapy program is. And I hope it inspires you to give today!
>
> You'll find enclosed a reply form you can use to choose your gift. And I would love if you would add your voice to our chorus and share a song that makes you feel emotional or brings back a memory you cherish. I promise we'll try our best to share your favourite melodies with our residents in the music room!

6. **Identifies what can be done right now to help**

> P.S. **Together, we urgently need to raise $20,000 to fund our Music Wish List and expand our delightful and critical music therapy program. Please, give today! And add your voice to our chorus!**

We used a full-size reply form (Fig. 1.2) and used segmentation to create a gift array tailored to the donor's previous giving. Such a small thing but very #donorloving.

We included a short wish list of items to demonstrate what the donor would help accomplish with different levels of giving and we included some space on the back for donors to add their voice!

Great branding creates space for donors to be a part of your story — because they are!

St. Patrick's Home of Ottawa Foundation

Yes, Ruth! I'll add my voice! Here is my special gift to support St. Pat's Home and your **music therapy program!**

❍ Ask 1 ❍ Ask2 ❍ Ask 3 ❍ I prefer to give $ _______

❍ I have enclosed my cheque, payable to St. Patrick's Home of Ottawa Foundation OR

❍ I prefer to pay by credit card. Please charge my ❑ VISA ❑ Mastercard

Card Number: ______________________ Expiry: ______________________

Signature: ______________________ Date: ______________________

Thank you! Your gift will go towards the items on our **Music Wish List!**

- 3 music carts (each cart includes a CD player, large print books, CDs, iPods and headphones), **$500 each**
- 5 portable electronic keyboards, **$1,000 each**
- 9 stereos, **$250 each**
- 9 wireless speakers, **$125 each**
- 18 professional musical performances, **$500 each**
- New sheet music and song books for each of the Resident Home Areas, **$500 each**

<Addressee>
<Address>
<City> <PR> <POSTAL>
Const ID/AppealCode XX-XXX-XXX

Please turn over and add your voice!

Your privacy is very important to us. The information you provide will be used to keep you informed of our activities or to contact you regarding your donation. You can read our full privacy policy at www.stpats.ca.

2865 Riverside Drive, Ottawa, Ontario K1V 8N5 www.stpats.ca

Charitable Registration #88897 0399 RR0001

Fig 1.2

St. Pat's Voices!

"Seeing my mom in your choir **melts my heart**, it was always her happy place singing at church"
– Sharon, daughter of Marjorie who loves singing in our choir!

"Teresa has lost most of her eyesight, and as a result can become disoriented, anxious, and agitated. I use music to draw Teresa's attention to the present, mirroring her agitation with up-tempo songs, then gradually changing to slow, gentle songs as she relaxes. Sometimes she'll even **open up to me with stories** about her children and her younger years." *– Elsa, Recreation and Choir Coordinator, St. Pat's*

"Among the many wonderful activities offered to my Mom at St. Patrick's Home, I have noticed anything involving music has been a very positive influence on her. Whether it's a musical concert being held in the Gathering Place, a group of local students singing holiday carols or the weekly gathering of choir members, it's inevitable that my Mom's mood improves almost instantaneously. In spite of her inability to recall basic daily tasks, she is still quite capable of remembering melodies and lyrics from music dating as far back as her teen years, and this always seems to put a smile on her face. **There is no doubt in my mind: music is magical for these residents!** Hopefully they will continue to reap the benefits and enjoyment from it in the future."
– Sheila, daughter of Estelle, a St. Pat's Home resident

St. Pat's Music Wish List

- **3 music carts** (each cart includes a CD player, large print books, CDs, iPods and headphones), $500 each
- **5 portable electronic keyboards**, $1,000 each
- **9 stereos**, $250 each
- **9 wireless speakers**, $125 each
- **18 professional musical performances**, $500 each
- **New sheet music and song books** for each of the Resident Home Areas, $500 each

Fig 1.3

Lastly, we added this small lift note (Fig. 1.3) to share some voices from St. Pat's who explain (in their own words) how important the music program is to residents. This is a perfect example of where to use some of that extra emotional content you get during an interview and can't use in the letter. A lift note can give it a home. It all adds to the case for support, and your donor has further proof of why this program is important.

Returning to that bit on the back of the reply form (Fig. 1.4). We are almost

Add your voice to our chorus!

We would love to hear from you about a song that makes you feel emotional or brings back a memory you cherish:

Thank you!

We'll do our best to share your song and story with our residents at St. Pat's!

Fig 1.4

constantly trying to give donors ways to talk back to their organizations. Not just at Christmas. All year round.

Direct response is a conversation and it can be powerful when you ask emotional questions of your donors. Emotional questions receive emotional responses.

These are some of the responses we got back.

Looking at this response, what is your donor telling you about herself? Why should that matter to you?

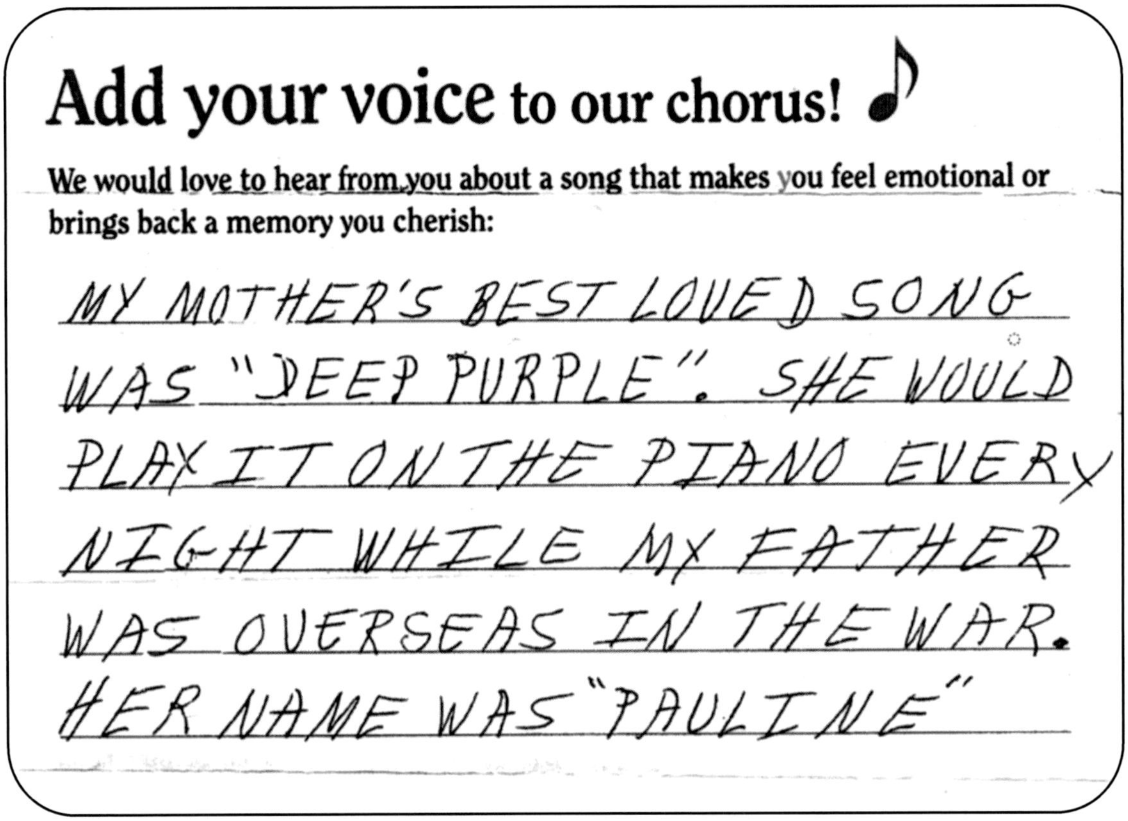

Add your voice to our chorus! ♪

We would love to hear from you about a song that makes you feel emotional or brings back a memory you cherish:

MY MOTHER'S BEST LOVED SONG WAS "DEEP PURPLE". SHE WOULD PLAY IT ON THE PIANO EVERY NIGHT WHILE MY FATHER WAS OVERSEAS IN THE WAR. HER NAME WAS "PAULINE"

I love this one.

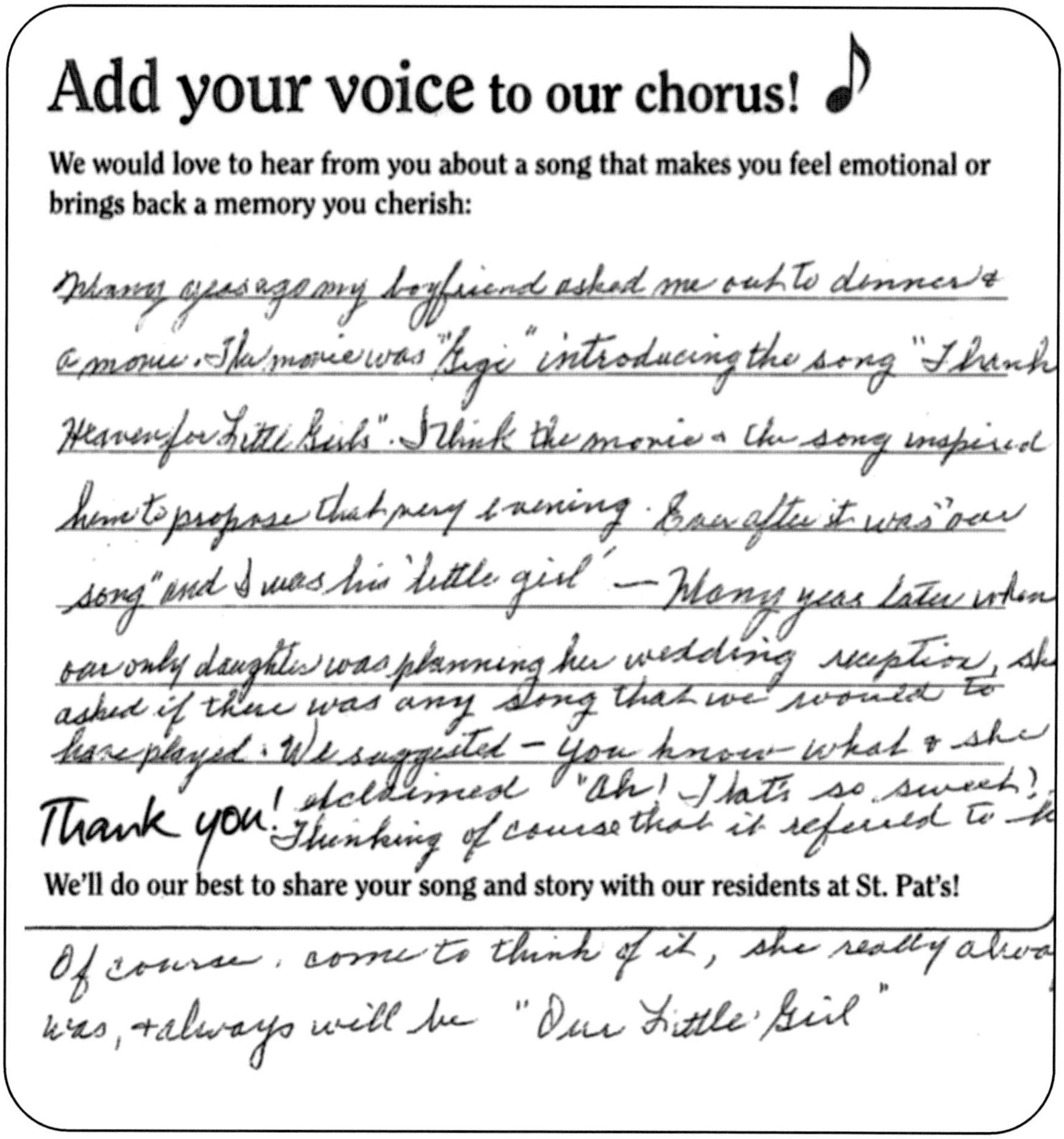

Add your voice to our chorus! ♪

We would love to hear from you about a song that makes you feel emotional or brings back a memory you cherish:

Many years ago my boyfriend asked me out to dinner & a movie. The movie was "Gigi" introducing the song "Thank Heaven for Little Girls". I think the movie & the song inspired him to propose that very evening. Ever after it was "our song" and I was his 'little girl' — Many years later when our only daughter was planning her wedding reception, she asked if there was any song that we would to have played. We suggested — you know what & she exclaimed "Oh! That's so sweet!" Thinking of course that it referred to h

Thank you!

We'll do our best to share your song and story with our residents at St. Pat's!

Of course, come to think of it, she really always was, & always will be "Our Little Girl"

"Many years ago my boyfriend asked me out to dinner and a movie. The movie was "Gigi" introducing the song, "Thank heaven for little girls." I think the movie and the song inspired him to propose that very evening. Even after, it was 'our song' and I was his 'little girl.' Many years later when our only daughter was planning her wedding reception, she was asked if there was any song that we would want to have played. We suggested — you know what, and she exclaimed "Ah! That's so sweet!" Thinking of course that it referred to her. Of course, come to think of it, she really was and always will be "our little girl!"

I appreciate that this donor took the time to share all of the things she wanted to share — not caring if she took more space than I gave her to do it!

What else is your donor telling you about herself in this message?

Add your voice to our chorus! ♪

We would love to hear from you about a song that makes you feel emotional or brings back a memory you cherish:

Listening to Violin music - orchestral particularly Classical Music / Hearing at end of life for my mom and as I understand are among the final pleasures of life

Singing - Ain't got a barrel of money, K K.K Katie, Twinkle Twinkle, Pop Goes the Weasel, How Great thou art. Mom at 98 remembers the lyrics and tunes to many many songs.

Thank you!

We'll do our best to share your song and story with our residents at St. Pat's!

Elsa has done so much to encourage the pleasure of singing through her choir I'm really happy to support this initiative to complement the music program. Hopefully some volunteers could help to go ~~room~~ person to ~~room~~ person to sing a song or two with them to brighten their days.

"Listening to: Violin music — orchestral particularly. Classical music and hearing it at the end of life for my mom and as I understand are among the final pleasures of life.

Singing: Ain't got a barrel of money, K.K.K.Katie, Twinkle Twinkle, Pop Goes the Weasel, How Great Thou Art. Mom at 98 remembered the lyrics and tunes to many, many songs.

Elsa has done so much to encourage the pleasure of singing through her choir and I'm really happy to support this initiative to complement the music program. Hopefully some volunteers could help to go person to person to sing a few songs or two with them to brighten their days."

This appeal doubled the revenue that St. Pat's expected, including getting five gifts of $1,000 or more. That was a big deal for an organization like St. Pat's.

St. Pat's decided to plan a special concert for donors using a lot of the song suggestions and memories that were sent back.

The day after this appeal hit donor mailboxes, our client Ruth was sitting at her desk when a knock came at the door.

Well, I'll actually let **Agent Jen Love** tell you this story:

I still can't share this story without crying.

She never calls me.

We've worked together for almost 10 years and she's never called me. She's the kind of Executive Director who emails me to ask if we can talk for half an hour a week from Thursday at 2:30 sharp.

So when Ruth called me the day after our appeal dropped, I immediately thought it was a direct response apocalypse scenario. Trembling, I answered the phone and my client said,

"Jen, I have a story for you."

"I just had an unexpected visitor," Ruth continued.

"I was sitting here in my office and there was a knock on my door. I looked up and saw a woman I'd never seen before holding the torn-open appeal in her hands. She said, 'I felt compelled to drive here and see you. You moved me.' Jen, all the hairs stood up on the back of my neck."

"She sat down and told me that as she was reading our letter, she heard music playing in her head. Old Irish lullabies her mother used to sing to her, songs her parents loved

and would play at home. She was reflecting on just how much music had meant to her all her life."

"She asked me about the music therapy program, what the residents said about it. We had a really lovely conversation. She'd lost her dad, and he had always been a proud supporter of many Irish Catholic charities, including St. Pat's."

Then she said, 'I've been thinking about making a more significant gift to something important, that really matters to me, but I didn't know what that was until today. Would it be OK if I wrote you a cheque for all $20,000 right now and fund the whole program?'

Jen, SHE asked ME!!!

I almost fell out of my chair. I thanked her and thanked her.

She was so happy, even happier than me! And the minute she left, of course, you know me, I looked her up in Raiser's Edge. Lapsed donor, hasn't given in three years. Cumulative giving on and off for about 10 years, totaling not even $600."

"I've been fundraising for 30 years and this has never happened to me. And you know, this is such a good reminder of 2 things. One, we send out appeals and we just don't know what's going on with people when they read it. And two, when you really connect with someone's values, magic can happen."

Over the next few weeks, donations continued to pour in. Terrific stretch gifts from donors at all levels. This campaign shattered the goals of previous spring appeals.

...and donors also shared their songs and memories.

Right?!

This is just a small sampling. This stuff literally makes me weep. Legit shaking and crying.

Isn't it beautiful?

Ruth and her staff have the delightful job of calling their donors and thanking them for their gift and for sharing their song. They have joyful, wonderful conversations about music and memories. They also ask if they would like to join a special concert being put on for amazing and generous donors, including them!

This is the stuff that fundraising dreams are made of, my friends. I know in my heart that this will inspire legacy conversations too.

Now, what about you? Are you ready to plan your next appeal to create a conversation with your donors?

The St. Pat's campaign is also an example of a classic case:

- **Why me** (the donor)?
- **Why now?**

We answered those questions and gave lots of space for the donor to be a part of the story. That's what great branding and storytelling does.

You won't get surprising and inspiring results like these from conventional approaches. When you give donors compelling reasons to help you, when you actively ask for and listen to their stories and let them share their values with you, when you get out of the way and make giving as easy as possible — amazing and beautiful things will happen.

Deviation Discoveries

We covered a lot of uncomfortable terrain in this deviation, but I want to leave you with a few considerations.

1. Yes. Who your organization is and what it stands for is important to donors, but only in the sense that who you are becomes a reflection of who **they** are. They **are** part of your story. The more your branding ignores them, the less they will care about the important work you are trying to do.
2. If your branding guidelines ignore the needs of your audience, they will get in the way of your potential to create successful fundraising appeals.
3. In fundraising, how your donor feels about your organization, what she sees in you and experiences with you has more to do with your brand than how **you** feel about your organization, see yourself and think your donor experiences you.

Creative Deviations

SIDE TRAIL

Watch out for shiny objects

THE MYTH OF BRANDING

Another week, another discussion about how an idea for an appeal was rejected because it isn't "on brand" enough.

"*But I used your Pantone colour,*" I sputtered.

"*The font is typeset according to your guidelines.*" I pleaded.

Nope. Brand police — 1. John — 0.

People, this madness must stop.

If you are an E.D., or work at a charity in a senior position, take a seat, grab a coffee and let's have a little chat about "branding" shall we?

First — this is important — if you have a branding or marketing manager whose job it is to give the thumbs up or down to any fundraising piece that you are responsible for, I'm so sorry, and I have good news. You probably don't really need them.

Branding is not rocket science. Branding is not something you need a degree for. Branding should not be confusing.

Your brand is what you are to your donors. It's how your donors perceive you. That's your brand. That's it.

There are "branding agencies" who will spend a lot of your (and your donors) money to do focus groups, to design hundreds of logo concepts, straplines, gorgeous design standard manuals, and letterheads. They will make big, pompous statements about how your charity is the leader in this and that and reiterate that you do all of these amazing things. They will hire photographers and shoot gorgeous images for your manuals and reports. They will dictate how to use this special little font that no one has heard of before and how you have to use this or it will all fall apart. Then, the glorious day will arrive and they will come to you, sporting the biggest smiles ever and present to you (queue the angels) your BRAND. Then, you will have to go out and hire a "brand manager," someone who has gone to university and studied marketing and understands how this "branding thing" works. They will lead you through every communications challenge and when they need to can retrieve the coveted "Brand Book" from the vault to show you why you, your designer and writer are wrong and why you are so off your "brand" you should get a quick slap.

Ok. Maybe I'm going a little far (but somehow, I don't really think I am).

Print this off in 54 pt courier and hang it by your desk.

Your brand is how your donors perceive you...

People get confused and think these mighty tomes produced by specialized agencies that contain fonts and colours and templates that no one uses with fancy words are your brand. Nope. Sorry.

Your brand is how your donors perceive you.

Ask your donors what your brand statement is. They probably won't know. They definitely won't care.

What they will say is,

- "Can you tell me what you did with my $100?"
- "Thank you for calling me the other day to say thanks for the donation."
- "What are your goals this year and how can I help?"
- "That letter that came last week really moved me and reminded me why I support you."
- "Every time I call, I find people so helpful."

Ask yourself about some of the charities or companies you support.

What is the brand to you? What do you think about them?

Your brand is how your donors perceive you.

Sorry, not sorry.

Deviation Two — The envelope

Day after day, your beloved donor reaches into her mailbox. She's looking for hope. She's searching for inspiration. She's longing for something special but her mailbox is filled with envelopes that look like bills; same size, same colour, same expectation of "nothing special." This deviation is an important part of your fundraising. Your envelope may be made of paper or it might be a small digital file that rolls into your donor's inbox — but if you get it wrong, then all the hard work you put into it will be for nothing.

I like to joke that I could do an eight-hour presentation on outer envelopes (OEs).

No one would come... but I'm pretty sure I could do one.

I obsess over the envelope more than anything else in direct response. I lie awake in the middle of the night thinking about them. I stand over my grill flipping burgers picturing them. I run along the trails in the forest imagining them.

I have to.

If I get the envelope wrong, then all the other hard work that went into that appeal will be for nothing. All the strategizing, all the segmentation, all the storytelling... for nothing.

I recommend you start obsessing over your OEs too. I see so many that fall short of being an effective piece for your donor to thoughtfully consider, be inspired or moved by, making it easy for them to cast it aside.

You have between one and three seconds to make an impression as your donor moves from her mailbox to her recycling bin.

The question is: what can you do to ensure that your donor stops for a moment to ask herself, "*Is this something I should look at closer?*"

This is where the rubber hits the road! This is how you tell if you're someone who *does* direct mail as opposed to someone who **obsesses** about direct response, doing everything you can to ensure a response.

Your "OE" might be an outer envelope. It might also be a subject line. It might even be a perfectly cropped image on Facebook.

But if you get it wrong, it doesn't matter how good the rest of the content is. You have failed.

1–3 seconds.

You need to **obsess** over them.

I have good news though.

The bar is very, very low, since most practitioners do not obsess over outer envelopes. That's why almost all the mail your donor receives looks the same.

In North America, "looks the same" means a white, #10 envelope, featuring some tiny, one-colour image plopped onto it with a nice little drop shadow. No thought is given to cropping, focus, or what the image is trying to say. It also typically appears alongside a tagline that says too much… or not enough… or simply gives it all away (Fig. 2.1).

The joke I use in presentations is that even if you had the most wonderful letter, written by God himself — if the envelope doesn't work and the donor doesn't open it — it would all be for nothing. The design and thoughtfulness you put into your direct mail envelope is so important, and yet, most envelopes I see look like an afterthought or worse... like there has been no thought about it at all.

In Canada, your donor might get between 30–40 of these types of envelopes in a week. That can balloon to 40–50 a day for someone living in the USA.

Fig. 2.1: This is not a real envelope.

JUNK MAIL, JUNK MAIL, JUNK MAIL

What can you do to ensure that your "outer envelope" stands out from the rest?

Yes, I am going to focus mostly on direct mail appeals, but if you wish, there are considerations here for other types of "OE" if you want to apply them.

First, I am going tell you a few secrets.

Anything other than a white #10 (or DL) that includes your logo and return address will likely beat almost anything else you can come up with. Ok? That's my starting place for outer envelope. I will dive into the "why" a bit later.

The more your envelope (and your appeal) looks like a personal piece of communication from you to me, the better it will perform.

Which would you open first?

I rest my case.

There are many, simple ways you can make your envelope stand out in a stack of white, #10 envelopes. And there is plenty of room for creativity. Here are some of my favourite considerations.

SIZE

At the risk of repeating myself (*and as you read through this book, I will repeat myself*) almost anything will be more effective than a white #10 envelope (or DL).

This past spring, I sat down to look through all of the mail my mother-in-law gets from her charities.

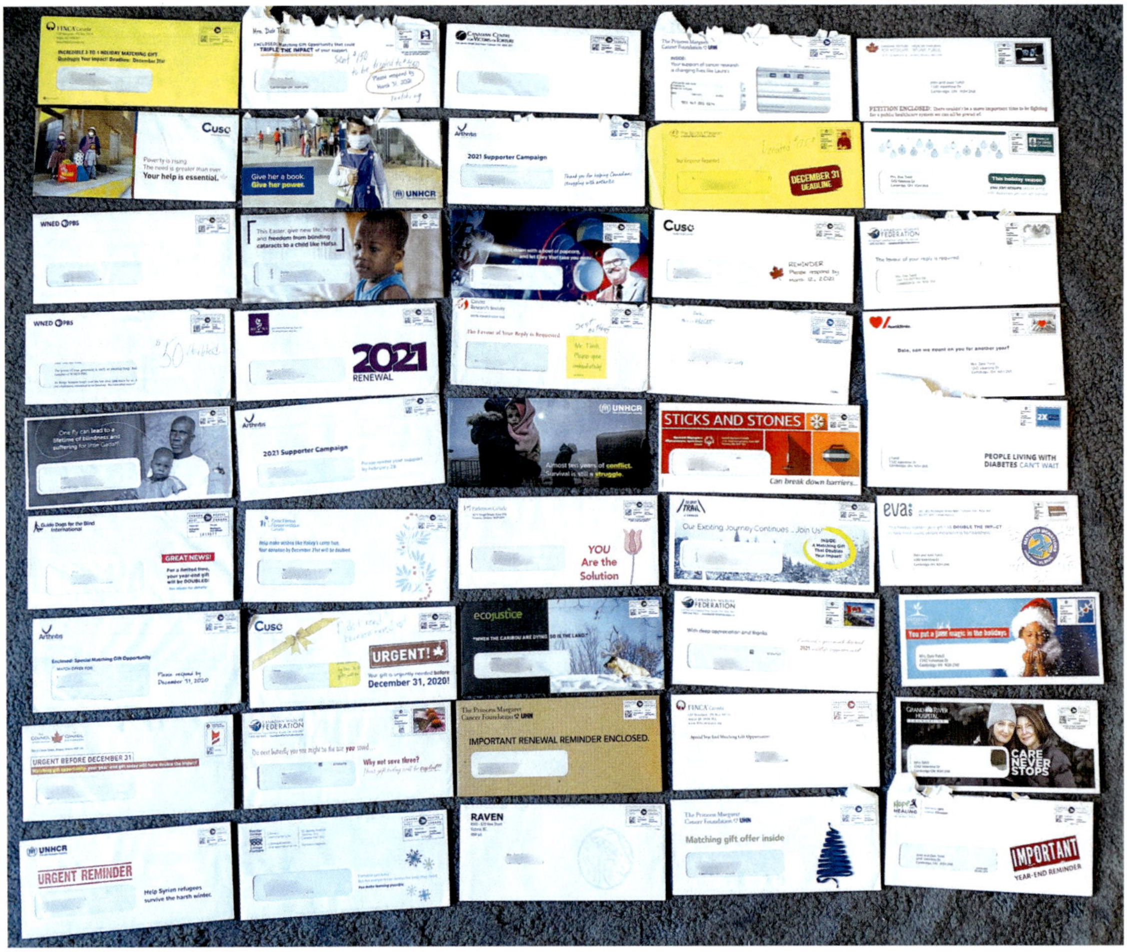

Of the 60 packs she got, 80% of them were #10 envelopes.

A basic truth of attention-getting is — if everyone is doing the same thing, just do the opposite.

When we start working with a new client, I look at everything the donor has seen from the organization in the past year or more and just do the opposite of that.

There are so many different sizes of envelopes.

Most of the direct mail packages created by Agents of Good use a 9.5″ x 5.875″ (similar to a C5) envelope, but we always consider the OE size as it relates to the audience, topic or ask.

We use 9″ x 12″ envelopes for mid-to-high value donors since an oversize envelope suggests that something quite important might be enclosed. We tend to look at using a more invitation sized envelope for things like monthly (regular giving) conversion or legacy appeal.

Always be thinking, "*What is an appropriate size envelope for who I am talking to?*" and, "*What I am asking them for?*"

By the way, you CAN use #10 envelopes in your appeals. Size is not the only determination in its effectiveness. But be aware that unless you are doing something quite clever with it, you might blend in with the mix.

Which takes me to the next point.

STOCK

Another overlooked consideration in the list of things that might make your pack more 'openable' is the stock you use for the outer envelope.

This seems so basic. Likely all of this does. But these things are part of the 1,000 things you need to obsess over and consider, since they can all impact the effectiveness of the pack.

Talk to your printer. Ask if they have something lingering on the shelves that is different than the typical white stock that they might want to clear out. They might have overstock that would be perfect for your next appeal!

Consider bulk printing your own special envelopes using a different paper.

Think about colour.

Using different coloured stock for your envelope can send its own clues about the contents of the package (aside from being dramatically different from the sea of white ones floating around your donor's mailbox).

Colours have meaning!

credit to Stephen Thomas Associates

Question: What does using a red stock envelope mean (in the eyes of your donor)?
Answer: The inside of this pack is so exciting or arresting or energetic that I MUST OPEN right this instant!

Red is perfect for that upcoming holiday appeal! Just as it is for something that is an emergency.

Consider weird stock. Stock that has flecks in it, ridges on it, stock that looks like a lunch bag.

These things work because they help your envelope do the opposite of every other envelope, so it can stand out from the crowd.

TAGLINES

Ugh.

One of the most misused, least understood techniques of direct response… the outer envelope tagline.

One of the biggest problems I see with direct mail is a total lack of understanding of what makes for an effective tagline.

It's like someone decided the plain envelope looked too boring and decided to chuck a tagline on it to make it more interesting.

Back to looking at my mother-in-law's mail. Of the 60 mail packs that she received,

97% had some sort of tagline.

Can a tagline make your mail pack or email more openable? Hell yes.

BUT!

Taglines work in testing if they are the "right" kind of tagline.

So, what's the "right" type?

A good tagline needs to pique the interest of the holder.

"What does this mean?"
"I need to find out more about this right now!"
"What's this about?"
"I need to do something about this! — RIGHT NOW!"
"I'm perplexed by this."

One of the very first direct mail packs I created with Tara Lepp and Stephen Thomas Associates for Schizophrenia Society of Canada, "Reminder" mailing. Circa 1998

Always be appropriate and thoughtful about your tagline.

If you have something inside that will be of interest or value to your donor, tell them!

Teasers that feature something that is a great deal (donors still love matching gift appeals) or an amazing offer (Your $1 = 3 meals) are always good.

Things that we sometimes don't want to work or don't want to like — also work.

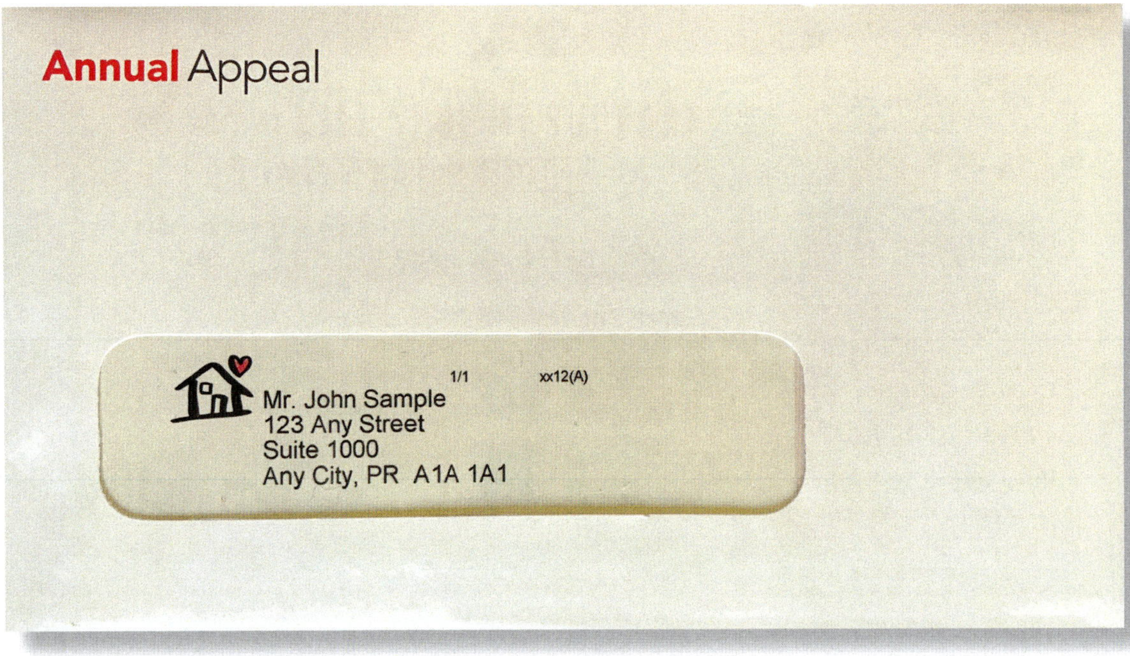

credit to Stephen Thomas Associates

The North American agency-contrived “Annual Fund” or “Annual Appeal” (more on this in *Deviation 5* on reply forms) can still work for certain organizations and for certain appeals.

The bottom line is — the absolute best teaser for your next appeal is likely NO TEASER.

Why? Because you aren’t giving anything away.

The donor wants to know why you are sending them something, and the only way to find out, is to open the mail pack.

Also, when you send a letter in the mail to your grandmother, do you type a teaser on it?

“**GRANDMA!** Want to hear what I did with the birthday money you sent me? **Open NOW to find out!**”

Ok that might work.

But most of the time, a logo, a return address and your postage will, statistically speaking, be just fine.

IMAGES

Like taglines, using images is another misunderstood part of envelope design. I see images used quite a lot on envelopes, but I don't see evidence of someone considering "Why are we using this image?" or "What do I want someone to think or feel when they see it?"

A few thoughts about images:

credit to Stephen Thomas Associates

- *Eye contact is everything.* Humans cannot avoid looking at something that is looking at them. My mom used to scold me for getting too close to her when I took her photo but I wanted her eyes as close as possible to the viewer. Eyes have stopping power. People look at people (or dogs, or trucks or bags, if they have eyes).
- *Images can tell powerful stories.* Think of that image of the boy washed up on the beach. You can imagine it right now. How many stories were told by that image? What story does your image tell? Don't use an image simply because someone thinks this plain envelope or letter needs one. You are a storyteller. What are you trying to say by using a particular image?

- *Sizing*. People. Sigh… please do not use tiny little thumbnails for your images. Use one big image instead of three small ones. The more detail in your image, the bigger it needs to be.
- *Cropping is key*. Just like my mom's eyes, what is the most important thing in your image? What is the subject matter of the image? What do you want me to look at that might move me to do something? A lot of amateur photographers miss the point of the subject matter and/or the focal point of the image. It can't be (*waves hands around in the air) everything. What do you want the reader to look at, and what do you want the reader to feel?

Photos work well in testing. They can really make your pack stand out, but only if they are the right type.

MYSTERY

credit to Stephen Thomas Associates

A pack for Interval House, a shelter for women and children in Toronto, Ontario.

Mystery works. Curiosity spurs action. Less is more. How can you make your donor wonder… what is this and why do I need to open this right now?

A long time ago, I remember Jeff Brooks sharing the story of how he put an image of a coffee ring on his envelope and tested it. It beat the plainer envelope.

Think of why it 'works'.

Why is there a coffee ring here? What does it suggest?

Through the years, I have used the coffee ring trick on lift notes, envelopes, in gratitude reports, newsletters… everywhere. It suggests that someone was looking

credit to Merchants Quay Ireland, Lisa Sargent and Denisa Casement

at this "thing" whatever it is, over their morning cup of joe or tea and wanted you to see it too. But by itself, without context, it's quite the mystery.

Sometimes when you put something in the pack, it also creates intrigue and mystery. For example, a newsletter can add bulk to a pack. The donor wonders — "Why is this pack so heavy? Best to open it and find out!" A paperclip adds a small bump inside.

There are a lot of things you can do that get your donor wondering — "What is this?

What's inside?"

Sometimes having nothing on the outer envelope, creates the most amount of mystery.

SURPRISE

How can you surprise your donor? We know how to do this in our real lives with people we love — why can't we get it sorted out for our donors?

What could you put on or do to an envelope that your donor would never expect?

I will cover more about using unexpected voices in your appeals in *Deviation 6* but even using a talking paper bag in your appeal gives you something to show on your envelope that makes it a surprise.

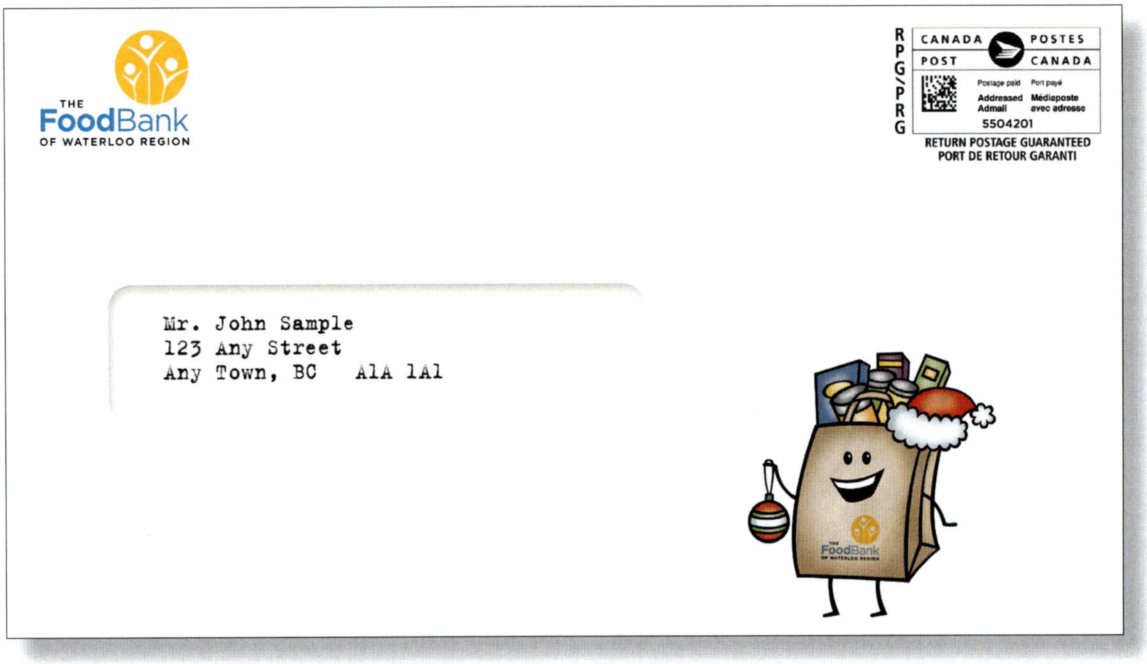

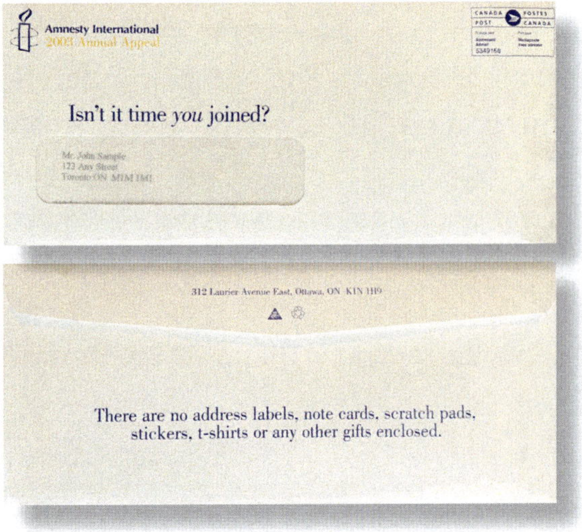

credit to Stephen Thomas Associates

Years ago, working on a prospect appeal for Amnesty International, Steve Thomas came up with a tagline on a #10 envelope that said, "There are no address labels, note cards scratch pads, stickers, t-shirts or any other gifts enclosed."

It worked! Not only did every other prospect pack out there contain so many of these items (and donors knew it,) but it was so against the norm that it became a delight and surprise.

NOSTALGIA

Nostalgia is a powerful feeling and an important tool in your outer envelope arsenal.

Nostalgia can be a gift to your donor. What can you do that makes them feel loved, happy or yearning for a simpler time?

Fig 2.2

Fig 2.3

Consider...

- A historical image that would be familiar to your audience **(Fig. 2.2)**
- A familiar phrase or quote or line from a song
- A typeface, like Courier, that harkens back to the days of typewriters and word processors
- Design that looks like something old and familiar, like a squishy photo album
- An illustration that represents a specific time and place, like the Coca-Cola Santa **(Fig. 2.3)**

Nostalgia draws the donor in. It creates warm feelings for a time past and depending on the content of the pack, can be a great mechanism for emotional engagement.

HUMAN TOUCH

The best direct response looks like a piece of personal communication from me to you. Few organizations understand this basic truth.

Handwriting your donor's name and address on the envelope, regardless of the

size, can be one of the most powerful things you can do to create an effective envelope.

This isn't smoke and mirrors at play.

We live in a world where everything looks amazing, glossy and perfect all the time. We live in a world where IMPERFECTIONS can, and should, be considered as cutting edge techniques.

I'm left-handed so when I write, I always smear the ink. Computers don't smear ink. Humans do.

Unless you are obsessive, when you put a stamp on an envelope, it rarely is perfectly straight or equally distant from the top and right. Computers don't put stamps on angles. Humans do.

Sometimes when we are writing a few cards over our morning croissant and cappuccino, you might leave a coffee ring or some delicious fatty crumbs behind. Computers don't leave fatty crumbs. Humans do.

Here it is — 2022, and I'm telling you that *fatty crumbs and stamps on an angle* is cutting edge fundraising.

Alert the media.

URGENCY

Urgency is such an important tool in the context of fundraising. But so often it is over or underutilized.

First, not EVERYTHING can be urgent all the time.

I am writing this book in the spring of 2021. We are well over a year into the COVID pandemic. Even though many organizations are still operating in an emergency state — not every appeal or email can be breathless and blaring. It's exhausting.

However, you are (theoretically) an organization that needs to raise funds to meet the needs of its mission and serve its beneficiaries. If you don't raise funds you won't be able to operate. So, you do urgently need donor gifts to keep going. Don't you?

Unfortunately, it often seems like mail appeals come across as an afterthought or some sort of weird journalistic observation or recording of something trivial.

How can you create urgency on your envelope?

- A bright-coloured stock or ink colour
- Using the word 'urgent'
- A deadline for gifts
- Design that looks rushed or hand made

Urgency is a powerful tool for the right appeal at the right time. It can get your piece looked at, and opened!

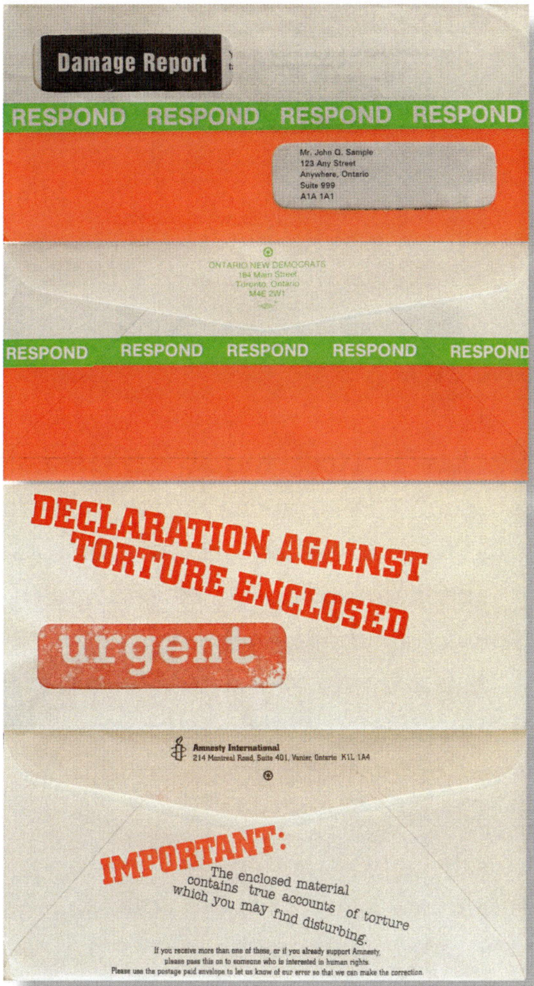

credit to Stephen Thomas Associates

credit to Stephen Thomas Associates

BRAND/LOGO

I mentioned earlier in this chapter that a good starting place for your next outer envelope is to only feature your logo, return address and postage.

IF your organization is brilliant at telling donors amazing stories, giving them donor-sized problems that they can help fix, and if you are terrific at saying thanks for their giving so they feel valued and appreciated by you, then good news… getting something in the mail from you is akin to a card from a friend. They know good feelings are ahead!

However.

If you send the same boring appeals over and over, if you never say thanks, never tell your donor what you did with their gift, and never show them any sort of love whatsoever, then your logo on the outer envelope may be hurting or hindering response.

When we look back at the mailings and touch points that a new client has sent to their donors over the past few years, we also look at the results of these pieces. If results are floundering, especially in main segments, I remove the logo for the first few mailings, since it might be getting in the way of responses.

As a result, I have often seen mailings immediately perform better.

I know it hurts, but facts are facts.

SHOCK

Shock is not a tool I turn to very often, since I have so many other tools at my disposal.

When used properly, at the right time, shock can perform immensely well, but it has to be used sparingly to ensure its effectiveness.

Shock doesn't always have to be a troubling image of a boy washed up on a beach. It can be more subtle too.

This is from a pack we did for Interval House many years ago. Enclosed was a story about a woman who was able to escape a troubling domestic violence situation. The appeal went on to ask the donor to help others do the same — and prevent more funeral announcements. Subtle shock given all of its context. (The appeal bombed by the way.)

credit to Stephen Thomas Associates

Use "shock" sparingly and with caution. It can turn off a donor if used incorrectly or repeatedly.

SENSORY

Although humans have five basic senses, most direct response packages will focus on only one. Sight. (And sometimes it fails even on that level, but that's for another deviation discussion.)

You can also use touch, sound and maybe even smell to create provocative outer envelopes.

As I mentioned previously, there is more to stock life than plain Jane, white stock

#10 envelopes. You can use stock that has ridges on it, or stock that is thicker or heavier. It may seem like such a small thing, but this one difference can make your donor dwell on the envelope for an extra moment or two, and that's the point.

credit to Stephen Thomas Associates

Sound also comes into play. For example, some organizations will send flower seeds for pollinators to their donors. You can hear the seeds as you move the envelope. This alone instantly makes your package more intriguing — more "openable." Envelopes lined with bubble wrap or crinkling paper as you squeeze it to feel what is inside, are sensory experiences that make opening the package all the more interesting.

Another old trick I learned was to start a popular song lyric (if it applies to the appeal obviously) on the outer envelope. It can get your donor humming, whistling and singing as they look at the pack. This is very powerful and a sure way to get the envelope opened.

I'm sure you are waiting for me to (eh-hem) "unpack" how to use smell in your mail.

Paper, all paper, has an inherent smell. This isn't something you can control. You can't make your outer envelope smell like fresh baked apple pie. (AS EFFECTIVE as that would be!) But, our minds are powerful. Using strong images of familiar smelly things can evoke an imagined smell.

INTRIGUE

We are curious beings.

Using intrigue can also make for a powerful envelope.

Adding something into the pack (especially if I can feel it through the paper Fig. 2.4) obviously makes it intriguing; but small, visual clues can also make your direct mail appeal interesting and worth considering.

Throughout my career I've used this bar (Fig. 2.5) on a lot of packages. Back in the day, we used chevrons or TELEMAIL stamped across it. Just like the holes in dot matrix printer paper, some of the meaning behind these things might be lost to us, but not your donors.

credit to Stephen Thomas Associates

Fig 2.4

What is it? What does it mean? Why is this bar here? What am I supposed to think?

Fig 2.5

These are good questions that makes a donor stop and consider. Donors asking themselves questions as they look at your envelope is a GOOD thing! Maybe the answer will lie inside.

The classic mistake is giving it all away to your donor on the front of the envelope. Telling too much of the story, or making it so obvious that it is an appeal for money. No intrigue. No delight in discovery.

Like so many things, less tends to be more. Telling or showing just a little can go a long way in making your piece more intriguing.

FROM

Yes! Showing WHO the letter is from can make your piece instantly openable or quickly chuckable.

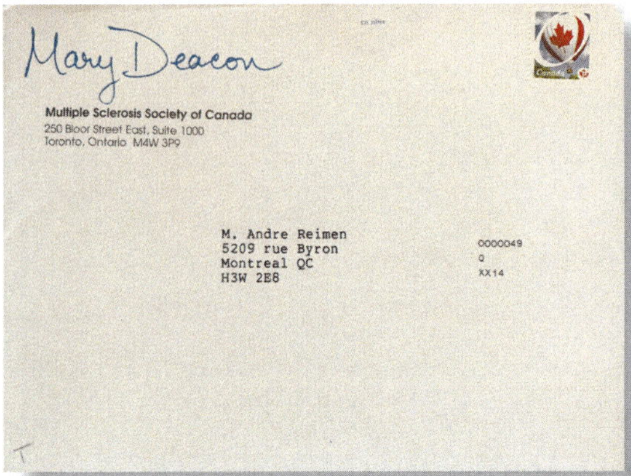

credit to Stephen Thomas Associates

It can also make your pack feel more special, more urgent, or more intriguing.

There is more to envelope life than just your logo, return address and postage.

We've sent mailings from celebrities,

high-profile individuals, directors, board members, bags, birds and talking hearts.

This leads right into the whole concept of personal mail. People send people mail. Organizations and businesses send bills and boring stuff.

POSTAGE

The most powerful visual on your outer envelope just might be the postage that you use.

Almost all the mail my mother-in-law gets uses a very standard, black indicia.

But people, we can be SO more creative than that.

In testing, there is a ranking of postage in terms of effectiveness. Yes — you can test the sort of postage you are using and see dramatic differences in how the appeal performs.

You can test the use of:

- multiple first-class stamps
- a commemorative stamp
- a standard first-class stamp
- a metered stamp
- a custom indicia
- a standard indicia
- no postage

The stamp can literally be your mail visual or tagline. We used to even make fake post marks around the postage area to add visual interest to the piece.

When I told you this stuff was super nerdy and obsessive, I wasn't kidding.

An example (credit to Derek Humphries) from Greenpeace Russia. If you tell me you wouldn't open this, you're lying.

IN SUMMARY

This list isn't exhaustive. There are many things that can make your donor consider your organization's envelope for even an extra second — and that's the goal.

Use just one of these ideas or a mixture of many to create a more powerful pack.

The job of direct marketers is to get the attention of donors and then make sure we reward them for it. Otherwise, we might not get it again. As we move through more deviations, we will look at the many ways we can *reward donors* for their time and consideration, but never doubt for one second that the hard work is in our hands. It's our responsibility.

For more nerdy reading, I would recommend you surf over to **http://www.sofii.org** and check out the brilliant **Jerry Huntsinger tutorial** on how to get your envelope ripped open.

Deviation Discoveries

Keep this in mind next time you think about your "envelope."

1. The more your "envelope" (online or offline) feels personal, like something sent from me to you, the more effective it likely will be.
2. Most of the "envelopes" your donor gets in her mailbox or inbox look exactly the same. How can you change yours so it stands out from the rest?
3. From testing we know that the most effective outer envelope (mail) is a simply designed 9.5″ x 5.875″ and features only your logo, return address and postage. So start there.

Deviation Three — Storytelling is dead

Everyone tells you that you need a good story. We search high and low for them all the time… but this deviation shows you that sometimes you don't need a story for effective fundraising. Sometimes what you actually need is right in front of you.

Ok. Ok.

Storytelling is not dead. You couldn't fundraise without stories.

However, we need to look at the *role of stories* in direct response, since so many organizations misunderstand how to use them effectively in their appeals to donors.

Stories are binders. We connect more deeply and intimately through the stories we share with one another. This is why, in most of the direct mail appeals Agents of Good creates, we give space for donors to talk, and tell you a part of their story.

You might ask donors why they give to you or who they think of when they give, or you might allow them to share a reflection about a place in nature that makes them feel at peace.

Far too often I will have a client ask me to review a letter that has an 'okay' story… but that's it. They haven't done the work to tell the right story.

In direct response and direct marketing, there are a few critical things that can make or break your appeals.

1. **List**

   These are the people you want to have a conversation with, to tell your story *to*.

   The quality of this list accounts for almost 50% of the success or failure of your piece.

   For example, if you have a list of donors that came to your in-person event for the last five years, and you send them your "Fall Direct Mail Appeal," that appeal, to that list, will likely fail. I can tell you that already.

   It will fail because the people on the list are event participants or event donors. That's what they like to do. That's how they like to give. Yes, you might find a few "mail donors" in the bunch, but I wouldn't hold your breath waiting for them to give to your mail pieces.

   As another example, if you have a list of donors who have been consistently giving to your mail appeals for the last five years, and you send them that same "Fall Appeal," it likely will do very well.

   This is why I highly recommend you *segment* your mailings and track the responses based on different audiences or different parts of your list. You segment your donors for each mailing so you can:

   - Track the performance of different types of donors (e.g., an current donor vs. an event participant)
   - Acknowledge that you know who they are (e.g., if they are a monthly donor, you refer to that)
   - Make sure you aren't asking a door who gave you $500 last year for $25 this year.

The three other critical make or break parts of your direct response appeal are:

2. **Offer**

   What are you asking for?

3. **Timing**

   Mailing a Christmas pack in September seems wildly crazy to me (and I know some orgs do it) but if you send your amazing pack at the wrong time it's just not going to work.

4. **Creative**

How it all looks and sounds and yes, the story(ies) you tell and how you tell them.

So, first and foremost as a storyteller, you *need to know what you are asking for and why the donor should care that you are asking for it.*

At the end of the day, every appeal, every Case for Support document, essentially has to answer those two questions: *Why me? Why now?*

UNIQUE REASON TO GIVE

Let's back up.

Every organization, be it charity or nonprofit, is extremely complex.

The structure of its staff, the complexities of its programs, how it serves its beneficiaries, how it fundraises, where it receives funding from, so on and so forth.

But that's not your donor's problem.

She doesn't care about your complexities. She certainly doesn't give to you to help figure them out. That's your job. You need to tap into the *essential reason of why you exist.*

In marketing, you'll hear the term USP — Unique Selling Position or Proposition. It's basically a fancy term that helps you figure out what you do best and why someone might want to buy "you."

But this is fundraising.

I'd like you to consider your URG (*hat tip to Ken Burnett for coining the phrase in his 1992 book, Relationship Fundraising*). **URG** = **U**nique **R**eason to **G**ive.

Every organization has one. It might be written down somewhere, might be lingering on a shelf or in the brain of its founder or original board, but it's out there.

48 hours before you were founded, a small group of (likely angry) humans made a decision to do something about what they perceived was a "wrong" in their world. They wanted to right that wrong. That "wrong" offended their values and they were determined to do something about it by finding other people who shared their values and also believed this wrong was a wrong. They would work together to try to fix it.

There is a version of your URG in there somewhere.

That version should express why you exist (what wrong you strive to fix), should be clear on why you and your charity are the very best at what you do, and how donors are vital to your success.

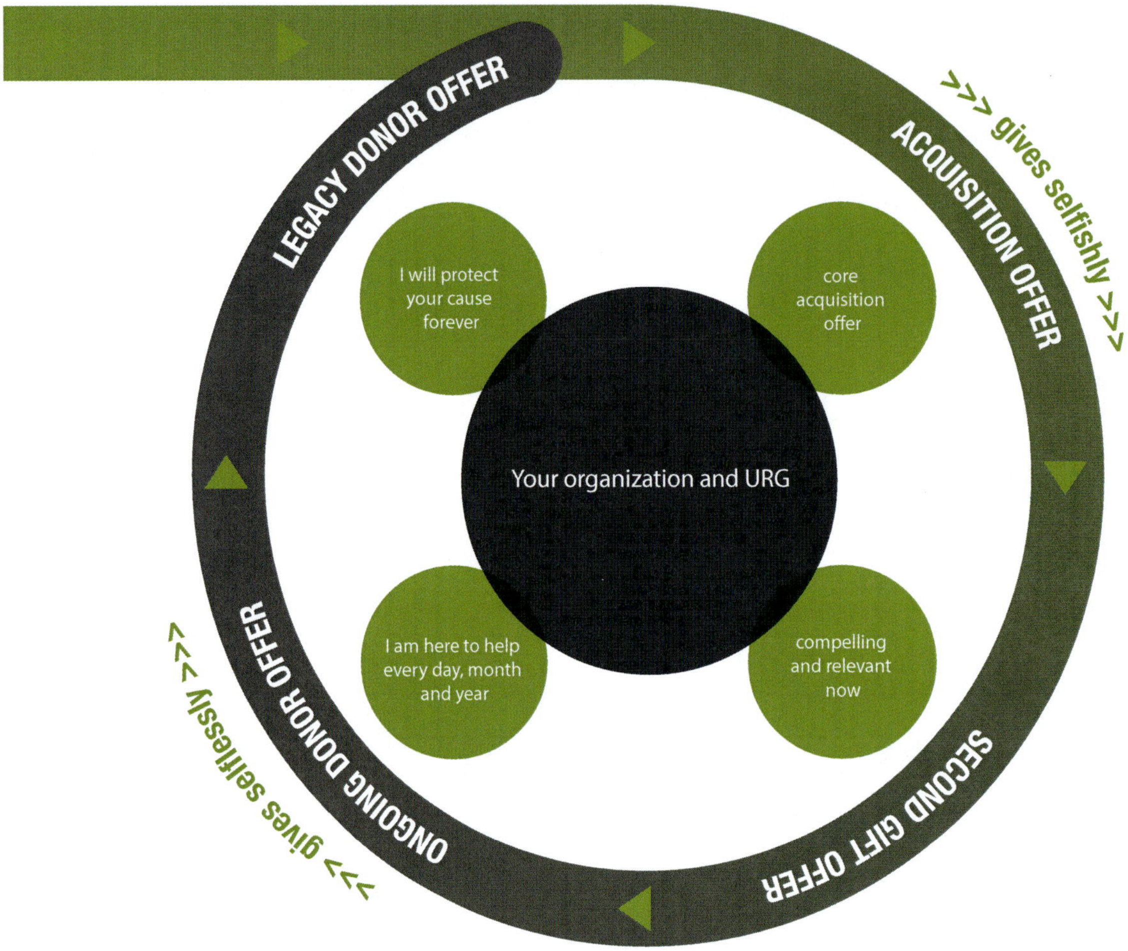

This sphere diagram represents how you connect to people and inspire them to support you. Outside the circle is the universe of potential donors for your organization, the people who care about what you do or share the same values with you. The center of the circle is your URG. From the original acquisition offer through to a thoughtful legacy piece, each and every contact with your donors is illuminated by your URG and brought to life with strong, clear offers.

Your URG shows how your donor can express *your* mission through *their* own values and reflects why your donors give to you: because you offer them a way to take action for something they believe in.

Donors give, not because they are educated by you or convinced by you, but because they are inspired and they share the same **beliefs** and **values** as you.

Here are a couple of examples.

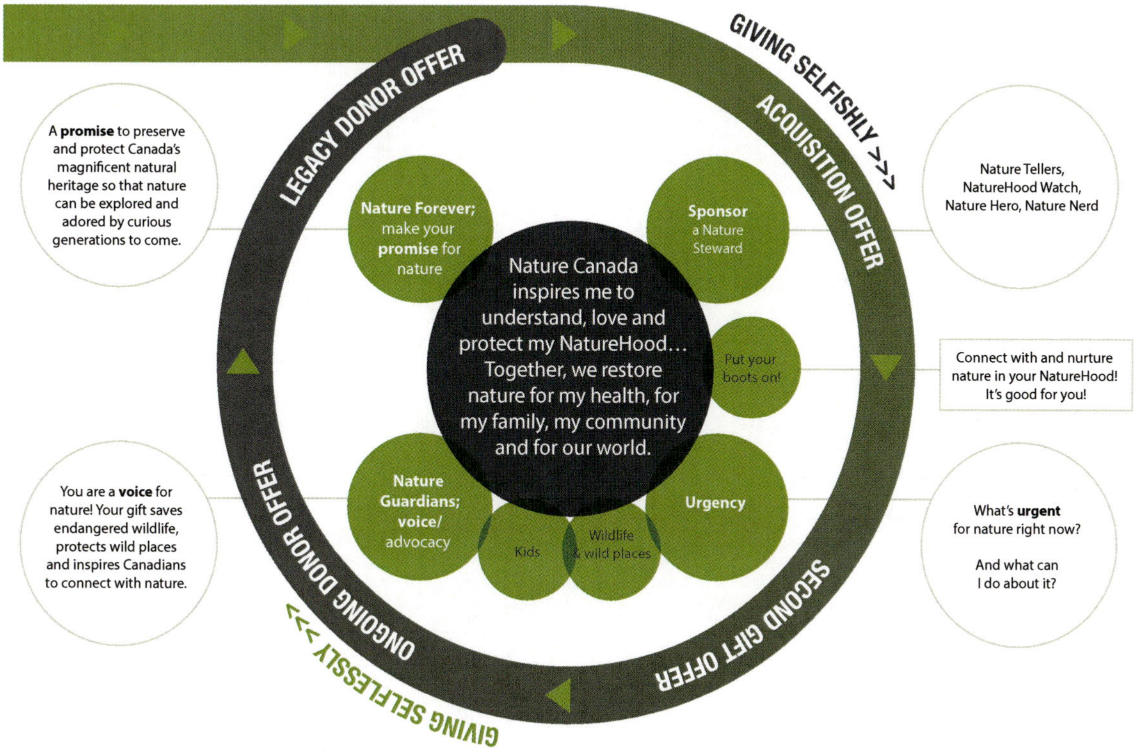

donor promise: I believe that the innovators of tomorrow need to express fearless creative energy today and every day. As a member of Station Gallery, I invest in my creativity and the creativity of children and grown-ups in Durham Region and beyond. Together, we are building the kind of citizen our world needs.

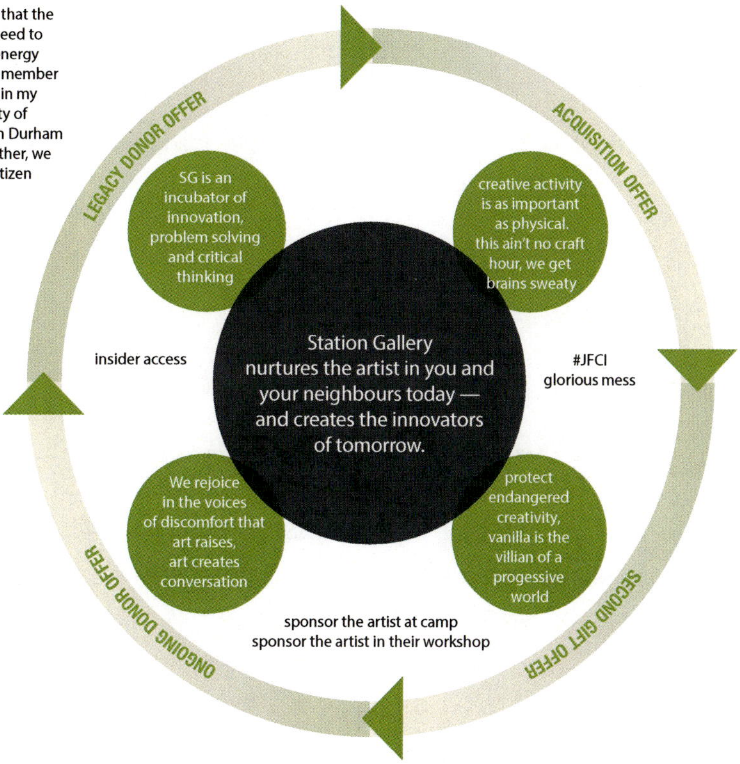

Your URG is about your donor. Not you. They can see themselves in the story. Its wording is succinct and conversational.

You need to do this work before you can effectively consider some of your core offers for your donors.

VALUES AND EMOTIONS

Your letter/offer/ask must utilize values and emotions.

This spring campaign for Ontario Nature was to save a piece of land that was

only accessible by boat. The outer envelope was designed for its donors.

The package included a two-page letter. Each paragraph touched on a value and emotion shared between the organization and its donors.

	value	emotion

You can help create the Sydenham River Nature Reserve	generosity	aroused
Protect your share of ontario nature's first-ever riverine nature reserve	attentiveness	angry/excited
Date, 2016		
Ms. Jane Sample 123 Anystreet Ave. Yourcity, ON 1A1 A1A		
Dear <Jane>,		
We need you to help us save a spectacular piece of land and create Ontario Nature's first riverine nature reserve!	selflessness	angry/frustrated
Because you're an Ontario Nature member who has generously supported our nature reserves in the past, I thought this story would intrigue you. And the story of this Sydenham River property is definitely one of intrigue.	loyalty	touched
Your best access is not on foot, but by canoe. You encounter strange creatures with exotic names, including an elusive turtle with an odd leathery shell, a bizarre bivalve called a snuffbox, and a fish called a brindled madtom. You see trees here you won't see anywhere else in Ontario. And, with 98% of Carolinian habitat like this gone forever, **you feel like you've entered a lost world**.	spirituality	excited/happy
You can protect your share of the Sydenham River Nature Reserve. **But please, we must act swiftly. There's an immediate threat**. Vast amounts of natural cover have already been lost in this biodiverse watershed. And there is very little protection for the riverbanks, woodlands, and meadows that remain.	courage	nervous/tense
Imagine you're joining me on a visit to the property to see for yourself exactly what is at stake.		excited
You slip your canoe into the calm, serene Sydenham River. This is the best way to visit—by paddling into the heart of the property. Your paddle slices through the Sydenham River, one of Ontario's most biodiverse waterways. **This ribbon of water is one of the last remaining connected green corridors in southwestern Ontario**.	spirituality	happy
A cerulean warbler trills and buzzes from the top of the forest canopy. You gaze up at the stunning trees like the Kentucky coffee-tree, blue ash and tulip—all only found here, in southwestern Ontario's Carolinian zone. During migration,	appreciation	happy
Ontario Nature 85th ANNIVERSARY 214 King Street West, Suite 612, Toronto, ON M5H 3S6 phone: 416-444-8419 toll free: 1-800-440-2366 ontarionature.org/protectnow *please turn over...*		
the trees teem with songbirds like scarlet tanagers, indigo buntings, Blackburnian warblers and wood thrush. Half of Ontario's bird species breed or pass through here. **Intact woodland like this is extremely rare.**	attentiveness	alarmed
The Sydenham River is home to some of the richest diversity of endangered and at-risk freshwater mussels in the world, with strange and beguiling names like wavy rayed lampmussel and round pigtoe. Most of these are globally rare, found here and **nowhere else in Canada**.	preservation	sympathetic
The river is also **critical habitat** for at-risk turtles including northern map turtles, Blanding's turtles and the rarely-seen spiny softshell.	compassion	sympathetic
You can help save this spectacular and important property forever by helping us create the Sydenham River Nature Reserve.	altruism	confident
We are collaborating with our local member groups, the Sydenham Field Naturalists and Lambton Wildlife, to acquire and maintain the Reserve. Their generosity and leadership on this project is inspiring. Together, we have already raised crucial funds from foundations, corporations and other partners, and now we're looking to members like you to protect your share.	good will	happy
Together, we urgently need to raise the remaining $240,000 by September 1st. Will you protect your share today?	cooperation	energetic
You'll find enclosed a special feature on the proposed Sydenham River reserve—I hope you enjoy reading more about it. You'll also find enclosed your reply form, where you can protect your share of our newest Nature Reserve today!	preservation	delighted
Please, join me and take action today to create our first-ever riverine nature reserve. Thank you for your vital support.	preservation	happy
 Yours for nature, *Caroline Schultz* Caroline Schultz, Executive Director		
P.S. Protect your share of the Sydenham River Nature Reserve by making your gift to Ontario Nature today!	preservation	happy

Have you ever looked at your own appeal letters this way?

George Smith said that all great fundraising should sound like someone talking. Using an emotional range in your letters does just that.

We do this every day with the people we know and love. Why do we stop when it comes to communicating with our donors?

If you find this difficult to do (especially the conversational part), I suggest you print your letter off and read it out loud to someone in your office. You will instantly change where you start and stop, how you structure your sentences and the words that you use.

I also want to point out that the above letter has no story.

It didn't need one, since it clearly articulated:

- the problem,
- the solution,
- the action they wanted donors to take, and then,
- overlaid a number of big values and emotions onto it.

FOCUS ON THE OFFER

The most classic direct response offer is: **Give us $7 NOW or the dog gets it**!

It's a classic, since it checks all four boxes of a great offer:

❍ **Problem**: The dog is going to "get it"
❍ **Solution**: Your $7 ensures the dog does NOT "get it"
❍ **Action**: Give us the $7
❍ **Urgency**: We need the $7 NOW

With *no* offer and *no* ask, you will get *no* money.

I know it seems obvious, yet like I mentioned earlier, I often get letters with a half decent story that never gets around to actually asking for anything.

Here are a few other great offers (Fig. 3.1, 3.2, 3.3) most of which can be found on http://www.sofii.org.

In *Deviation One*, I shared an example from St. Patrick's Home of Ottawa to show that when you have a good offer, and you clearly articulate the problem, solution and action you need the donor to take, you don't necessarily need a story.

Here is another example of how you can create effective fundraising without using a story.

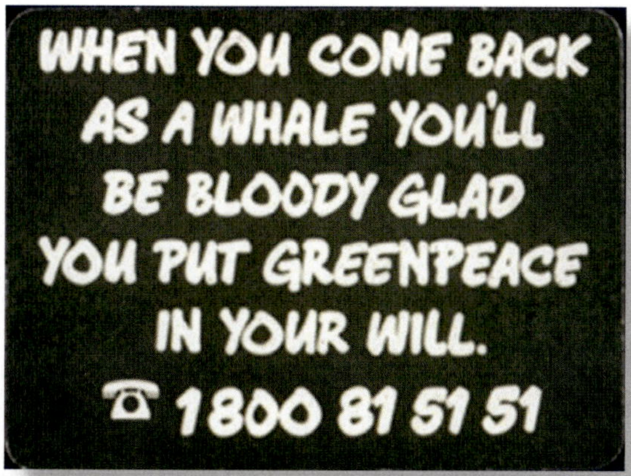

Fig. 3.1: Greenpeace Australia: Famous legacy offer on a beer mat

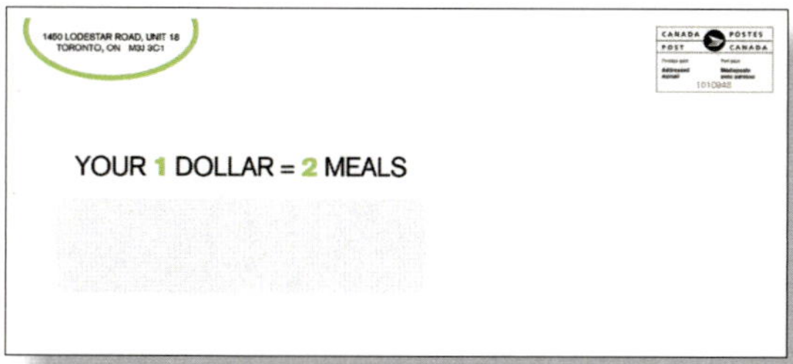

Fig. 3.2: Second Harvest: Prospect pack

Fig. 3.3: RNLI UK: Press ad for single cash gift

The following pack tells a story without really telling a story. Not in the traditional sense. Instead, this pack really leans into the *offer.*

Second Harvest needed to raise $130,000 to buy a new refrigerated truck to add to its fleet of other trucks that weren't refrigerated. Second Harvest uses their trucks to literally zip all over Toronto rescuing food before it goes to waste. They then work diligently to get that food to people in need.

This was the outer envelope sent to donors. It was printed on kraft stock, (the same stock used for paper bags) and showed an image of a little truck driving into the pack. "BEEP! BEEP!"

Special Note: the truck facing into the bottom right of the envelope is a visual clue to get the envelope turned over and opened. As a rule, you don't want images of things with eyeballs facing off the page, since eye movement studies show your reader will follow the direction of the eyes and move their view away from the words you want them to read. Usually, you want eyes facing into the page — but in this case — we actually wanted the reader to move their eyes off.

The back of the envelope had the Second Harvest logo and return address. This envelope was obviously a lot different than what donors tended to get from the Second Harvest. I mean, have you ever gotten an envelope like this?

And what about a letter from a truck (Fig. 3.4)?

The truck makes a simple Case for Support in its letter, and on the back we included a simple graphic about the "who" and "how" Second Harvest was feeding people around the city.

A lift note (Fig. 3.5) from Joe Chesham focuses again on **what** they were asking donors for, the **problem** as they saw it, the **solution** they envisioned, and the **action** they were asking their donor to take to help solve the problem.

We also got a late message that there was a matching gift, so we added a buckslip (Fig. 3.6) into the pack to share the exciting news.

Finally, we added two additional pieces. The reply form (Fig. 3.7) and a simple peel-off sticker with a "set of keys" for the truck so that the donor could put the keys next to the gift level they wanted to give at.

Engaging, simple involvement devices like this sticker really do work in appeals.

On the reply form, you'll notice we added a gift option of $65,000 and a note that read "*I'll buy the other half of the truck.*"

Yes, we were secretly hoping that someone would send in a cheque for $65,000! Although no one did for this appeal, it's something that can work.

At the very least, the donor gets a cheeky chuckle that we would ask for such an outrageous amount and thinks, well I can't do that but maybe I can give a bit more than I tend to.

This simple piece grabs the donor's attention since it is so different.

The appeal worked.

Second Harvest got their new truck. In fact, the appeal did so well that we scrapped the reminder pack we had pulled together and spent some of the budget on doing a heartfelt thank you letter and email instead. (Fig. 3.8) It was from the truck, of course.

This campaign raised twice as much money as the previous spring and the average gift was much higher than usual.

BEEP!
BEEP!

March 30, 2011

You can help Second Harvest buy ME!
I'm a shiny new truck and I want to rescue food that would otherwise go to waste and deliver it to hungry people!

Dear Jen,

I have a dream.

I have a dream that I start up every morning and rev my engine with joy knowing that today, I will be driving around Toronto delivering food to hungry men, women and children in our city.

Sure, I could be bought by some fancy company and maybe deliver diamonds or plasma TVs, but I believe I was built for something more.

As soon as my spark plug fired, I knew I was destined for greatness.

And you can help!

Right now, I'm sitting on this lot waiting to be bought. And I hear the sales guys here in their shiny suits talking about the interested customers, but I only care about one customer -- and I know you care about them too.

Second Harvest.

I hear you are a supporter of Second Harvest. Good for you! You'll also find in this package a letter from Joe over at Second Harvest and he can tell you more about exactly <u>why</u> they need this truck <u>right now</u> and what <u>you can do</u> to make it happen.

Please, help Second Harvest deliver more food to hungry people -- and fulfil my destiny too!

Beep Beep,

Future Truck of Second Harvest

Fig. 3.4

25 YEARS
SECOND
HARVEST

March 30, 2011

Dear Friend,

I know it may seem a bit strange for you to receive a letter from a truck (bet that's never happened to you before!) but we wanted you to feel the energy – and urgency – of this opportunity.

Right now, there is a truck sitting on a lot somewhere in this city.

Second Harvest has a pressing need for it.

And all we need is you.

Will you help us buy this new truck today? Will you make your gift to Second Harvest today and help us buy our truck and continue delivering fresh food across the city?

Second Harvest exists to feed hungry people by rescuing fresh fruits, vegetables, dairy and meat that would otherwise go to waste. Our trucks hit the streets each and every day and stop at grocery stores, food manufacturers and restaurants to pick up food and deliver it right away to our partners – over 200 social service agencies including women's shelters, breakfast programs, drop-in centres and more.

Your support already helps us provide more than 16,000 meals a day. You're helping feed a hungry child, a senior on a fixed income, a woman who has fled abuse, a struggling family.

But here's what else we know:

- more children are attending school on an empty stomach;
- more parents skip meals so their children can eat;
- more elderly people have inadequate diets because they live in poverty;
- more working-poor families have to choose between eating and paying the rent.

At Second Harvest, we take a common-sense approach to hunger. And part of that means that we recognize when we can solve a problem.

We can solve the problem of increased demand. With our new truck.

1450 LODESTAR ROAD, UNIT 18, TORONTO, ON M3J 3C1 t: 416.408.2594 f: 416.408.2598 SECONDHARVEST.CA

Our fleet of 7 trucks has been on the road for the last 4 years – and in that time, we've gone from delivering 5.4 million pounds of food to 6.4 million pounds of food – that's an increase of over 15%!

With a new truck, we can deliver enough food for an additional 2,500 meals per day. You'll be helping fill those empty stomachs with fresh, nutritious food...

...And the child who came to the community centre for tutoring can concentrate a bit more on his homework.

...And the dad who is looking for work can focus on his resume.

...And the abused woman can gain energy, strength and confidence.

...And gathering around a table to eat together will instil a sense of community in every single life.

You're giving much more than a truck. But we need the truck to make it all happen.

You'll find a sticker enclosed. Please, make your gift to help us turn the key and start up our brand new truck. Your gift today will help us deliver 2,500 extra meals each and every day across our city! Please, help us fill empty stomachs with fresh, nutritious food!

Yours for a city without hunger,

Joe Chesham
Volunteer President, Second Harvest

P.S. Amazing news! Just as we were finishing our letter to you, The Pottruff Family Foundation came through offering to match your gift to buy our new truck! Check out the slip we enclosed at the last minute!

Fig. 3.5

25 YEARS
SECOND
HARVEST

We are delighted to tell you that The Pottruff Family Foundation has just offered to match your gift today!

Marie from The Pottruff Family Foundation has a special message for you. She said, "We hope this inspires others to give! We will match all donations up to half the value of the truck. Join us in supporting this terrific initiative and help Second Harvest buy their new truck!"

That means we need to raise $65,000 from our caring supporters to purchase our new truck! Please, send your gift today and it will be matched!

Fig. 3.6

YES, TRUCK! Here are your keys! I'll help buy you for Second Harvest! Here is my gift of:

…ker to …ice	Please attach sticker to your choice	Please attach sticker to your choice	Please attach sticker to your choice
❍ $X	❍ $XX	❍ $Other_____	❍ $65,000 (I'll buy the other half of the truck!)

Mr. John Sample
123 Any Street
Any Town, BC   A1A 1A1

Remember your gift will be matched today!

❍ I have enclosed a cheque payable to Second Harvest OR
❍ I pr…
Card …
Signa…
Thank … your su… can su… gift in y…
❍ Ple…
Informa…
My pho…
1450 LOD…

Fig. 3.7

Hi <Jen>!

Beep Beep!

You did it! You helped Second Harvest surpass their goal and they are going to be able to buy me, a shiny new truck, and deliver more fresh food to hungry people.

Your gift means Second Harvest will be able to buy me and build me just the way they need to. As you know, Second Harvest rescues food that would otherwise go to waste and delivers it within 48 hours to hungry people across the city.

Here is where I'll be with my new happy friends at Second Harvest, thanks to you!

Your support is absolutely amazing. Thank you so much for being a great partner of Second Harvest. See you on the streets in the fall!

Beep Beep!

THE **NEW** SECOND HARVEST TRUCK!
(I've been waiting my whole truck life to say that!)

Fig. 3.8

Deviation Discoveries

Stories have been used to connect humans since the beginning of time, but often, in pursuit of the *right* story for the appeal, other more important things can be overlooked.

1. Understand your URG. What's the **U**nique **R**eason I should **G**ive to you and not to another organization that looks and sounds a bit like you? Every organization is complicated, but that's not your donor's problem. Think about the moment, 24 hours before your organization was founded, and it will be there where you will likely find the purest expression of why your organization exists.
2. Start by answering these questions: What are you asking the donor for? What do you want them to do? Why should they care right now?
3. Ensure that every appeal utilizes a full range of values and emotions, because that's what we do when we have conversations with other humans. Sharing your values and emotions will create deeper connections with your donors.

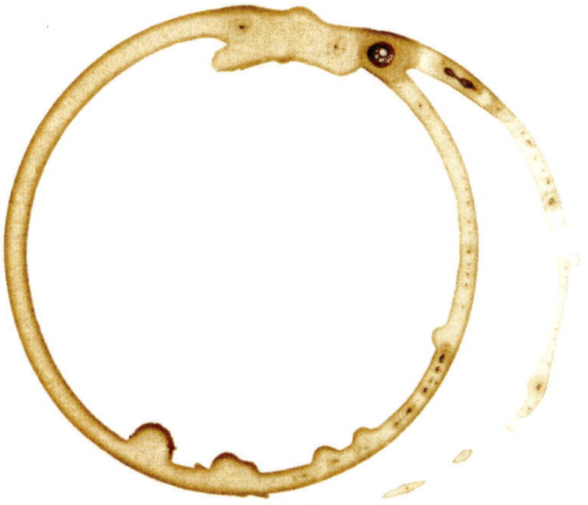

Deviation Four — It's all the small things

Great design and fundraising is like everything else in life. It's made up of 1,000 small things you need to do to make it all work. This deviation looks at a number of small things you can incorporate into your work to make it stand out and rise above everything else your donor sees and feels.

You've probably heard the expression "death by a thousand cuts." In life and work, it's not the one thing you can do, it's the thousand that will make a difference.

I've sat in board room meeting after board room meeting where the intent is to come up with that BIG, breakthrough idea. You're chasing ghosts, my friend. It's the thousand small ideas that will change your organization.

I obsess over small things. Colleagues find it strange that after so many years I still want to talk about rubber stamps and courier type, but these are the things that still can make a difference to an appeal — so why wouldn't I?

On their own, small things are easily dismissed, and very rarely mentioned at conferences. They can be boring to think or talk about, but collectively they can revolutionize your fundraising.

Why?

It is because small (and very human) things add up to a unique and personal experience for your donor. It's similar to your entire fundraising program. It would be a strategic mistake to look at a mailing and remove it because it didn't "perform" well. Every piece in the mailing, every mailing itself, every touch point with your donor all add up to a collective noise. Is the program you're running Chopin or death metal?

I'll let you think about that.

THE REAL MAGIC BULLETS

My friend and colleague Francesco Ambrogetti shared a fascinating test he ran when he was Director of Development in the #donorlove department at UNICEF Italy.

He found that if he sent a hand-written thank you card within 48 hours of a donor's gift and if he called them on the anniversary of their giving or on their birthday, he saw a **30% increase in their retention** and a **50% increase in their "Lifetime Value."**

There's your BIG idea!

Two simple, low-tech things that anyone could do right now can yield significant results. Yet we get wrapped up in the latest technology or shiny new metric while trying to squeeze out every last dollar.

I share Franki's finding with people all the time and they still don't do it. It's dismissed. Too simple. Not sexy enough.

So, that's *one* and *two* of *1,000* small things.

THE POWER OF A PAPERCLIP

Hear me out.

When we ask our clients to print, personalize and mail a portion of their appeal in-house, we ask them to paperclip their business card to the top of the letter or attach a photograph that shows the donor's gift in action or potential impact of their gift. We suggest that maybe they just clip all of the components of the pack together.

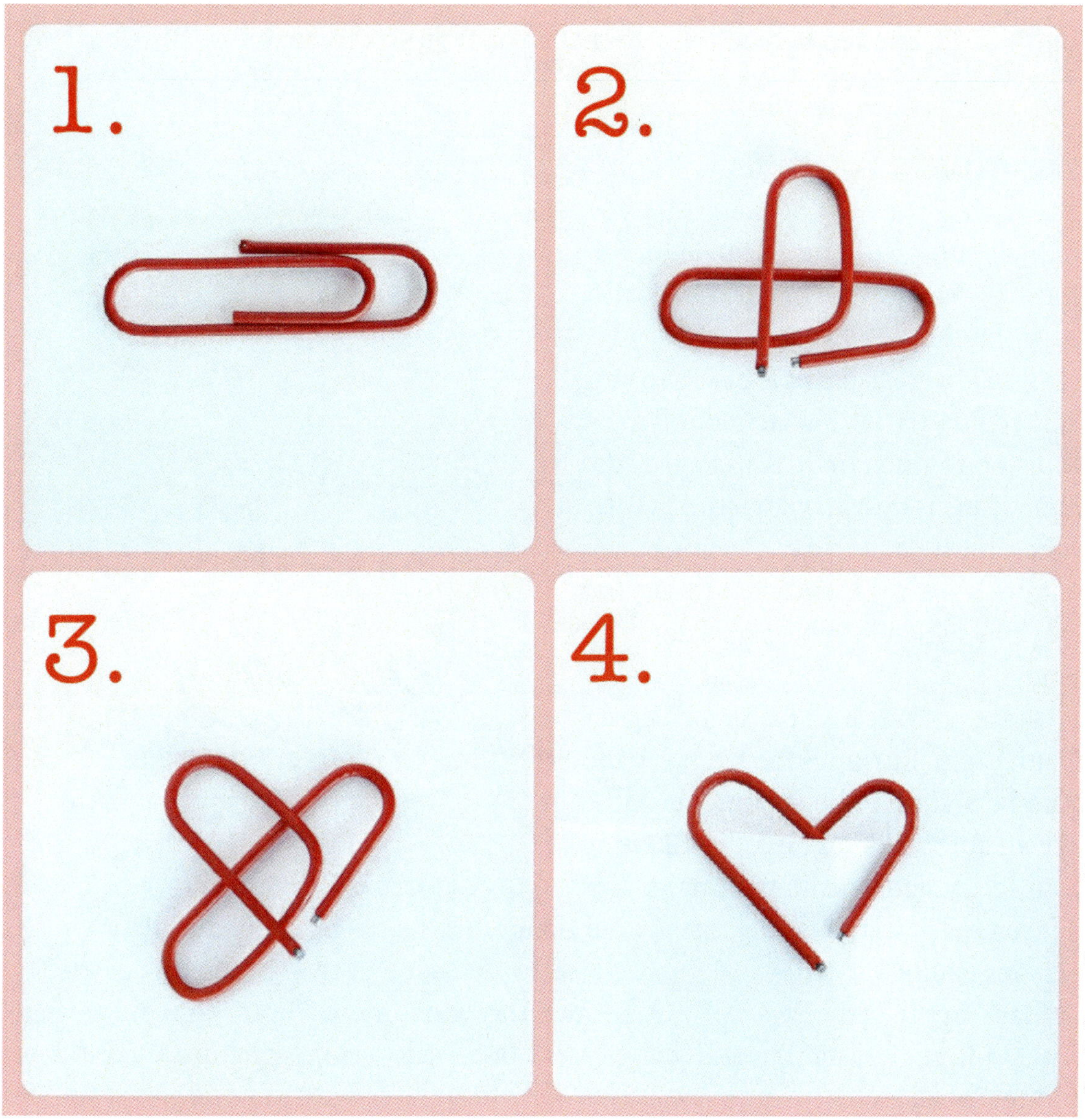

credit to Liz Fourez of lovegrowswild.com

Paperclips have power for a few reasons.

First, you know what doesn't like paperclips? Machines. Not only do they not possess the dexterity to attach a paper clip to a piece of paper, it also gums up the system. So, a paperclip suggests that a human was involved. Someone sat down and put this "thing" together for another human. That, in the context of direct marketing, has power.

Also, paperclips have presence. They take up space. They have texture. They can be felt through an envelope. They have enough power to get that envelope opened. Which makes your mailing more effective and helps it to raise more money.

It's 2022, and I'm here to tell you that a paperclip is the next new BIG idea.

SIGNATURES

The *signature* of the letter signer is another "small thing" that can have a huge impact.

This is a great example of something that seems trivial but actually isn't if you stop to think on it. A basic truth of fundraising is this: people give to people. When I, (the donor) flip the letter over to find out who is sending it to me and I see this signature, what signal does this send?

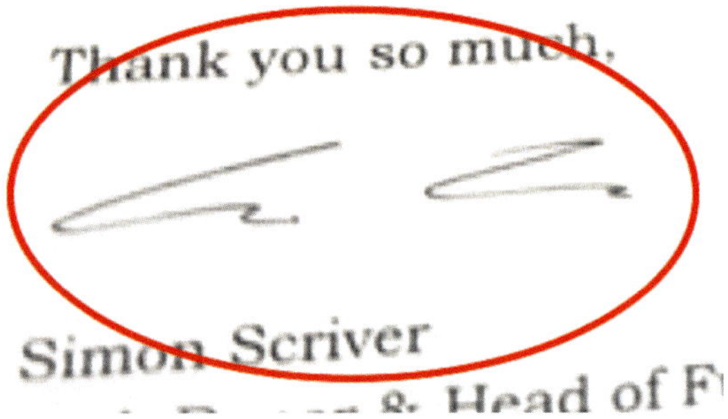
Thank you so much,

Simon Scriver

that I know President Reagan
support.

Sincerely,

Bob Packwood

Bob Packwood
Chairman

President Reagan's dream of
n your $100 is absolutely

credit to Stephen Thomas Associates

I joke with my Irish pal Simon Scriver that he actually isn't Bono from U2 and thus he shouldn't be signing his name like an autograph on his letters. Letting your letter signer write their name like this sends a quick visual message to your donor that the signer is too important for the person reading the letter as demonstrated by the fact that their name isn't readable.

Back in my early days, we would open the signature in Photoshop and trace it with a thicker pen tool to add weight to it. Bob Packwood's signature is confident and readable!

COFFEE RINGS & SMEARED INK

This seems strange to bring up, but a coffee ring visual can do so much for your appeal or communication.

Just give in to the idea.

When you see a newspaper on the kitchen counter and it's got a coffee ring on it, what does that mean? It means someone else has touched it, read it, experienced it, maybe even left it there for you. It's like a fingerprint that says, "I was here." When you write to people, you want them to feel your presence, and know that you are sharing this specific and beautiful message or note just with them. We've actually used coffee rings in our designs, because it says to the reader, this is a shared moment between you and me.

Computers do not leave coffee rings on things. Humans do.

Same for smeared ink. I'm left-handed, so when I write anything, the ink gets a bit smeared on the page from the edge of my palm.

Computers do not smear ink. Humans do.

We need to acknowledge who our donors actually are. If you are fund-raising in Canada, the United States of America, the United Kingdom, Australia, or most of the main markets in the world, then your donor likely is over the age of 65 and she tends to be female.

Which brings me to another small deviation.

FONT SIZE

Almost everyone over the age of 45 has some type of visual impairment. Again, this is one of those things that every designer or fundraiser should know and think about as they craft communications for their donor.

Don't typeset your letters in a font size smaller than 14 point. Ever.

Don't cram your letter onto one side of a sheet of paper in 8 point font size. Explain to the person who is asking you to do this that not only are you making your appeal letter unreadable, but that a longer letter will almost always perform better (i.e., make more money) than a short letter.

Years ago, CNIB (Canadian National Institute for the Blind and visually impaired) did a study about typography with the RGD (Registered Graphic Designers) in Canada. The conclusion they came to was that in print, large, san-serif fonts were best for readability and comprehension.

I always wonder if we are going out of our way to make our donors feel old and stupid because:

- using small type means they can't easily read it
- teeny boxes on your reply form is how they are supposed to provide their credit card number, which can hurt their hands if they have arthritis
- using reverse-out type, which is difficult to read
- writing letters at a Grade 12 reading level with complex sentence structures makes it sound like a computer wrote it, and could leave your donor unable to understand what you are talking about

I don't think we are in the business of making donors feel old and stupid are we? Small things folks.

GRATITUDE

I talk a lot about gratitude in *Deviation 11,* but one of the simplest things you can do right now that will make a monumental difference in your fundraising program is to make sure your donor feels acknowledged and thanked as soon as possible after making a gift.

The first bit of "love" a donor receives from you should NOT be a soul destroying, transactional and boring tax receipt. (Or worse, nothing at all!)

For one client, we worked with illustrator Jessica Rae Gordon to craft this simple thank you card.

The moment a gift came in, the fundraiser could handwrite a simple and heartfelt thank you and send it immediately back to the donor.

I recall sitting next to my friend and colleague, Ann, during a presentation, watching her handwrite hundreds of cards that she was going to send out to her donors. I applauded her efforts (and still do) to make donors feel appreciated, but I also took a sample of her handwriting and sent it off to a type designer in the USA!

This allowed Ann to just type out what she wanted her cards to say in her own handwriting! The service I used doesn't exist anymore, but there are still a number of design services that will allow you to create a font out of your (or your boss's) handwriting. Super simple trick to help you add handwriting touches to your packs.

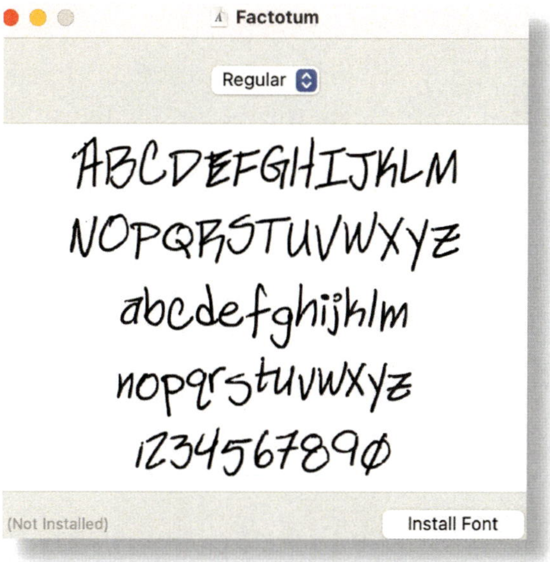

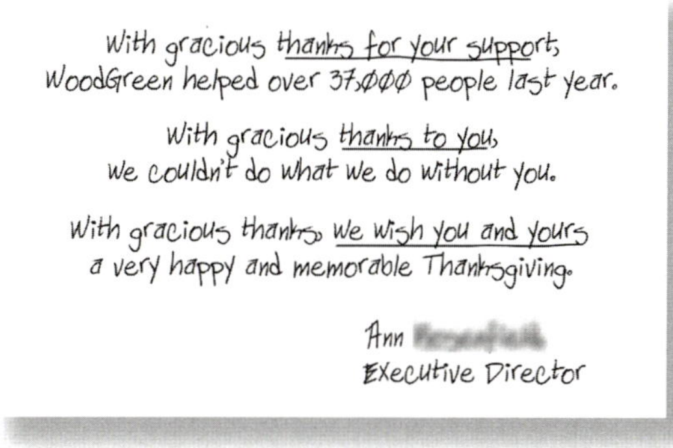

EYESCANS AND SKIMMERS

In 1984, Dr. Siegfried Vogele wrote a book, *"Handbook of Direct Mail."* It was first published in German, but now you can get an English version. Just like George Smith's *"Asking Properly,"* you'll find much of the content is still relevant.

I really wish more people would take the time to learn about some of these fundamentals.

One of the things Dr. Vogele writes about is "the reading behaviour of the recipient of your letter."

Understanding how a donor "reads" your letter is a small thing that you must fundamentally understand.

Very few donors actually read your letter from beginning to end.

The donor will pull out the letter and first look at their name and address at the top, if it appears there.

They will look down to the bottom right corner of the page, hopefully see a note that says "please turn over... ", then flip the letter over and look at the name of the person who is writing to them. They'll read the P.S.

Some donors will make a decision to give or maybe read more based on these two things.

For those of you who have a boss that dislikes a good old-fashioned P.S., let them know they are leaving a lot of money on the table by not including one.

The P.S. (postscript) serves an important purpose in your letter. It should reiterate or state what it is you are asking for, ideally with some urgency.

Not having one or putting anything else in your P.S. puts you at risk of not getting a gift.

Then you have the skimmers.

These are the donors who will go back to the front to quickly skim through the appeal, reading only the words and lines that are emphasized in bold, underlined or highlighted.

Only add emphasis to what you are asking the donor to do (give!) or to remind them how amazing and important they are.

Ask yourself: what would the donor think and feel if all they read were the bolded and underlined parts of your letter?

Some of your donors will make a decision to give or not based on the words you have emphasized.

A couple other small things as they relate to your letter.

I know a lot of people dislike it when the paragraph on the bottom of the page is cut off mid-sentence or worse... when the top of the next page only has a word or a single partial line.

I, on the other hand, know this is GREAT!

Unfinished sentences or dangling words entice the donor to turn the page over to complete the thought and/or finish reading what you are writing about.

Same for adding a little "please turn over... " to the bottom right corner of your pages. It keeps the skimmers and readers moving along!

We always add a photo of the letter signer to our appeal letters (Fig. 4.1). This is even more critical in your legacy appeals (more on that in *Deviation 12*).

Jeff Brooks asked me once if we ever tested the impact of using that photo beside the signature. To date, we have not — nor do I know of anyone who has tested it.

to treasure for a family facing cancer …and that's a priceless gift for the days ahead for a family holding on to hope.

Yours with my deep personal thanks,

Catrin Devonald
CEO
Sweet Louise

PS: <<Salutation>>, we <u>must</u> raise $29,680 by Christmas Eve to protect

Fig. 4.1

But, as I explained to Jeff, in the context of people giving to people and allowing the donor to picture who is writing to them, what would be the downside? It is just another tiny way you can remind your donor that another human, just like them, crafted this letter for them.

Have you ever heard of the "loneliest paragraph"?

In the context of eye scans and skimmers… you will find the loneliest paragraph on the top of page 2. You can almost be positive that if there is a paragraph or two that no one will ever read, it's these ones on page 2.

At Agents of Good, we like to joke with our clients that this is the place to bury all the boring stuff your boss wants you to put in your appeals: stats, facts, the numbers, bullet points and figures. All the things that will hardly persuade a donor to give.

Make sure that all of the content in your letter is relevant and adds to the overall case — but, if you are forced to add something else in, the top of page 2 is where you can put it.

SEGMENTATION

Another small thing, that really is one of the biggest of the small things, is segmentation.

Specifically, I am talking about the type of segmentation that shows the donor you actually know who you are talking to. This seems basic, yet so often I look at appeals that suggest there was no segmentation of any type in the mailing. Every donor got exactly the same appeal with the same generic ask.

ACTIVE VARIABLE

Today I'm writing because you can make a meaningful impact on the lives of kids and adults who need transfusions at this special time of year. I know you've already made a difference this year. With deep gratitude, I urge you to make a special year-end gift of <$Ask1>, <$Ask2>, <$Ask3> or more.

NEW VARIABLE

Today I'm writing because you can make a meaningful impact on the lives of kids and adults who need transfusions at this special time of year. As one of our newest donors, your support is especially cherished. With deep gratitude, I urge you to make a special year-end gift of <$Ask1>, <$Ask2>, <$Ask3> or more.

LAPSED VARIABLE

Today I'm writing because you can make a meaningful impact on the lives of kids and adults who need transfusions at this special time of year. I know you've been a donor in the past, and we've really missed your support this year. With deep gratitude, I urge you to make a special year-end gift of <$Ask1>

Segmentation is a fundamental principle of direct marketing, my friends. Please take the time to do this work appropriately.

DONOR-FOCUSED DESIGN

Years ago, we had a meeting with our friends at Canadian National Institute for the Blind. On our way into the boardroom, we walked past a wall of posters that featured the ten design principles that CNIB uses in all of its marketing/ communications/ fundraising.

As a designer and donor champion, I spend a lot of time thinking about the needs of donors. We all should, so these massive posters really stuck with me. They might also provide you with some design considerations for your next appeal (especially those of you who are also designing information about legacy giving).

01

Contrast

Use a high contrast colour for text and background.

Good examples are black or dark blue text on a white or yellow background, or a white/yellow text on a black/dark blue background.

02

Type Colour

Print material is most readable in black and white.

If using coloured text, restrict it to things like titles, headlines or highlighted material.

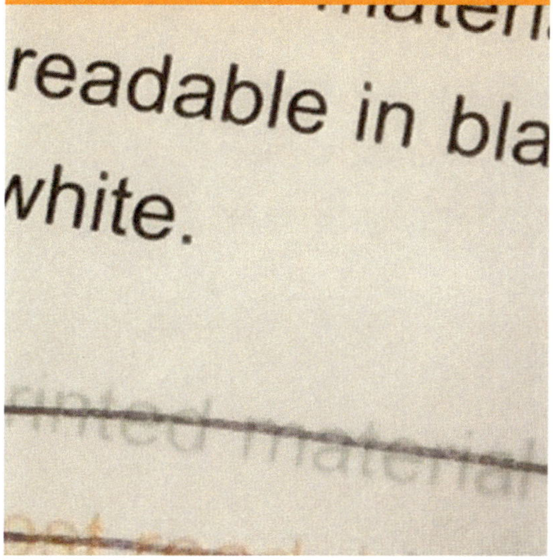

03

Point Size

Bigger is better. Keep your text large. Preferably between 12 and 18 point (depending on the font — point size varies font to font).

Consider your audience when choosing point size.

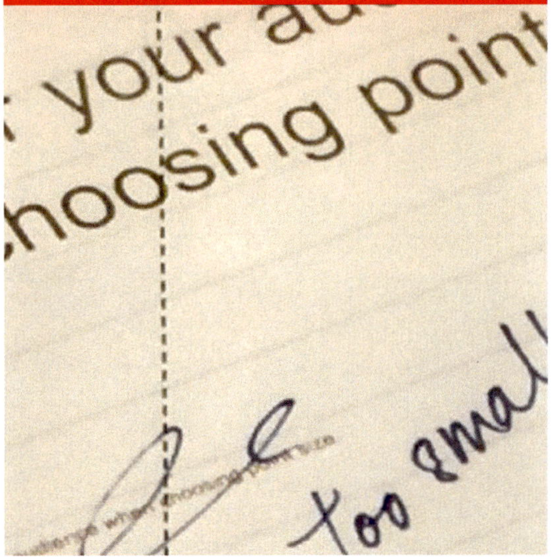

04

Leading

Leading is the space between lines of text and should be at least 25%–30% of the point size. This lets readers move more easily to the next line of text.

Bolder type will need slightly more leading.

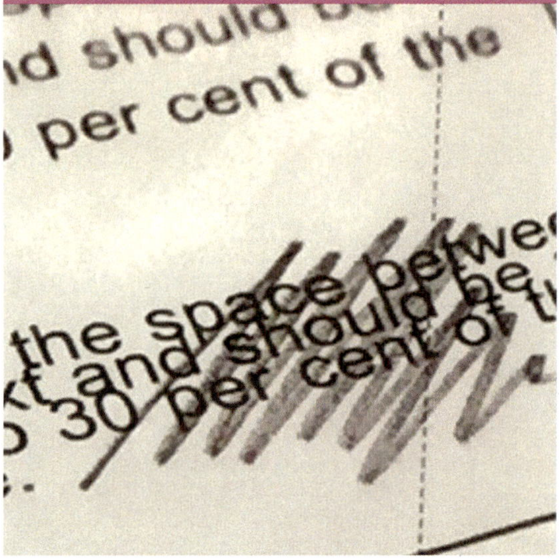

05

Fonts

Avoid complicated or decorative fonts.

Choose standard fonts with easily-recognizable upper and lower-case characters.

06

Font

Opt for fonts with medium weight (or heaviness) and avoid light type with thin strokes.

When emphasizing a word, italics and upper-case are not recommended.

07

Letter Spacing

Don't crowd your text.

Keep a wide space between letters.

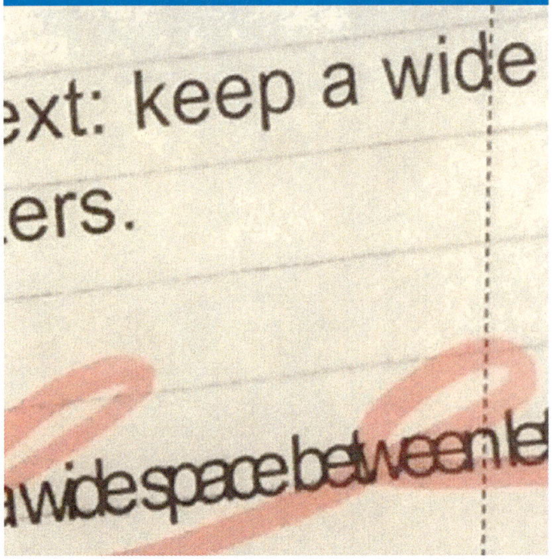

08

Margins & columns

Separate text into columns to make it easier to read, as it requires less eye movement and less peripheral vision.

09

Paper Finish

Use a matte or non-glossy finish to cut down on glare.

Reduce distractions by not using watermarks or complicated background designs.

10

Simple design

Use distinctive colours, sizes and shapes in your design but ensure that each element supports the message of the piece.

Let me tell you something. A good designer can make your "thing" pretty, but a *great* designer will make sure your "thing" communicates your point well and is clearly understood. The more you force a designer to add colours, swooshes, photos, fonts, bars and embellishments, the more you inhibit the ability of someone to comprehend what you are asking them to do or what you want them to know.

Do not mess with the focus and concentration of your donors. Ask for one thing. Get the point across as quickly and as simply as possible. Every single design element should be there to help support the message.

Often the design or mailing that may seem the most graphically boring is the most effective.

1,000 THINGS

There are literally a thousand more things that I could share with you, like when you add your stamps to an envelope, make sure they sit on a bit of an angle, because that's what humans do! Our imperfections are subtle clues!

Also, I almost always add little handwritten stars, arrows, marks or highlighting to parts of the letter or reply form copy. Again, I focus on highlighting copy that reiterates what you are asking for or reminds the donor how amazing they are.

Consider changing your contact emails from info@yourcharity.org to john@yourcharity.org, and use direct telephone numbers, even for the bosses.

The point of all of the 1,000 things that I hope you will now start obsessing over, is that they are almost all human touches that remind donors they are indeed having conversations with other humans. They are connectors.

You and I already know that these sorts of things can create stronger bonds in the most valuable relationships in our lives. We use sticky notes, a quick text to check in, some freshly picked flowers, a simple love note or "I miss you" card, or maybe even a surprise trip to Paris for those we love the most. These are the things that can monumentally deepen our connections with each other.

Do not dismiss them in your fundraising program. Obsess over them all.

Deviation Discoveries

We spend too much time looking for one big idea, and think that if we change one thing, then everything will improve and we'll instantly raise more money. Successful fundraising is like life. It's about the 1,000 small (and sometimes annoying) things you need to think about and make decisions about that will create unique experiences for your donors. This is where you can start to get really obsessive about the "artform" of direct response!

1. It's often the simplest and least high-tech solutions that can have the most impact on your donors.
2. Acknowledge who your audience is and where you need to meet them – in your design, your writing, or whatever channel you are using. Put their needs around accessibility, readability, and comprehension before yours.
3. Great fundraising programs embrace and cherish connections between humans. They make a point of reminding donors that behind that nice name and logo is a collection of humans fighting for and protecting the same things that your donor believes in.

Deviation Five — Getting a reply!

In fundraising, you usually need to get your donor to "do something." You want them to take action, give a gift. This deviation focuses on the role of the reply form in a direct mail piece and how to make your form potentially perfect.

Ah, the poor, misunderstood, under-appreciated (and possibly icky) reply form.

I imagine some fundraisers holding the top corner of their reply form with two tiny-pinched fingers, holding their nose with the other and throwing it in the direction of an envelope… ugh.

But let's be honest, mess this up and you can kiss any potential gift goodbye.

Why do we insist on making the act of giving so difficult?

Surprisingly, (and luckily!) most donors stick with it and find a way to give regardless of our efforts to get in their way!

Reply form. Coupon. Remittance form. It goes by a lot of different names but this is the piece of paper that your donor hopefully sends back, with a donation.

Let me remind you of this: the **letter** in your pack is for you to start a conversation with your donor. The **reply** form is for your donor to talk back to you... if they wish to do so.

Unfortunately, many fundraisers have a tendency to forget that the reply form should be about communication. They make their forms overly confusing and transactional. But it doesn't have to be that way.

Jeff Brooks writes a blog, https://www.futurefundraisingnow.com. In it, he recommends that when you start writing a direct mail appeal, you start with the reply form, before anything else. Especially your affirmation or "yes" line.

"Yes Jane! I will help feed my hungry neighbours today!"

You work onwards from there.

At Agents of Good, we always start with what the problem is, but from a storytelling sense. What are we asking donors for and why should they care right now? I don't even start to think about what the pack or piece will look like until this part is done. Often, Jen Love and I work side by side having that conversation. As we work through the story we want to tell, we start to talk about the best way to tell it.

But I digress.

I have already discussed that in North America, 80% of all direct mail arrives in a white #10 envelope. I would also suggest that 80% of the reply forms in those packs will be 8.5″ x 3.5″ and attached to the bottom of the letter, either with a perforation or simply floating free in the envelope. This is cheap and transactional, offering no space for conversation. (Maybe still a little icky.)

THE PERFECT REPLY

Let's start by taking a look at what I consider to be "close" to perfect when it comes to a reply form (Fig. 5.1).

1. It is full letter sheet size. More often than not, when you test this (e.g., you mail half of your donors a full sheet size reply form and mail the other half of your donors a smaller reply form) the full size reply will do better (e.g., get more replies and raise more money). Yes, I have seen exceptions, but at Agents of Good, we often use a full size reply form because (like a lot of things) what's the downside?

2. It is personalized. I almost always try to add the donor's name in really big type at the top of every reply form! This form is for them to do something amazing! At the very least, make sure that your donor's name and address is on it so if they send it back, you know who the gift came from.

Special Reply Form for:

Ms. Caring Donor
123 Generosity Street
Lovely, ON X0X 0X0

Children's HEALTH FOUNDATION

Yes, Dr. Andrade! I'll help you treat more children with epilepsy using the amazing Rosa. Please MATCH my renewal gift of:

❍ $50 X 2 = **$100** ❍ $75 X 2 = **$150**

❍ $100 X 2 = **$200** **OR** ❍ **Surprise us $________**

❍ I have enclosed my cheque, payable to Children's Health Foundation.

OR

❍ I prefer to make my gift using my credit card.
Please charge my ❍ VISA ❍ MasterCard ❍ AMEX

Card Number:

Expiry Date:

Name on Card:

Signature:

Telephone #:

OR

❍ I prefer to give online at **childhealth.ca/donation/**

OR

❍ I prefer to **make a monthly gift** and have filled out the information on the back.

Thank you for helping sick children!

Children's Health Foundation • 345 Westminster Avenue, London, Ontario N6C 4V3
1-888-834-2496 • 1-519-432-8564 • childhealth.ca

We receipt gifts over $20 unless otherwise requested. Charitable Business # 11885 2482 RR0001

RE ID/Appeal Code

Fig. 5.1

3. It acknowledges the call to action in a positive manner! Yes! I'm taking the action you asked me to take!

4. It has a lot of "YOU" in it. "YOU" is glue. It keeps me reading along. It makes me an important part of your mission. It keeps me connected to my giving and the impact it will make.

5. It is segmented for different donors. If I gave you $50 last time, it makes no sense to ask me for $500 (usually). There are a lot of different strategies when it comes to segmentation and what to ask your donors to give. We tend to start with a simple:

❍ $last gift
❍ $last gift (+25%)
❍ $last gift (+50%)
❍ $last gift (+100%)
❍ Other $______.

You can get creative with your testing here if you want.

Test print your gift array from highest to lowest, or lowest to highest. I've used a "❍ Surprise us $_______" as an option, instead of "Other."

That works especially well when you are looking for a stretch gift. You could also test circling the second or third gift option in the array. And on and on.

If you have a matching gift or a good offer, do the math for the donor on the reply so they can see the difference their gift will make.

There is a lot of science around gift arrays. It can get all kinds of nerdy but as mentioned, at the bare minimum, make sure the gift array you present to your donor is appropriate to their previous giving.

6. It asks for one thing. Agents of Good reply forms, usually only ask for a single, cash gift. This can be a bit contentious. Almost every reply form you see these days provides the option to make a single gift, but also has a monthly, regular gift option. I recently went through my mother-in-law's mailbox and reviewed 60 packs side by side. 80% of them asked for a single gift <u>and</u> a monthly gift. I'll get into this more later in this chapter but here's what you need to know.

In testing, more often than not, asking for a "one off" cash gift will do better than adding the option to make a monthly, regular gift. Why? Two reasons. First, analysis paralysis is a thing. The more work it is to make a decision, the less likely I will make any decision at all. Second, and to that point, anything that slows response, lowers response. This goes for online and offline.

So many reply forms I see look like this. Does yours?

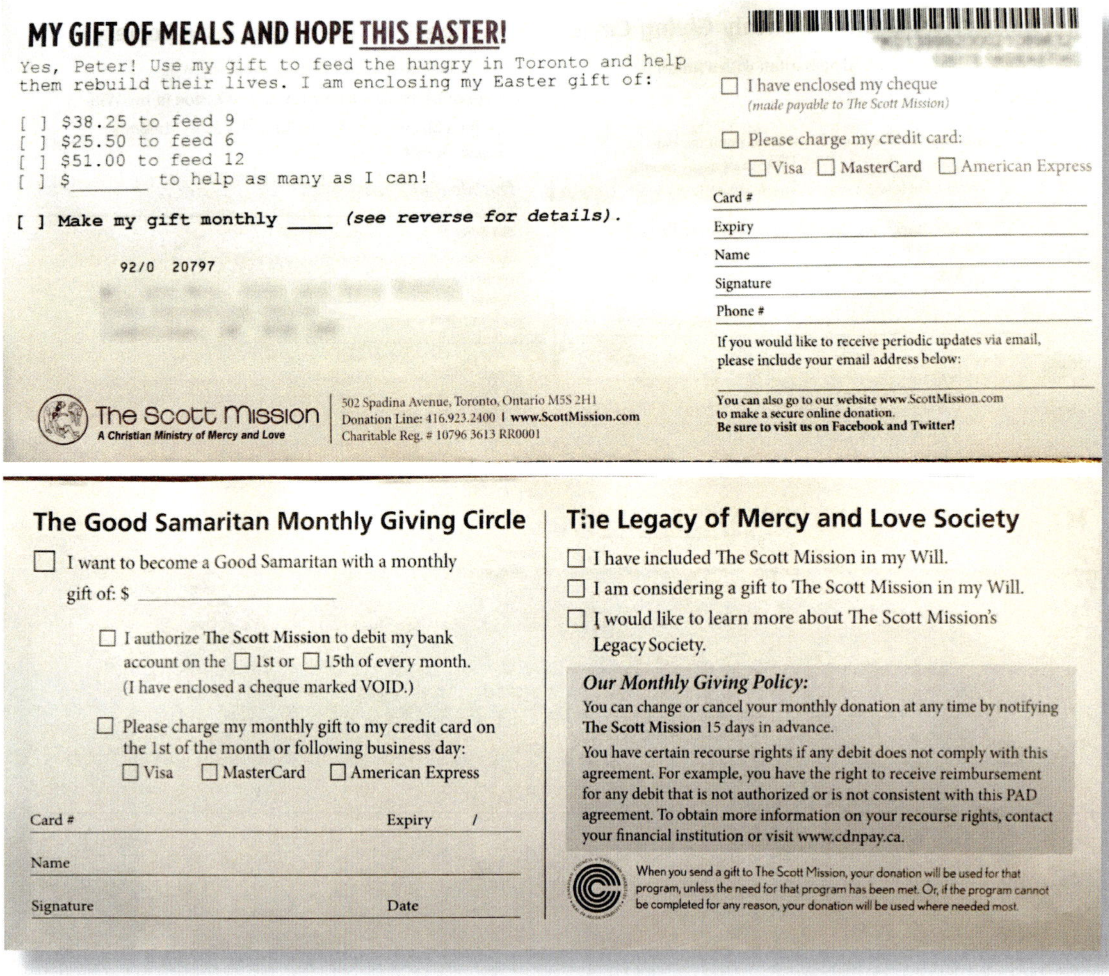
MY GIFT OF MEALS AND HOPE THIS EASTER!

Yes, Peter! Use my gift to feed the hungry in Toronto and help them rebuild their lives. I am enclosing my Easter gift of:

[ ] $38.25 to feed 9
[ ] $25.50 to feed 6
[ ] $51.00 to feed 12
[ ] $_______ to help as many as I can!

[ ] Make my gift monthly ____ *(see reverse for details).*

92/0 20797

☐ I have enclosed my cheque
(made payable to The Scott Mission)

☐ Please charge my credit card:
☐ Visa ☐ MasterCard ☐ American Express

Card #

Expiry

Name

Signature

Phone #

If you would like to receive periodic updates via email, please include your email address below:

The Scott Mission
A Christian Ministry of Mercy and Love

502 Spadina Avenue, Toronto, Ontario M5S 2H1
Donation Line: 416.923.2400 I **www.ScottMission.com**
Charitable Reg. # 10796 3613 RR0001

**You can also go to our website www.ScottMission.com to make a secure online donation.
Be sure to visit us on Facebook and Twitter!**

The Good Samaritan Monthly Giving Circle

☐ I want to become a Good Samaritan with a monthly gift of: $ ____________

☐ I authorize **The Scott Mission** to debit my bank account on the ☐ 1st or ☐ 15th of every month. (I have enclosed a cheque marked VOID.)

☐ Please charge my monthly gift to my credit card on the 1st of the month or following business day:
☐ Visa ☐ MasterCard ☐ American Express

Card # Expiry /

Name

Signature Date

The Legacy of Mercy and Love Society

☐ I have included The Scott Mission in my Will.

☐ I am considering a gift to The Scott Mission in my Will.

☐ I would like to learn more about The Scott Mission's Legacy Society.

Our Monthly Giving Policy:
You can change or cancel your monthly donation at any time by notifying **The Scott Mission** 15 days in advance.
You have certain recourse rights if any debit does not comply with this agreement. For example, you have the right to receive reimbursement for any debit that is not authorized or is not consistent with this PAD agreement. To obtain more information on your recourse rights, contact your financial institution or visit www.cdnpay.ca.

When you send a gift to The Scott Mission, your donation will be used for that program, unless the need for that program has been met. Or, if the program cannot be completed for any reason, your donation will be used where needed most.

Take a closer look and count how many decisions need to be made to fill out the reply completely.

The reply form above requires 27 decisions! One of the packs my mother-in-law received required 41 decisions! That's crazy!

On the other hand, asking for a monthly gift is sometimes a good idea.

As discussed later in this chapter, I prefer to provide a monthly gift option on its own in a dedicated "monthly invite" pack. This allows you to make a case for monthly giving and not have it simply be a check box option.

However, in the case of your annual appeals, asking for a single or monthly gift on your reply can also make a lot of sense. You want regular, monthly givers for your organization. They make for excellent legacy prospects and they have a better lifetime value to your organization. Agents of Good generally will give options for both (on the reply form) at the beginning of the year and during the holidays.

7. It has a ton of white space. I know that the smaller, slip reply forms are cheaper to make but the irony of being an organization that helps the visually impaired or folks with arthritis and only giving them 3/16″ of space to write their credit card number or name into isn't lost on me. We must honor the shaky handwriting we see on the reply forms that are sent back to us!

8. It features very large type.

9. It doesn't have tiny little boxes for your donor to try to fill out.

10. It says "thank you." Seriously, why does your donor have to wait for that soul-destroying tax receipt that might arrive 8 months later to be (and I use the term very lightly here) "thanked?"

And a bonus item for the top ten list...

Less is more. Only ask for what you need and get out of the way. If you are asking for other bits of information, at least tell the donor why you are asking for it.

ASKING FOR ONE THING

The late, great George Smith suggested, in *Asking Properly*, that every appeal should be "special." This means that every appeal and every ask should be about a specific problem that can be solved with your donors' help.

For fundraisers in North America, that might sound a bit strange.

A lot of organizations follow an "Annual Renewal" cycle of mail.

The nutshell is that you send dedicated "Renewal" mail packs throughout the year with the objective of getting donors to "renew their support" (i.e.: give) to your organization.

Modified Annual Renewal Campaign

	House Renewal	House Specials		House Lapses →	Acquisition
Jan	1				X
Feb					
March	2				X
April					
May	3				
June		X			
July	4				X
August	Phone	X			X
Sept					
Oct					
Nov		X			X
Dec					
Jan '95	1				X

"Donor, thank you for being so

generous to us last year. I hope that you will support our mission again in 2021 by making a gift today."

You remind the donor throughout the year with that basic ask and you keep mailing them until they do renew their support. Once they do, you don't send them any more renewals.

You also send out "House Special Appeals." A special appeal is a dedicated pack focused on a specific topic or issue. All donors get these mailings.

In other markets, they only send out Special Appeals. Every mailing is about a "special" topic. I'm not saying that no one in North America does that, I'm just pointing out that the "Annual Renewal" is a very typical approach here and it does work.

In the context of real human relationships, I want you to remember that you are having *emotional conversations* with your donors.

Just like in real life, if you are having a coffee or lunch with a friend or colleague, you might share the challenges and successes that you're facing and you may ask for help with a particular challenge.

Throughout the conversation, you might keep mentioning what you need help with and what you need me (as a friend) to do.

At the end of the lunch you may say, "Will you help me with this?"

The person on the other side of the conversation has a single decision to make. Will I help or will I not help?

Effective mailings work the same way. Here is an example.

Camp Oochigeas is a camp in northern Ontario where kids who have or had cancer can go and just be a kid and enjoy camp life.

The goal of the 'Camp Ooch' appeal was to raise funds to send as many kids to camp as we possibly could.

The mail pack went out in a 9″ x 6″ outer envelope. We didn't want it to get missed in the stack of #10 envelopes the donor was probably getting.

The envelope is playful and fun.

Just like camp.

The envelope also makes the donor ask questions.

It was different than the typical pack they normally received from the organization that they love so much. It didn't use their logo. It was larger than usual. It was heavier than usual (I'll get to that) and the back had a teaser that read, "Camp is right this way."

The two-page letter was personalized and came from Alex, the ED.

CAMP OOCHIGEAS

Date, 2018

Ms. Jen Love
123 Lover's Lane
Muskoka, ON X0X 0X0

Dear <Jen>,

☞ Do you believe in magic?

You will now! I've enclosed for you a very special map. When you look at it, you'll be magically transported right here to Camp Ooch and you'll see and feel your incredible support in action helping kids affected by childhood cancer experience the Magic of Ooch.

Matthew, an Ooch camper, shared that if there was a magic wand that could send him to Ooch right now, he'd be with his friends, out on the paddleboards trying to knock each other off and ganging up on the counsellors...

"The Ooch waterfront is a big part of my memories: fishing, canoeing, swimming—everyone can enjoy their own activity and still feel like part of one community. It's small enough that you feel like a family but big enough that you feel like you have your own space. Because of Ooch, I know that cancer can mean something other than a hospital. It really does mean friendship and fun! To me, the Magic of Ooch is the infinite positives that make an extreme ultimate positive—the friends you make there, the amazing location, everything you want to try, there are no limits to what you can do!"

<Jen>, can you see yourself in this story? Because you are there. You're everywhere on the Ooch map, because you make the Magic of Ooch possible. Thank you!

Right now, campers from your community and around the province are crossing their fingers and hoping they can come to Camp this summer. Your gift today—of <$50> or whatever you choose—will help send more kids to Camp this summer!

Just a few months from now, Ooch will come alive with laughter,

CAMP OOCHIGEAS 464 Bathurst Street, Toronto ON M5T 2S6
Tel: 416.961.6624 Fax: 416.961.2267 ooch.org

singing and games. Kids at all stages in their cancer experience will meet up on Flagpole Field, an amazing and totally accessible space where they'll greet each other, connect with their cabin mates and counsellors, and start to explore Ooch.

Matthew's mom Ana remembers first arriving at Ooch: *"You're breathing a different air up there. Fresh air, yes, but you just feel that you're entering a magic place. And there's something else magic, for me. I love Matthew, and I would give my life for him in a second.* ***But Ooch gives Matthew something I can't give. The experience of sharing the most difficult part of his life with other kids.*** *As much as I try, I can never fully understand what he went through. And Ooch turns something so scary into something so bright. Ooch is emotional treatment for cancer. And it's magic."*

I hope you enjoy taking a closer look at your magic map and exploring Ooch, knowing that you make it come alive with stories just like Matthew's.

You can be part of the story this summer, too! Your gift today will make more the Magic of Ooch possible for kids with cancer right now in hospital, and in communities across Ontario. And you'll be part of the story this summer at Ooch Muskoka.

You'll find enclosed a reply form you can use to make your gift to Ooch today. And on that form there is also a space for you to share a message with Ooch campers, so you can really can be part of the story!

Thank you, so much, for your kind, caring and compassionate support of Ooch.

Yours, forever believing in magic,

Alex

Alex Robertson, CEO

P.S You can share the Magic of Ooch! Please send in your gift today to send more kids like Matthew to Camp Ooch this summer. Thank you for believing in the Magic of Ooch!

Right now, campers from your community and around the province are crossing their fingers and hoping they can come to Camp this summer. Your gift today—of <$50> or whatever you choose—will help send more kids to Camp this summer!

I want to zero in on the ask. The letter was about a camper named Matthew and how every gift will help send more kids like him to camp this summer.

A key to great storytelling is to change the perspective. Sometimes a story that's been told over and over again can seem completely fresh and new when you change the voice or angle. This is the case for this appeal. Ultimately every Camp Ooch appeal is about sending kids to camp, but we are always looking for ways to make it interesting for donors to interact with, and to give the donor a fresh perspective on their potential impact.

We really wanted to do that for this appeal. Historically, the organization used lots of nice photos of kids having fun at camp, which is perfect, but over time it meant that all their appeals started to look the same. The images began to lose their emotional impact. We often use illustration in our work for this reason.

Our goal was to immerse a donor into the "ask" of sending a kid like Matthew to camp. How could we do that?

We decided to "show" the donor around camp so they could see all of the different activities that were possible. It would help them to understand the ways the camp was structured for fun, yet with the care and safety of these precious kids always top of mind.

For our mid to high-value donors, we like to create special packs. I go into more detail on this in *Deviation 9*.

For this pack, we worked with Jessica Rae Gordon to create an oversize map of Camp Ooch **(Fig 5.2)**.

You really need to see Jessica's work up close to appreciate the artistry that goes into every detail. I've had clients ask if the cost of working with illustrators are worth it? To be honest, it's a cost that we absorb and don't charge our clients extra for because it makes the work outstanding — and more importantly, it makes for more effective direct response. How can any human (donor or otherwise) not engage with it? It's imaginative, and fun, giving the donor a fresh look and new perspective into the impact of their giving.

For our mid to high-value pack, the map insert was set on a 11″ x 17″ sheet. On the back we added this **(Fig. 5.3)**:

Fig. 5.2

CAMP OOCHIGEAS

☞ With your magic map, you'll be magically transported right here to Camp Ooch—and you can see and feel your incredible support in action, including:

The adventure swings and high ropes course—for brave hearted kids to challenge themselves in a safe, loving and supportive environment. And as Matthew says, "*everyone sets their own limits for how high they want to go and everyone cheers you on, no matter what you do!*"

In the **Slaight Arts & Music Centre** kids unleash their creative power! All the fabulous supplies you can imagine, plus dedicated space for the growing music program including a recording studio! Matthew remembers learning to play the ukulele at Ooch!

Gatts' Lodge—rebuilt last year thanks to you! Now fully winterized and expanded to accommodate 50% more campers so that we can keep our promise that no child is ever turned away. The woodshop and dining hall also provide indoor programming space for year-round campers or in poor weather.

The **Med Shed** is where kids receive chemotherapy and other types of care. More rest and isolation rooms for campers, and expanded working space for nurses and doctors means faster and more effective treatment, so kids can get back to being kids.

Do you see **all those animals**? Kids explore the wild side of Camp Ooch and learn about Muskoka wilderness. We've named all the different wildlife you can spot here at Ooch—Justin Beaver, Franklin the turtle, Flicker the deer, Stevie the snake, Chicago the bear and more! Our campers fill out Ranger Reports when they catch a glimpse of our wild friends! And don't forget "Mooch the Moose", a magic moose statue who comes to life at night and moves around Camp!

Thank you for being a part of our magic map, and for helping kids with cancer experience the Magic of Ooch!

Fig. 5.3

The map insert was included to add detail about the camp grounds, showing the places where kids could sing and do art, as well as how the campground was organized to accommodate the kids who might still be undergoing cancer treatment. More importantly, the map showed donors on a more granular level how their gifts were helpful and needed.

For the mid to high-value donors we also created two more inserts.

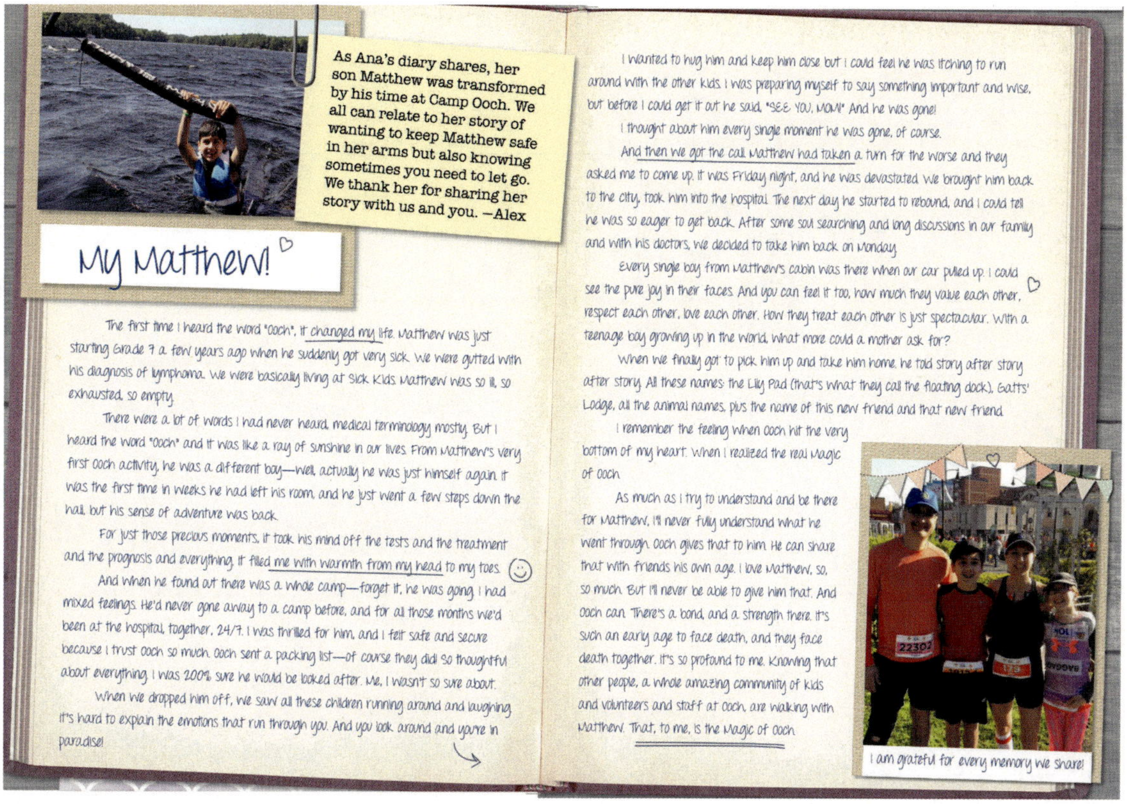

The first was made to look like a diary entry from Matthew's mom, Ana. It included plenty of human touches: paperclips, handwriting, and smiley faces. We interviewed her as part of the appeal and her words and thoughts about the importance of Camp, especially as it related to her son Matthew, really informed so much of the appeal. We wanted to share those thoughts with donors.

The final insert was from Matthew **(Fig. 5.4)**.

The insert was written in his own words and shared what going to camp meant to him. These extra pieces may seem like overkill, but it allowed Ooch's amazing donors to hear many different perspectives on why their giving mattered.

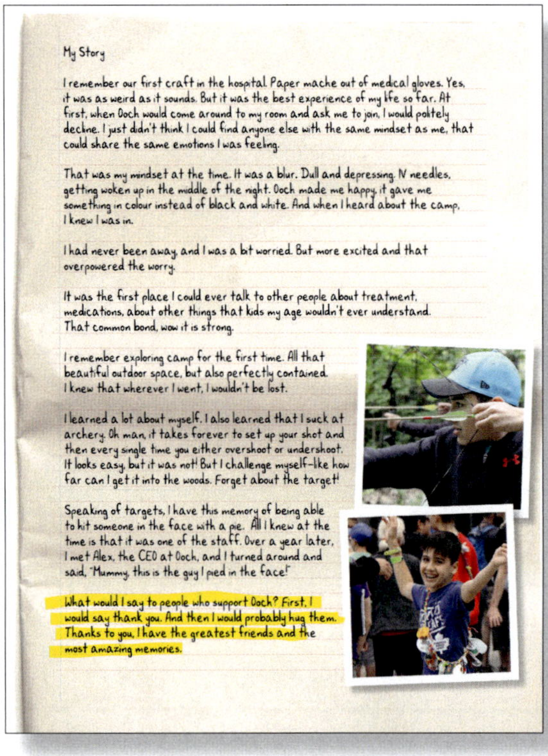

My Story

I remember our first craft in the hospital. Paper mache out of medical gloves. Yes, it was as weird as it sounds. But it was the best experience of my life so far. At first, when Ooch would come around to my room and ask me to join, I would politely decline. I just didn't think I could find anyone else with the same mindset as me, that could share the same emotions I was feeling.

That was my mindset at the time. It was a blur. Dull and depressing. IV needles, getting woken up in the middle of the night. Ooch made me happy, it gave me something in colour instead of black and white. And when I heard about the camp, I knew I was in.

I had never been away, and I was a bit worried. But more excited and that overpowered the worry.

It was the first place I could ever talk to other people about treatment, medications, about other things that kids my age wouldn't ever understand. That common bond, wow it is strong.

I remember exploring camp for the first time. All that beautiful outdoor space, but also perfectly contained. I knew that wherever I went, I wouldn't be lost.

I learned a lot about myself. I also learned that I suck at archery. Oh man, it takes forever to set up your shot and then every single time you either overshoot or undershoot. It looks easy, but it was not! But I challenge myself–like how far can I get it into the woods. Forget about the target!

Speaking of targets, I have this memory of being able to hit someone in the face with a pie. All I knew at the time is that it was one of the staff. Over a year later, I met Alex, the CEO at Ooch, and I turned around and said, "Mummy, this is the guy I pied in the face!"

What would I say to people who support Ooch? First, I would say thank you. And then I would probably hug them. Thanks to you, I have the greatest friends and the most amazing memories.

Fig. 5.4

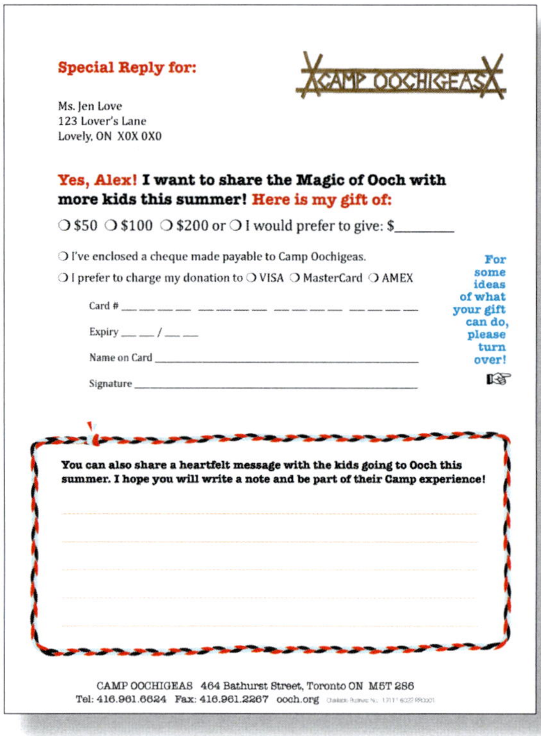

Special Reply for:

CAMP OOCHIGEAS

Ms. Jen Love
123 Lover's Lane
Lovely, ON X0X 0X0

Yes, Alex! I want to share the Magic of Ooch with more kids this summer! Here is my gift of:

❍ $50 ❍ $100 ❍ $200 or ❍ I would prefer to give: $________

❍ I've enclosed a cheque made payable to Camp Oochigeas.

❍ I prefer to charge my donation to ❍ VISA ❍ MasterCard ❍ AMEX

Card # ____ ____ ____ ____

Expiry ___ / ___

Name on Card ______________________

Signature ______________________

For some ideas of what your gift can do, please turn over! ☞

You can also share a heartfelt message with the kids going to Ooch this summer. I hope you will write a note and be part of their Camp experience!

CAMP OOCHIGEAS 464 Bathurst Street, Toronto ON M5T 2S6
Tel: 416.961.6624 Fax: 416.961.2267 ooch.org

Fig. 5.5

Finally, the reply form (**Fig. 5.5**).

The front of the coupon was personalized and the gift array tailored to be relevant to the donor's previous giving. We also included some space for a heartfelt message if a donor wanted to share one.

On the back, we included examples of what a $50 gift or $4,000 gift could do. Being specific around what a donor's gift will do increases response rates and average gifts because so often donors don't actually know what impact their giving will make. Yes, this hard work is on you, and yes, I understand that sometimes being specific like this isn't possible. However, the more you can provide donor-sized problems, the more your donor will want to help and be a part of the solution.

Here are some ideas of exactly how your gift will help!

$50 provides board games for kids with cancer in the hospital

$150 gives a kid with cancer an afternoon at Ooch Downtown

$300 gives a kid too sick to travel one day at Ooch Day Camp

$600 gives a kid with cancer a weekend at Camp Ooch

$1,500 gives arts and craft supplies for kids with cancer in the hospital

$2,000 gives a kid with cancer a week at Ooch Overnight Camp

$4,000 gives a kid with cancer 2 weeks at Ooch Overnight Camp

$5,000 provides 25 ukuleles, percussion instruments and other equipment so kids can make beautiful music with Ooch

Every appeal you send to donors should be like this one; as specific as possible in what you are asking for, including why you're asking for it and the impact it will have.

The last thing I want to highlight is the idea of including space for the donor to share a "heartfelt" message. This is something we try to include as often as possible on our reply forms.

Direct response is a conversation between you and your donor. How can that happen if you aren't creating moments for your donor to talk to you? You want them to tell you things about themselves, their giving and their lives.

You will also get to read beautiful things like this:

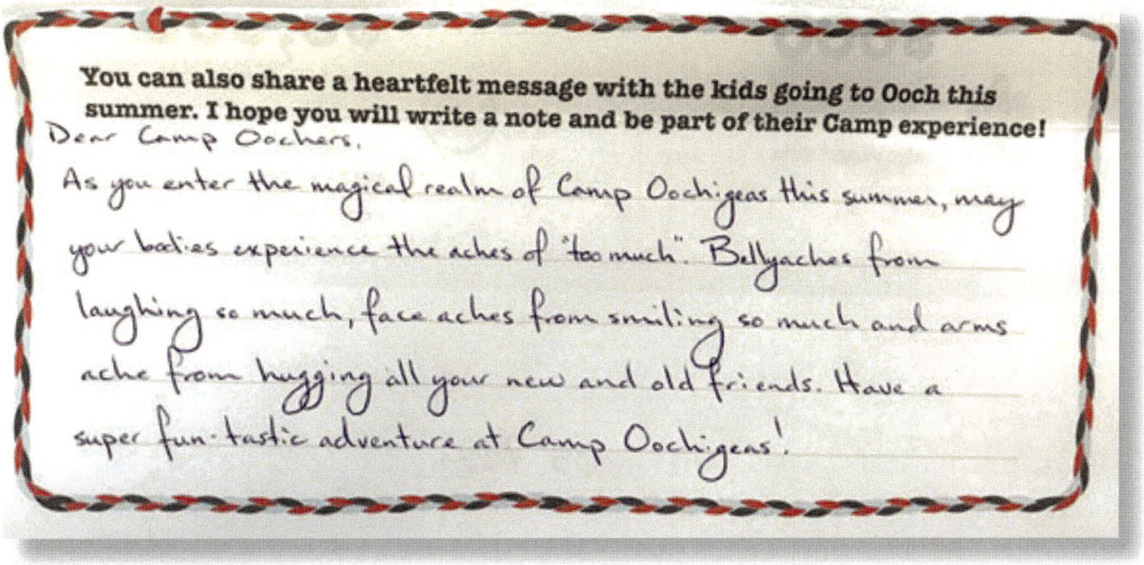
You can also share a heartfelt message with the kids going to Ooch this summer. I hope you will write a note and be part of their Camp experience!

Dear Camp Oochers,
As you enter the magical realm of Camp Oochigeas this summer, may your bodies experience the aches of "too much". Bellyaches from laughing so much, face aches from smiling so much and arms ache from hugging all your new and old friends. Have a super fun-tastic adventure at Camp Oochigeas!

Dear Camp Oochers,
As you enter the magical realm of Camp Oochigeas this summer, may your bodies experience the aches of "too much". Bellyaches from laughing too much, face aches from smiling so much and arms ache from hugging all of your new and old friends. Have a super fun-tastic adventure at Camp Ooch!

How beautiful is that?

This donor is giving with love in her heart and a large smile on her face. This obviously is not a transactional moment for her. And unbelievably, about 65% of donations to this campaign came back with feelings like this. This speaks to the high level of engagement the donors feel with their organization.

This mailing touched donors in a way that others hadn't, mostly since we creatively showed them the impact of their giving in a way they had never seen before.

This appeal had a 30% increase in gifts, a jump of 40% in revenue and the average gift went up over 200%. Yes, that is extraordinary and speaks to both the generosity of Camp Oochigeas donors and the impact of asking for something quite specific in a creative way.

MORE ABOUT BOUNCE BACKS

How often do you give opportunities for your donor talk to you? To tell you something about themselves?

Do you let your donors express their values and emotions as it relates to your cause?

I believe it to be one of the most important aspects of direct response.

Direct response = conversation.

You are (hopefully) having conversations with your donors in this work. Regardless of the channel.

Your donor is getting 5, 10, 30 or more appeals from charities a day.

Ask, ask, ask… take, take, take… We can do better. We must do better.

We must constantly be thinking about ways that we can let our donors talk to us, tell us a story about themselves, or share why they decided to give today.

Again, remember to HONOUR the shaky handwriting. Your donor will tell you a lot about themselves through their words, their writing and the swoop in their letters, the things they share, the space they take, and the references they make to the past.

This is the power of an effective "bounce-back" piece, either included on your reply form or added separately

ConstID/Appeal-Seg Code

St.Thomas Elgin General Hospital Foundation

Special Holiday Reply for:
<Addressee> -MAIN
1234 Generous Street
Anytown, ON. XoX oXo

Yes, Jacqueline! Here is my special life-saving holiday gift of:

❍ $50 ❍ $100 ❍ $200 OR ❍ I prefer to give $______

❍ I have enclosed my cheque, payable to St. Thomas Elgin General Hospital Foundation.

OR

❍ I prefer to make my gift using my ❍ VISA ❍ ❍

Card Number: ______ Expiry Date: ______

Name on Card: ______

Signature: ______

Telephone #: ______

Email: ______

New regulations from VISA may require us to contact you by phone to confirm your CVV. If you choose to give using your VISA, please include your telephone number. Thank you!

Due to COVID-19, we are asking our donors and supporters to please consider giving online at ItsOURHospital.ca

189 Elm Street, St. Thomas, Ontario N5R 5C4 • 519.631.2030 x 2246 • foundation@stegh.on.ca • ItsOURHospital.ca

Dear <**Salutation**>,
Please keep this ornament as a reminder of the lives you're impacting with your generosity. Wishing you and your loved ones a healthy and happy holiday season.

WISHING YOU A Healthy & happy HOLIDAY SEASON!

ConstID/Appeal-Seg Code

Fig. 5.6

into your direct mail appeal.

Your year-end or holiday appeal is a great time to add something simple, like an ornament as the bounce back **(Fig 5.6)**.

It can be included on the bottom of the reply form. One can be kept by the donor to hang on their fridge or the Christmas tree. The other can be used for her to write a few words about your organization, who she thinks of when she gives, or to share a meaningful memory, heartfelt wishes, or something else entirely.

This donor is rarely asked anything (aside from giving a gift). She will take delight in the opportunity and she will share some of the feelings that are swirling around her heart.

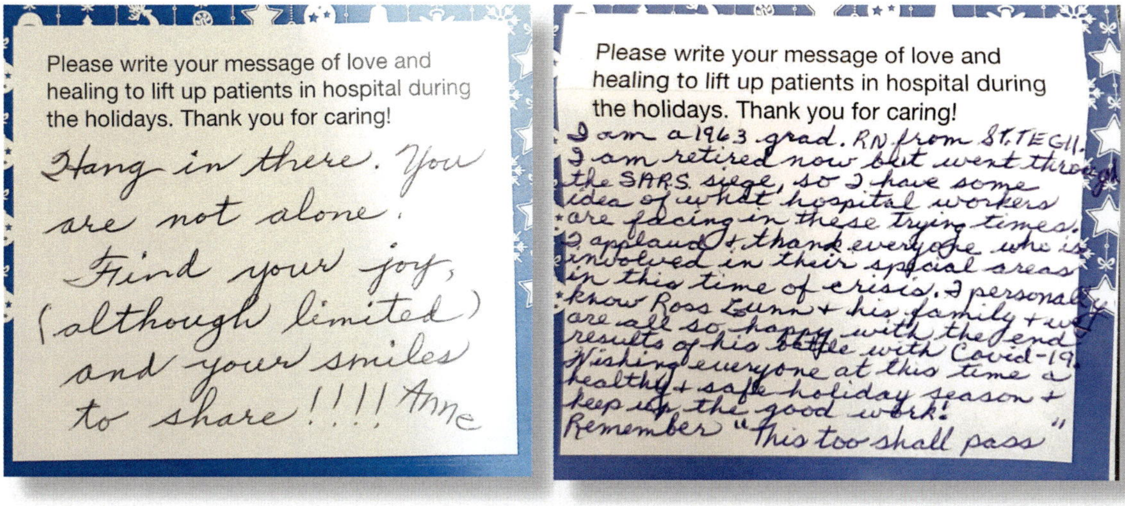

These donors may even decide to give *more* to accompany their message. Regardless, they will be giving with love in their hearts and smiles on their faces.

These are the sorts of things that are very difficult to explain to boards and bosses. How do you calculate an ROI on this sort of thing?

The answer, of course, is that you can't. Because these conversations represent something much deeper than a simple ROI equation.

GETTING A REPLY TO A MONTHLY CONVERSION MAILING

So maybe you have tested it. Maybe you found that asking donors for a single gift (vs. asking for a single or monthly gift) got a better response.

But you DO want regular/monthly donors. You need them. They are better donors in terms of lifetime value and can help do more to meet the ongoing needs of your mission.

I'm not an expert on all the ways to convert single cash gift donors to monthly donors, but I wanted to share one example that can work well for you. And that's a good old-fashioned monthly conversion mailing.

These can work very well for you for a number of reasons.

First, because it is mail.

Most of your best donors love mail. You can be very targeted by sending this mailing only to the most loyal of your donors to start with and then working your way through your file. You can be personal and make the piece feel quite invitational and different than your other mail.

Also, you can be specific and state a different type of case to your donors for their consideration. You should state: i) why your donor should consider making this sort of gift, ii) why it would be helpful to you, iii) the impact it will have on your mission, and iv) any benefits there might be for the donor.

Plus, you're back to asking for one thing. Which gives you a better shot at getting it.

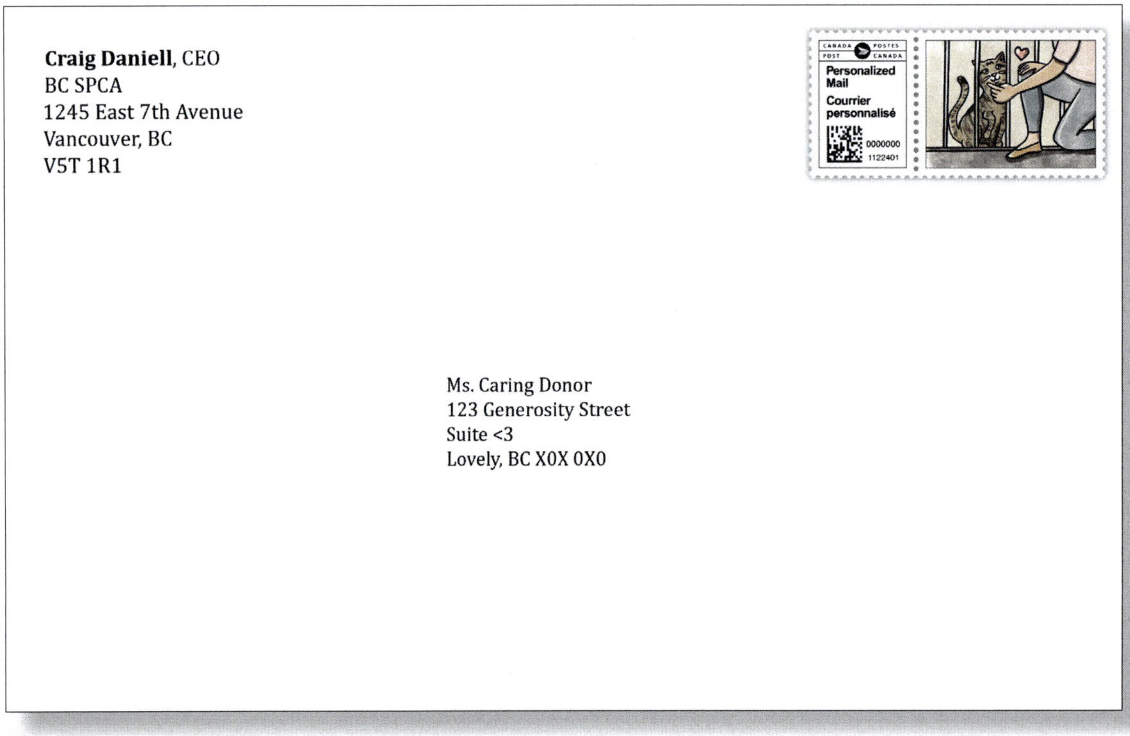

Fig. 5.7

This is an example from the British Columbia SPCA (Fig. 5.7).

A monthly conversion pack can lean into the idea of a personalized piece of mail from "me to you" in order to stand out.

We sent this out in an oversized 9.5″ x 5.875″ envelope. No logo or branding was used, just simple type with the letter signer's name and return address. For some donors, we suggest using first class postage and for others, like BC SPCA, we create a specialized indicia.

Postage can be a massive factor in getting your mail noticed. The more stamps you use, or more visually interesting they are, the more likely someone will look at it and open it.

The envelope was closed faced (no window) and had the donor's name and address lasered on at the mailhouse.

It was very personal.

The two-page letter came from Craig, the CEO of BC SPCA. This mailing was going to recent new donors, so we started with a quick thank you for recently joining the pack! We gave a voice to Jenny and Trooper, a cat and dog who were recently treated thanks to these donors. We asked and gave examples of amounts for a regular gift.

Craig's letter makes a straightforward case for monthly giving, explaining why these types of donors are so important for organizations like the BC SPCA.

BC SPCA PAW Plan
Monthly Giving Program

Date, 2020

Ms. Caring Donor
123 Generosity Street
Suite <3
Lovely, BC X0X 0X0

Dear <Caring>,

You joined our BC SPCA "pack" recently. **Thank you for your caring and compassionate heart**!

Each and every day, your kind and helpful support is there for innocent animals in their most desperate hour.

You were there for Jenny: *"Just weeks ago, my family left me without saying goodbye. They took the furniture, they took their clothes, they took the food...they took everything but me. I was boarded inside with no way out. I meowed as loudly as I could inside my cold, dark house, but no one could hear me. I cried for food and water but no one was listening..."*

And you were there for Trooper: *"OUCH! My paw is in agony and I can't even walk. I can't even lick it because it smells and tastes disgusting. I hope I don't get attacked. I'm helpless here on the streets and I'm very hungry and thirsty and scared..."*

You can read more about Jenny and Trooper—**and how you are a critical part of saving their precious lives**—on the enclosed note.

Right now, I want to tell you about how you can join me, and other loyal and friendly animal lovers, to provide ongoing, crucial support to animals who are abused and neglected.

<Caring>, can you put your love for animals into action and join our PAW Plan monthly giving program? Your monthly gift of $X, or even $XX will be put into action right away, helping animals in our care right now.

Please turn over...

The British Columbia Society for the Prevention of Cruelty to Animals
1245 East 7th Avenue, Vancouver BC V5T 1R1 | 604-681-7271 or 1-800-665-1868
The Standards Program Trustmark is a mark of Imagine Canada used under licence by BC SPCA.
Charitable Registration BN 11881 9036 RR0001
spca.bc.ca facebook.com/bcspca @BC_SPCA

Strong Charities · Imagine Canada

Your ongoing and loyal support is also a promise to the animals who will need help tomorrow, next month and every month.

When you join the PAW Plan, you belong to an amazing group of animal lovers who make an important sacrifice to provide love to animals. And what that means here at the BC SPCA is you are here to provide the safety net for animals in their most desperate hour, anytime and anywhere. It's so helpful! Monthly donors are our lifeblood.

Nobody expected a pandemic, but thanks to our PAW Plan donors, desperate animals were still protected as COVID-19 turned our lives upside down. In a matter of days, with our PAW Plan donors beside us, we were able to provide help for hungry animals by rapidly expanding our pet food bank program.

PAW Plan donors allow us to quickly help animals during emergencies, including wildfires, and also plan ahead with confidence.

Please take a moment to read more about the stories of Jenny and Trooper on the enclosed note. Our PAW Plan donors helped rescue and rehabilitate Jenny, Trooper and many other beautiful and brave animals.

You can use the enclosed reply form to sign up as a PAW Plan donor today. You can also give online at www.spca.bc.ca/pawplan or contact our Generosity Services team at 1-855-622-7722 or donations@spca.bc.ca.

Thank you again for your generosity and for being there for animals who need you.

With gratitude,

Craig Daniell

CEO and proud PAW Plan Monthly Donor

P.S. Thank you for being a true friend to animals like Jenny and Trooper! Please join me and other animal lovers in the PAW Plan monthly giving program today.

The full-size reply form offered a gift array that was appropriate to each donor in terms of their initial gift.

The donor needed to make four decisions:

1. Do I want to give monthly to the SPCA? **and**
2. How much do I want to give them each month? **and**
3. Do I want to send in a VOID cheque? **or**
4. Do I want to make my gift using my credit card?

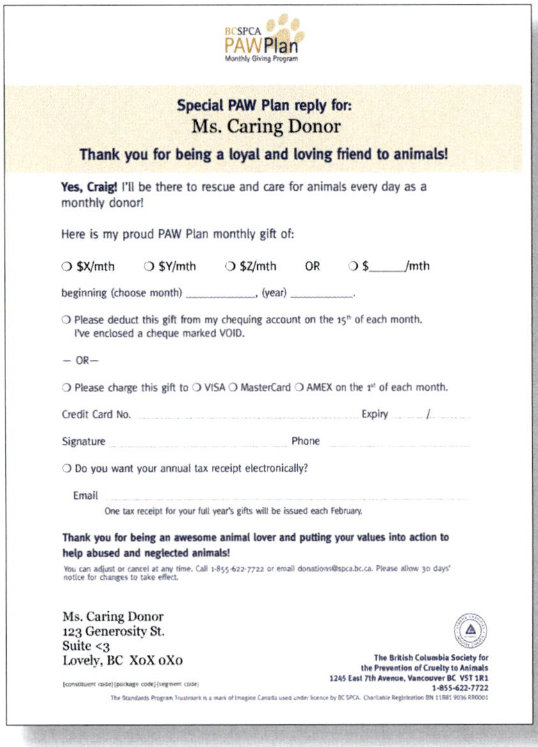

BCSPCA PAW Plan
Monthly Giving Program

Special PAW Plan reply for:
Ms. Caring Donor
Thank you for being a loyal and loving friend to animals!

Yes, Craig! I'll be there to rescue and care for animals every day as a monthly donor!

Here is my proud PAW Plan monthly gift of:

❍ $X/mth ❍ $Y/mth ❍ $Z/mth OR ❍ $______/mth

beginning (choose month) ____________, (year) __________.

❍ Please deduct this gift from my chequing account on the 15th of each month. I've enclosed a cheque marked VOID.

– OR –

❍ Please charge this gift to ❍ VISA ❍ MasterCard ❍ AMEX on the 1st of each month.

Credit Card No. ______________ Expiry ____/____

Signature ______________ Phone ______________

❍ Do you want your annual tax receipt electronically?

Email ______________

One tax receipt for your full year's gifts will be issued each February.

Thank you for being an awesome animal lover and putting your values into action to help abused and neglected animals!

You can adjust or cancel at any time. Call 1-855-622-7722 or email donations@spca.bc.ca. Please allow 30 days' notice for changes to take effect.

Ms. Caring Donor
123 Generosity St.
Suite <3
Lovely, BC XoX oXo

[constituent code][package code][segment code]

The British Columbia Society for the Prevention of Cruelty to Animals
1245 East 7th Avenue, Vancouver BC V5T 1R1
1-855-622-7722

The Standards Program Trustmark is a mark of Imagine Canada used under licence by BC SPCA. Charitable Registration BN 11881 9036 RR0001

Ask and get out of the way. Make it as simple as you can for your donor to respond.

Finally, we included an insert. It was 8.5″ x 11″ but folded down to fit into the pack. The top of the insert used images of Jenny and Trooper; two great pals with lots of loving eye contact. The piece was engaging and warm.

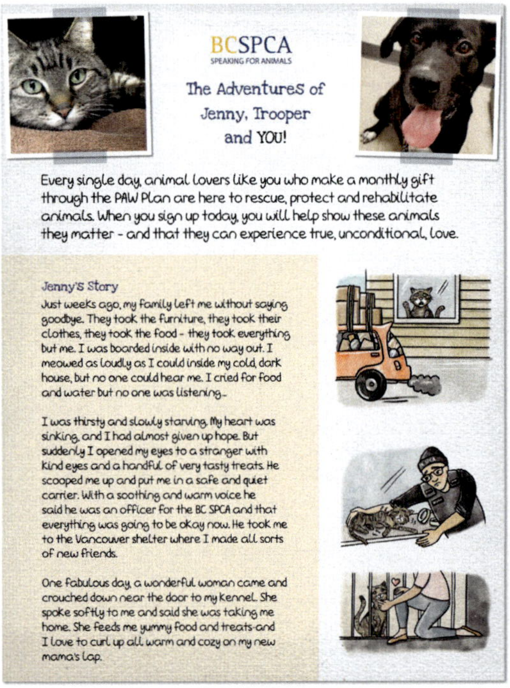

BCSPCA
SPEAKING FOR ANIMALS

The Adventures of Jenny, Trooper and YOU!

Every single day, animal lovers like you who make a monthly gift through the PAW Plan are here to rescue, protect and rehabilitate animals. When you sign up today, you will help show these animals they matter - and that they can experience true, unconditional, love.

Jenny's Story

Just weeks ago, my family left me without saying goodbye. They took the furniture, they took their clothes, they took the food - they took everything but me. I was boarded inside with no way out. I meowed as loudly as I could inside my cold, dark house, but no one could hear me. I cried for food and water but no one was listening...

I was thirsty and slowly starving. My heart was sinking, and I had almost given up hope. But suddenly I opened my eyes to a stranger with kind eyes and a handful of very tasty treats. He scooped me up and put me in a safe and quiet carrier. With a soothing and warm voice he said he was an officer for the BC SPCA and that everything was going to be okay now. He took me to the Vancouver shelter where I made all sorts of new friends.

One fabulous day, a wonderful woman came and crouched down near the door to my kennel. She spoke softly to me and said she was taking me home. She feeds me yummy food and treats and I love to curl up all warm and cozy on my new mama's lap.

We used the voices of Jenny and Trooper intentionally so we could tell the story from their perspective, which had a completely different impact than if Craig told the story.

Adding in an extra piece like this was a departure for the SPCA, but it gave them an opportunity to add to their case and share a complimentary story in a totally different way.

We also used some simple illustrations to "show" parts of the story we

Trooper's Story

OUCH! My paw is in agony and I can't even walk. I can't even lick it because it smells and tastes disgusting. I hope I don't get attacked. I'm helpless here on the streets and I'm very hungry and thirsty and scared...

But a kind person found me and helped me get surgery because my leg muscles had almost completely deteriorated. I was also very underweight and unhealthy from living as a stray. I was cared for with tenderness and affection by the BC SPCA. I lost my paw, but gained a loving, joyful life!

I've adapted to life on three legs with just a few hiccups and I have the most perfect furever family. They said, "He has become a certified couch potato and loves cuddles in bed. He loves car rides and treats and makes new friends wherever he goes." That's true! I love meeting animal lovers like you! Animal lovers are the best people!

If I could give you and all BC SPCA supporters a gentle but loving "high paw" I would!

obviously didn't have images for. This allowed us to bring some visual emotion into the piece that we couldn't have otherwise.

Jenny watching her family pack up and drive off gets me in the feels every time.

On the back, Trooper also got to share his story and use his sweet voice to ask donors to raise a paw and join the program as well.

Of course, a reply envelope was also included in the mail pack.

The BC SPCA used this mailing as a complement to a number of other means of converting new donors to monthly donors, so their results might differ from yours. However, I urge you to consider adding a pack like this to your annual mail cycle. Complementing it with some telephone follow-up is just one example of how you can find new monthly donors for your organization.

INVOLVEMENT DEVICES

Lastly, let's look at an easy way to get donors "involved" in their giving, beyond just checking a box. This is a simple way that will instantly make your appeal more interesting.

It used to be that you'd get fantastic mailings from Publishers Clearing House — or other organizations — inviting you to win $10,000,000 by filling out a form, putting a sticker in the box, sliding the piece into this envelope and so on. This created involvement and excitement.

A similar principle of involvement was used for the Second Harvest appeal (full appeal in *Deviation 3*) to raise enough funds to purchase a new truck. We created a cheap and cheerful sticker of some truck keys that donors could peel off and place above the amount they wanted to donate.

YES, TRUCK! Here are your keys! I'll help buy you
for Second Harvest! Here is my gift of:

Please attach sticker to your choice | Please attach sticker to your choice | Ple attach s your c | Please h sticker to ır choice

❍ $X | ❍ $XX | ❍ $Other_____ | ❍ $65,000 (I'll buy the other half of the truck!)

Remember your gift

It seems like such a simple thing, but it can really boost response because your donor can more actively be a part of giving.

Deviation Discoveries

Is there a more important piece in the mail pack than the reply form? Getting a response is the most important metric.

1. The reply form is there so your donor can take the action that you hope they will take. Make it as easy to use as possible. The more the donor needs to think about how to fill it out, the less likely it will get completed.
2. Giving to you isn't just a transactional exchange for your donor. Create space for your donors to feel joy and involved in this important act.
3. Give your donors the chance to talk to you and share a bit of their own story with you. Even if they don't do it, they will appreciate the opportunity.

Deviation Six — Who gets to tell your story?

Who (or what?) gets to tell your story is a key consideration for any great fundraising appeal. This deviation looks at how you can use different voices or perspectives to tell your story.

Stories bring us together. That's why we share them. They reflect our values as individuals and as a collective tribe. They teach us about who we are and where we came from. They tell us where we might be headed and how we will be when we get there.

As charities, the stories we tell donors can remind them why they care about us while inspiring them to keep helping. Hopefully.

I'm sure you know an amazing storyteller. Hopefully we all have at least one in our lives.

I know quite a few, but one of my favourite storytellers was my mom.

My mom, Sandra, was never the loudest person in the room but when she decided to share a story (even one you had heard a few times before), you couldn't help but take notice. She would become more animated. Her voice would change, depending on who she was speaking about. Her face would move and contort and sometimes, she would get so into it that she would burst out laughing at herself and the absurdity of it.

Every organization has stories to share, and every organization has a collection of voices and storytellers at its disposal to help share these stories.

Even if you only have one story, changing the voice that is telling it instantly makes it more interesting, since every voice will tell it differently.

I am a big fan of surprising and delighting donors by using creative voices.

Fundraising can be fun! A fun approach is not always appropriate, but sometimes it makes for even more effective fundraising than the typical doom and gloom.

This may come as a shock, but your donors actually *enjoy* being surprised by you.

They love receiving something that they never would have expected. It makes them pay attention and potentially enjoy the act of giving.

Donors giving with a smile on their face is a beautiful thing my friends.

I know. I can hear your head exploding.

When was the last time you received a call from a donor who was laughing or smiling from an appeal they just got from you?

Never?

Then this might be the deviation for you.

THE STORY OF RUBY

This was one of the first packs I designed. It was a House 2 Renewal Reminder pack for the Schizophrenia Society of Canada. Circa 1997. The pack didn't come from our elephant pal but it was a departure from the usual envelope that donors tended to get. It was appropriate, memorable and effective.

Another direct mail package that was appropriate, memorable and effective was the "Ruby" pack.

I don't think the following 12-year-old pack was the pinnacle of my career, but many people keep coming back to it.

The "Ruby" pack is a classic example of a trick that probably shouldn't be buried in the middle of this book, but nonetheless, here we are. The trick is, whenever Agents of Good starts working with a new client, one of the first things we do is look at everything their donors have seen for the past 12–16 months. Most of the time, this means their mail appeals.

I want to see everything a donor has been receiving in their mailbox and inbox from the client charity. I need to get a sense of what that experience has been like for the donors who might be paying attention.

Depending on the client, the appeal, the story, the ask, the timing and so on… we pull a "Ruby" out of our hat.

This idea is this: when you send a pack that looks and feels like nothing a donor has seen before, it sends a quick message to your donors that they are in for a slightly different experience when they pull the envelope out of their mailbox.

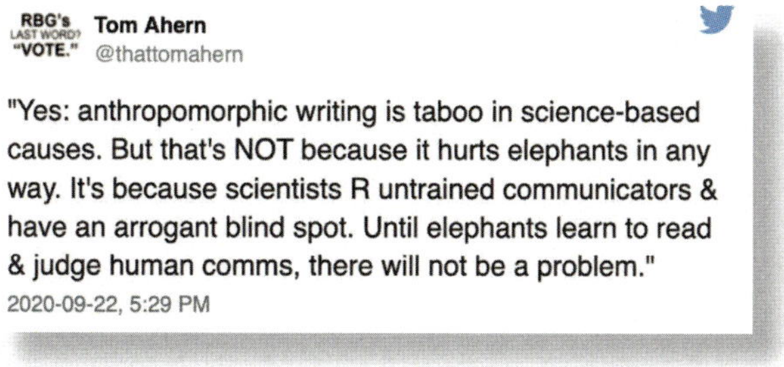

The whole idea of "anthropomorphizing" (attributing human characteristics to an animal or inanimate object) is largely frowned upon in professional fundraising.

Because it's cheesy. Not serious enough. Childish.

This is a shame, because when used creatively, it will raise you a ton of money.

I'm asked time and time again about how to sell ideas like this to your boss, and if I had a magic answer for you, I'd share it.

But I can tell you that **trust** is key.

Everyone tells you they want something "different" when it comes to the next fundraising campaign, but the rubber really hits the road when you put something truly different in front of them.

So let's look at the pack. This "special" mailing was for Ontario Nature. At the time, they followed a pretty traditional schedule of renewals and specials for their donors.

The "problem" was that every year millions of birds die when they crash into office buildings because they are distracted or blinded by the glare of city and office lights.

Ontario Nature had launched a lawsuit against developers and business owners of these buildings to make sure that the lights were turned out at night.

In this mailing, we specifically wanted to focus on the migration of hummingbirds. Even more specifically, the ruby-throated hummingbird.

Like all of the best ideas, no one can quite remember who came up with it or exactly how it came about.

But, together, we made the decision that the best voice to rage against the villainy of developers was the voice of a tiny, 3.5 gram, ruby-throated hummingbird named "Ruby." (I mean what else would we call her?)

This special mailing went out in a cheap and cheerful, white #10 envelope. The front only featured a strange marking.

I tend to avoid using jargon since it may alienate people, but this marking was a special kind of jargon.

Most Ontario Nature donors would have known what this strange marking was.

It was, of course, the footprint of a hummingbird.

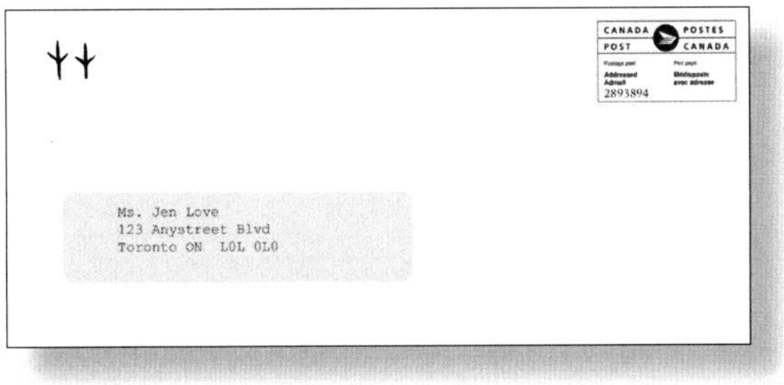

The back of the envelope featured a small "label" with the return address of Ruby's home in the Boreal Forest.

Kimberley McKenzie, our amazing client, said (and I quote) "*WTF?! You want me to pitch what?*"

This, of course, was outside Ontario Nature's usual norm of envelope that would have featured their logo mixed with some visual or tagline.

The key to an appeal like this is that you really have to go all the way. Sometimes writers or fundraisers decide they want to try this sort of approach to storytelling but chicken out when it comes to committing to the voice, the character, the story. But you must — otherwise it doesn't always come across well.

The donor received a very simple, 8.5″ x 14″ letter/reply combo. This format is very common in Canada.

Ruby attached a photo of herself, "A shot taken of me just before we left Costa Rica... it's my good side."

The use of that language was quite intentional. It instantly gave Ruby a vulnerable and relatable voice.

"Dear Jen,
I bet you've never received a letter from a bird before.

A shot taken of me just before we left Costa Rica... it's my good side...

John L Richbourg

Ms. Jen Love
123 Anystreet Blvd
Toronto ON L0L 0L0

Dear Jen,   June 11, 2010

I bet you've never received a letter from a bird before.

That's OK. I've never written a letter before! Caroline Schultz and the team at Ontario Nature wanted you to hear my story from my point of view.

What a journey it was for me this year!

I just arrived back home here in Ontario's spectacular boreal forest after my annual 4,500 kilometre migration from Costa Rica.

Flying across the Gulf of Mexico was different for me this year - did you know that there is a massive and foul oil spill there? I had a lump in my ruby throat flying over that disaster.

But my journey was just beginning.

The northern United States is always treacherous for me. Clouds of pesticides from airplanes are the worst - but by now, I and other hummingbirds have become used to it, and we know to steer clear.

And then, I was elated to fill my lungs with fresh, clean air. I'm home in Ontario! I can smell the boreal forest and the wonderful, wild, natural space. What a beautiful province we share!

I'm guided toward the Rouge River, and I'm home free. My heart beats 1,200 times a minute when I fly. And it skips a few

Yes, Ruby! I hear your chirp and I'll speak up for you!

Here is my special gift to Ontario Nature of: ❒$50 ❒$100 ❒$200 ❒ Other $______

beats when I find the Rouge.

I follow the river north.

WHAT!?

What was that? I thought I saw another ruby-throated hummingbird right in front of me, and as I skirted left, so did he. I skirted right, so did he. I hovered. So did he.

I was looking at me! There was a monstrous structure, clear like a window, right in front of me. I flew straight up until the strange image was gone. And I continued.

I know now what that was. The deadliest building for birds in Toronto. To us birds, it is a wall of windows, right on the shore of a path that we all take to get home to the boreal forest – and we can't see it!

I was lucky. I can hover in the air, so I avoided a collision. Many others suffer a horrible fate. I hear that thousands of migrating birds die every year hitting this building!

Friends of Ontario Nature – these bird deaths are preventable!

Caroline from Ontario Nature can tell you more about Ontario Nature's action to prevent bird strikes, and I hope that you'll help out in any way that you can. You'll also find a map of my migration path on the back of Caroline's note – see for yourself why some buildings are so dangerous!

Today, as I chirp to you, I'm home and safe in the boreal forest. Your support helps me get home every single year. Thank you.

Yours truly,

Ruby

You can make a lasting gift to Ontario Nature and make a difference every single day by

I would like to join the Friends of Nature program and make a monthly gift of:

❐ $10 ❐ $15 ❐ $20 ❐ Other $________

That's ok. I've never written a letter before!"

I've heard Agent Jen Love read these words a thousand times in conference rooms around the world, and I still think it is one of her best leads ever.

I hope you will take the time to read the letter, because it is cleverly simplistic and a masterclass in exceptional appeal writing.

It was typeset in Courier font. Nice and big. It looked like a personal letter from Ruby to the donor.

The reply form was perforated along the bottom so it could be torn off and put into the business reply envelope.

Ruby signs the letter using her footprints.

No PS — which usually would be a no-no, but Ruby is not a seasoned direct response expert. She's a hummingbird!

We created a migration map insert because, like every good insert or lift piece, we wanted to add to Ruby's case and present her story in a totally different way.

The donor can see Ruby's plight as she tries to make her way from sunny Costa Rica, past the BP Oil Spill in the Gulf of Mexico, up towards the Boreal Forest.

On the back of the insert was a note from Caroline Schultz, the executive director, who brings donors in on the

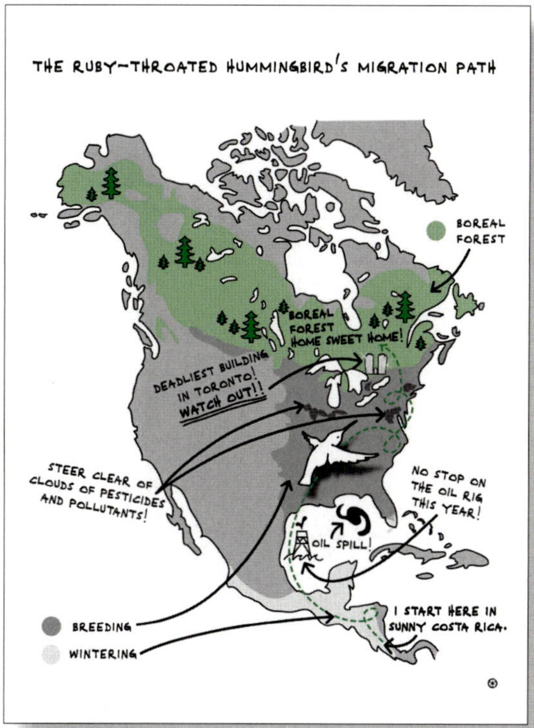

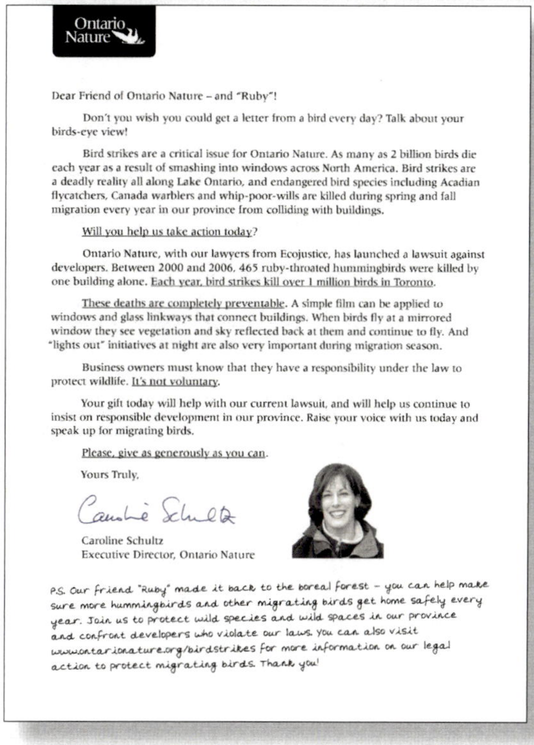

Ontario Nature

Dear Friend of Ontario Nature – and "Ruby"!

Don't you wish you could get a letter from a bird every day? Talk about your birds-eye view!

Bird strikes are a critical issue for Ontario Nature. As many as 2 billion birds die each year as a result of smashing into windows across North America. Bird strikes are a deadly reality all along Lake Ontario, and endangered bird species including Acadian flycatchers, Canada warblers and whip-poor-wills are killed during spring and fall migration every year in our province from colliding with buildings.

Will you help us take action today?

Ontario Nature, with our lawyers from Ecojustice, has launched a lawsuit against developers. Between 2000 and 2006, 465 ruby-throated hummingbirds were killed by one building alone. Each year, bird strikes kill over 1 million birds in Toronto.

These deaths are completely preventable. A simple film can be applied to windows and glass linkways that connect buildings. When birds fly at a mirrored window they see vegetation and sky reflected back at them and continue to fly. And "lights out" initiatives at night are also very important during migration season.

Business owners must know that they have a responsibility under the law to protect wildlife. It's not voluntary.

Your gift today will help with our current lawsuit, and will help us continue to insist on responsible development in our province. Raise your voice with us today and speak up for migrating birds.

Please, give as generously as you can.

Yours Truly,

Caroline Schultz

Caroline Schultz
Executive Director, Ontario Nature

P.S. Our friend "Ruby" made it back to the boreal forest – you can help make sure more hummingbirds and other migrating birds get home safely every year. Join us to protect wild species and wild spaces in our province and confront developers who violate our laws. You can also visit www.ontarionature.org/birdstrikes for more information on our legal action to protect migrating birds. Thank you!

joke. The change in voice from something very light and conversational to one that was more authoritarian drives home the importance and seriousness of the issue.

Fundraisers, and those who work with them, need to remember that we are having emotional conversations with donors and as such, must create appeals with emotional range.

We also converted Caroline's handwriting into a font so that she could write the PS at the bottom. This has also allowed us to add her handwriting all over packs in subsequent years — a nice little personalization hack.

And out it went.

"I don't mind telling you that as the new director of development I was terrified when this mailing went out. Not because I didn't like it — I loved it and advocated for it. But because it was so different from anything the organization had done. The Ruby mailing felt really risky. It's good to feel that way a few times a year. It is also a gift to work somewhere that is willing to try new approaches." –Kimberley MacKenzie.

So… how did it do?

The reaction was pretty quick. Phone calls and emails from donors, board members, volunteers delightfully came in, as did little notes along with donations.

One donor, a wonderful fellow named Jack (an active member and donor for almost 50 years) even wrote back (Fig. 6.1) to Ruby and dropped off his letter in person.

Jack's letter was the first time I truly felt the power of this type of emotional, vulnerable and even FUN — fundraising.

As you can imagine, Ruby just had to write back to Jack (Fig. 6.2). Agent Jen relished the opportunity to up her pun game since Jack set the bar so high.

As we share in our presentations, the love story continued on between Jack, Ontario Nature and Ruby. We found out that Jack was remembering the organization in his Will and continued to be a vocal, active supporter and donor to an organization he obviously felt deeply connected to.

Our pals at Ontario Nature wanted to do something to honour Jack as a special donor, so we commissioned Jessica Rae Gordon to create a portrait of Ruby for Jack for the holidays (Fig. 6.3).

Caroline from Ontario Nature and Agent Jen were able to go out for a little visit to Jack's and hand-deliver this portrait and a little card from Ruby back to Jack.

This is one beautiful story of one beautiful donor. Obviously you can't go out of

[redacted]
Toronto ON [redacted]
August 22 2010

Dear Ruby,

You win the bet! I have indeed never before received a letter from a bird, not even from a cute young chic, and I am thrilled and delighted. I hope that you won't send any letters to glow-worms because they don't want to be delighted! I can't think of any other species of bird that I would rather receive a letter from; I certainly would not like to receive a letter from a vulture.

I have always admired the fantastic aerial acrobatics which you hummingbirds are so capable of. I am particularly amazed by the nuptial display which the male hummingbirds use to impress the females. If you, Ruby, are a female as your name suggests, you must be especially impressed and excited to witness these stunts. I have concluded, however, that you must be a male because you said that you had a lump in your ruby throat, and only male ruby-throats have a ruby throat. Also, you refer to the reflected image of yourself as seen in a building window, as 'he'. It doesn't matter to me which you are; in either case you are a real jewel.

We humans have an expression 'travelling in the best of circles' which means associating with famous and important people. You male hummingbirds travel in the best of semi-circles. How do you make such perfect circular arcs? It looks as if you are suspended from an invisible string with the other end attached to a fixed point. I can't imagine a helicopter pilot doing stunts like this, and even if he could, he make a heck of a lot more noise than you do.

I am trying to visualize you, hovering over the keyboard of your typewriter and using your incredibly thin bill to operate the keys while writing your letter to me. We humans have an expression 'hunt and peck' to describe people like me who use only two fingers, one on each hand, and who have not memorized the crazy order of letters on the keyboard. This seems to apply more to your typing than to mine or perhaps it should be hover and peck for you.

Perhaps you use a computer to type your letters. When they first came out with computers I was hoping that they would adopt a more logical arrangement of the keys but they simply copied the old QWERTY etc. I still use a typewriter; I don't even have a computer.

A few years ago I wanted to look up on the internet the label and number of a CD which was aired on CBC radio, and which contained some classical music which I wanted to buy. I went to the local library and the computer assigned to me had a blank screen but there was a sign saying 'To activate the screen, press any key'. The only key I had was my house key, so I got it out of my pocket and pressed it firmly but nothing happened. I was puzzled but soon decided that what this sign meant was that I was supposed to press keys A N Y K E Y in that order. I started to do so, but when I pressed the first key the computer was so smart that it knew what other letters were coming and the screen lit up!

(over)

Fig. 6.1

The instruction given by the announcer on the radio was to go to the CBC website and then follow the lynx. I couldn't find any lynx on the screen; there was also no bobcat, no puma, no panther no lion or any other kind of cat. It occurred to me that they could't use any member of the cat family because it would undoubtedly eat the mouse! I then realized that perhaps the word was links, not lynx. However, I couldn't find any golf course on the screen either. And even if I could find a lynx or a golf course on the screen, how could I follow it,

We humans seem to find many things to do with computers hooked up to the internet. I suspect that many animals are also benefitting from the internet. The spider probably improves its chances of attracting a fly by telling it to "visit my website". The job situation is much improved for mice because each computer requires one. There is one type of mouse whose job prospects are limited; the poor little doormouse can't get a job with a computer using a Windows program.

In conclusion, I wish you well on your annual trip south for the winter. It must be nice to be able to fly to Costa Rica without dealing with customs officials, going through airport security checks, or having to produce passports and visas. It must also be nice to be able to stop whenever you want to feed and rest without worrying about reservations and credit cards.

Thanks again for your letter; it was a real humdinger.

Yours sincerely,

Jack Gingrich

Jack Gingrich

P.S. Why did it not say
AIR MAIL on your envelope?

P.S. Number 2 When a male
hummingbird performs his
semi-circular swinging from
side to side, do you call him
a 'real swinger'?

P.S. Number 3 Do you birds
use the TWITTER website to keep
in touch with each other?

Dear Jack,

Tweet Tweet! What a treat! I just arrived back in Ontario and am simply buzzing with delight about your letter.

We hummingbirds have an expression, "wearing your heart on your wing" when you just can't help but show your feelings. Jack, my heart is on my wing. Thank you, so much, for taking the time to write to me. And for supporting Ontario Nature as a way to stand up for the little creatures like me!

Speaking of standing up, I hear Caroline was in court a few weeks ago. I'm just so honoured to have fine human friends like you. I buzzed over the courthouse and chirped my encouragement from the skies. I hope it helped!

That was the only real detour on my journey this year. I felt the "call of nature" near the courthouse, but I held on until I could get to that deadly building you guys are fighting. I hope that helped too!

Jack, I simply loved your letter.

You asked me about making such perfect circular arcs. I wish there was a better story for you, but it really is just very natural for me. This may sound strange, but we hummingbirds have another expression, "hummer nature", for thoughts, feelings and actions that just happen naturally. Do you have that expression – "human nature"? Boy, I wonder what that would be? Is it human nature to be so darn terrific? Must be! You sure are!

There's something I really admire about humans too, Jack. Stillness. If I close my eyes, I picture you with your feet up and this paper in your hands. I hope that's what you are doing.

Fig. 6.2

How funny that you ask about how I "hover and peck". You are so right! But, I find it so hard to think while I hover over the computer, so I actually write out what I'm going to say first. I have another expression that I'm sure will sound odd to you. I call it "chicken scratches" when I write something down. A good friend of mine is a chicken and his penmanship is atrocious!

That reminds me. You mentioned using a typewriter instead of a computer. I really think we may be kindred spirits! Sometimes when I am super hungry on my migration I come upon these feeders that must have been designed by NASA. They are so confusing it makes my head hurt. Nothing beats a good old flower for me.

Speaking of which, my tummy is humming so I have to find something to eat. Luckily, up here in the boreal forest there are lots of wild flowers for me to enjoy. You fine folks who are protecting my home up here are just super. If you're ever up here, give me a buzz. Haha. That's another hummingbird expression. It means give me a call. Wait! That's also one for the birds.

Oh well. I hope you know what I mean and how I feel. There are only two words I can think of, Jack, my dear friend.

Thank you.

Yours truly,

Ruby

your way to do this sort of thing for all of your donors but you do have donors like Jack.

And, you do have voices like Ruby that you can utilize in your storytelling if you wish. Your donors will likely thank you for it in all sorts of ways that you can't imagine.

I've heard it more than once. "Yeah, but we could never do a Ruby pack."

Maybe you're right. Maybe you never could do the Ruby pack, but you do have a Ruby. I promise.

It takes some work and creativity to find your "other" voices. It will also take a supportive and trusting boss and some courage to put a name to it and present it. It will TOTALLY take some deep breaths to drop it into the mailboxes of donors.

Fig. 6.3

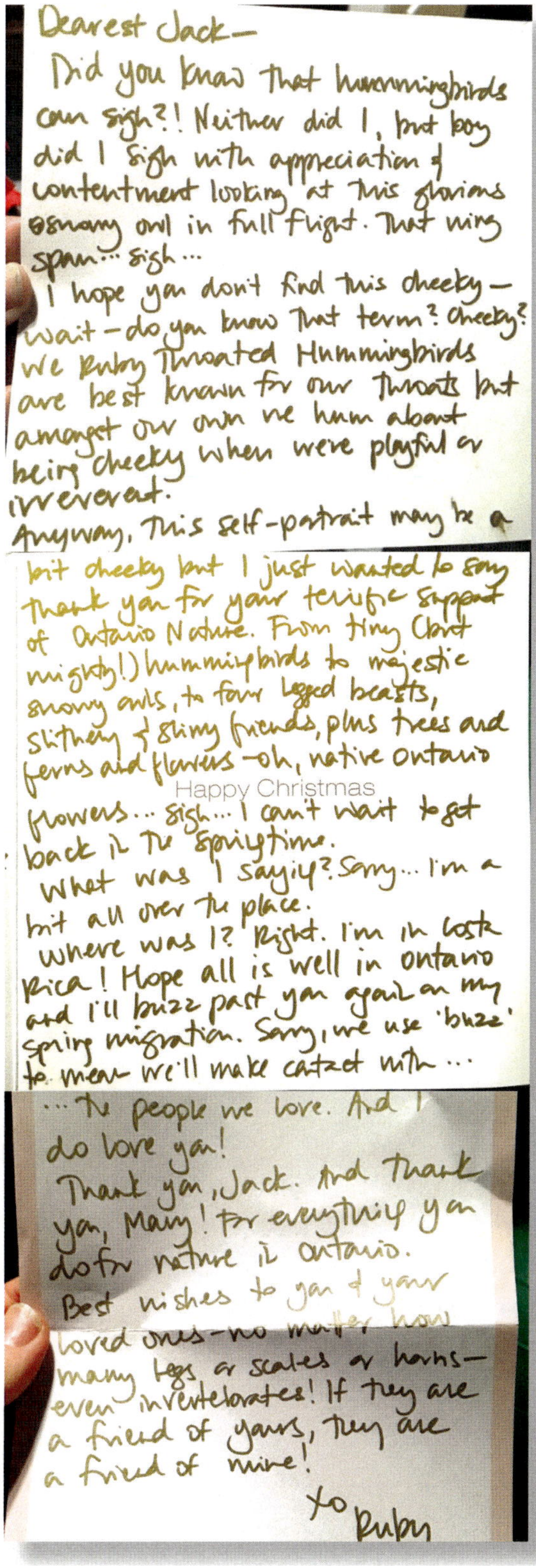

Dearest Jack—
Did you know that hummingbirds can sigh?! Neither did I, but boy did I sigh with appreciation & contentment looking at this glorious snowy owl in full flight. That wing span… sigh…
I hope you don't find this cheeky— wait—do you know that term? Cheeky? We Ruby Throated Hummingbirds are best known for our throats but amongst our own we hum about being cheeky when we're playful or irreverent.
Anyway, this self-portrait may be a bit cheeky but I just wanted to say thank you for your terrific support of Ontario Nature. From tiny (but mighty!) hummingbirds to majestic snowy owls, to four legged beasts, slithery & slimy friends, plus trees and ferns and flowers—oh, native Ontario

Happy Christmas

flowers… sigh… I can't wait to get back in the springtime.
What was I saying? Sorry… I'm a bit all over the place.
Where was I? Right. I'm in Costa Rica! Hope all is well in Ontario and I'll buzz past you again on my spring migration. Sorry, we use 'buzz' to mean we'll make contact with…
…the people we love. And I do love you!
Thank you, Jack. And thank you, Mary! For everything you do for nature in Ontario.
Best wishes to you & your loved ones—no matter how many legs or scales or horns— even invertebrates! If they are a friend of yours, they are a friend of mine!
xo Ruby

I have often been told,
"This is too juvenile for our donors."
"Our donors are too smart for this... "
"Our donors only respond to figures and statistics... "
"Our donors only like... "
"Our donors only respond to... "

Stop making excuses for your personal or organizational insecurities.

Your donors love to be surprised. They love to laugh and be delighted. Just like we all do. They love the thrill of getting something from you they would have never expected.

JADA'S DREAM

An unexpected voice doesn't have to be a truck, or a bird, or a bag or a heart. It can also be human.

Here's another example from a targeted mid-level appeal that Agents of Good created for Camp Oochigeas.

Camp Ooch needed to rebuild the space around their waterfront to make it more accessible for all kids. Some children had limitations to getting close to the campfire by the waterside.

Like so many of the appeals AOG works on, the words and stories of the organization's beneficiaries guide us in how to share those words and stories with donors.

Jada was no different.

Jada (short for Jadarose), was in grade 8 and had an aggressive form of cancer. Part of the way through treatment, Jada

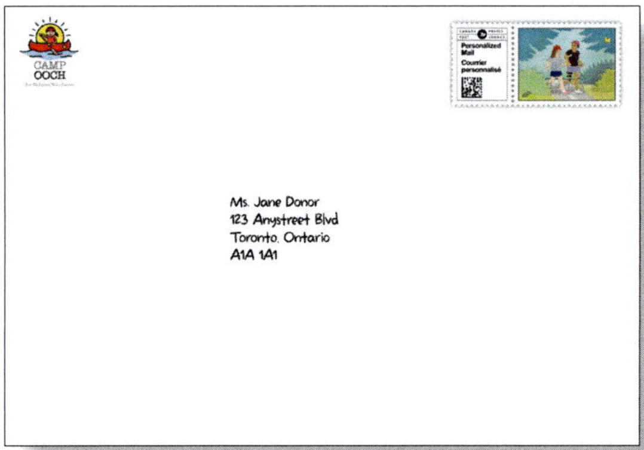

CAMP OOCH

Date, 2019

Ms. Jane Donor
123 Generosity Street
Suite <3
Lovely, ON X0X 0X0

Dear <Caring>,

You have a very special place in the story of Camp Ooch. Your kindness and generosity is felt by our Campers and their families every single day. Thank you for your amazing support!

You're hearing from me today because we want you to be part of the next chapter in the story of Ooch. And, like a good story told by the campfire or by flashlight in our cabins, it's got excitement, adventure and just the right amount of heart-thumping, race-against-time urgency!

Right now, we have a magnificent opportunity to rebuild the Camp Ooch waterfront and "Camphitheatre", where we have our campfires and sing-a-longs. With your help, we can renovate the heart of Camp, and make it more accessible for kids using walkers, crutches and wheelchairs, helping our Campers get around with full independence.

Your gift of $500 or $1,000 will help make dreams come true. Let me tell you how.

Let me tell you how you can make dreams come true. I want to introduce you to one of my friends, a firecracker of a kid named Jadarose, but we call her Jada. Jada had a very aggressive, rapid-onset form of cancer when she was in grade 8. Part way through Jada's intense treatment, the doctors told Jada and her mom Jennifer that they recommended amputating one of Jada's legs below the knee.

True to form for our Ooch Campers, Jada's spirit is stronger than you can believe, but she needs a little extra help to get around at Camp. For kids using walkers, wheelchairs, canes or crutches, getting down to the waterfront and Camphitheatre without help can be a struggle. And our kids are independent!

464 Bathurst Street, Toronto ON M5T 2S6
Tel: 416.961.6624 Fax: 416.961.2267 ooch.org

I'm sharing this with you now, before we share this project with others, because you are a cherished donor and you have made very generous gifts to Ooch. We count you in a very special group of donors and I hope you are inspired to give your biggest gift to Ooch yet!

You'll find enclosed a special storybook, created just for you and few other of our very loyal donors and friends. A local artist and friend of Ooch did these illustrations to help bring Jada's dream to life for you.

And we want you to be part of this story.

You can be part of making our outdoor spaces as accessible as our indoors, where kids like Jada splash and play in the water, swim, kayak, and more. And they will do all this independently—with your caring and generous support.

Our ambitious plan includes updating Camphitheatre, so that kids with any kinds of assistive devices can participate fully and independently in sing-a-longs, jams and campfires.

Your gift of $X this renovation will make dreams come true. You'll find enclosed your reply form, and as you can see, we are making a big and bold ask of you today. You'll also find enclosed a couple more photos and reflections from Jada and Jennifer.

Thank you, from the bottom of my heart, for your kind and compassionate support of Ooch and kids like Jada. I know we are asking you for a lot today, but I hope you'll reflect on this request and give as generously as you can. If you want to talk to us about ways to give or have any questions at all, please don't hesitate to reach out. We would love to talk with you and help make this happen!

With gratitude,

Alex

Alex Robertson, CEO

P.S. Will you be part of this story with your gift today? You will help us rebuild the heart of Camp Ooch!

and her mom were told they would need to amputate one of Jada's legs below the knee. As you can imagine, for a kid like Jada, getting down to the Campitheatre without some help could be a struggle — which is why Camp Ooch wanted to make it more accessible.

I wanted to make this package feel as personal as possible. The oversize outer envelope was hand-addressed and featured a personalized mail indicia. Some donors even received it with a first-class stamp!

The pack was a little bit heavier and "squishier" since it included a few more pieces than usual. These are all good things.

The two-page letter came from Alex, the executive director. That was fairly typical and in the context of what they were asking donors for, was a very appropriate voice to make that ask.

At AOG, we try to be very thoughtful about adding emphasis to our letters. We don't use an excessive amount of bolding or underlining — but we make sure anything that we do add emphasis to is either reiterating what we are asking the donor for, telling them how important they are to us (the org), or celebrating what they make possible.

In addition, Jen Love and I always apply the *Tom Ahern red pen test* (from: *How to Write Fundraising Materials that Raise More Money*) to our letters.

Lovely, ON X0X 0X0

Dear <Caring>,

You have a very special place in the story of Camp Ooch. Your kindness and generosity is felt by our Campers and their families every single day. Thank you for your amazing support!

You're hearing from me today because we want you to be part of the next chapter in the story of Ooch. And, like a good story told by the campfire or by flashlight in our cabins, it's got excitement, adventure and just the right amount of heart-thumping, race-against-time urgency!

Right now, we have a magnificent opportunity to rebuild the Camp Ooch waterfront and "Camphitheatre", where we have our campfires and sing-a-longs. With your help, we can renovate the heart of Camp, and make it more accessible for kids using walkers, crutches and wheelchairs, helping our Campers get around with full independence.

Your gift of $500 or $1,000 will help make dreams come true. Let me tell you how.

Let me tell you how you can make dreams come true. I want to introduce you to one of my friends, a firecracker of a kid named Jadarose,

CAMP OOCH

SPECIAL REPLY FORM FOR:
Ms. Jane Donor

✔ **Yes, Alex! I will be a leader in making nature more accessible at Camp Ooch!**

Here is my leadership gift of:
❍ $500
❍ $1,000
❍ $2,000
❍ I prefer to give $______

Thank you!
If you have any questions about your giving or our work, please reachout at 647-557-6503 or Shighfield@ooch.org
Thanks!
Stephanie

❍ I've enclosed a cheque made payable to Camp Oochigeas.
❍ I prefer to charge my donation to ❍ VISA ❍ MasterCard ❍ AMEX

Card # ____ ____ ____ ____

Expiry __ / __

Name on Card ________

Signature ________

Telephone ________

New regulations from VISA may require us to contact you by phone to confirm your CVV. If you choose to give using your VISA, please include your telephone number. Thank you!

Ms. Jane Donor
123 Generosity Street
Suite <3
Lovely, ON X0X 0X0

Some ideas of what your gift will do are on the back!

464 Bathurst Street, Toronto ON M5T 2S6
Tel: 416.961.6624 Fax: 416.961.2267 ooch.org
Charitable Business No.: 13111 6022 RR0001

Get a red pen. Then select an important donor communication such as an appeal letter or newsletter. You could also print out your website's home page. Apply red pen to paper each time the word you appears — in any of its forms (*yours, you'll*) — circle it.

A good piece of donor communication will look like it has the measles.

You is the most powerful (and warmest) word in fundraising.

"*You*" is glue. It keeps your donor reading.

The group of donors who received this appeal were given gift amounts that aligned with their previous giving. Some of the fundraising team added handwritten personal notes where appropriate, inviting the donor to contact them if they had any questions.

I think it's incredibly important that you make it easy for your donor to talk to a real human.

On the back, we took the time to break down some tangibles of what the donor's gift could accomplish. Yes, this requires some leg-work for you and your organization. The reward is that donors tend to give more (or more than they usually do) since they actually understand what their giving will do!

CAMP OOCH

What Your Gift Will Do

$500 Pathways for All: You'll help grade and resurface a section of paths, allowing Campers to go between their cabins, buildings, and activity areas without assistance.

$1,000 Landscaping Features: You'll ensure the natural beauty of Camp Ooch is preserved after construction is completed!

$2,500 Roadway Improvements: You'll ensure a portion of the roads to the Barn (our indoor recreation facility), MedShed, sports court and camp garden are upgraded and accessible.

$5,000 Waterfront Boardwalk: You'll contribute to boardwalk upgrades, allowing all Campers to easily access waterfront activities and docks.

$7,500 Camphitheatre Benches: You'll provide additional, improved seating at our upgraded Camphitheatre, making this space more welcoming for all our Campers.

$10,000 Camphitheatre: You'll make a portion of our Camphitheatre—the heart of Camp Ooch—accessible for all, and help towards our goal of allowing 50% more Campers around the campfire!

We potentially could have stopped there. A lot of organizations do.

We wanted to tell the story of Jadarose more visually for Camp Ooch's donors. We wanted to take them *beyond* the typical facts and figures.

Time to dive into feelings.

With storytelling, with direct response, with everything, the story dictates the delivery.

I rarely spend a second trying to figure out how something will look, until I know what we are trying to say. What would be the point?

Agent Jen and I talked about the Jada narrative.

We knew the essence of the story we wanted to share with donors. We knew that the end objective was to show how a re-imagined camp could allow all the amazing kids like Jada to have the same camp access that everyone else did.

We talked about creating a storybook to allow our mid-level folks to imagine this story too.

I worked with Jessica Rae Gordon on sketching out the illustrations I wanted to bring life to Jada's story.

Jada's dream

Jada can't wait to get back to Camp Ooch. What will be her first adventure? She can't wait to smell the forest, hug her old friends, and make new ones.

But her heart falls just a bit. She loves everything about Camp. And even though there is always someone to help, she worries she won't be able to walk down to the Camphitheatre and waterfront on her own. Since her amputation, rough terrain and uneven paths can make walking alone more difficult.

FINALLY! After her long trip north, Jada makes her way off the bus, excited to be at Camp. The smells of the forest! The sounds of laughter! The music and singing!

The final insert was a 5.5″ x 5.5″ storybook that shared Jada's story as we imagined it.

Jada's Dream is a simple little story that shares the future vision of what Camp Ooch will be like when they are able to make the Campitheatre more accessible. It's not a list of "we will do this" and "we will do that." It is a moving story that visually shows the impact these changes will have on kids like Jada.

We created one more lift note — from Jada and her mom **(Fig 6.4)**.

The lift note was designed to look handmade with taped photos and highlighter emphasis. For the donors who just skim your direct mail pieces, what does this piece say?

"I can see in people's eyes when they watch me knee-board or swim—they're like, "Whoa, that's awesome!" — The donor can feel the sense of accomplishment Jada feels about herself being able to do these things.

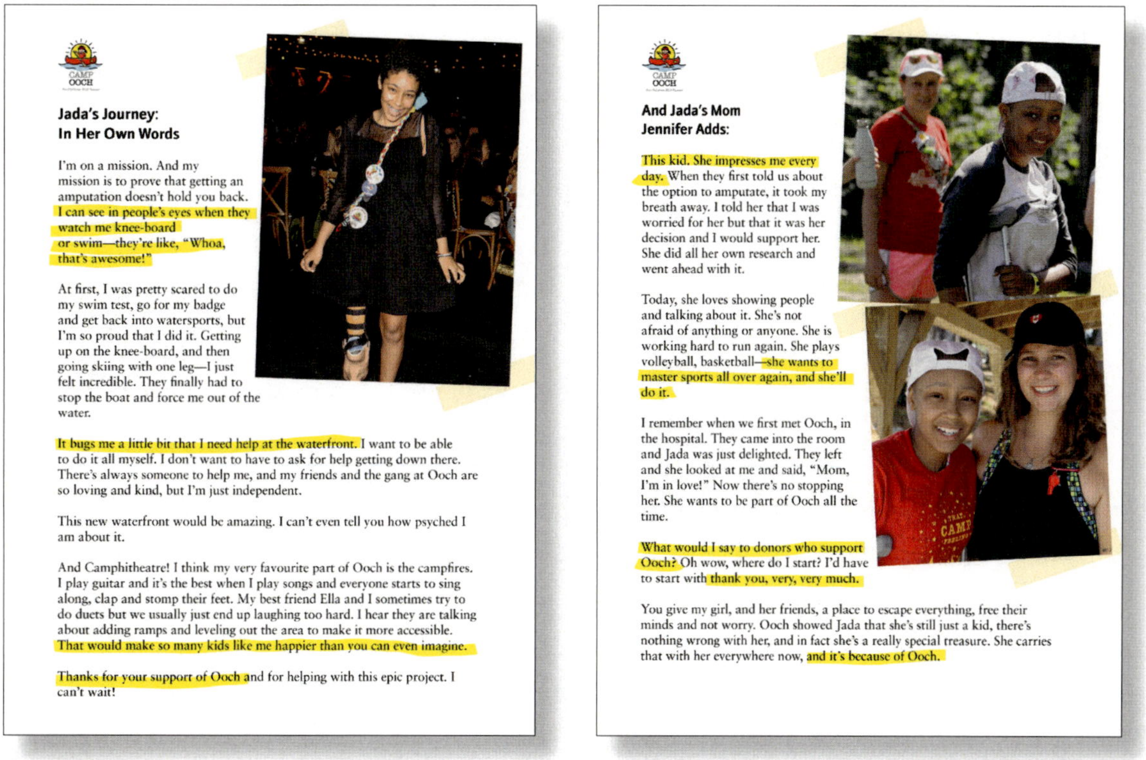

CAMP OOCH

Jada's Journey: In Her Own Words

I'm on a mission. And my mission is to prove that getting an amputation doesn't hold you back. I can see in people's eyes when they watch me knee-board or swim—they're like, "Whoa, that's awesome!"

At first, I was pretty scared to do my swim test, go for my badge and get back into watersports, but I'm so proud that I did it. Getting up on the knee-board, and then going skiing with one leg—I just felt incredible. They finally had to stop the boat and force me out of the water.

It bugs me a little bit that I need help at the waterfront. I want to be able to do it all myself. I don't want to have to ask for help getting down there. There's always someone to help me, and my friends and the gang at Ooch are so loving and kind, but I'm just independent.

This new waterfront would be amazing. I can't even tell you how psyched I am about it.

And Camphitheatre! I think my very favourite part of Ooch is the campfires. I play guitar and it's the best when I play songs and everyone starts to sing along, clap and stomp their feet. My best friend Ella and I sometimes try to do duets but we usually just end up laughing too hard. I hear they are talking about adding ramps and leveling out the area to make it more accessible. That would make so many kids like me happier than you can even imagine.

Thanks for your support of Ooch and for helping with this epic project. I can't wait!

CAMP OOCH

And Jada's Mom Jennifer Adds:

This kid. She impresses me every day. When they first told us about the option to amputate, it took my breath away. I told her that I was worried for her but that it was her decision and I would support her. She did all her own research and went ahead with it.

Today, she loves showing people and talking about it. She's not afraid of anything or anyone. She is working hard to run again. She plays volleyball, basketball—she wants to master sports all over again, and she'll do it.

I remember when we first met Ooch, in the hospital. They came into the room and Jada was just delighted. They left and she looked at me and said, "Mom, I'm in love!" Now there's no stopping her. She wants to be part of Ooch all the time.

What would I say to donors who support Ooch? Oh wow, where do I start? I'd have to start with thank you, very, very much.

You give my girl, and her friends, a place to escape everything, free their minds and not worry. Ooch showed Jada that she's still just a kid, there's nothing wrong with her, and in fact she's a really special treasure. She carries that with her everywhere now, and it's because of Ooch.

Fig. 6.4

"*It bugs me a little bit that I need help at the waterfront.*" – This is the heart of the appeal. There are a lot of kids like Jada who feel negative about needing help from anyone. They also might make the decision to not join in so they aren't having to bother anyone.

"*That would make so many kids like me happier than you can even imagine.*" – The representative voice of all the kids, all of the beneficiaries of this appeal to the donor who can make it all possible!

"*Thanks for your support of Ooch…* " – Gratitude. Appreciation. Acknowledgement.

On the back:

"*This kid. She impresses me every day.*" – A mom's pride in her child.

"*…she wants to master sports all over again, and she'll do it.*" – You the donor are making that possible for her by making it easier for her to access the water and do the things that she loves.

"*What would I say to donors who support Ooch … Thank you, very, very much.*" – Gratitude. Appreciation. Acknowledgment.

"*…it's because of Ooch.*" – this organization (and its donors) do so much to help kids like mine.

These three voices; Alex, Jada, and Jennifer give the donor a 360 degree emotional perspective on the impact and importance of her gifts. All three make the donor feel seen, and appreciated, and acknowledged.

Always harness the full power of the various voices, human and otherwise, associated with your organization. These voices can remind donors how cherished and valued they are, and how critical they are to achieving your mission.

SANTA CLAUS AND THE CARIBOU

From the moment they reach into their mailbox and wade through the stack of appeals that they have received, or click open their inbox, you have one shot to get the attention of your donor.

As you should now realize, a common question at AOG HQ is who, or what, is the right voice for the story. I think you'll agree that almost anything would be better than the droning, overly-professional tones of your Executive Director. (No offense to your droning, overly-professional Executive Director of course.)

Here is one last example to drive home the point.

There was an appeal I worked on many years ago (with the Godfather of Good, David Love) for an organization called the Canadian Arctic Resources Committee (CARC), protectors of the arctic and the caribou.

We pitched the concept of a direct mail pack that would come from Santa. The outer envelope featured an illustration of an angry Santa writing a note while looking out his window. Some oil tanker had run aground spilling its contents, and as a result the reindeer were falling over sick. I really wish I had a copy of this pack, but I'm sure you can imagine it. The letter, from Santa, told donors why he was upset and was asking them for help.

The client was terrified. Thankfully, they took a chance. It raised a shed-load of money.

In fact, it raised more funds than any appeal they had done before. Donors were enchanted. They heard about a familiar issue in an unfamiliar sort of way.

Using a different voice to tell your story can do that for you.

Don't miss an opportunity to ask yourself: Who, or what, is the right voice for our story?

Deviation Discoveries

A lot of organizations use the same letter-signer, appeal over appeal. However, your organization is made up of a collection of humans (and other things) that have their own perspective on your story. Ask yourself, who (or what) is the right voice right now in the eyes and ears of your donor that might help convince them to help.

1. Using unique voices that can tell emotional stories can unlock deeper connections for donors longing for a more intimate conversation.
2. Your organization is made up of many different voices and perspectives. Brainstorm your own list. Think of staff, program and front-of-the-line people, beneficiaries, their families (human or otherwise). Ask yourself, based on what you need your donor to do today, who would be the best person to ask your donor for help.
3. Story or voice dictates execution. Not the other way around. Once you've determined what you are asking the donor to do, and the voice you are using to ask for that, then you should determine the best way to tell that story.

Deviation Seven — More is more

This deviation examines any other piece in your mail pack that isn't your outer envelope, letter or reply form. A good insert or lift note can be like finding a new trail you've never been on before. It can take your appeal in an unexpected but delightful direction. Your ideas are only limited by your creativity.

They're called "lift notes" for a reason. When you use them, they tend to lift response.

Tried and tested.

That being said, all lift notes are not created equal. Not all lift notes will increase response rates — but the right one(s) will.

Lift notes can take many forms, but usually the "right" one is a piece that rounds out the case for support that you've made in the letter, presenting additional information in a different way.

A good starting place is to ask yourself this question, "What else, aside from this letter, does this appeal need to make the case more understandable, relatable, actionable or emotional?"

Your boss may question if the extra expense is worth it, "*What's the ROI of adding this insert?*"

I have no absolute answer to this question. It's like the saying, "how long is a piece of string?" And like so many other things, it also depends. Testing might give you an idea, but I wouldn't suggest it.

How many lifts should I add to our direct mail pack?

In the context of storytelling, the answer is: as many as you need to fully tell the story or round out your case. It's similar to your direct mail letter. Make it as long as it needs to be to do the job it needs to do.

Yes, every lift piece you add to your pack will add extra expense, potentially more postage or bigger envelopes; and no, you obviously can't do that for all of your donors. (See more on this in *Deviation 9*.) However for those very special donors, who are giving 80% of your revenue appeal over appeal, it IS worth the expense.

Add this once a year

At Agents of Good, we recommend our clients add a once-a-year insert that shares thanks for the "one, two or three things your support helped us accomplish this past year" and, "looking ahead, your continued support will help us to move ahead on these one, two, three new issues."

We typically add this type of insert early in the year to a mailing.

This was the first mailing of the year for Ontario Nature.

The outer envelope was 9″ x 6″ and included a teaser and visual of the membership card that was enclosed. When you put things like this in a pack, it's often good to tell your donors that you have done it!

The letter was a double sided, 8.5″ x 11″ (Fig. 7.1). The main ask was for the donor to renew their support of the organization.

We used a full-size 8.5″ x 11″ (Fig. 7.2) reply form to offer donors the opportunity to renew their support with a single gift or to join the monthly giving program.

The member card (Fig. 7.3) was "tipped on" to the letter (which means it has a low tack stick on the back so it could be attached and personalized to the top of the letter).

And finally, we added this extra insert (Fig. 7.4).

This lift was printed full size on 8.5″ x 11″ paper. It highlighted key accomplishments from the previous year while looking ahead to the year to come. It also included

Ontario Nature

<Date>

<Addressee>
<Address 1>
<Address 2>
<City>, <PROV> <POSTAL>

Dear <Salutation>,

Ontario is yours to protect and your voice for nature is critical in 2021. Together, we will protect and advocate for Ontario's most vulnerable species and their habitat. Right now, more than ever, we must stand together and take action for nature.

<Salutation>, your membership renewal for 2021 is absolutely crucial. Your gift of <$Ask1> today will protect and defend cherished wild species and restore and preserve habitats across Ontario.

Over the past year Ontario suffered numerous assaults on the laws and policies meant to keep our wild species and wild spaces safe. We have been overwhelmed by your support. By signing onto our petitions through our Action Alerts your voice is making a difference. The challenges will continue. We promise Ontario Nature will work even harder on your behalf to protect Ontario's wild species and wild spaces over the coming year.

We have listened to what is most important to you, our members, to identify urgent priorities for nature protection in 2021. You'll find enclosed an update on how we'll put your membership into action protecting nature. Here are a few highlights:

On Our Nature Reserves: Your gifts will support research projects at our nature reserves across Ontario, like a BioBlitz on our newest Nature Reserve, Gananoque Lake where we have already identified more than 25 species at risk. At Sydenham River Nature Reserve, you'll support a planting

214 King Street West, Suite 612, Toronto, ON M5H 3S6
phone: 416-444-8419 toll free: 1-800-440-2366 ontarionature.org

Please turn over...

project to restore disused farmland into native Carolinian tallgrass prairie and woodland habitat to increase protection for 38 species at risk. You'll also help build a wheelchair accessible trail at our H.N. Crossley Nature Reserve in Muskoka. Right now, we are also working to acquire a new property to protect even more precious habitat. You'll hear more about this exciting project soon!

Taking Action for Nature: Tens of thousands of our members and supporters spoke up last year to hold the line to keep existing environmental protections. We continue to see our leaders tear apart our environmental laws and policies at a breakneck pace, and our support in 2021 is essential so that we can continue to demand action and respond quickly when issues arise. And when all else fails, we'll turn to the courts to overturn unlawful actions.

Nurturing Environmental Leaders: Your gifts will support our Youth Circle for Mother Earth and our Youth Summit. You will help bring more youth together from across the province to collaborate with experts and peers to bring the crucial voice of young environmental leaders to decision makers. They will develop leadership skills, share environmental knowledge, and organize conservation volunteering events.

You can use the enclosed reply form to make your gift and provide essential support for nature in our province. Thank you for taking action for nature in 2021 with your membership gift.

Yours, for nature,

Caroline Schultz

Caroline Schultz, Executive Director

P.S. Your membership gift today will go to work for nature immediately. Please, take action to protect nature right now. Thank you!

Fig. 7.1

YOUR 2021 ONTARIO NATURE MEMBERSHIP RENEWAL

Yes! I'll protect nature in Ontario in 2021 with my membership gift today!

Here is my gift of:
❍ $30
❍ **$50** ← You'll receive our quarterly ON Nature magazine with a gift of $50 or more!
❍ $75
❍ I prefer to give $________

❍ I have enclosed my cheque, payable to **Ontario Nature OR**
❍ I prefer to give by credit card. Please charge my: ❍ VISA ❍ MasterCard ❍ AMEX

Cardholder's Name: ________
Card Number: ________ Expiry: ____/____
Signature: ________ Telephone: ________
Address: ________
City: ________ Province: ____ Postal Code: ________

❍ I would like to receive my tax receipt by email.
Please email my receipt to: ________
By providing your email address, you consent to us contacting you from time to time. Ontario Nature respects your privacy and does not share email addresses.

Thank you! If you prefer, you can give online at **www.ontarionature.org/renewal2021** or call Kiran at **1-800-440-2366, extension 234**. Your enclosed membership card will be activated when you make your gift today!

Please turn over to join our ***Friends of Nature*** monthly giving program and for information on our legacy giving program!

<ADDRESSEE>
<ADDRESS>
<ADDRESS>
<City> <PR> <POSTAL>

Ontario Nature

214 King Street West, Suite 612, Toronto, ON M5H 3S6
phone: 416-444-8419 toll free: 1-800-440-2366 ontarionature.org Charitable Registration # 10737 8952 RR0001
Const ID/Appeal-Seg Code

Yes! I'll protect nature everyday of the year and join the *Friends of Nature* monthly giving program!

I'd like to make a monthly gift of:
❍ <$Ask 1>/month ❍ <$Ask 2>/month
❍ <$Ask 3>/month ❍ I prefer to give $______/month

❍ I have enclosed my cheque, marked **VOID**.
❍ I prefer make my monthly gift using my credit card.
Please charge my: ❍ VISA ❍ MasterCard ❍ AMEX

Cardholder's Name: ________
Card Number: ________ Expiry: ________
Signature: ________
Telephone: ________

Becoming a *Friend of Nature* monthly donor provides a convenient way to ensure your membership is current without the need to renew each year.

Have you considered protecting nature forever with a gift in your Will?

Legacy gifts have tremendous impact on our work and help to ensure that this province's spectacular natural heritage is protected for generations to come. Even a small gift in your Will can make a huge impact for nature.

❍ Please contact me about protecting nature forever with a gift in my Will.
I prefer:
❍ Phone: ________
Best time to reach me is (circle one) Morning Afternoon Evening Anytime
❍ Email: ________
❍ Please send me materials in the mail.

You are also encouraged to contact me anytime with questions or for a confidential conversation. – Kirsten Dahl, Director of Development, 416-444-8419 ext. 235, kirstend@ontarionature.org

"I joined Ontario Nature to protect the species that have no voice. We are their voice. Remembering Ontario Nature in my will is how I want to leave my mark when I'm gone." – Joanne, For Nature Forever Circle Member and Proud Grandma

Fig. 7.2

issues that Ontario Nature would be focusing on.

These inserts are fairly easy to create, because typically, you already have the information sitting around the office. It doesn't have to look overly designed, just something visually interesting and readable.

Let's take a look at some other common types of lifts that can be used in many of your appeals.

Thank you for being an Ontario Nature member!
Together we are working to save wild species and protect wild spaces in Ontario.

Learn how your membership is making a difference. Visit **ontarionature.org** today or call **Kiran 1-800-440-2366, extension 234.**

Ontario Nature

Photo by Megan Lorenz
Effective through February 2022

Fig. 7.3

YOURS TO PROTECT: URGENT PRIORITIES TO PROTECT NATURE IN ONTARIO IN 2021

Your voice for nature is critical in 2021. Your generosity today will protect and defend cherished wild species and restore and preserve habitats in Ontario.

YOURS TO PROTECT:
Nature Reserves—and Wild Species!

Here are a few ways we'll put your membership to work on our Nature Reserves:

- **Gananoque Lake:** You'll support our staff and local volunteers from the Nature Network who will be completing a BioBlitz to identify species that require special conservation consideration. We've already found a variety of rare and at-risk species like the golden winged warbler and gray ratsnake!
- **Sydenham River:** You'll support a major planting project to help restore farm fields into tallgrass prairie and woodland, expanding natural Carolinian habitat to help an astounding 38 at-risk species found on and near the reserve to thrive. These include cerulean warbler, Acadian flycatcher and freshwater mussels. The Carolinian Zone is one of the most biodiverse and threatened ecosystems in Canada.
- **H.N. Crossley:** You'll help build a wheelchair accessible trail to protect the sensitive wetland habitat including the provincially rare white-fringed orchid and unique carnivorous plants like the pitcher plant.
- You'll help expand our nature reserve network: stay tuned for details!

YOURS TO PROTECT:
Citizen Science Projects

Your support enables us to collaborate with thousands of volunteers from as far south as Pelee Island to Hudson's Bay in the north on the upcoming Breeding Bird Atlas. Volunteers, many of whom are part of our Nature Network, play a key role in connecting with birders from across the province to collect vast amounts of data which will help us map approximately 300 species of breeding birds and inform bird conservation planning. One neat addition to the Breeding Bird Atlas is the use of new technology to help with remote counts and reach areas where we have previously lacked knowledge.

You will help us to establish a ginseng survey protocol so landowners can better manage populations of this endangered plant on their property and help aid in the recovery of populations in Ontario.

Canada warbler

We are also developing a long-term snake monitoring protocol which will bring landowners and conservation staff together to monitor populations of snakes in our province, many of which are endangered, like the eastern foxsnake and blue racer. With your support we will use this information to inform future conservation planning to protect snake biodiversity in Ontario.

YOURS TO PROTECT:
Critical Environmental Laws and Policies

Your support means we will continue to speak up for nature and hold our leaders accountable. Together with our partners, we have filed a judicial review to challenge the government's non-compliance with the Environmental Bill of Rights. We are also joining with partners for legal action to stop the destruction of Lower Duffins Creek, a provincially significant wetland in Pickering. We'll provide you with updates as soon as we have any news.

YOUR 2021 CONSERVATION ACTION REPORT

In your latest issue of *ON Nature*, you'll find a Conservation Action Report that shares more information about these projects—and others! Together, we are nature's watchdog in Ontario. And right now, we must stand together and demand action for nature. Please, take a moment right now and renew your commitment to nature in 2021 today. **Thank you!**

Fig. 7.4

ORNAMENTS

Simple ornaments are an easy, once-a-year way to create dialogue with your donors.

This is an example from a Camp Ooch holiday mailing.

Ornaments are low production and printed on regular stock. "Cheap and cheerful," as they say. Yet this simple ornament can do a lot in the context of donor giving.

It provides an opportunity for you to show some (personalized) gratitude and appreciation to your donor that they can proudly display on their fridge, tree, or mantle.

It also gives your donor an opportunity to tell you something about themselves: why they give, who they think of or honour, how old they might be. Donors disclose all sorts of things about themselves by what they share. Also, donors are so RARELY asked or given an opportunity to share something about themselves. So even if they don't act on your invitation — you can bet it's still appreciated.

The key to these simple ornaments (and any piece you want the donor to return) is that you ask a *simple, emotional question*. In other words, an ornament isn't the place to ask your donor to share their stance on a complicated issue.

Donors do return the ornaments.

Dear <Caring>,
Your woodland animal friends—and everyone here at Camp—wishes you and your loved ones joy and peace this holiday season. Thank you for your kind and generous heart!

CAMP OOCH | Camp Trillium

Here you can share your message or a story with our Campers who are in the hospital this holiday season. Thank you for brightening up lives!

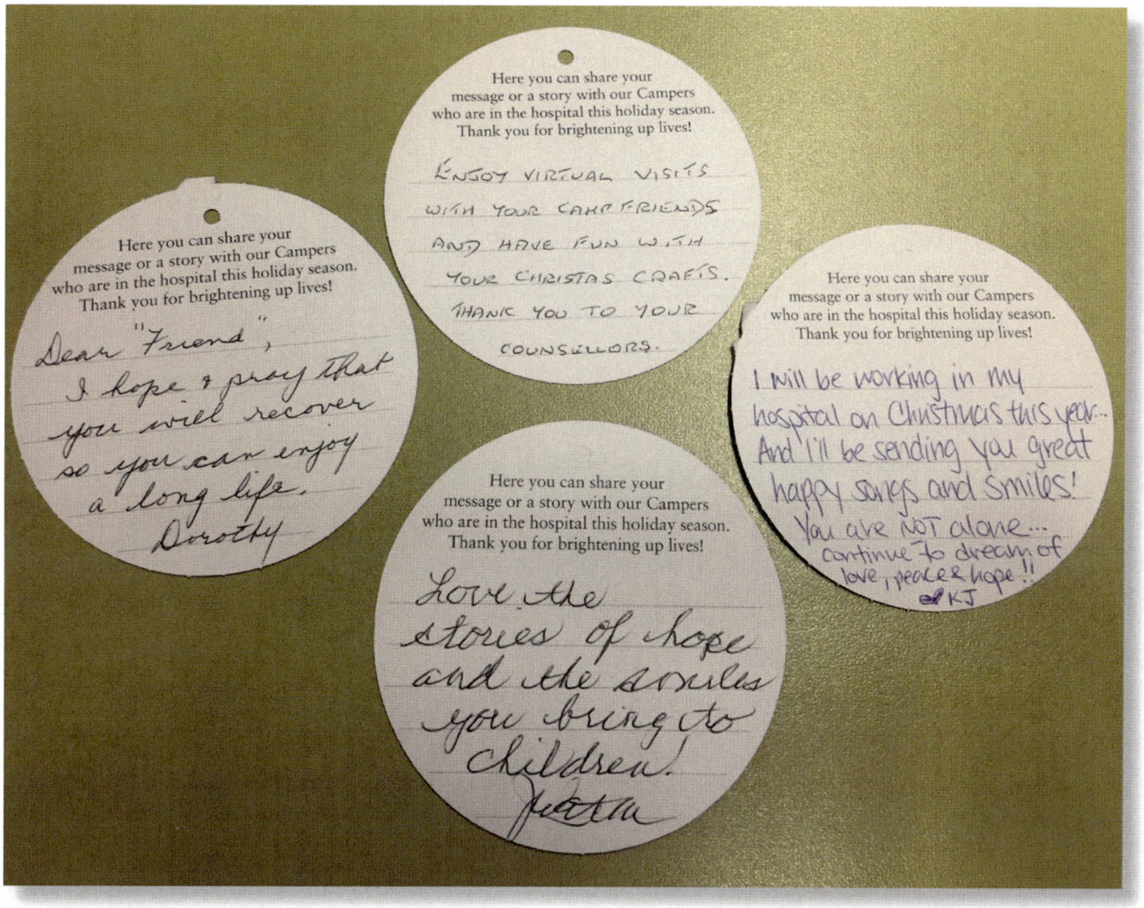

So, what's the point?

There were many lessons learned in fundraising during the COVID-19 pandemic. I strongly believe this is an example you can use in any fundraising climate.

Donors don't get tired of giving. They get tired of boring asks. They get tired of hearing the same voice. They get tired of being talked at. They get tired of hearing about how amazing the organization is.

Our/your job is to share compelling reasons why donors should give to our organization. Our job is to create donor-sized problems they can help solve. Our job is to create space for our donors to be a part of the story.

The hard work is ours. Not theirs. Never blame donors for their lack of action.

One final thing to consider about the value of asking your donor to send you back something like this ornament in the mail: they may not have planned to send a gift, but will often include a cheque when they send back the ornament, simply because they're taking that action!

BUCKSLIPS

A 'buckslip' can be a lot of things. Obviously named because traditionally it was the size and shape of "a buck" or "a dollar bill", almost anything can be a buckslip, but here is an example.

This same Camp Ooch package also included a simple "buckslip" to thank the matching gift donor and reiterate the urgency of replying to the appeal.

You could have mailed the appeal without an ornament or a buckslip, but when you see how they support the main message, they become easy inclusions.

ABRACADABRA!

Fox is here to double your gift!

Fabulous Mr. Fox is here to enchant you—but there is no hocus pocus here! It's the amazing news that our friends at Volkswagen Canada are proud to be **matching your gifts up to $100,000 between now and December 31st!**

When you give, your holiday donation will be matched, doubling your impact! Double the magic! **Double the joy!**

Please, take a moment right now to return your enclosed reply form—or you can give online at **www.ooch.org.**

Thank you! **And thank you to our magical friends at Volkswagen Canada!**

PHOTOS

A picture is truly worth 1,000 words.

This is an appeal from St. Thomas Elgin General Hospital Foundation.

A few things to note about the mail pack:

- For the outer envelope, the donor's name and address was lasered right onto the outside of the envelope (more effective than using a window on the envelope). It featured a personalized indicia with an image of lilacs filling the air with their perfumy scent, quite familiar to donors living in southwestern Ontario. Playing with the senses of donors makes for more engaging appeals.
- The letter was a direct ask for $198,000 for the purchase of a new piece of equipment called a "C-Arm." The lead-in sentence utilizes another human sense. The sense of sound.

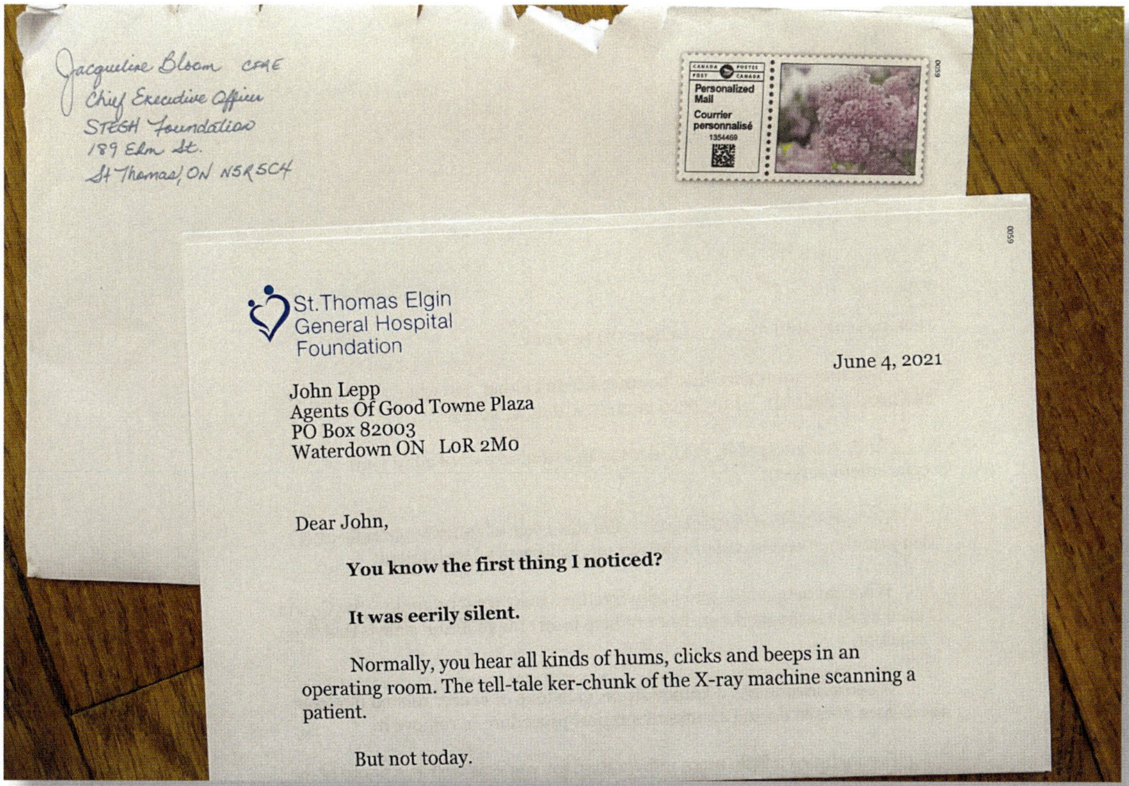
Jacqueline Bloom CFRE
Chief Executive Officer
STEGH Foundation
189 Elm St.
St Thomas, ON N5R 5C4

Personalized Mail
Courrier personnalisé

St.Thomas Elgin
General Hospital
Foundation

June 4, 2021

John Lepp
Agents Of Good Towne Plaza
PO Box 82003
Waterdown ON LoR 2Mo

Dear John,

You know the first thing I noticed?

It was eerily silent.

Normally, you hear all kinds of hums, clicks and beeps in an operating room. The tell-tale ker-chunk of the X-ray machine scanning a patient.

But not today.

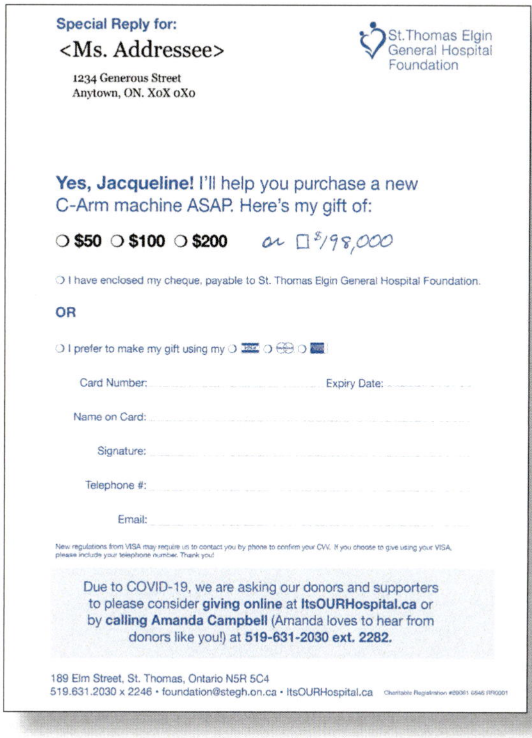
Special Reply for:
<Ms. Addressee>
1234 Generous Street
Anytown, ON. XoX oXo

St.Thomas Elgin
General Hospital
Foundation

Yes, Jacqueline! I'll help you purchase a new C-Arm machine ASAP. Here's my gift of:

❍ **$50** ❍ **$100** ❍ **$200** or ☐ $198,000

❍ I have enclosed my cheque, payable to St. Thomas Elgin General Hospital Foundation.

OR

❍ I prefer to make my gift using my ❍ ❍ ❍

Card Number: Expiry Date:

Name on Card:

Signature:

Telephone #:

Email:

New regulations from VISA may require us to contact you by phone to confirm your CVV. If you choose to give using your VISA, please include your telephone number. Thank you!

Due to COVID-19, we are asking our donors and supporters to please consider **giving online** at **ItsOURHospital.ca** or by **calling Amanda Campbell** (Amanda loves to hear from donors like you!) at **519-631-2030 ext. 2282.**

189 Elm Street, St. Thomas, Ontario N5R 5C4
519.631.2030 x 2246 • foundation@stegh.on.ca • ItsOURHospital.ca

The reply form has a tailored gift array tied to the donor's previous giving.

You might notice I added the option to give the entire $198,000. When you know exactly how much you need to raise for an appeal, why not ask for it? Some donors might find this a little cheeky, but there just might be that one donor who will check the box. It has happened. At the very least, you could see a lift in the average gift since some donors might not be able to give you the $198,000 but realize they can do better than the $50 they usually give.

I'll admit that we struggled over the idea of including anything else in this

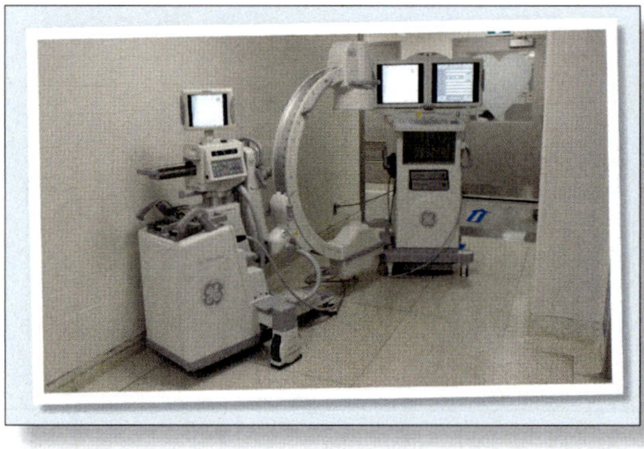

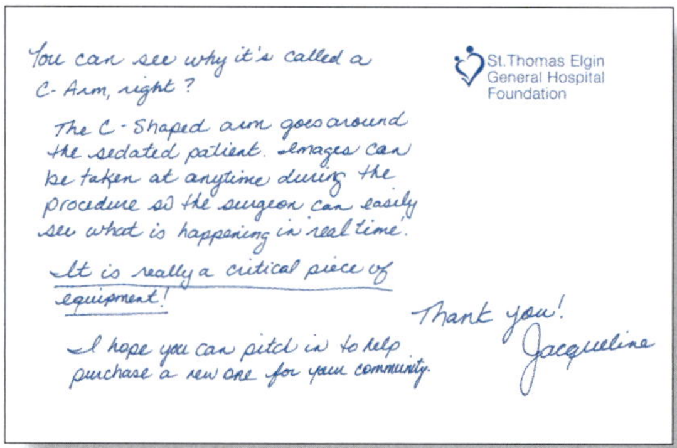

You can see why it's called a C-Arm, right?

The C-Shaped arm goes around the sedated patient. Images can be taken at anytime during the procedure so the surgeon can easily see what is happening in real time.

It is really a critical piece of equipment!

I hope you can pitch in to help purchase a new one for your community.

Thank you!

Jacqueline

package. What else could we add to the pack that might strengthen the case and be the difference between getting a gift or not?

Well — we decided to add an image of what the C-Arm looks like!

I also asked Jacqueline to handwrite a short message for the back, which was scanned in and printed.

This was a simple inclusion that added to the case for support in a slightly different way.

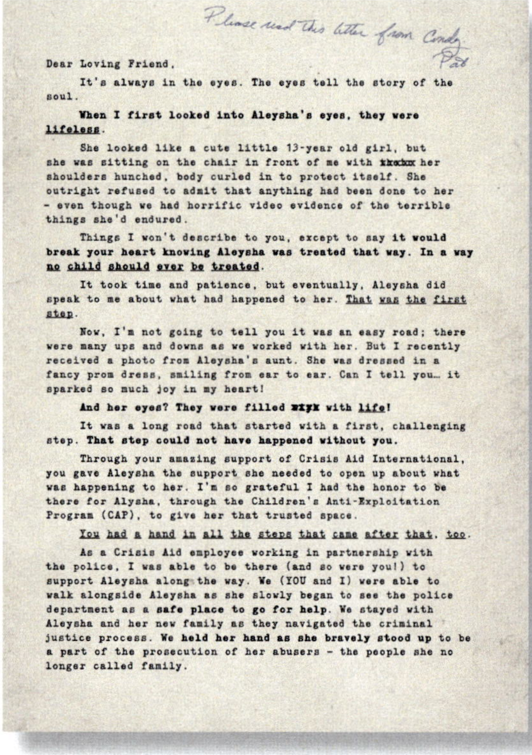

Please read this letter from Cindy
Pat

Dear Loving Friend,

It's always in the eyes. The eyes tell the story of the soul.

When I first looked into Aleysha's eyes, they were lifeless.

She looked like a cute little 13-year old girl, but she was sitting on the chair in front of me with her shoulders hunched, body curled in to protect itself. She outright refused to admit that anything had been done to her - even though we had horrific video evidence of the terrible things she'd endured.

Things I won't describe to you, except to say **it would break your heart knowing Aleysha was treated that way. In a way no child should ever be treated.**

It took time and patience, but eventually, Aleysha did speak to me about what had happened to her. That was the first step.

Now, I'm not going to tell you it was an easy road; there were many ups and downs as we worked with her. But I recently received a photo from Aleysha's aunt. She was dressed in a fancy prom dress, smiling from ear to ear. Can I tell you… it sparked so much joy in my heart!

And her eyes? They were filled with life!

It was a long road that started with a first, challenging step. **That step could not have happened without you.**

Through your amazing support of Crisis Aid International, you gave Aleysha the support she needed to open up about what was happening to her. I'm so grateful I had the honor to be there for Alysha, through the Children's Anti-Exploitation Program (CAP), to give her that trusted space.

You had a hand in all the steps that came after that, too.

As a Crisis Aid employee working in partnership with the police, I was able to be there (and so were you!) to support Aleysha along the way. We (YOU and I) were able to walk alongside Aleysha as she slowly began to see the police department as a **safe place to go for help**. We stayed with Aleysha and her new family as they navigated the criminal justice process. **We held her hand as she bravely stood up** to be a part of the prosecution of her abusers - the people she no longer called family.

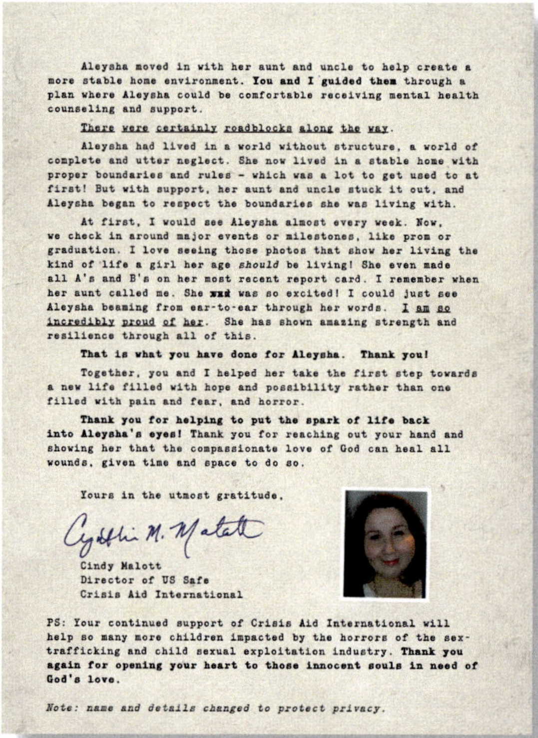

Aleysha moved in with her aunt and uncle to help create a more stable home environment. **You and I guided them** through a plan where Aleysha could be comfortable receiving mental health counseling and support.

There were certainly roadblocks along the way.

Aleysha had lived in a world without structure, a world of complete and utter neglect. She now lived in a stable home with proper boundaries and rules - which was a lot to get used to at first! But with support, her aunt and uncle stuck it out, and Aleysha began to respect the boundaries she was living with.

At first, I would see Aleysha almost every week. Now, we check in around major events or milestones, like prom or graduation. I love seeing those photos that show her living the kind of life a girl her age *should* be living! She even made all A's and B's on her most recent report card. I remember when her aunt called me. She was so excited! I could just see Aleysha beaming from ear-to-ear through her words. I am so incredibly proud of her. She has shown amazing strength and resilience through all of this.

That is what you have done for Aleysha. Thank you!

Together, you and I helped her take the first step towards a new life filled with hope and possibility rather than one filled with pain and fear, and horror.

Thank you for helping to put the spark of life back into Aleysha's eyes! Thank you for reaching out your hand and showing her that the compassionate love of God can heal all wounds, given time and space to do so.

Yours in the utmost gratitude,

Cynthia M. Malott

Cindy Malott
Director of US Safe
Crisis Aid International

PS: Your continued support of Crisis Aid International will help so many more children impacted by the horrors of the sex-trafficking and child sexual exploitation industry. **Thank you again for opening your heart to those innocent souls in need of God's love.**

Note: name and details changed to protect privacy.

Fig. 7.5

THE POWER OF A TESTIMONIAL

Another straightforward idea for a lift note is to include words from your program staff or a beneficiary **(Fig. 7.5)**.

Often, when you interview and talk to staff or beneficiaries, you have more content or stories than you could possibly fit into a single appeal letter. These individuals might not necessarily be the right person to "ask" donors for a gift. But you still may want to share their words and their compelling story.

MORE INFORMATION

Finally, adding an insert for a segment of donors (like your mid-level donors) is an easy way to send them tailored content that is appropriate to them.

This type of insert is personal and specific to your donor. The goal is to invite contact and remind your donor about the conversations and connections they have to an organization they care about. A feeling that is obviously mutual.

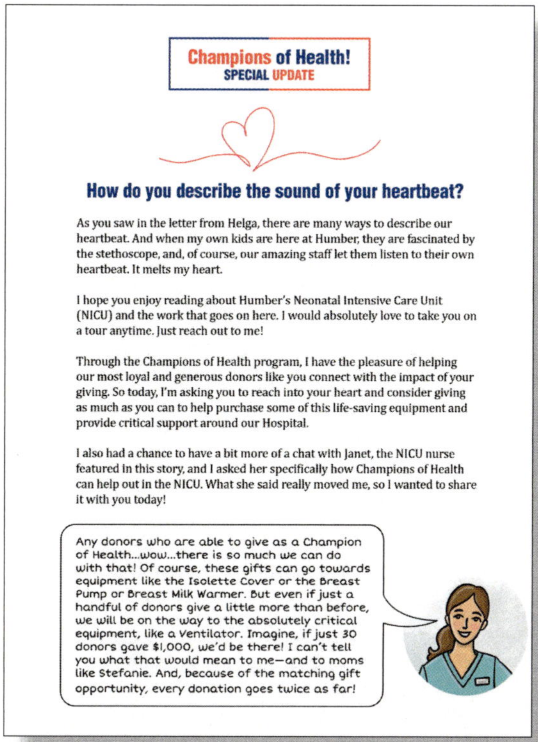

Champions of Health!
SPECIAL UPDATE

How do you describe the sound of your heartbeat?

As you saw in the letter from Helga, there are many ways to describe our heartbeat. And when my own kids are here at Humber, they are fascinated by the stethoscope, and, of course, our amazing staff let them listen to their own heartbeat. It melts my heart.

I hope you enjoy reading about Humber's Neonatal Intensive Care Unit (NICU) and the work that goes on here. I would absolutely love to take you on a tour anytime. Just reach out to me!

Through the Champions of Health program, I have the pleasure of helping our most loyal and generous donors like you connect with the impact of your giving. So today, I'm asking you to reach into your heart and consider giving as much as you can to help purchase some of this life-saving equipment and provide critical support around our Hospital.

I also had a chance to have a bit more of a chat with Janet, the NICU nurse featured in this story, and I asked her specifically how Champions of Health can help out in the NICU. What she said really moved me, so I wanted to share it with you today!

Listen to your heart, and please give as generously as you can. This amazing matching gift opportunity is the perfect time for you to enhance your giving, if you can! Thank you!

Daniela Campoli

Daniela Campoli, Development Officer
Phone: 416.242.1000, ext. 81529
Email: dcampoli@hrh.ca

Become a Champion of Health in 2020!

As a reminder, when you give $500 or more to Humber, you become part of our Champions of Health leadership program. Champions like you receive special updates and invitations to events and opportunities to get an insider's look into the impact of your giving. For more about this program, you can contact me anytime.

From the desk of
Jennifer

April, 2015

"Mummy, Daddy! Look! That one's almost ready! Oh boy! When can we go in?"

Our 4-year old son Christian bounces in his car seat and waves his little arms with excitement when we drive past the Habitat for Humanity build on Kehl Street. **But it's not exactly what you think.**

You see, our dreams have come true and one of those beautiful houses will be ours very soon, but Christian doesn't know yet. Ever since he could talk, he has asked us to stop at any model home, open house or for sale sign so that he can explore inside. He charges up the stairs, finds the bedrooms and tells stories about the kids that live there.

"This boy loves airplanes. He wants to be a pilot and fly way, way up to the sky!"

"Look at all these stuffed animals. I feel like I'm at the zoo, Mummy!"

Christian has never had his own bedroom. He sleeps in a cot in the corner of ours. Sometimes when his 2 older sisters Juliana and Olivia aren't home, he takes a few of his toys, sets them up in their room and pretends it's his own bedroom. The first time I saw him do this, I remember feeling it was adorable and heartbreaking at the same time.

The day we found out about our new home, my husband Adrian and I were overjoyed like you can't even imagine! And as we stayed up late crying, laughing and making plans, we decided that this was an opportunity to do something really special for our sweet little boy.

So, we've got it all planned. When we are ready to move, he'll spend the weekend at my mum's place and we'll set up his bedroom. We saved up for a big boy bed and a new comforter. He actually showed me the comforter once out shopping but I told him we didn't have the money or space for a big boy

continued...

bed for him yet. I waited until the price came way down and I've stashed it at my mum's. We'll move all his toys and books and set up his room perfectly.

And then we'll drive past, and we know he'll say: *"Mummy, Daddy! Look! Oh boy! Can we go and look inside?"* He'll be delighted when we finally say *"sure, buddy, let's check it out!"* He'll charge up the stairs and find the bedroom.

And then we'll be right on his heels and say, *"this is your very own bedroom Christian, and we're staying here tonight and forever!"*

Oh, I just can't wait for August!

The folks at Habitat asked me to share my story with you, and I jumped at the chance to be able to tell you myself just how much your support of Habitat means to me and my family. And it's a growing family...because we have a new baby on the way in just a few weeks. In our current apartment, we didn't even have space for Christian, let alone a newborn.

It made my heart ache, raising our kids in a small apartment. It's like a weight you can't take off when you live in a not-so-great neighbourhood. I've always wanted a home so badly. Something nice, safe and simple and that belonged to us. But our new home is so much more than that—it's also so beautiful! And we've already met some of our warm and friendly new neighbours!

Thank you, so very much, from the bottom of my heart, for your amazing support of Habitat. You made my dreams come true, and you have given my family the most precious gift.

Sincerely yours,

Jennifer

A personal note from a beneficiary designed on "her letterhead."

YOUR HD RESEARCH TIMELINE:

Your Support In Action to Solve the Puzzle of Huntington Disease

1973 Ralph and Ariel Walker founded the Huntington Society of Canada

Huntington Society of Canada
HUNTINGTON
Société Huntington du Canada

1976 Discovery that the HD gene was on the tip of chromosome 4 led to a genetic test

1984 Predictive testing centre established in Vancouver, one of only 3 such projects in the world

1993 HD gene discovered! Direct testing becomes available, giving anyone at-risk a definitive answer as to whether they will develop HD

"This discovery inspired a new wave of genetic research. It really inspired a paradigm."
– Dr. Marcy MacDonald

1998 We launch our Navigator Program, making HSC funding available to HD scientists across Canada

"Our findings are important because they tell us exactly what we need to do next."
– Dr. Rona Graham

2006 Researchers stop progression of HD in a mouse!

2009 PREDICT-HD study renewed, the largest pre-symptomatic HD research study to date, active in 32 international sites, including 4 in Canada

"I want to thank the participants for the amazing contributions they've made. Not only do we advance HD research, but other researchers have come to us and wanted to borrow the research design for other diseases.
– Dr. Jane Paulsen

2011 Discovery of a common link between Alzheimer's and HD, leading to increased scientific collaboration

"For a relatively small organization, HSC has targeted its research dollars in a place where they can have maximum impact." – Dr. Jeff Carroll

2012 Researchers reverse HD motor symptoms in a mouse!

2013 Discovery that huntingtin protein bends differently than protein from a normal gene, and proves that the normal shape can be restored

2014 Treatment breakthrough: researchers isolate and block a glutamate receptor in the membrane of brain cells, resulting in a 90% decrease in presence of mutant huntingtin protein which causes HD

2015 5 clinical trials launched, first human trials addressing the root cause of HD

"As we advance towards treatments addressing the root cause of Huntington disease, this innovative research initiative and partnership with Brain Canada has the potential to transform HD research."
– Bev Heim-Myers, CEO

2016 Partnership with Brain Canada to fund virtual networks connecting clinicians, scientists and families, to expedite discovery of treatments to slow and prevent HD

2017 Research investment into "gene-silencing", a huntingtin-lowering therapy that targets the disease right at its root

"We have brought something all the way from the test tube to the patient. And it's working! Now we are going back to the lab and saying, 'How can we make this more efficient? How can we make this better?'"
– Dr. Blair Leavitt

YOU

"We are very grateful to all the donors—large and small! Important achievements don't happen overnight, but each step brings us closer to treatments. It's a little bit like composing a big puzzle with hundreds of different pieces. Each piece matters. You can't complete the picture until you have all the pieces."
– Dr. Simonetta Sipione

Every piece matters. Your piece matters!
Will you please give today and support urgent and promising HD research? Thank you!

A research timeline.

This is the face I do when I'm feeling a little bit silly. I have lots of energy now, so playtime is my favourite time! LOVE
Today, I feel safe and loved. I didn't think I would ever feel this happy.
It's so nice not feeling hungry or thirsty every day. I know I'll always have enough food and water because I have nice people looking out for me.
And I don't feel so tired and weak like I used to all the time. Now, I can run around!
The people at The Home looked after me when I needed it most. They told me that you helped me. You are so kind helping to pay for all the medicine and food I needed to get better (and lots of other things!).
I want to say a big THANK YOU!
This is my story
By Dolly the puppy
Before I came to The Lost Dogs' Home, life wasn't good for me.
It was dark and loud where I was born.
I was huddled in a corner with my brothers and sisters. We would tremble all the time because we were so scared.
I was so hungry and thirsty every day.
Then we were taken to the shelter at The Home and everything changed for me.
This is what I looked like when I arrived at The Home. I was very skinny. You could see my ribs. I was so afraid when someone picked me up but too weak to show it.
I remember arriving with my littermates and I hid in the back corner of our carrier. I didn't know what was going on and I was frightened.
Soon after my litter arrived, I was separated from my brothers and sisters. Someone told me I needed to go to the vet clinic because I was really sick.
I felt dizzy so I closed my eyes and fell asleep. When I opened them, I was lying on a table with a lady named Elena patting me gently. She spoke to me very kindly, so I started to feel less scared.
Me at the vet clinic. Everyone was so nice to me. I think they knew I wasn't feeling very well.

I stayed at the vet clinic for about two weeks while the vets and nurses took care of me. They gave me lots of delicious food and water. I felt a little bit better every morning when I woke up. And someone was always there to give me a pat.
Elena and her team said I needed to have a big sleep for my desexing surgery.
One day, Elena said I was ready to go and live in a foster home for a while because I wasn't so sick anymore.
How exciting!
I don't think I've ever seen inside a house before.
This is my foster carer. Her name is Ellie and she's really friendly. I like to cuddle with her.
I was still feeling fragile when I arrived at Ellie's place. She made sure I kept warm by putting a special jacket on me and giving me a soft blanket to curl up in.
It made me feel calm and relaxed.
I made a new pal at Ellie's house.
His name is Hercules, and we love to play together. I like to steal toys from him and sometimes we play tug-of-war. Maybe one day I'll be as strong as Hercules.
I'm feeling MUCH better now! This is me with my special cuddly toy that Ellie gave me. I'm very cosy sitting in this bed and I hope Ellie comes over to give me more pats. I'm too comfortable to move.

A scrapbook.

Mail

Subject: **Boss's Injuries**

From Jaime <Jaime@rspcansw.org>

to Jeffrey <Jeffrey@rspcansw.org>

Hi Jeffrey,

Please can I ask you to review and advise on these x-rays? They're of a three-year-old Staffy cross called Boss who we rescued after a cruelty report. He fell from a second-floor balcony and received no pain relief or veterinary treatment for two days.

As the x-rays indicate, he landed heavily on his left hand side resulting in clear fractures to the left front leg and left back leg (hip).

We performed the emergency surgery and Boss is now currently in ICU. I believe there's every hope surgery could effectively repair the back leg, but I am concerned about the long-term outlook and the likelihood of chronic pain and further surgeries being needed.

Front leg (left) – we've used a splint and a plaster. Fracture already healing well.

Back leg (left) – surgery was successfully carried out and a plate inserted into Boss's back leg to repair the fracture.

Many thanks,
Jaime

RSPCA New South Wales

Jaime
Veterinary Surgeon RSPCA New South Wales

Page 1 of 1

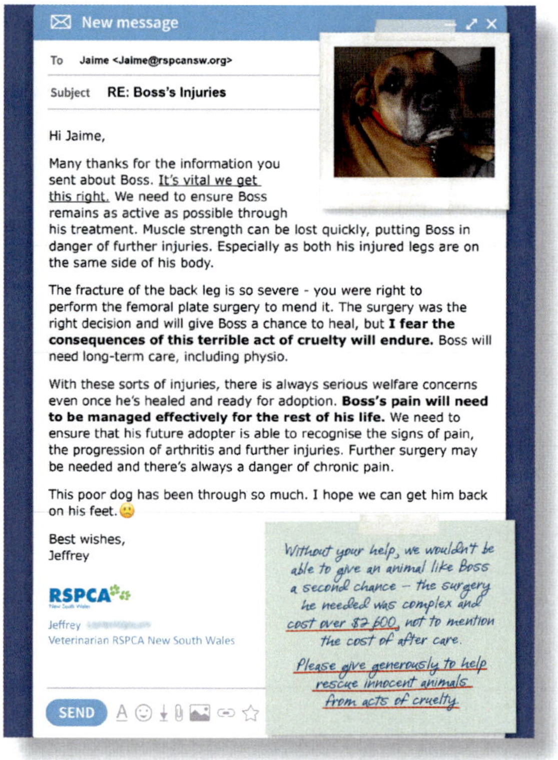

New message

To Jaime <Jaime@rspcansw.org>

Subject **RE: Boss's Injuries**

Hi Jaime,

Many thanks for the information you sent about Boss. It's vital we get this right. We need to ensure Boss remains as active as possible through his treatment. Muscle strength can be lost quickly, putting Boss in danger of further injuries. Especially as both his injured legs are on the same side of his body.

The fracture of the back leg is so severe - you were right to perform the femoral plate surgery to mend it. The surgery was the right decision and will give Boss a chance to heal, but **I fear the consequences of this terrible act of cruelty will endure.** Boss will need long-term care, including physio.

With these sorts of injuries, there is always serious welfare concerns even once he's healed and ready for adoption. **Boss's pain will need to be managed effectively for the rest of his life.** We need to ensure that his future adopter is able to recognise the signs of pain, the progression of arthritis and further injuries. Further surgery may be needed and there's always a danger of chronic pain.

This poor dog has been through so much. I hope we can get him back on his feet. 🙁

Best wishes,
Jeffrey

RSPCA New South Wales

Jeffrey
Veterinarian RSPCA New South Wales

SEND

Without your help, we wouldn't be able to give an animal like Boss a second chance – the surgery he needed was complex and cost over $7,600, not to mention the cost of after care.

Please give generously to help rescue innocent animals from acts of cruelty.

An email.

An illustration that visually represents what you are asking for in the mail appeal.

These examples are by no means exhaustive; rather they represent some of the more common types of lift notes or extra pieces you could consider adding to your direct mail appeals.

The only limit is your own creativity! Here are a few other ideas to help you brainstorm: buckslips, newspaper clippings (real or mocked up), maps, photos, photo album, involvement devices, ornaments, schedules, budgets, seals, decals, stamps, press releases, tickets, wallet cards, posters, fridge art, kids drawings, business cards, magnets, cards, handwritten apologies, freemiums, calendars, newsletters...

Deviation Discoveries

"More" stories will almost always result in "more" gifts. What other sorts of pieces can you add to increase the "storytelling" aspect of your appeal? How can you make it more engaging? How can you show the problem from a different perspective or add to your overall case? Be creative!

1. The inclination to think that more is wasteful or too expensive is reasonable. But sometimes a simple two-page letter doesn't go far enough to make the case.
2. Often, the content that doesn't fit easily into your "ask" letter is perfect for some other type of insert: a photo, an extra story, some statistics, a drawing.
3. At least once a year, consider adding a piece to your mailing that gives donors a chance to share some of their thoughts with you. It might be a specially designed ornament or simply a few lines at the bottom of your reply form. It creates a powerful opportunity for connection between you and your donor.

Deviation Eight — Design your boss hates

This deviation might make you feel gross. Icky, even. But I want to show you this little overgrown side trail away from the perfectly manicured one you may be used to walking down. I want to show you that, from your perspective something might look childish and silly, or overly simplistic, but in fact is intentionally "designed" that way to make donors notice and open their cheque books.

I remember the meeting pretty well.

It was with a new client to talk about the first mailing we were working on together.

The client knew, philosophically, how Agents of Good tended to work. There was a level of trust that we would put the organization's donors at the forefront of our storytelling and thinking around any new appeals. That's always a great place to begin a new relationship.

And then… we presented this envelope with a bug eyed "H" on the front of the envelope and a tagline that read "*NICE TO MEETCHA.*"

No logo. Nothing else.

The envelope was a bit ugly. A bit clumsy. A bit cheesy. A bit unprofessional.

And, it was perfect! (There's more on this pack in the *Bonus Deviation*!)

You can probably imagine the client's reaction.

Crickets.

You could hear someone's stomach growl from the room next door. Sideway glances at each other. (*Ok. I might be exaggerating a little.*)

This wasn't the first time I had encountered this sort of 'are you kidding me?' reaction from a client.

"*We can't mail this!*"

"*Can you jazz it up a bit?*"

Throughout my career, non-designer types had demanded that I 'jazz up' the design! Make it more interesting! Nicer! Prettier! More professional!

It's not that I'm a bad designer.

It's just that I design with the donor in mind. My subjective opinion on the colours and fonts that I like have nothing to do with the art form that is direct response design. I have also spent most of my career trying to de-program the brains of the designers I have hired.

Every single extra design element that gets added to a page only decreases the potential of that page getting the response you want.

Time and time again I've seen it play out. If you, your boss, Chad from marketing, Sally in accounting and Patricia, who manages your data, all hate the direct mail package design I present, it usually means it will be more effective in getting your donor to actually donate.

Why?

In his 2012 book, *The Fundraisers Guide to Irresistible Communications*, Jeff Brooks shares three design laws for effective direct response:

1. **Make it obvious.**
2. **Keep it plain.**
3. **Make it corny.**

Let's unpack this.

1. Make it obvious.

Your donor already knows why she is holding this direct mail package from you in her hands. She understands that your organization is one of the causes she cares deeply and passionately about. She "gets" that her job is to send you a few of her hard-earned dollars to help fix a problem. It's a problem that might be very small or it might be way bigger than her, but she feels that, in this moment, she can be a part of the solution because you will show her how.

Why beat around the bush? Get to the point as quickly as you can, and then please get out of the way. Too many fundraising appeals take far too long to get to the point.

Be clear on what you are asking for! And ask for it! Over and over. Explain why! A classic case for support needs to answer: Why me and why now?

On the reply form, clearly show your donor how to take the action you've hopefully been asking them to take! Make it obvious.

Ask and *get out of the way*. Don't build in barriers for giving! The easier and more obvious you make it, the more likely you will get a positive result.

2. Keep it plain.

People who don't understand effective design and communications believe more is better. It isn't. Less is better. (Yes, I know this directly contradicts *Deviation 7*. This is a complicated business my friends.)

Every line, every starburst, every word, every element you add to your fundraising, the more likely you *will not* get the result you want.

If I am sending you a personal email, or a personal letter, I don't "design" it, do I? You want your communications with your donor to feel like a personal communication from you to them.

The best, and most effective, fundraising and communications materials are the simplest, in terms of design.

I'm not saying it *always* has to be plain or simple but, like most things in life, it's not a bad place to start. Be confident that less is more when it comes to your design and messaging.

3. Make it corny.

If you know me, then you know corny is my jam. Because it works. Donors love corny. Corny gets attention.

To your boss, corny feels icky. It feels unprofessional. It gets sneered at, looked down at.

BUT, donors love it and respond to it.

Let's take a look at some examples that demonstrate the three design laws.

PHIL, THE BAG

This is my pal "Phil the Bag" from the Fill the Bag campaign that Agents of Good created to support the 2016 fundraising efforts of a local food bank in Waterloo, Ontario.

Phil is the epitome of cheesy.

Through the years, we have encountered a lot of resistance to the idea of any type of anthropomorphizing (see more about this in *Deviation 6*).

"*It's juvenile.*" "*Unprofessional.*" "*It's insulting to donors.*" "*We don't like it.*" "*Our donors are too smart to like this.*" "*It's too cheesy.*"

I'm here to tell you that it works. As in, this technique will help you raise a lot more money.

Like I keep saying, *get out of the way*.

The creative brief for this appeal said we needed to create a mail pack that "*educated, engaged and inspired supporters by focusing on donor impact and by sharing stories.*" It also said, "*tie into Thanksgiving.*" Easy, peasy.

In Canada, Thanksgiving is celebrated earlier than it is in the United States.

How we got from 'tie into Thanksgiving' to Phil the bag is like most great ideas, lost in the sands of time, but with a straight face we presented this to the client. (Thanks to Veronica Davies, one of our exceptional artists and designers for her inspiring work on bringing Phil to life!)

Three character sketches showed how Phil could look (Fig. 8.1).

This was far different than any outer envelope this organization had mailed to its donors before.

Fig. 8.1 — Some character sketches for Phil, the bag.

The tagline presented the offer — a great deal for donors.

Phil was an unexpected surprise to donors. He was cheesy, cute and fun!

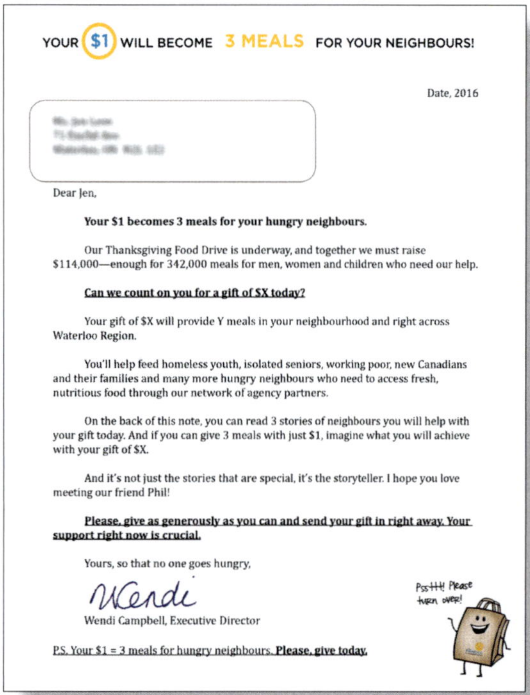

YOUR $1 WILL BECOME 3 MEALS FOR YOUR NEIGHBOURS!

Date, 2016

Dear Jen,

Your $1 becomes 3 meals for your hungry neighbours.

Our Thanksgiving Food Drive is underway, and together we must raise $114,000—enough for 342,000 meals for men, women and children who need our help.

Can we count on you for a gift of $X today?

Your gift of $X will provide Y meals in your neighbourhood and right across Waterloo Region.

You'll help feed homeless youth, isolated seniors, working poor, new Canadians and their families and many more hungry neighbours who need to access fresh, nutritious food through our network of agency partners.

On the back of this note, you can read 3 stories of neighbours you will help with your gift today. And if you can give 3 meals with just $1, imagine what you will achieve with your gift of $X.

And it's not just the stories that are special, it's the storyteller. I hope you love meeting our friend Phil!

Please, give as generously as you can and send your gift in right away. Your support right now is crucial.

Yours, so that no one goes hungry,

Wendi

Wendi Campbell, Executive Director

P.S. Your $1 = 3 meals for hungry neighbours. **Please, give today.**

Psstt! Please turn over!

The pack was meant to be "cheap and cheerful," inexpensive and to the point. It was mailed in a standard white #10 envelope with a combined letter/reply form printed on 8.5″ x 14″ paper. A simple Business Reply Envelope was also included.

Of course, Phil shows up at the bottom of the letter saying, "*Psstt! Please turn over!*"

Phil (and characters like this) can say all sorts of things (Fig. 8.2) that your overly professional and serious boss might not be comfortable saying in a conversational manner!

Another fun thing about these sorts of characters is that you can easily integrate them into your social and digital channels (Fig. 8.3).

This type of creative treatment can really help your organization to stand out. It's more engaging than using a standard stock image combined with a

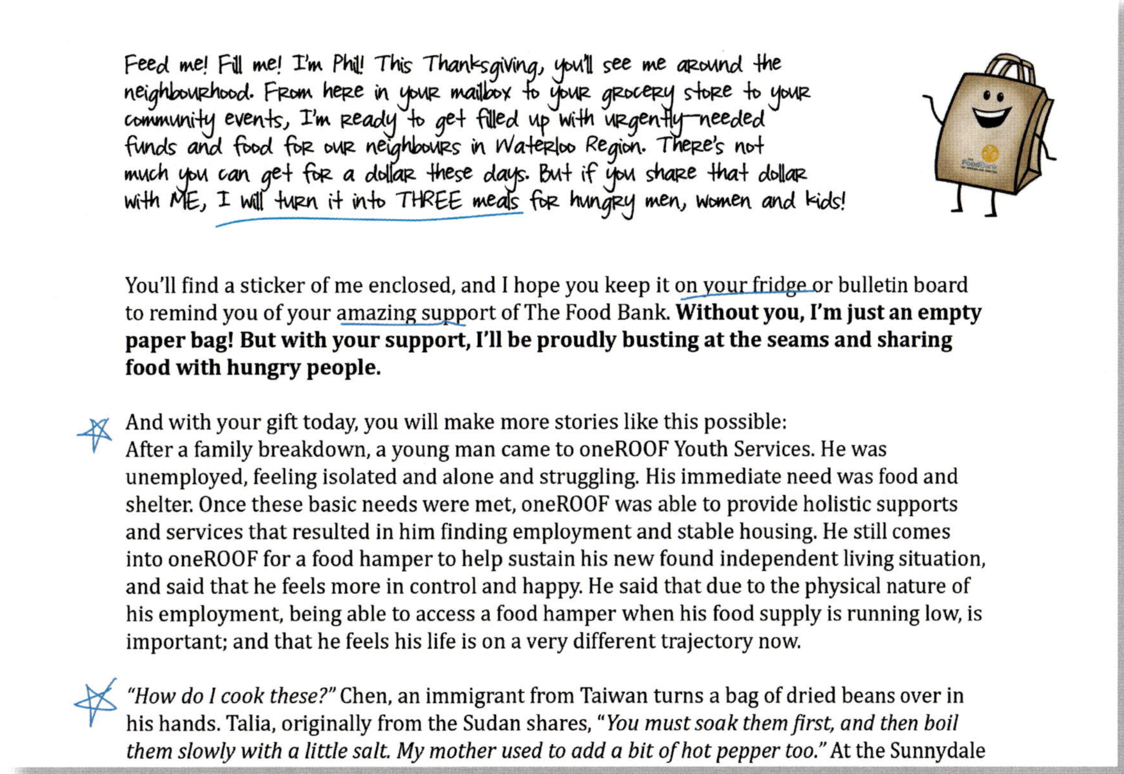

Feed me! Fill me! I'm Phil! This Thanksgiving, you'll see me around the neighbourhood. From here in your mailbox to your grocery store to your community events, I'm ready to get filled up with urgently-needed funds and food for our neighbours in Waterloo Region. There's not much you can get for a dollar these days. But if you share that dollar with ME, I will turn it into THREE meals for hungry men, women and kids!

You'll find a sticker of me enclosed, and I hope you keep it on your fridge or bulletin board to remind you of your amazing support of The Food Bank. **Without you, I'm just an empty paper bag! But with your support, I'll be proudly busting at the seams and sharing food with hungry people.**

And with your gift today, you will make more stories like this possible:
After a family breakdown, a young man came to oneROOF Youth Services. He was unemployed, feeling isolated and alone and struggling. His immediate need was food and shelter. Once these basic needs were met, oneROOF was able to provide holistic supports and services that resulted in him finding employment and stable housing. He still comes into oneROOF for a food hamper to help sustain his new found independent living situation, and said that he feels more in control and happy. He said that due to the physical nature of his employment, being able to access a food hamper when his food supply is running low, is important; and that he feels his life is on a very different trajectory now.

"How do I cook these?" Chen, an immigrant from Taiwan turns a bag of dried beans over in his hands. Talia, originally from the Sudan shares, *"You must soak them first, and then boil them slowly with a little salt. My mother used to add a bit of hot pepper too."* At the Sunnydale

Fig. 8.2 — The back of the appeal letter where we could use Phil's playful voice.

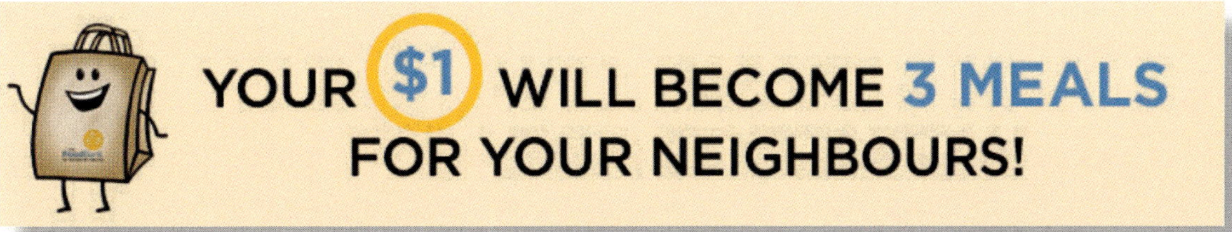

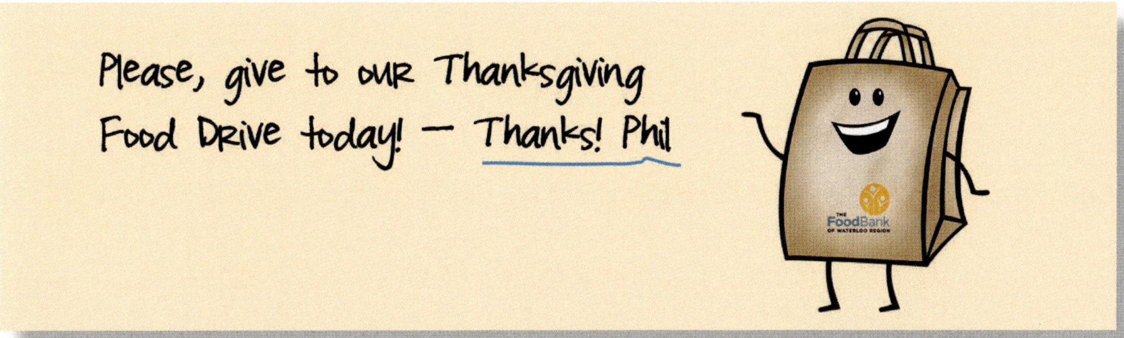

Fig. 8.3 — We used Phil's voice across all social media including home page banners and twitter.

generic-sounding voice that most direct mail letters use.

This was a completely different approach that paid off for this organization. Donors responded well enough to Phil that people were able to breathe again.

While there wasn't another appeal in the schedule until closer to the Christmas holiday, there was another "holiday" coming up where we saw an opportunity for the organization to use Phil.

As Halloween approached, Agent Jen and I thought we could have some fun getting Phil dressed for the occasion. We did some brainstorming and wondered, what would Phil look like dressed as a vampire or superhero?

My favorite was Phil at the top left. I have a strange sense of humour, and Phil the bag dressed as a paper bag tickles my funny bone. However, I was out-voted and Phil got dressed as a ghost for Halloween!

I really hope you're smiling because that was the point of Phil! Fundraising can be FUN my friends. For you and your donors!

The organization shared this FUN side of Phil through social channels and emailed out a creative appeal to donors they had email addresses for.

There is no greater gift than allowing donors to give with both a smile on their face and love in their heart, as they support a cause they care deeply for.

After Halloween, it was time to turn our attention to the holiday appeal. Phil was working well and there was no reason to deviate from continuing to use him as a device for storytelling. We got Phil all decked out for the holidays.

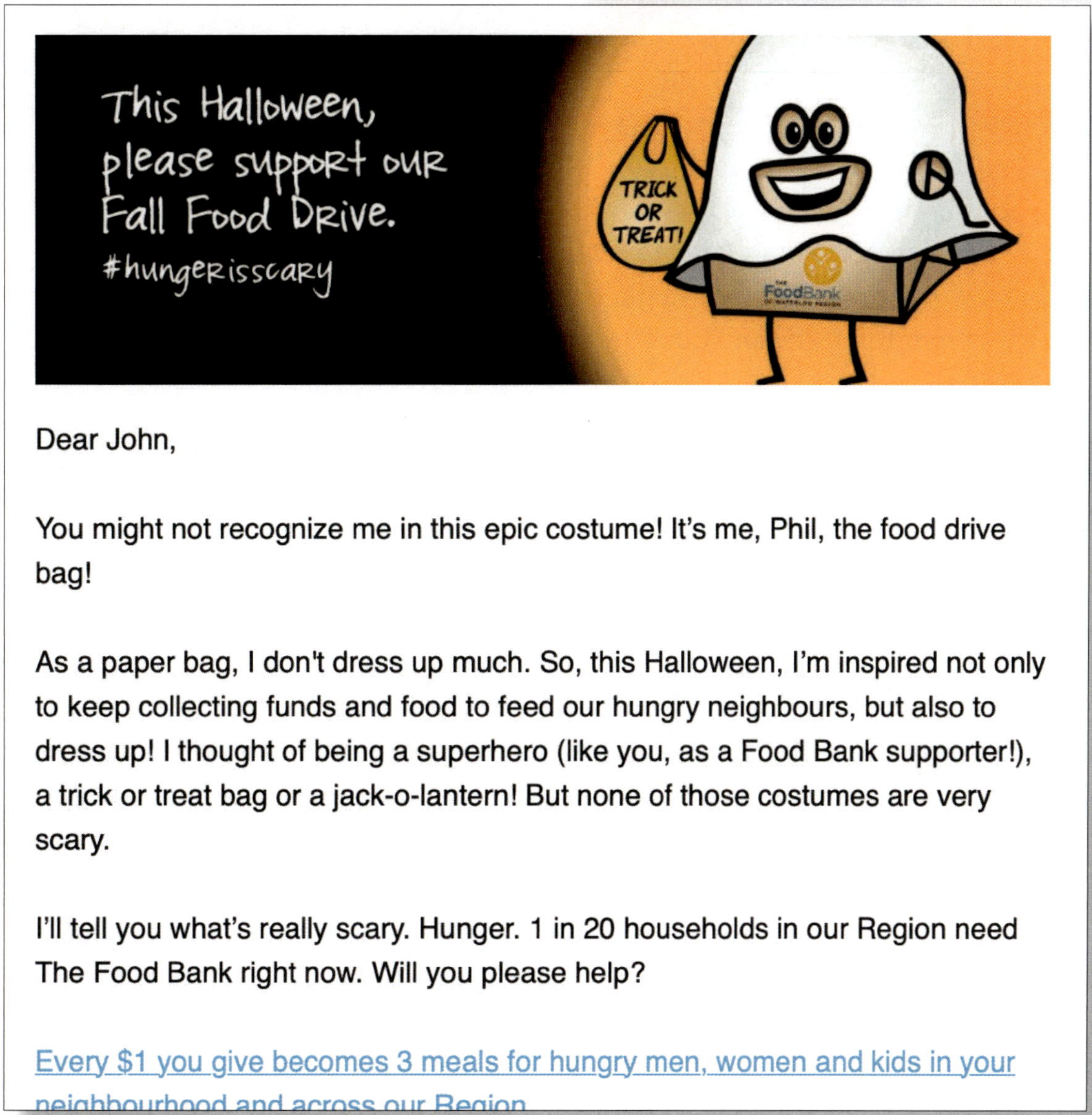
This Halloween, please support our Fall Food Drive.
#hungerisscary

TRICK OR TREAT!

FoodBank

Dear John,

You might not recognize me in this epic costume! It's me, Phil, the food drive bag!

As a paper bag, I don't dress up much. So, this Halloween, I'm inspired not only to keep collecting funds and food to feed our hungry neighbours, but also to dress up! I thought of being a superhero (like you, as a Food Bank supporter!), a trick or treat bag or a jack-o-lantern! But none of those costumes are very scary.

I'll tell you what's really scary. Hunger. 1 in 20 households in our Region need The Food Bank right now. Will you please help?

Every $1 you give becomes 3 meals for hungry men, women and kids in your neighbourhood and across our Region

We made the decision to send a mail pack directly from Phil to donors. This time, the package was mailed in a 9″ x 6″ outer envelope to ensure it stood out from the typical #10 envelope.

No tagline. Just this increasingly familiar face smiling on the front.

The letter was highly engaging and conversational. Phil shared what the problem was and how donors could be a part of the solution. It was obvious, plain and very corny.

I recommend you run your copy through a readability app from time to time.

Historically, we have used the Flesch Kincaid scoring in Microsoft Word. You can see this copy has a reading ease of 80.5% (ideally you want a score of 80% or higher) and written at a grade level of 5.1 (ideally your copy should be between 4 and 6).

These two things mean your letter is easy to read, it is understandable, and it

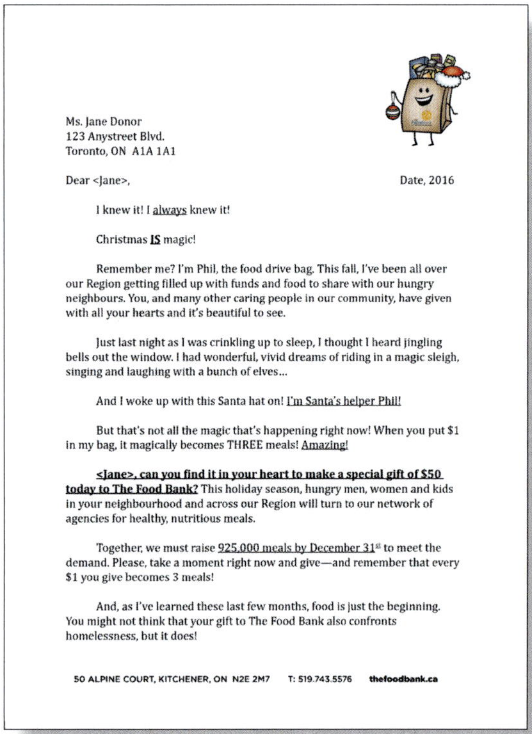

Ms. Jane Donor
123 Anystreet Blvd.
Toronto, ON A1A 1A1

Dear <Jane>, Date, 2016

I knew it! I always knew it!

Christmas **IS** magic!

Remember me? I'm Phil, the food drive bag. This fall, I've been all over our Region getting filled up with funds and food to share with our hungry neighbours. You, and many other caring people in our community, have given with all your hearts and it's beautiful to see.

Just last night as I was crinkling up to sleep, I thought I heard jingling bells out the window. I had wonderful, vivid dreams of riding in a magic sleigh, singing and laughing with a bunch of elves...

And I woke up with this Santa hat on! I'm Santa's helper Phil!

But that's not all the magic that's happening right now! When you put $1 in my bag, it magically becomes THREE meals! Amazing!

<Jane>, can you find it in your heart to make a special gift of $50 today to The Food Bank? This holiday season, hungry men, women and kids in your neighbourhood and across our Region will turn to our network of agencies for healthy, nutritious meals.

Together, we must raise 925,000 meals by December 31st to meet the demand. Please, take a moment right now and give—and remember that every $1 you give becomes 3 meals!

And, as I've learned these last few months, food is just the beginning. You might not think that your gift to The Food Bank also confronts homelessness, but it does!

50 ALPINE COURT, KITCHENER, ON N2E 2M7 T: 519.743.5576 **thefoodbank.ca**

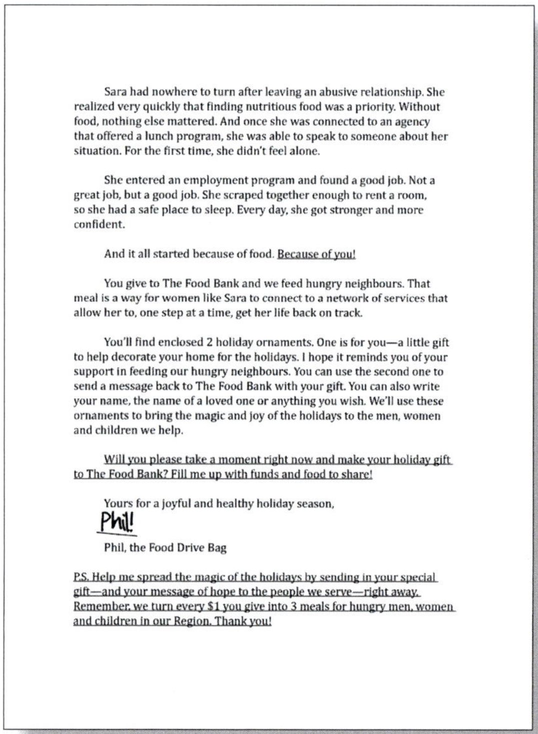

Sara had nowhere to turn after leaving an abusive relationship. She realized very quickly that finding nutritious food was a priority. Without food, nothing else mattered. And once she was connected to an agency that offered a lunch program, she was able to speak to someone about her situation. For the first time, she didn't feel alone.

She entered an employment program and found a good job. Not a great job, but a good job. She scraped together enough to rent a room, so she had a safe place to sleep. Every day, she got stronger and more confident.

And it all started because of food. Because of you!

You give to The Food Bank and we feed hungry neighbours. That meal is a way for women like Sara to connect to a network of services that allow her to, one step at a time, get her life back on track.

You'll find enclosed 2 holiday ornaments. One is for you—a little gift to help decorate your home for the holidays. I hope it reminds you of your support in feeding our hungry neighbours. You can use the second one to send a message back to The Food Bank with your gift. You can also write your name, the name of a loved one or anything you wish. We'll use these ornaments to bring the magic and joy of the holidays to the men, women and children we help.

Will you please take a moment right now and make your holiday gift to The Food Bank? Fill me up with funds and food to share!

Yours for a joyful and healthy holiday season,

Phil!

Phil, the Food Drive Bag

P.S. Help me spread the magic of the holidays by sending in your special gift—and your message of hope to the people we serve—right away. Remember, we turn every $1 you give into 3 meals for hungry men, women and children in our Region. Thank you!

sounds conversational. As a result, your letter will be easier for your donors to engage with and act upon.

The reply form was printed on 8.5″ x 11″ paper because historically these perform well and will help you to raise more money than using a smaller reply. The form shows the donor the exact impact of their gift in terms of the number of meals they'll provide. Plus, there's an ornament included.

As previously noted in *Deviations 5* and 7, these types of send-back pieces are great ways to encourage donor engagement and learn more about your donors.

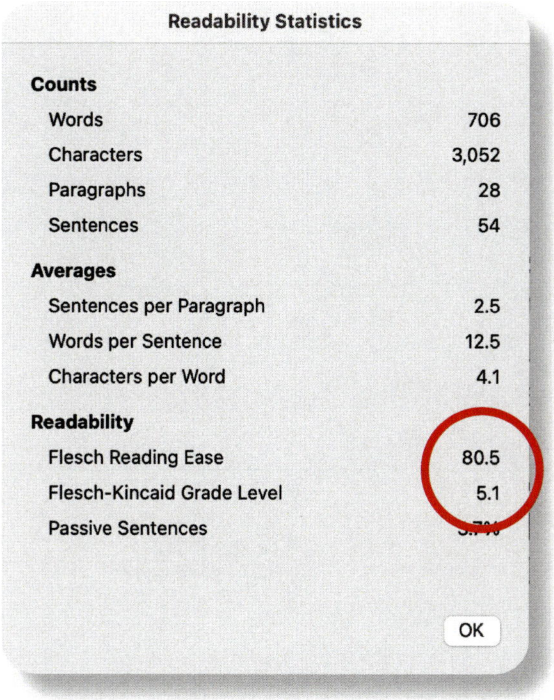

Readability Statistics

Counts	
Words	706
Characters	3,052
Paragraphs	28
Sentences	54
Averages	
Sentences per Paragraph	2.5
Words per Sentence	12.5
Characters per Word	4.1
Readability	
Flesch Reading Ease	80.5
Flesch-Kincaid Grade Level	5.1
Passive Sentences	

OK

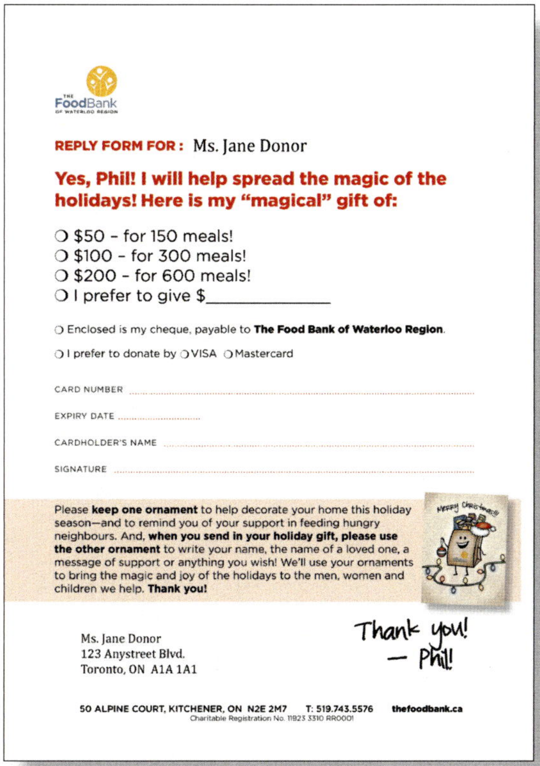

THE FoodBank OF WATERLOO REGION

REPLY FORM FOR : Ms. Jane Donor

Yes, Phil! I will help spread the magic of the holidays! Here is my "magical" gift of:

❍ $50 - for 150 meals!
❍ $100 - for 300 meals!
❍ $200 - for 600 meals!
❍ I prefer to give $______________

❍ Enclosed is my cheque, payable to **The Food Bank of Waterloo Region**.

❍ I prefer to donate by ❍ VISA ❍ Mastercard

CARD NUMBER ....

EXPIRY DATE ....

CARDHOLDER'S NAME ....

SIGNATURE ....

Please **keep one ornament** to help decorate your home this holiday season—and to remind you of your support in feeding hungry neighbours. And, **when you send in your holiday gift, please use the other ornament** to write your name, the name of a loved one, a message of support or anything you wish! We'll use your ornaments to bring the magic and joy of the holidays to the men, women and children we help. **Thank you!**

Ms. Jane Donor
123 Anystreet Blvd.
Toronto, ON A1A 1A1

Thank you!
— Phil!

50 ALPINE COURT, KITCHENER, ON N2E 2M7 T: 519.743.5576 thefoodbank.ca
Charitable Registration No. 11923 3310 RR0001

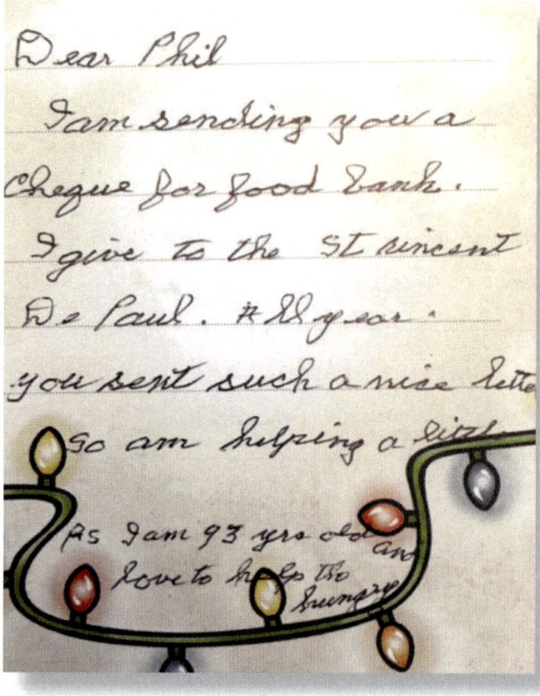
Dear Phil
I am sending you a
Cheque for food bank.
I give to the St vincent
De Paul. All year.
you sent such a nice lette
so am helping a littl
PS I am 93 yrs old and
love to help the
hungry

Phil asks the donor to share their name or a name of a loved one — or a simple message of support to those who benefit from the Food Bank.

This gave the organization the opportunity to share images of the ornaments that were sent back via social media and newsletters; a powerful example of social proof. You can show your donors bits of themselves in the shared thoughts of other donors. It creates a deeper connection to the organization, because your donor will feel part of a community of people who feel the same as they do.

Also, you can get some beautiful messages back, like this example.

It reads: *Dear Phil. I am sending you a cheque for the food bank. I give to the St Vincent de Paul. All year. You sent such a nice letter so I am helping a little. PS I am 93 years old and love to help the hungry…*

First off, can I just point out that this woman is **talking to a paper bag**?

And second, how unfortunate is it that we have created a sector where time and time again we see notes like these from donors to "characters" like Phil but very rarely to real humans like Executive Directors?

Phil was a cheesy hit with donors. So much so that the organization created a walking, talking mascot who participated in community parades and could be seen dropping pucks at local hockey games.

As you can imagine, there was some organizational push-back on the idea of Phil. There were concerns that Phil was unprofessional and juvenile. He certainly wasn't on "brand." "*Food insecurity is serious business,*" we were told.

But Phil gave us the opportunity to be emotional and vulnerable and use a different voice to speak to donors. I believe that's why donors responded so positively.

Don't be afraid to use a character like Phil — if you can. They're fun and engaging and super effective for fundraising.

Don't hide behind the idea of "being professional" as an excuse for boring, cookie cutter direct response.

EYEBALLS

Fun fact: In 2012, a bunch of behavioural scientists tested eyeballs. Or, to be more precise, the effect that eyeballs have on fundraising response.

They conducted an 11-week field experiment using donation jars that sit on the counter at your local grocery store. They glued some round, googly eyeballs onto one while they left the other the way it was.

What do you think they found? The one with eyeballs raised more (or had more money stuffed into it!). To the tune of almost 50% more. Delightful!

Read about the full study here: (https://www.engadget.com/2019-05-03-study-eye-images-make-people-more-charitable.html)

I admit that, throughout my career, I've put eyeballs on almost everything (much to the chagrin of my clients and their bosses)! Agents of Good continues to see this approach result in more funds raised for our clients. You can't argue with science and real human behaviour.

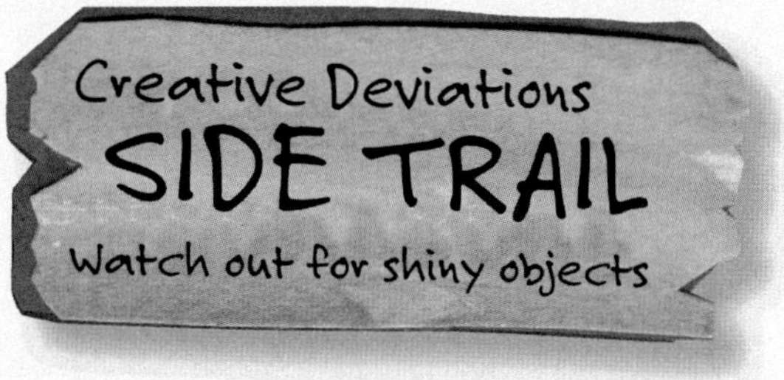

THE 10 PILLARS OF GREAT RELATIONS BETWEEN CHARITIES AND CONSULTANTS

At almost every conference Agents of Good attends, we are asked how we get ideas like "things with eyes" past the traditional, cross-armed boss who thinks these sorts of ideas are dumb.

If I had a magic bullet answer for you, I'd be a rich fella. However, through the years, I have discovered 10 basic pillars for creating an environment where work like this can bloom. I would suggest that these should exist for every working relationship — not just that of a charity and a consultant.

Pillar One: Conversation

All great things stem from conversations. Not 86-page RFP's, not demands of knowing what "all of this" costs, not 140 character tweets — con-ver-sa-tion.

I don't care if you are looking for a new Agency of Record, or if you are having difficulties with getting payments, or trying to think about some objectives for next year, or not happy with the tone of the emails going back and forth.

Pick up the phone, get in your car and drive to a coffee shop, fire up Skype or Zoom and talk. Chat. The best results come when you can see facial expressions and body language.

Without conversation, there is no relationship.

Pillar Two: Love

Yeah, I said it. Love.

It doesn't have to be the head over heels kind of love, and it may not exist the moment you lay eyes upon one another, but yes — love is a very important pillar in the best relationships.

With love, from both parties, comes an unspeakable bond, an indescribable understanding, a constant desire to remain together and keep on working hard, no matter the challenge.

With love, everything is possible.

Pillar Three: Knowledge

You know stuff and I know stuff. I tell you the things I know about anything that is relevant (and sometimes not) and you tell me about the stuff you know that is relevant (and sometimes not).

See Pillar 1: Conversation.

I don't need to know everything you know and vice-a-versa, but the more we understand what we are both up against — be it other staff or departments, or competition, or plans, or history, or design, or other work we have seen and done — the better we will all be. We will all be smarter, better, faster and more productive.

Don't come to the table with your cards held close to your chest. Lay it all out.

You have knowledge and I have knowledge.

Let's share.

Pillar Four: Trust

Trust means knowing that when you say, "*this stays under the cone of silence*" it does.

Trust means that when I say, "*I'll have this to you by Friday*" I will.

Trust means that we all know, day after day, that we do EVERYTHING with the best intentions and with your best interests at heart.

Trust means I tell you the truth, even when it hurts — and often it will — no offense. Trust means that when something just doesn't seem right — we say it and fix it because (back to Pillar 2) we love one another enough to fix it.

Trust means that I've got your back and you've got mine and we help each other do better.

Without trust, forget it.

Pillar Five: Expectations

This one is often overlooked. I expect my clients to be nice to me.

You expect me, your consultant, to not sell your donor list. I expect a half decent coffee when I come to meet with you and you, expect that I will call if I'm going to be late.

Sometimes, it is better to discuss what we expect of each other before we move along too far in our journey, but often we don't know WHAT we expect until the other party doesn't do it.

Then, we need to make sure we tell each other in the most loving and caring way we can. I expect that my clients will always do that, and they expect I will listen.

See how this works?

I am expecting you will agree, but remember, you can always tell me that I can't expect that. Which leads me to…

Pillar Six: Respect

You'll notice that a lot of these pillars are closely connected.

Respect is so important. I automatically give anyone I meet 100% respect, until they show that they don't do the same.

What is respect? To me, it's an acknowledgement of ability, of needs or experiences that are similar and different from mine. It's an age thing, it's a human thing. There is no room for ego, being self-serving or completely focusing only on one-sided needs. This obviously applies to your donors as well.

When you respect your donors, usually they will respect you back.

Unlike the song, now you know what R-E-S-P-E-C-T means to me.

Pillar Seven: Creativity

We are all creative.

We are shaped by our knowledge, experiences, our lives and our careers. The funny thing is that creative is scary. Creative is unknown destinations through deep water, creative is "outside the box," especially when it really is inside the box or better yet, doesn't even acknowledge there IS a box.

My job is to approach every one of your problems or challenges creatively.

Your job is to approach every one of your problems or challenges creatively.

There is no room for "This is what was done last year," in creativity.

Pillar Eight: Honesty

I have been honest with you, when I've told you I don't care so much about you and your charity.

My deepest wish is to help you connect your donors to the good work they do for your mission.

You have been honest with me when you've told me that my idea is not very good.

Don't mistake honesty with hurtfulness.

This also goes back to respect.

Being honest means we say what needs to be said because we know that we will all be better for knowing it. Being honest means we share our fears and our nervousness. It means we show each other we are human and not perfect.

With loving honesty, the whole world will be changed.

Pillar Nine: Collaboration

Another Agents of Good key word here!

This essentially means we work together.

It's not us vs you. It's not you vs us.

It doesn't mean if the mailing bombs, it's our fault or yours.

It doesn't mean that we do all the thinking and come to you with the same solution we sold to our other clients.

Collaboration means we are in the same boat. If it sinks, we all sink. If we find the promised land, we all celebrate together. This also loops back to knowledge. I tell you what I know, you tell me what you know and we do amazing stuff. All the time.

If you don't want to roll up your sleeves and work hard alongside your agency, consultant, or donor — then don't bother.

Pillar Ten: Loyalty

No one speaks of loyalty anymore.

Few in our sector even know what it means.

The best clients and the best consultants are the ones who (time and time again) put their butts on the line for each other.

Let's throw caution to the wind and have each other's back and best interests in our hearts. Let's stand by each other when the sky is falling and offer protection from it.

There isn't much loyalty left, with so many people in it for themselves.

Call me idealistic, but I believe you need to be loyal for the very best kind of relationship.

DEVIATION DISCOVERIES

On the surface, it looks like this deviation mostly focuses on using cheesy illustrated characters. But it's more about stepping away from the idea of "professionalism" that so often gets in the way of human storytelling. Just like in our personal life — sometimes our work can be a hot mess.

1. Don't design for design's sake. Every element, every box, every line, every extra "thing" you add to the appeal should have a clear purpose otherwise it will only distract and detract from the likelihood of getting a gift.
2. Ugly design is human design. Not-so-pro is excellent and effective for direct response purposes.
3. Imperfections are perfection in direct response. They stand out. They get attention. They get sympathy. The remind us that humans are at work. Not robots.

Deviation Nine — Automation will not save you

Have you ever considered moving away from your well-manicured lawn to something much more natural and organic? This deviation focuses in on why getting your hands and knees dirty and working up a bit of a sweat will help you to raise more money for your organization. Today and tomorrow.

Automation means profit, right?

The less we have to be involved with a task, using people who charge less per hour to do something so we don't have to, the more money we make, right?

We live in a world that celebrates automation and making a profit. We obsess over return on investment (ROI). We work in a sector that focuses on spending as little as possible while being expected to raise more and more money, year after year.

We also work in a sector that is, more often than not, forced to "bring in the money now" while having trouble investing in the future.

Short game vs. long game.

Direct response (especially direct mail) is an investment in the long game. If you're just starting up a direct mail program, the returns are not going to be immediate, and the long term impact can't always be measured. Furthermore, the overall success of your program can't be determined by the response to one specific appeal.

Direct response, in any channel, means that you are having a conversation with another human and you are asking for them to do something. Usually, in fundraising, it means you're asking them to send you a monetary gift.

Here's the thing about that.

The more you lean in to the idea of one human having a conversation with another human and asking for something specific — the more successful it will be.

That's it.

That's the key to revolutionizing your organization... along with the 1,001 other things you can do which will only make you even more successful. (See *Deviation 4.*)

But...

And there is almost always a but.

I consistently hear excuses as to why we can't do the one thing (or 100 things) that would instantly take your fundraising off the charts.

"*It's too much work.*" "*It's too hard.*" "*We don't have time for that.*"

I didn't say it was easy, but, it is simple.

I will even give you the magic bullet you look for at every conference and never find.

Take a look at your desk.

Pick up your recently-mailed spring appeal or holiday pack.

How many donors did you send it to?

How many of those donors got exactly the same pack? Same outer envelope. Same letter. Reply.

All? Half? (I hope you at least did some basic segmentation!)

Your donors walk to their mail box and pull out a stack of white, #10 envelopes. They flip through them, sorting over the recycling blue bin... junk, junk, junk, bill, bill, bill.

They are used to the endlessly perfect and fabricated messaging they get. It barely registers in their brain anymore.

"*Junk, junk, junk, bill, bill... oh hold on!*"

This one has handwriting. And a stamp! Wow. This must be something worth looking at.

Donors are savvier then we give them credit for.

They don't like to feel like they are a walking ATM for anyone. They don't want to be treated like ID number 9577584.

Remember: The best direct mail feels like a personal piece of communication from me to you.

So how do we do this?

PARETO

Almost everyone holding this book will know what the Pareto principle is. It's the good old fashioned 80/20 rule.

In fundraising, it means that generally speaking, you raise 80% of your revenue from 20% of your donors.

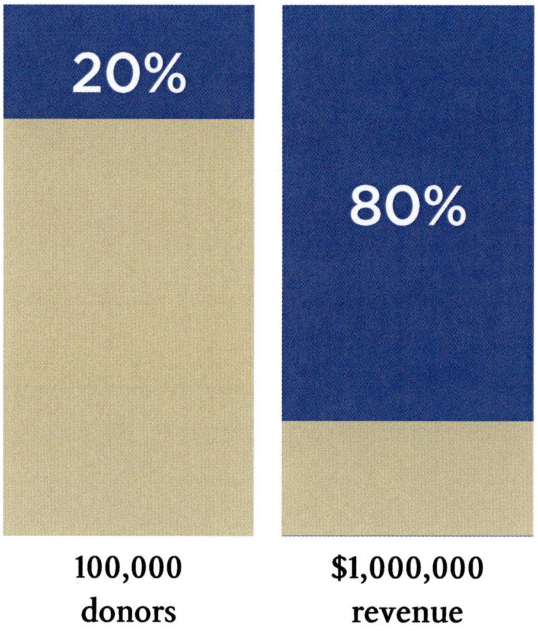

Do you agree?

If so, I have already made a strong case for you to stop sending the same mail to everyone.

Have you ever looked at who the 20% people are?

They will likely be your monthly donors, your legacy donors, your "mid-to-high-level" donors and your loyal donors.

If you are raising 80% of your revenue from these amazing humans, why are you sending them the same appeal as everyone else?

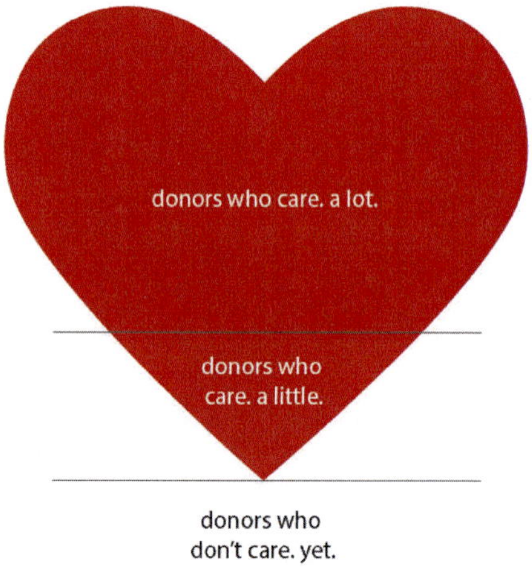

Let's assume you have taken a look at the 20% donors and have segmented them out from the other 80%.

What I am going to ask you for is very simple. It is also a lot of hard work. But that's the job.

What I want you to do is take these amazing folks and try to finish as much of the mailing as you can "in house," or in other words, from your office.

This is what we call "high human touch."

First, your mailing should go in an oversized, non-window envelope. Ideally you will also use a first class or commemorative stamp on it and you or someone in your office will take the time to handwrite the donor's name and address.

Bonus points for:

- a little bit of smeared ink, because maybe the writer is left-handed like me, and we smear everything!
- the stamp being placed on a slight angle — or using multiple stamps
- applying an extra sticker, or stamp or seal

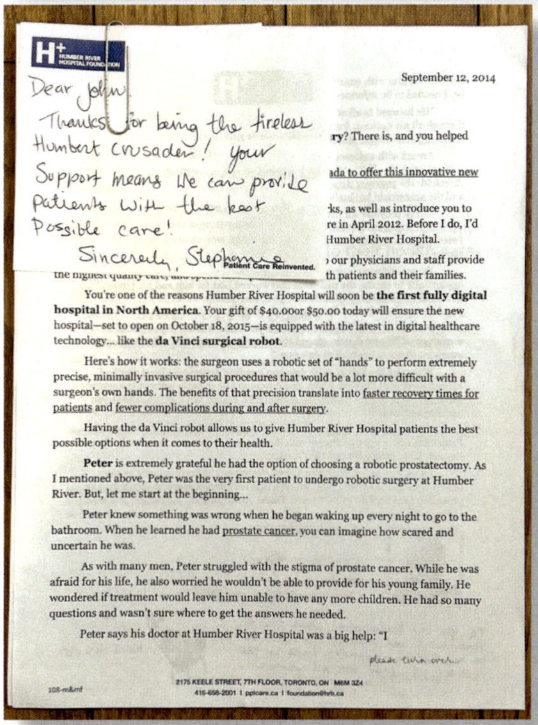

These are small things, but serve as visual reminders to your donor that a real human was involved in the creation of their mail pack.

The letter should be brilliantly written, filled with emotion, touching on the donor and organization's shared values featuring a specific story and compelling offer.

You can print it on your laser printer, or you can have it printed at a print shop and then shipped back to you for personalization. It should most certainly be personalized, and every single one should be hand-signed.

If you know the donor personally, a

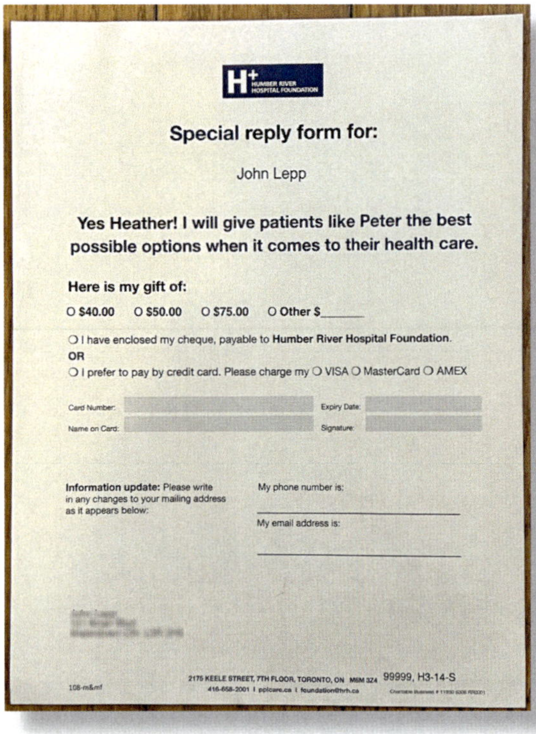

H+ HUMBER RIVER HOSPITAL FOUNDATION

Special reply form for:

John Lepp

Yes Heather! I will give patients like Peter the best possible options when it comes to their health care.

Here is my gift of:

O $40.00 O $50.00 O $75.00 O Other $_____

O I have enclosed my cheque, payable to **Humber River Hospital Foundation**.

OR

O I prefer to pay by credit card. Please charge my O VISA O MasterCard O AMEX

Card Number: Expiry Date:

Name on Card: Signature:

Information update: Please write in any changes to your mailing address as it appears below:

My phone number is:

My email address is:

108-m&mf

2175 KEELE STREET, 7TH FLOOR, TORONTO, ON M6M 3Z4 99999, H3-14-S

416-658-2001 | pplcare.ca | foundation@hrh.ca

small note at the beginning or the end referencing something you know about them, like a birthday or recent milestone, will go a long way. Also, consider adding your direct telephone number (yes, really!) and an open invitation to contact you at any time.

The more levels of human touch you can apply to this appeal, the better it will do.

Some other things to try:

- a note in the margin
- crossing out "Dear Ms. Sample" and writing "Dear Jane,"
- something paper clipped to it, like a photo or a business card
- a sticky note applied, etc.

The full sheet, 8.5″ x 11″ reply form can be done in Word and printed from your office printer. It should also be personalized and ask for only one thing: a single gift. The gift array should repeat what you are asking for in the letter with a few other options.

- Last gift
- Last gift + 25%
- Last gift + 50%
- Last gift + 100%
- A blank field for them to give whatever they want

If you're mailing a monthly donor, maybe you are asking for a special, one-time gift, or you might be asking them to upgrade their monthly gift. It should be clear on the reply form.

The reply form should have plenty of white space and large type (14 pt or higher) for your donor to take all the space she needs to fill out her info.

If your mailing included some sort of insert or lift note, print extra so you can insert it by hand or paper clip it along with the letter and the reply. If you have a photo or something similar that demonstrates your mission in action, go to your local photography store, get a bunch printed on photo paper. Then, write a simple note on the back, something like, "you made this moment possible" or, "Susy thanks you" or, "I had this image on my desk and I really wanted you to see it."

Be creative.

And finally,

Don't forget the BRE (Business Reply Envelope)!

If you can, ditch the BRE and use a personalized reply envelope with a stamp on it for the best of the best donors! It will make a big difference. If you think that it will cost too much money, then at least try to add a sticker or a handwritten touch along with some personalization to your standard BRE.

This is not the time to spend as little as possible. Lavish love and attention on these people.

Obviously if you are a charity with 1,000,000 donors, doing a pack like this for your top 20% of donors will not be possible.

The scalability of this idea will be up to you, but don't do nothing. You can do this for some of your donors and they will thank you for it. They will "perform" much better almost immediately.

Try to repeat this "high human touch" (and low tech) approach for every single mailing.

It's easy! And also very difficult.

GORGEOUS GEORGE

Here is another example of how you can use the Pareto principle along with the combined power of a moving story and effective design to create a winning appeal.

Thank you to Jonathon Grapsas at Flat Earth Direct and the folks at TeamKids (Australia) for letting me share this. We created this appeal in partnership with their teams.

This is the story of Georgia, or Gorgeous George as she was known to her family and friends. Georgia was born with extremely complex needs. When she was born, doctors told her mom Kirsteen that she might only live a year.

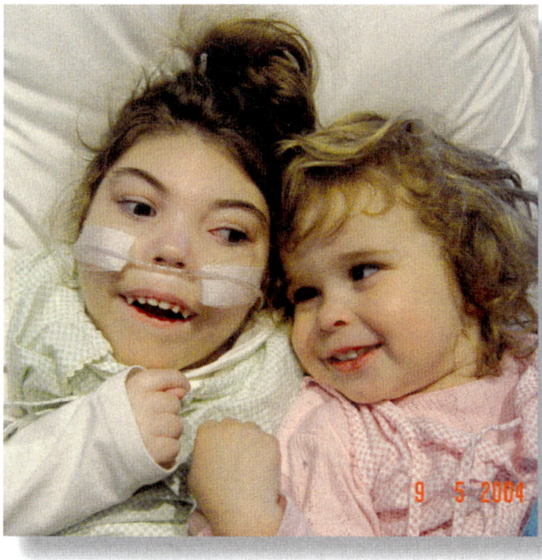

"*When I first held Georgia in my arms,*" says Kirsteen, "*I told her I would do everything in my power to make her life happy — make every day special — and surround her with love while I still could.*"

#sob

Gorgeous George lived long past the age of one. Kirsteen kept her promise to her daughter — sacrificing everything to care for her little girl around the clock, trying to pack as many happy memories into her life as possible.

Georgia loved playing games with her little sister, being outdoors as much as possible and enjoyed, most of all, her family holidays to a beach house.

The beach house that Kirsteen managed to find for her family was lovely, but it was not well-equipped for Georgia's needs.

Kirsteen would have to pack their entire house with them when they went: medicines, medical equipment, a wheelchair, diapers...the list went on.

There was no special bed for Georgia to sleep in, so they had to make do. Kirsteen carried stress with her every trip. What if something were to happen to Georgia? There was no hospital close by. On top of the emotional stress, there was no lift at the beach house to help get Georgia and her wheelchair up and down all the stairs. The family had to manage on their own.

Despite the difficulties, Kirsteen knew how much holidays like this meant to Georgia, and to her sister Chelsea. They never knew if it would be Georgia's last summer. Kirsteen knew that they were making memories they'd hold onto for the rest of their lives.

Kirsteen kept her promise of special moments and happy memories to Gorgeous George for 14 years.

For this appeal, the case for support was that every family deserves to make

happy memories, but sadly, not every family in palliative care is able to, and those who are, become burdened with the same stress and difficulties that Kirsteen was. It's not a vacation *AT ALL for the parents.*

The goal was to create an appeal that would allow donors to help TeamKids affect change for families with children in palliative care at the Women's and Children's Hospital.

With generous help, TeamKids was going to create a very special beach house where families with high medical needs could take holidays together and create lasting happy memories. It would be a place where the parents and siblings could have a much-needed break from stress and worry, and a place where the sick child could laugh and smile with the people they loved most in the world.

This is the mail pack they created for their very top donors: **the top 20% of the 20%.**

These special donors received their mailing in a specially-designed tube. The same type of tube that rolled up building plans are often stored in (you'll see why in a bit!).

The letter was highly personalized. It was also four pages long and repeated a lot

"Many of the very sickest kids have never been on holiday. And they never will. They may never see the ocean again, hear waves lapping on the beach or feel the sea breeze on their face. This new beach house could change everything and give families the chance to make happy memories together. And I know how important those memories are."
Kirsteen, mum to Georgia and Chelsea

<Serial No>/<Segment>
<Title> <First Name> <Surname>
<Address 1>
<Address 2>
<Suburb> <State> <Postcode>

[Mailing Date]

IN MEMORY OF GORGEOUS GEORGE

We've made a promise to give terminally ill kids the best Christmas present ever…
…Please will you send a special Christmas gift< of $Ask1> that could give a kid like Georgia the chance to see the ocean – for what sadly may be the last time in their lives?

Dear <Salutation>,

I'm sure, like me, your heart goes out to children like Georgia, who spend so much of their lives in hospital. Even when they are at home they're undergoing medical treatment, and missing out on so many of the joyful experiences of childhood.

It really should be the other way around.

For children like Georgia, every day should be special – full of smiles, laughter and love. **Because their families live with the heartbreaking knowledge that every day could be their last.**

Kirsteen knew when her beautiful little girl was born that every moment they had together would be precious. After doing a brain scan and assessing her complex medical condition, doctors said they thought Georgia might live for a year. Just a year.

That's when Kirsteen made her a promise.

"When I first held Georgia in my arms," says Kirsteen. *"I told her I'd do everything in my power to make her life happy – make every day special – and surround her with love while I still could."*

It was an extremely brave thing to do. I'm sure you would have wanted to do the same if that had been your child, but Kirsteen only discovered later how hard it would be.

This Christmas, inspired by Kirsteen, we're making a promise of our own to kids who are receiving palliative care at the Women's and Children's Hospital – to give them the chance to escape, enjoy a break with their families and see the ocean, perhaps for the last time in their lives.

<Personalised, p/P>lease will you help us keep this promise to kids who may never live long, full lives?

With Christmas coming, I'm asking you to support an exciting, new project – to create a special beach house and open it to terminally ill kids like Georgia and their families.

TeamKids — WCH Foundation | Locked Bag 5, Adelaide SA 5001, AUSTRALIA
T 08 8464 7900 | F 08 8464 7999 | www.teamkids.com.au

We already have a site. We have plans all drawn up. I now urgently need to raise $<target TBC> which will be used to adapt the beach house to the needs of the very sickest children. That means installing a lift, making it entirely wheelchair accessible, and putting in place hoists so each child can easily take a bath or get in and out of bed.

And when I say it's urgent, it really is. I have until Friday, 18 November to raise the funds for this vital stage of work – that's only a few weeks away.

Please will you send a special Christmas gift< of $Ask1> that could give a sick kid like Georgia the chance to see the ocean?

I'm turning to you knowing how generous you are when I write, and I'm so thankful for that. Your recent gift<s> show<s> me how determined you are to help sick kids. I feel sure you'll understand why this project is so important. It's almost unbearable to think of children who are in palliative care spending their lives undergoing medical treatment at home and in hospital – never once having a holiday.

This Christmas, I desperately hope you'll help change that.

As Kirsteen discovered, family life is hard when you have a terminally ill child.

"In the early days, we spent a lot of time in hospital, with Georgia seeing a whole team of specialists," she remembers. *"But Georgia surprised them all – she was determined to be with us far longer than the doctors thought possible. As time went by, we were able to give her more care at home. If she was ill, we'd go straight to the intensive care unit at the Women's and Children's Hospital, but the rest of the time the palliative care team helped me look after her at home."*

There was no cure for Georgia's condition. No way she'd ever be better. Instead her treatment was based around giving her the best quality of life. But that still meant a lot of time in hospital or surrounded by medical equipment at home.

If it hadn't been for the promise Kirsteen made to Georgia when she was a baby, she might have lived her life without so many precious experiences – getting out on the road, travelling as a family, going to the beach and having a big, happy Christmas together.

Sadly, many children facing desperately short lives never enjoy any of those things.

"You need to understand how hard it is, just to go out and get a carton of milk when you have a seriously ill child," says Kirsteen. *"It might take half an hour to pack everything we'd need, including oxygen, nappies, the wheelchair and Georgia's other medical equipment. Then I'd try and get Georgia and her little sister, Chelsea, in the car. More time would go by. I'd probably need two hours just to get milk – something that anyone else might do in minutes."*

It's no wonder then that packing for a holiday is impossible for many families, especially when you realise that money is often tight, with one or even both parents having to give up work to offer fulltime care.

That's why I'm asking you to do something extra special and give the sickest kids the best Christmas present ever, <Personalised>.

Please will you send a generous gift< of $Ask1> that could create a very special beach house that's fully fitted out to suit the needs of terminally ill kids and their families?]

The house would be open to as many as 65-80 children who are in palliative care at the Women's and Children's Hospital, and their families, who have no other chance of a break. And they'd be able to enjoy a holiday knowing everything had been thought of.

That's because, with your help, the beach house will:

- Be fully accessible to wheelchairs, with a lift and hoists installed, and extra wide hallways and doorways.
- Have fully accessible bathrooms or all kinds of special needs.
- Have a sheltered decked with sea views.
- Be close to a hospital in case of emergency and local medical staff will be trained to offer support.

It's such an exciting plan, but that's all it will ever be without your support. And it needs to come to life. It needs to be up and running to give children like Georgia and their families a holiday to remember together.

I don't know what your childhood memories of Christmas are, but for many of us, it was all about long days on the beach, swimming, splashing, feeling the warm, golden sand underfoot and, of course, being with family and friends.

Happy times. Happy times that every child should enjoy, especially if this could be the last Christmas they'll have.

Because the tragic truth is Kirsteen felt they had to celebrate every Christmas like it was Georgia's last – the family never knew if their 'beautiful soul, their shining light' would still be with them a year later.

Long before we made plans for a dedicated beach house for terminally sick kids and their families, Kirsteen had managed to find one where she could take her kids. She wanted so badly to give her little girl a life filled with incredible experiences. So she endured the stress and difficulties that came along with taking a high-needs child on holiday on her own. That beach house wasn't fully wheelchair accessible, it wasn't equipped with hoists and it wasn't as close to a hospital as Kirsteen would have liked. But despite the stress and worry this caused Kirsteen, every now and again, she managed to take both her girls there because she knew how happy it made them.

"It was really hard work and I always came back physically exhausted from having to lift Georgia or squeeze her wheelchair into places it wouldn't really go," Kirsteen said, *"There was no special bed for her, so that was another worry. But I did it, because I knew how happy it made Georgia. Some of our most precious memories are of the time we spent together by the ocean."*

For Kirsteen, Georgia and Chelsea, every day away from hospital, home and medical treatment was special.

"If the weather was good, we could sit out on the deck and Georgia could enjoy the sea air," explains Kirsten. *"We'd go for walks, listen to music, play games, watch movies – simple things that anyone else might take for granted. But not us. These were special days that made us feel close and connected. Today my most priceless memories come from those times by the ocean."*

Every child should see the ocean, and huge blue sunlit skies stretching to the horizon. Every child should feel warm sand run through their fingers and toes. Every child should smell the salt in the air and feel the fresh sea breeze.

And of course, most do. But not maybe the ones who need it the most.

I'm talking about kids like Georgia who spend most of their life indoors, in hospital, surrounded by medical equipment, being treated by doctors and nurses.

This Christmas, I'm asking you to change that. Because it's now in our hands – yours, mine, and our incredibly generous community here in South Australia.

We have a site and plans for the beach house. Now we need to raise the money to adapt it to the special needs of kids like Georgia.

Please will you send a generous gift< of $Ask1> that could give a terminally ill child the chance to enjoy sunlit days on the beach, making happy memories with their family?

Tragically, that's all Kirsteen and her family are left with now – memories. And they're thankful for every happy one, because life is so, so hard when you lose a child, a sister, a grandchild.

For fourteen brave and determined years, Georgia surprised her doctors and brought happiness to everyone she met. But four years ago, she passed away.

"Georgia left us on the first day of spring, September 1st," remembers Kirsteen. *"It's been very hard to go on without her. Christmas is especially painful, because we would have big get togethers, with Georgia at the very heart of our celebration. We miss her every day, but our memories of those happy times are a huge comfort. And no one can take them away."*

And for her sister Chelsea, it's not the cemetery where she wants to go to feel close to Georgia. It's the bench that marks the spot where Georgia used to look out over the beach to the ocean during those precious days at the beach house. On it, there's a plaque that reads, *'In loving memory of Georgia 'Gorgeous George'. Your smile lit up the world.'*

You won't be surprised then to learn that Kirsteen and her family are doing everything they can to support the beach house that TeamKids plans to open in Georgia's memory.

"The thought that there will be a specially adapted and equipped beach house for families with terminally ill kids is so exciting," says Kirsteen. *"It means there will be somewhere to go that's all set up for them and they can experience a family holiday, and create lots of wonderful memories with their child without that stress and worry that they normally have to live with every day. That's so important."*

Kirsteen and her family know what the new beach house would mean to a child and their family. And now so do you<, Personalised>.

Please will you send a special Christmas gift< of $Ask1, $Ask2 or even, if you can, an exceptionally generous $Ask3> to help give a child, who may have only a short time to live, the chance to see the ocean?

Christmas is coming, a time when we traditionally put kids first. With your gift, you can put the needs of the very sickest children first – and that would mean so much to them and their families.

Yours sincerely,

Sam Tolley

Chief Executive Officer

TeamKids – Women's & Children's Hospital Foundation

P.S. This Christmas, I'm asking you to give kids receiving palliative care the best present ever – the chance to take a break from hospital and go on a family holiday, perhaps for the first and last time in their lives. Please will send a gift< of $Ask1, $Ask2 or even $Ask3> that could help create a very special beach house so it is all set up to meet their needs? Please give as generously as you can.

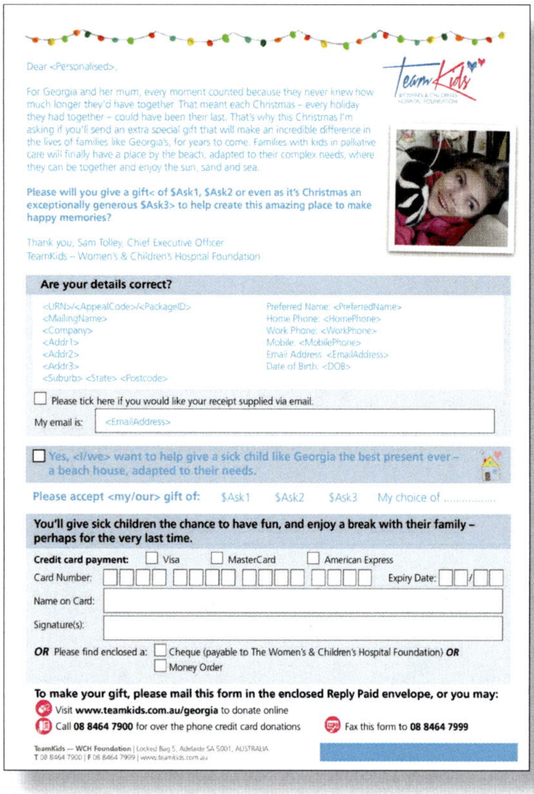

Dear <Personalised>,

For Georgia and her mum, every moment counted because they never knew how much longer they'd have together. That meant each Christmas – every holiday they had together – could have been their last. That's why this Christmas I'm asking if you'll send an extra special gift that will make an incredible difference in the lives of families like Georgia's, for years to come. Families with kids in palliative care will finally have a place by the beach, adapted to their complex needs, where they can be together and enjoy the sun, sand and sea.

Please will you give a gift< of $Ask1, $Ask2 or even as it's Christmas an exceptionally generous $Ask3> to help create this amazing place to make happy memories?

Thank you, Sam Tolley, Chief Executive Officer
TeamKids – Women's & Children's Hospital Foundation

Are your details correct?

<URN>/<AppealCode>/<PackageID>
<MailingName>
<Company>
<Addr1>
<Addr2>
<Addr3>
<Suburb> <State> <Postcode>

Preferred Name: <PreferredName>
Home Phone: <HomePhone>
Work Phone: <WorkPhone>
Mobile: <MobilePhone>
Email Address: <EmailAddress>
Date of Birth: <DOB>

☐ Please tick here if you would like your receipt supplied via email.

My email is: <EmailAddress>

☐ **Yes, <I/we> want to help give a sick child like Georgia the best present ever – a beach house, adapted to their needs.**

Please accept <my/our> gift of: $Ask1 $Ask2 $Ask3 My choice of ....

You'll give sick children the chance to have fun, and enjoy a break with their family – perhaps for the very last time.

Credit card payment: ☐ Visa ☐ MasterCard ☐ American Express

Card Number: Expiry Date: /

Name on Card:

Signature(s):

OR Please find enclosed a: ☐ Cheque (payable to The Women's & Children's Hospital Foundation) ***OR*** ☐ Money Order

To make your gift, please mail this form in the enclosed Reply Paid envelope, or you may:

Visit **www.teamkids.com.au/georgia** to donate online

Call **08 8464 7900** for over the phone credit card donations

Fax this form to **08 8464 7999**

TeamKids — WCH Foundation | Locked Bag 5, Adelaide SA 5001, AUSTRALIA
T 08 8464 7900 | F 08 8464 7999 | www.teamkids.com.au

Merry Christmas from Georgia's family to yours

Thank you for helping give sick children the best present ever.

All donations of $2 or more are tax deductible.

Personal information is collected to process donations, issue tax receipts and to send you updates. For these purposes, your information may be shared with trusted third parties and our service providers (and their directors, servants and agents), either in Australia or overseas. Failure to provide personal information may result in the WCH Foundation being unable to provide you with certain information and offers. Our Privacy Policy, which you can read in full at www.teamkids.com.au contains information about: (i) how you can access and correct your personal information; (ii) how you can lodge a complaint regarding the handling of your personal information; and (iii) how any complaint will be handled by the WCH Foundation. You may contact our privacy officer with any queries via email: info@wchfoundation.org.au or mail: Locked Bag 5, Adelaide SA 5001 or telephone: 08 8464 7900. Occasionally we allow like-minded organisations to contact you with information that may be of interest, including some organisations located outside Australia. They allow us to do the same so we can reach more people with vital information.

☐ Please tick here if you do NOT want to receive communications from organisations we trust. If you do NOT want to receive future communications from the WCH Foundation, please call our friendly team at 1800 008 483.

of the story I just shared with you.

A full size, A4, reply form used every bit of space (front and back) for storytelling. Extra space wasn't jammed with other asks, check boxes or random pie charts.

We created an insert that looked like a scrap book from Kirsteen to the donors of TeamKids. It included personal photos and her words and reflections. There was a lot of overlap between the insert and letter, but the creative execution of the insert draws donor interest in a totally different way than a letter.

As part of the appeal, we created some simple gift tags, a simple premium for the pack. This gave the donor something that could be used during the Christmas holidays, reminding them of their support for TeamKids and children like Georgia.

Finally, we created a third insert that would allow the donor to feel like a valued partner in the building of this very special home. This was printed on a very large A3 sheet and folded down. This is the front of the lift.

Then the lift opened to more photos from the beach house and some hand-written sticky notes with the features of the new home.

This included an architectural rendering of the house that brought the donor

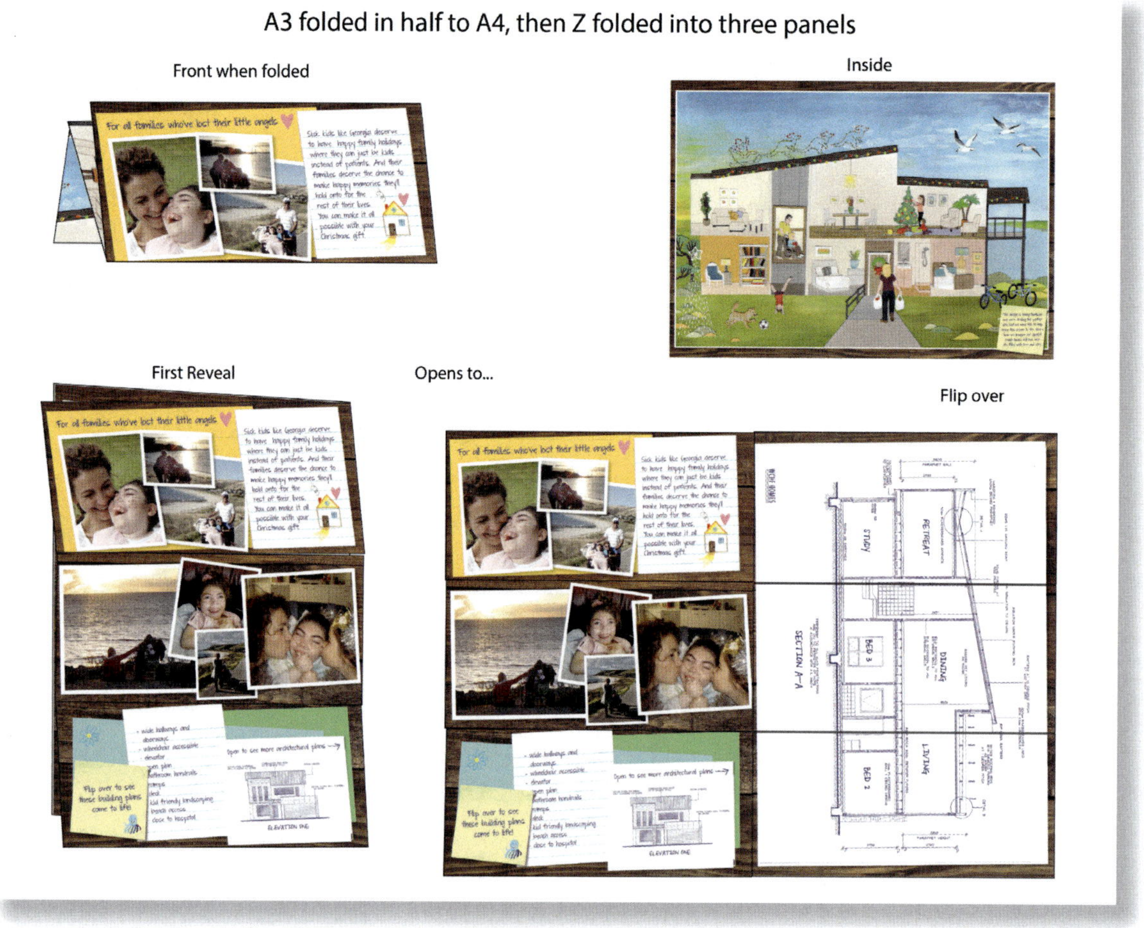

"inside." We could have stopped there, but this cold rendering was missing something.

The inside opened to this very large format, gorgeous "imagining" of what the home will look like when it is filled with life; there for any family who needs it.

The donor would ensure THIS dream would become a reality.

Everything was rolled up nice and neat and delivered to the donor in a special mailing tube.

Can you imagine a scenario where this is NOT opened?

This mail pack, to the very best donors used a:

- mail tube
- full colour 4-page letter
- full colour reply form
- full colour insert like a diary entry
- full colour Christmas labels

- full colour and oversized insert, featuring more story, an architectural rendering and illustration of the new, yet to be built, home

Mail packs like this, especially utilizing express post envelopes or mailing tubes, can get open rates of 90% or higher. And yes, they are expensive to design, print and mail, but when you acknowledge that 80% of your revenue is coming from 20% of your donors, it is a smart investment.

Also, you can scale these mail packs down depending on the segment of donors.

Your mid-level donors could get an oversized (9″ x 12″ or 9″ x 6″) envelope, 4-page letter, 2-page reply form, the Christmas labels (or not) and a smaller version of the insert. Your base donors (80%?) would get an outer envelope, 2-4 page letter, reply form and simple insert using the illustration and some photos, for example.

DEVIATION DISCOVERIES

We tend to associate automation with profit since processes and robots make things faster, better and sometimes cheaper. By slowing things down and making some things up as you go along, you will be able to adapt to a rapidly-changing world and create stronger and more effective fundraising appeals.

1. Faster is not always better. So much of fundraising is like real life. We need to be thoughtful and mindful of how we reach out and connect with our donors.
2. Low tech is better than high tech. The more donors feel your fingerprints along the edges of your envelopes, the more they will engage with it.
3. Donors do not dislike long stories. They do, however, ignore grandiose self-pandering that does little to acknowledge their role in your work. For the right donors, more is more — and will result in more giving!

Deviation Ten — Off the trail!

The first nine deviations didn't stray too far off the main trail. This deviation invites you to drive further down the road to somewhere you probably haven't been before. This is a place where smooth pavement ends and rough gravel begins. Let's pull off here. It's time to tighten up your laces and start walking down a "barely there" path that will take you to somewhere new. It is also a place that just might take your storytelling to an entirely new level. This deviation will look at how custom illustration, photography and thoughtful design can take your appeals (and your donors) to a place they've never been before.

Back in my agency days, we always had a creative in the studio who could sketch, paint or illustrate a complex concept that you just wouldn't be able to capture in a photo.

I always liked having that available as an option.

It is the same for stock photography. I know budgets are tight, but I want the donor to hold something in their hands that they haven't seen on a billboard or ad in the local paper.

A colleague told me that they would love to use custom photography or illustration in their work but their clients would never approve the budget. These were big, big name clients.

I explained that we never ask for extra budget to do it this kind of work. I take it out of our budget. It's worth it to me.

Custom illustrations or custom photographs can go that extra mile and can make such a difference in fully capturing your organization's unique story.

PATRICIA

Patricia was a lovely woman who lived at St. Patrick's Home of Ottawa (a long-term care home located in Ottawa, Canada).

Agents of Good was asked to do a gratitude video for St. Pat's after a long capital campaign to rebuild the home for people like Patricia.

Originally, we were going to do a short video using found and stock images with some supers (text overlaid onto the images in the video), but it didn't have a personal enough feel. We also wanted to feature a beneficiary so that the donors really could get a deeper sense of the direct impact of their giving on someone who lived at the Home.

Enter Patricia, who graciously agreed to be our featured beneficiary.

We packed up the cameras, went to Ottawa, and found Patricia waiting for us! We spent the day chatting and taking photos of Patricia going about her daily life in and around the facility.

We ended up using these shots for the short gratitude video. Patricia became an overnight sensation in and around St. Pat's! How could she not? She was truly a lovely woman whose personality shone through in the photographs.

The holiday appeal was scheduled next for St. Pat's. We knew we had to feature Patricia in that appeal too, since donors loved her so much in the video.

We sent the appeal in an oversized 9.5″ x 6″ envelope.

A NOTE about window positioning: We've tested the positioning of the window in the past with other clients. The best performing outer envelopes tend to not have a window at all. We've also tested having the letter show through the envelope vs having the reply form show through (which needs to be the address carrier if you use a standard 9.5″ x 5.875″ window envelope, since it sits about 3/4″ from the bottom).

Our tests showed that having the letter show through the window on the envelope (thus being the first thing the donor saw when they opened it) did better than having the reply form as the address carrier. So that's why the window placement is higher on this envelope than on your standard envelope!

The tagline used a fragment of a popular Christmas carol. This can get a donor humming along, which instantly makes the outer envelope more "openable." We also included a line about the enclosed ornament.

There are two reasons this works. First, we always like to tell the donor if we have put something in the pack just for them and second, it reads, "Fragile: Your 2015 ornament is enclosed."

The pack is completely flat. The donor is thinking, how can it be fragile? I don't feel anything. They want answers, and there is only one way to get them!

The two-page letter (Fig 10.1) was from Ruth, the Executive Director and talks about Patricia and the changing of the seasons and how gifts will be used to light up the Christmas trees, fund holiday outings, and provide blanket-warming machines and other vital equipment.

In other words, comfort and joy.

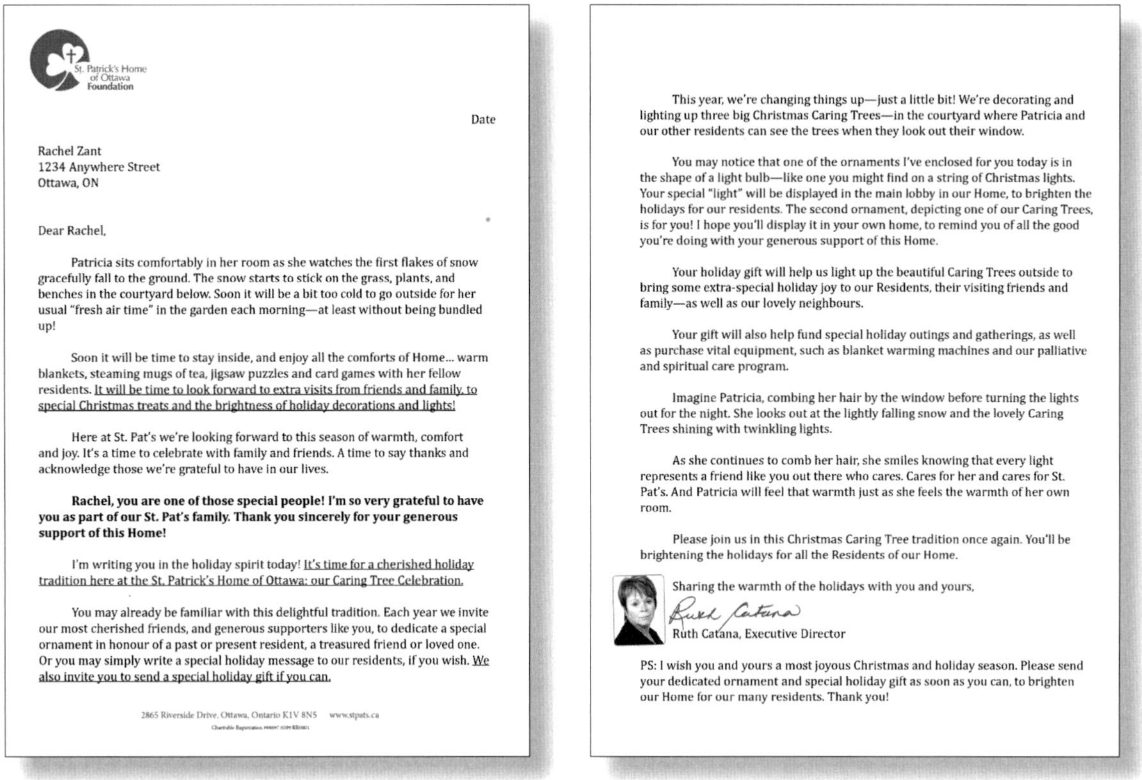

St. Patrick's Home of Ottawa Foundation

Date

Rachel Zant
1234 Anywhere Street
Ottawa, ON

Dear Rachel,

Patricia sits comfortably in her room as she watches the first flakes of snow gracefully fall to the ground. The snow starts to stick on the grass, plants, and benches in the courtyard below. Soon it will be a bit too cold to go outside for her usual "fresh air time" in the garden each morning—at least without being bundled up!

Soon it will be time to stay inside, and enjoy all the comforts of Home... warm blankets, steaming mugs of tea, jigsaw puzzles and card games with her fellow residents. It will be time to look forward to extra visits from friends and family, to special Christmas treats and the brightness of holiday decorations and lights!

Here at St. Pat's we're looking forward to this season of warmth, comfort and joy. It's a time to celebrate with family and friends. A time to say thanks and acknowledge those we're grateful to have in our lives.

Rachel, you are one of those special people! I'm so very grateful to have you as part of our St. Pat's family. Thank you sincerely for your generous support of this Home!

I'm writing you in the holiday spirit today! It's time for a cherished holiday tradition here at the St. Patrick's Home of Ottawa: our Caring Tree Celebration.

You may already be familiar with this delightful tradition. Each year we invite our most cherished friends, and generous supporters like you, to dedicate a special ornament in honour of a past or present resident, a treasured friend or loved one. Or you may simply write a special holiday message to our residents, if you wish. We also invite you to send a special holiday gift if you can.

2865 Riverside Drive, Ottawa, Ontario K1V 8N5 www.stpats.ca
Charitable Registration [illegible]

This year, we're changing things up—just a little bit! We're decorating and lighting up three big Christmas Caring Trees—in the courtyard where Patricia and our other residents can see the trees when they look out their window.

You may notice that one of the ornaments I've enclosed for you today is in the shape of a light bulb—like one you might find on a string of Christmas lights. Your special "light" will be displayed in the main lobby in our Home, to brighten the holidays for our residents. The second ornament, depicting one of our Caring Trees, is for you! I hope you'll display it in your own home, to remind you of all the good you're doing with your generous support of this Home.

Your holiday gift will help us light up the beautiful Caring Trees outside to bring some extra-special holiday joy to our Residents, their visiting friends and family—as well as our lovely neighbours.

Your gift will also help fund special holiday outings and gatherings, as well as purchase vital equipment, such as blanket warming machines and our palliative and spiritual care program.

Imagine Patricia, combing her hair by the window before turning the lights out for the night. She looks out at the lightly falling snow and the lovely Caring Trees shining with twinkling lights.

As she continues to comb her hair, she smiles knowing that every light represents a friend like you out there who cares. Cares for her and cares for St. Pat's. And Patricia will feel that warmth just as she feels the warmth of her own room.

Please join us in this Christmas Caring Tree tradition once again. You'll be brightening the holidays for all the Residents of our Home.

Sharing the warmth of the holidays with you and yours,

Ruth Catana, Executive Director

PS: I wish you and yours a most joyous Christmas and holiday season. Please send your dedicated ornament and special holiday gift as soon as you can, to brighten our Home for our many residents. Thank you!

Fig. 10.1

For the full-sized reply form, (Fig. 10.2) we didn't need to head back to Ottawa to get a photo of Patricia sitting at her window, enjoying the lovely falling snowflakes, and admiring the tree outside. Instead, we asked Veronica Davies to come up with a compelling illustration based on one of the images we'd taken months before for the video.

We often use illustrations as a way to bring the donor close to their giving. Seeing lovely Patricia sitting in her room admiring the decorated trees? This is about as close as you can get to understanding the impact of your gift!

Last, we included this "fragile" Christmas light ornament (Fig. 10.3) for donors to write on and send back with their gift.

We also created banners for the St. Patrick's Home of Ottawa website for those donors who might put the pack down and head online to give.

Creating personal connections to beneficiaries, whenever you can, creates deeper connections to giving.

Humans give to humans. Full stop.

But sometimes, they will give to animals too.

Fig. 10.2 — We shot this photo (above) of Patricia in her room back in the summer time but we wanted an "updated" image for the holiday appeal without having to trudge all the way back to Ottawa to reshoot it in the winter. Luckily for us, Veronica Davies was able to put Patricia (right) into this perfect illustration for the holiday reply form.

Yes, Ruth! I'll brighten the holidays for the residents of St. Pat's with my gift of:

❍ $XX ❍ $XXX ❍ $XXXX OR ❍ $______

❍ I have enclosed my cheque, payable to St. Patrick's Home of Ottawa Foundation OR

❍ I prefer to pay by credit card. Please charge my ❑ VISA ❑ MC

Card Number

Expiry

Cardholder Name

Signature

Rachel Zant
1234 Generosity Street
XXXX, XX, XXXXX
XXXX, XX, XXXXX
XXXX, XX, XXXXX

Your ornaments are enclosed! Please send one in, along with your holiday message and your special gift, as soon as possible, so we can display it for our residents. Thank you for your generous support!

Your privacy is very important to us. The information you provide will be used to keep you informed of our activities or to contact you regarding your donation. You can read our full privacy policy at www.stpats.ca.

Const ID/AppealCode XX-XXX-XXX

2865 Riverside Drive, Ottawa, Ontario K1V 8N5 www.stpats.ca

For you...

For our residents like Patricia...

Here are your special ornaments from the residents of St. Pat's!

One ornament is for you. We hope you'll put it on display at home as a reminder of our gratitude for your caring support.

On the other ornament, we've left a space for you to share a special holiday message or the name of someone you would like to honour. Please return it to us, along with your special gift, as soon as possible so that we can display it in our Home and brighten the holidays for our residents.

Thank you for sharing your warmth and light with us this Christmas season.

St. Patrick's Home of Ottawa Foundation

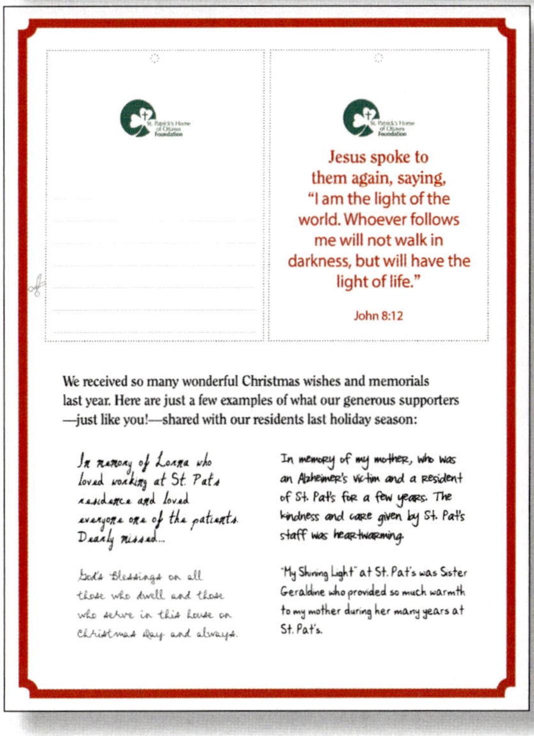

St. Patrick's Home of Ottawa Foundation

Jesus spoke to them again, saying, "I am the light of the world. Whoever follows me will not walk in darkness, but will have the light of life."

John 8:12

We received so many wonderful Christmas wishes and memorials last year. Here are just a few examples of what our generous supporters —just like you!—shared with our residents last holiday season:

In memory of Lorna who loved working at St. Pats residence and loved everyone one of the patients. Dearly missed...

God's Blessings on all those who dwell and those who serve in this house on Christmas day and always.

In memory of my mother, who was an Alzheimer's victim and a resident of St. Pat's for a few years. The kindness and care given by St. Pat's staff was heartwarming.

"My Shining Light" at St. Pat's was Sister Geraldine who provided so much warmth to my mother during her many years at St. Pat's.

Fig. 10.3

As I write this chapter, we are hopefully emerging from two years of a pandemic (COVID-19, if you are reading this many, many years in the future).

The year we created this next example was 2020.

The above photo was a pretty typical scene from Camp Ooch the summer before COVID hit but overnight, they went from crowds of kids to this:

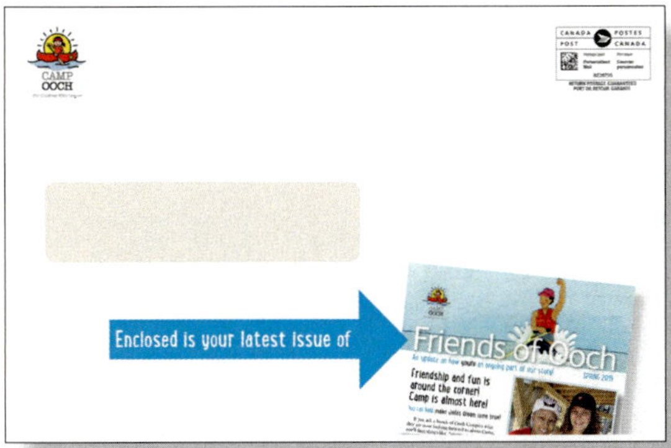

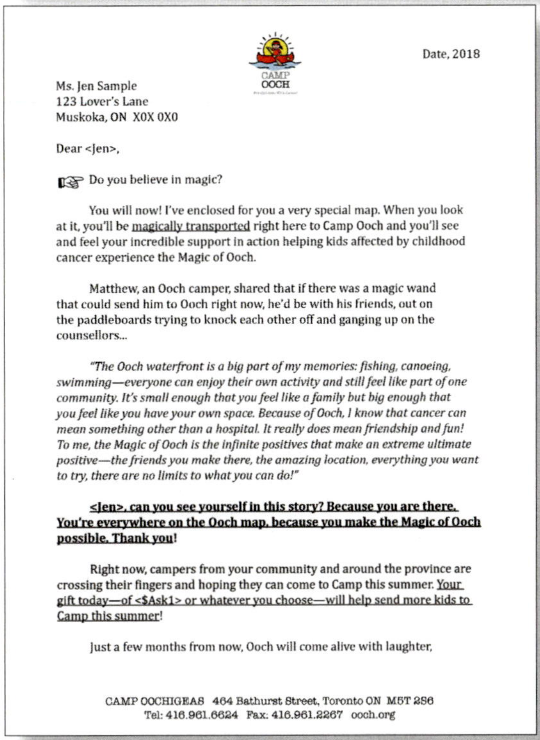

CAMP OOCH

Date, 2018

Ms. Jen Sample
123 Lover's Lane
Muskoka, ON X0X 0X0

Dear <Jen>,

Do you believe in magic?

You will now! I've enclosed for you a very special map. When you look at it, you'll be magically transported right here to Camp Ooch and you'll see and feel your incredible support in action helping kids affected by childhood cancer experience the Magic of Ooch.

Matthew, an Ooch camper, shared that if there was a magic wand that could send him to Ooch right now, he'd be with his friends, out on the paddleboards trying to knock each other off and ganging up on the counsellors...

"The Ooch waterfront is a big part of my memories: fishing, canoeing, swimming—everyone can enjoy their own activity and still feel like part of one community. It's small enough that you feel like a family but big enough that you feel like you have your own space. Because of Ooch, I know that cancer can mean something other than a hospital. It really does mean friendship and fun! To me, the Magic of Ooch is the infinite positives that make an extreme ultimate positive—the friends you make there, the amazing location, everything you want to try, there are no limits to what you can do!"

<Jen>, can you see yourself in this story? Because you are there. You're everywhere on the Ooch map, because you make the Magic of Ooch possible. Thank you!

Right now, campers from your community and around the province are crossing their fingers and hoping they can come to Camp this summer. Your gift today—of <$Ask1> or whatever you choose—will help send more kids to Camp this summer!

Just a few months from now, Ooch will come alive with laughter,

CAMP OOCHIGEAS 464 Bathurst Street, Toronto ON M5T 2S6
Tel: 416.961.6624 Fax: 416.961.2267 ooch.org

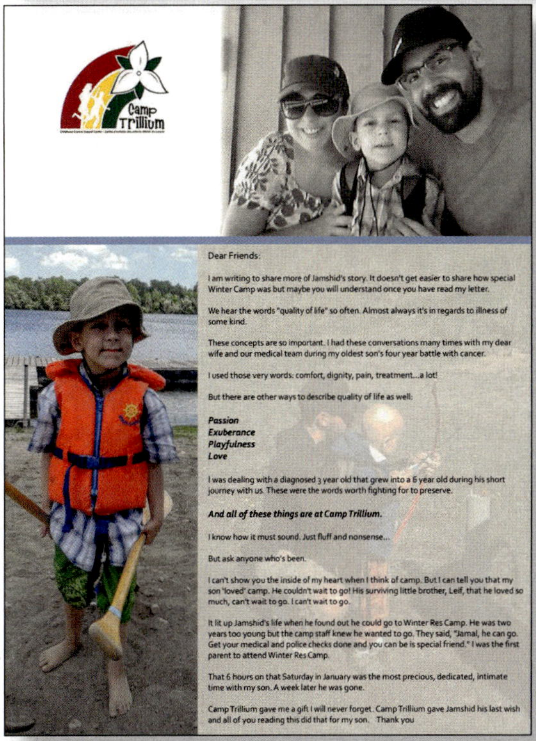

Camp Trillium

Dear Friends:

I am writing to share more of Jamshid's story. It doesn't get easier to share how special Winter Camp was but maybe you will understand once you have read my letter.

We hear the words "quality of life" so often. Almost always it's in regards to illness of some kind.

These concepts are so important. I had these conversations many times with my dear wife and our medical team during my oldest son's four year battle with cancer.

I used those very words: comfort, dignity, pain, treatment...a lot!

But there are other ways to describe quality of life as well:

Passion
Exuberance
Playfulness
Love

I was dealing with a diagnosed 3 year old that grew into a 6 year old during his short journey with us. These were the words worth fighting for to preserve.

And all of these things are at Camp Trillium.

I know how it must sound. Just fluff and nonsense...

But ask anyone who's been.

I can't show you the inside of my heart when I think of camp. But I can tell you that my son 'loved' camp. He couldn't wait to go! His surviving little brother, Leif, that he loved so much, can't wait to go. I can't wait to go.

It lit up Jamshid's life when he found out he could go to Winter Res Camp. He was two years too young but the camp staff knew he wanted to go. They said, "Jamal, he can go. Get your medical and police checks done and you can be is special friend." I was the first parent to attend Winter Res Camp.

That 6 hours on that Saturday in January was the most precious, dedicated, intimate time with my son. A week later he was gone.

Camp Trillium gave me a gift I will never forget. Camp Trillium gave Jamshid his last wish and all of you reading this did that for my son. Thank you

Like all of us, Camp Ooch had entered a new reality. The ability to meet their core mission of sending kids to camp had evaporated overnight.

This occurred at the same time Camp Ooch was merging with another organization, Camp Trillium. They were two camps doing similar things but certainly had different ways of talking to donors.

Agent Jen Love and I knew from the start that we would have to be thoughtful about how to mix two different "design" approaches as well as two distinct pools of donors.

Organizationally, you might get all kinds of fired up when a merger happens or when you go through a rebrand. But to be honest, donors don't care much about that. They DO care when all you do is talk about the merger and stop giving them compelling reasons to give or tangible problems they can help solve.

I wasn't too worried from a storytelling point of view.

I knew we just needed to keep telling great stories, and show donors the potential impact of their gifts. I also knew we could simply keep following good direct response design practice and we'd be okay.

But then… COVID. No more camp. Not for a while.

That's when we knew we were going to have to get creative with our storytelling.

This was the envelope I designed for the spring appeal — the one that dropped just after COVID arrived — and the first after the merger. It wasn't made to look like an emergency pack of any kind. We used both logos side by side and a visually interesting indicia with no image or tagline. Simple and effective.

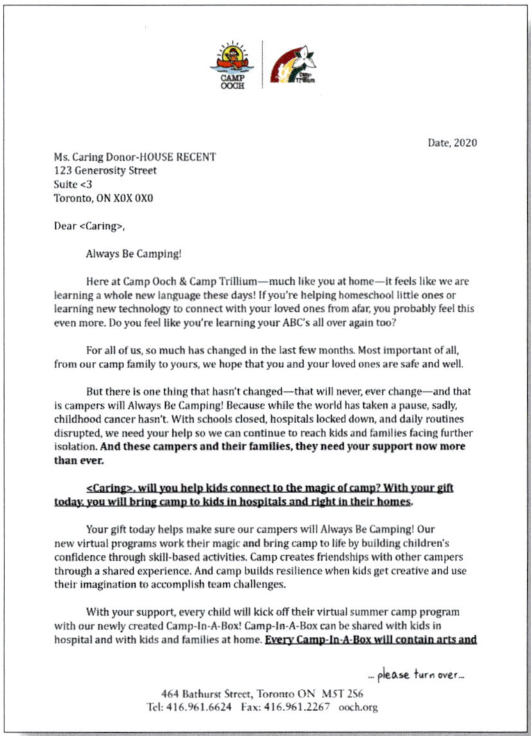

CAMP OOCH

Date, 2020

Ms. Caring Donor-HOUSE RECENT
123 Generosity Street
Suite <3
Toronto, ON X0X 0X0

Dear <Caring>,

Always Be Camping!

Here at Camp Ooch & Camp Trillium—much like you at home—it feels like we are learning a whole new language these days! If you're helping homeschool little ones or learning new technology to connect with your loved ones from afar, you probably feel this even more. Do you feel like you're learning your ABC's all over again too?

For all of us, so much has changed in the last few months. Most important of all, from our camp family to yours, we hope that you and your loved ones are safe and well.

But there is one thing that hasn't changed—that will never, ever change—and that is campers will Always Be Camping! Because while the world has taken a pause, sadly, childhood cancer hasn't. With schools closed, hospitals locked down, and daily routines disrupted, we need your help so we can continue to reach kids and families facing further isolation. **And these campers and their families, they need your support now more than ever.**

<Caring>, will you help kids connect to the magic of camp? With your gift today, you will bring camp to kids in hospitals and right in their homes.

Your gift today helps make sure our campers will Always Be Camping! Our new virtual programs work their magic and bring camp to life by building children's confidence through skill-based activities. Camp creates friendships with other campers through a shared experience. And camp builds resilience when kids get creative and use their imagination to accomplish team challenges.

With your support, every child will kick off their virtual summer camp program with our newly created Camp-In-A-Box! Camp-In-A-Box can be shared with kids in hospital and with kids and families at home. **Every Camp-In-A-Box will contain arts and**

…please turn over…

464 Bathurst Street, Toronto ON M5T 2S6
Tel: 416.961.6624 Fax: 416.961.2267 ooch.org

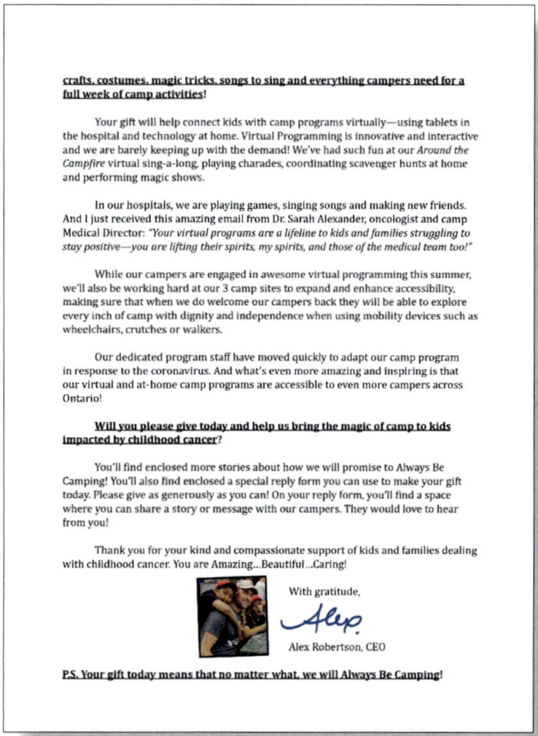

crafts, costumes, magic tricks, songs to sing and everything campers need for a full week of camp activities!

Your gift will help connect kids with camp programs virtually—using tablets in the hospital and technology at home. Virtual Programming is innovative and interactive and we are barely keeping up with the demand! We've had such fun at our *Around the Campfire* virtual sing-a-long, playing charades, coordinating scavenger hunts at home and performing magic shows.

In our hospitals, we are playing games, singing songs and making new friends. And I just received this amazing email from Dr. Sarah Alexander, oncologist and camp Medical Director: *"Your virtual programs are a lifeline to kids and families struggling to stay positive—you are lifting their spirits, my spirits, and those of the medical team too!"*

While our campers are engaged in awesome virtual programming this summer, we'll also be working hard at our 3 camp sites to expand and enhance accessibility, making sure that when we do welcome our campers back they will be able to explore every inch of camp with dignity and independence when using mobility devices such as wheelchairs, crutches or walkers.

Our dedicated program staff have moved quickly to adapt our camp program in response to the coronavirus. And what's even more amazing and inspiring is that our virtual and at-home camp programs are accessible to even more campers across Ontario!

Will you please give today and help us bring the magic of camp to kids impacted by childhood cancer?

You'll find enclosed more stories about how we will promise to Always Be Camping! You'll also find enclosed a special reply form you can use to make your gift today. Please give as generously as you can! On your reply form, you'll find a space where you can share a story or message with our campers. They would love to hear from you!

Thank you for your kind and compassionate support of kids and families dealing with childhood cancer. You are Amazing…Beautiful…Caring!

With gratitude,

Alex

Alex Robertson, CEO

P.S. Your gift today means that no matter what, we will Always Be Camping!

The two-page letter talked about the importance of camping for Camp Ooch/Trillium kids and the ABCs! Always Be Camping! The donor could help bring camp to kids by giving to the "Camp in a Box" idea.

The letter used a 14pt font and was typeset to look like a personal letter from Alex to "Ms. Caring Donor."

The full size reply form utilized every bit of space we had. It had lots of white

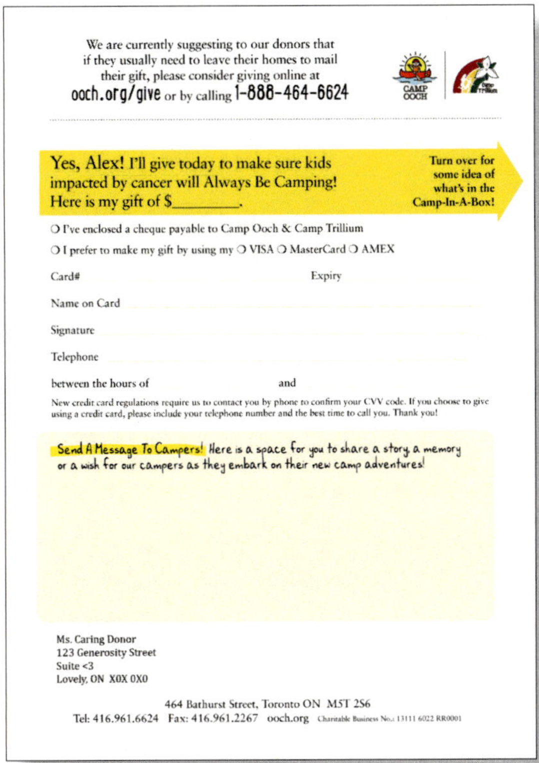

We are currently suggesting to our donors that if they usually need to leave their homes to mail their gift, please consider giving online at ooch.org/give or by calling 1-888-464-6624

CAMP OOCH

Yes, Alex! I'll give today to make sure kids impacted by cancer will Always Be Camping! Here is my gift of $________.

Turn over for some idea of what's in the Camp-In-A-Box!

❍ I've enclosed a cheque payable to Camp Ooch & Camp Trillium

❍ I prefer to make my gift by using my ❍ VISA ❍ MasterCard ❍ AMEX

Card# Expiry

Name on Card

Signature

Telephone

between the hours of and

New credit card regulations require us to contact you by phone to confirm your CVV code. If you choose to give using a credit card, please include your telephone number and the best time to call you. Thank you!

Send A Message To Campers! Here is a space for you to share a story, a memory or a wish for our campers as they embark on their new camp adventures!

Ms. Caring Donor
123 Generosity Street
Suite <3
Lovely, ON X0X 0X0

464 Bathurst Street, Toronto ON M5T 2S6
Tel: 416.961.6624 Fax: 416.961.2267 ooch.org Charitable Business No.: 13111 6022 RR0001

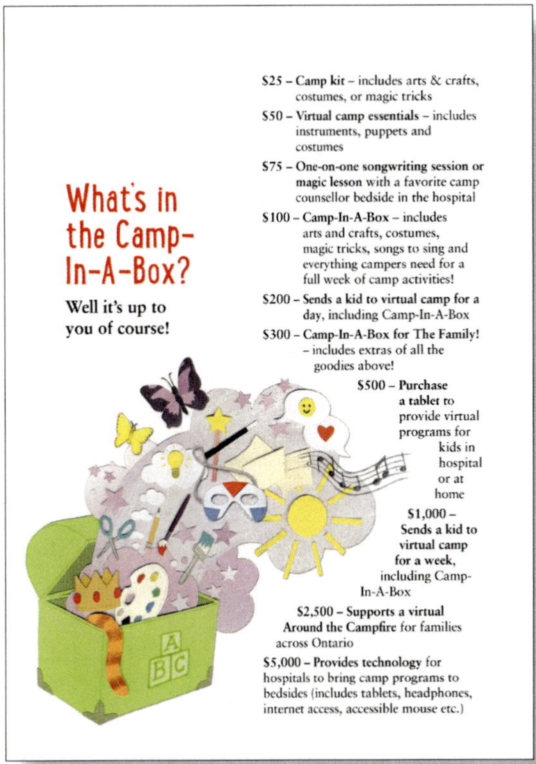

What's in the Camp-In-A-Box?

Well it's up to you of course!

$25 – **Camp kit** – includes arts & crafts, costumes, or magic tricks

$50 – **Virtual camp essentials** – includes instruments, puppets and costumes

$75 – **One-on-one songwriting session or magic lesson** with a favorite camp counsellor bedside in the hospital

$100 – **Camp-In-A-Box** – includes arts and crafts, costumes, magic tricks, songs to sing and everything campers need for a full week of camp activities!

$200 – **Sends a kid to virtual camp for a day**, including Camp-In-A-Box

$300 – **Camp-In-A-Box for The Family!** – includes extras of all the goodies above!

$500 – **Purchase a tablet** to provide virtual programs for kids in hospital or at home

$1,000 – **Sends a kid to virtual camp for a week,** including Camp-In-A-Box

$2,500 – **Supports a virtual Around the Campfire** for families across Ontario

$5,000 – **Provides technology** for hospitals to bring camp programs to bedsides (includes tablets, headphones, internet access, accessible mouse etc.)

space and included room for the donor to write their credit card details and send back a note to campers if they wished to do so.

For the first time ever, we suggested to donors that if they thought it would be safer to give online or call in their gift, they could do that. Traditionally, we would avoid that. You have donors in a moment. If they are holding your reply form in their hands, ready to write a cheque or scribble in their credit card number, the last thing you want to do is distract them. But these were not normal times.

On the back, we asked Jessica Rae Gordon to help imagine all of the fun things that would be included in our "Camp in a Box"– flying out for all of the kids that would be receiving one. We also "unpacked" the box to show donors what their gifts could do. This always helps raise the average gift since your donor will understand what their $200 can accomplish.

We included a simple lift note featuring the words of a beneficiary's mom.

CAMP OOCH

Thatcher loves loves *LOVES* Ooch. Like so many families, we met the Ooch team the same day that Thatcher was diagnosed with leukemia. I cannot even imagine what our cancer journey would be like without the love and kindness we get from Ooch. When I heard that camp was cancelled this year, *my heart was broken and crushed to think about kids and families* who wouldn't have the same experiences as us. You don't know just how alone you feel when your child is that sick. You're already isolated and distancing from friends and even family members. Right now it would be just devastating if families with sick kids didn't have Ooch.

I'm overwhelmed with joy and relief to know that the hospital programs are still going strong and that virtual camp is up and running. It absolutely warmed my heart to join the Around the Campfire virtual event recently. It was like a 4 hour activity in our home. *We all got our Ooch shirts*, braids and bling, *set up a little fort* with our Ooch blankets and drank hot chocolate in our Ooch mugs. *We sang with friends* and shared stories. And then *we chatted about it* for hours afterwards. Thatcher was so thrilled and he's looking forward to even more new camp adventures! He's also obsessed with Star Wars right now and he's working that into his camp crafts and songs here at home.

I also know that you are someone who gives to Ooch, and I want to thank you from the very bottom of my heart. I am so grateful for your generosity. And I want you to know that even though camp is changing, it's just as important as ever—maybe even more important right now. Anything you can give means more magic for even more kids. Thank you!

— **Erin**, Jedi Knight Thatcher's mom

Obviously, at the time we thought this might get us over the hump. The whole COVID thing would be gone soon right? Right?

Nope.

This was the new reality for Camp Ooch and Camp Trillium and the kids and families they served. Our challenge was how to keep telling stories without using lots of images of kids on iPads and participating in zoom calls.

We wanted to remind donors that camp was still happening. Just in a totally different way. We certainly didn't want to lose the warm feelings associated with camping by using lots of images of kids behind cold screens.

Often in storytelling, it's not the story you need to change. It's the perspective.

Or the *way* you tell it.

Or *who* tells it.

Next up in the Camp Ooch schedule was a newsletter pack, meant to report back

on the impact of donor gifts.

This pack had a cover letter that went along with the newsletter. It was light in tone, pointed out a few articles, made an ask, and invited donor feedback.

The reply form featured the donor's name and address very prominently at the top. Then, we included this note

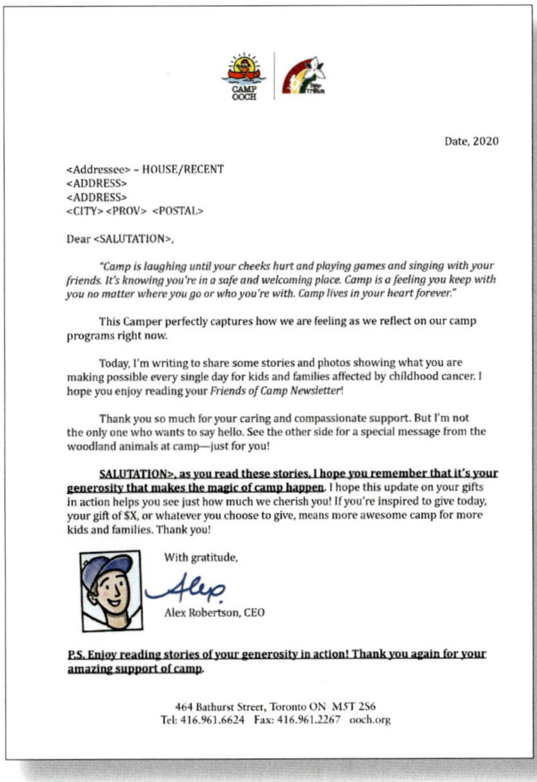

CAMP OOCH

Date, 2020

<Addressee> – HOUSE/RECENT
<ADDRESS>
<ADDRESS>
<CITY> <PROV> <POSTAL>

Dear <SALUTATION>,

"Camp is laughing until your cheeks hurt and playing games and singing with your friends. It's knowing you're in a safe and welcoming place. Camp is a feeling you keep with you no matter where you go or who you're with. Camp lives in your heart forever."

This Camper perfectly captures how we are feeling as we reflect on our camp programs right now.

Today, I'm writing to share some stories and photos showing what you are making possible every single day for kids and families affected by childhood cancer. I hope you enjoy reading your *Friends of Camp Newsletter*!

Thank you so much for your caring and compassionate support. But I'm not the only one who wants to say hello. See the other side for a special message from the woodland animals at camp—just for you!

SALUTATION>, as you read these stories, I hope you remember that it's your generosity that makes the magic of camp happen. I hope this update on your gifts in action helps you see just how much we cherish you! If you're inspired to give today, your gift of $X, or whatever you choose to give, means more awesome camp for more kids and families. Thank you!

With gratitude,

Alex

Alex Robertson, CEO

P.S. Enjoy reading stories of your generosity in action! Thank you again for your amazing support of camp.

464 Bathurst Street, Toronto ON M5T 2S6
Tel: 416.961.6624 Fax: 416.961.2267 ooch.org

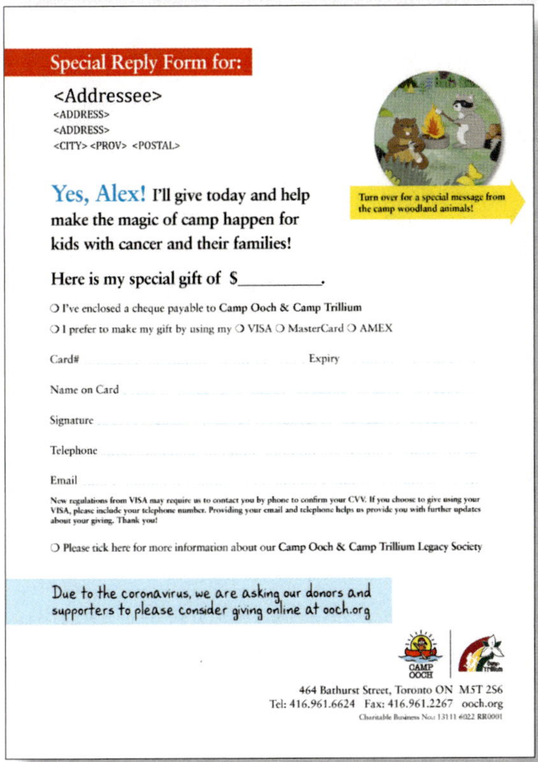

CAMP OOCH

Special Reply Form for:

<Addressee>
<ADDRESS>
<ADDRESS>
<CITY> <PROV> <POSTAL>

Turn over for a special message from the camp woodland animals!

Yes, Alex! I'll give today and help make the magic of camp happen for kids with cancer and their families!

Here is my special gift of $________.

❍ I've enclosed a cheque payable to **Camp Ooch & Camp Trillium**

❍ I prefer to make my gift by using my ❍ VISA ❍ MasterCard ❍ AMEX

Card# Expiry

Name on Card

Signature

Telephone

Email

New regulations from VISA may require us to contact you by phone to confirm your CVV. If you choose to give using your VISA, please include your telephone number. Providing your email and telephone helps us provide you with further updates about your giving. Thank you!

❍ Please tick here for more information about our **Camp Ooch & Camp Trillium Legacy Society**

Due to the coronavirus, we are asking our donors and supporters to please consider giving online at ooch.org

CAMP OOCH

464 Bathurst Street, Toronto ON M5T 2S6
Tel: 416.961.6624 Fax: 416.961.2267 ooch.org

— GREETINGS FROM —

CAMP OOCH

Thank you so much for your kind and caring heart!

It certainly has been a different year here at camp without the hustle and bustle of kids and families. But we know that your virtual camps have been awesome.

All of us woodland animals sure do miss the sounds of laughter and singing and splashing!

We know that you are one of the terrific people who give to camp and make magic possible. Even if the campers weren't here in person this year, you sure made their summer special and brought them smiles and laughter and love just the same. And we think that makes you a really, really good friend. Thank you!

Anyway, take care of your loved ones—and we'll look forward to welcoming camper families and helpers like you back to camp sometime soon! We'll take care of camp for you; you keep taking care of our campers!

XOXO Love,

Your Woodland Animals!

with a special message from the camp woodland friends.

Using the voice of "woodland friends" on the back completely changed the tone of the message. These creatures could say all sorts of things a "professional" human wouldn't.

There is something to be said for bringing this kind of levity into your messaging.

These woodland animals were holding down the fort and taking care of camp until the kids could come back.

The detail in this illustration by Jessica Rae Gordon is sublime.

The four-page newsletter **(Fig. 10.4)** checked a lot of boxes for a great donor news-

letter but I want to focus on this one part **(Fig. 10.5)**.

Donors (and campers!) really enjoyed the idea of woodland friends taking care of things around camp and staying ready for when the camp would re-open.

Fast-forward to June of 2021, we found out that camp would return.

And so our direct mail package returned to the animal friends who were still

Fig. 10.4

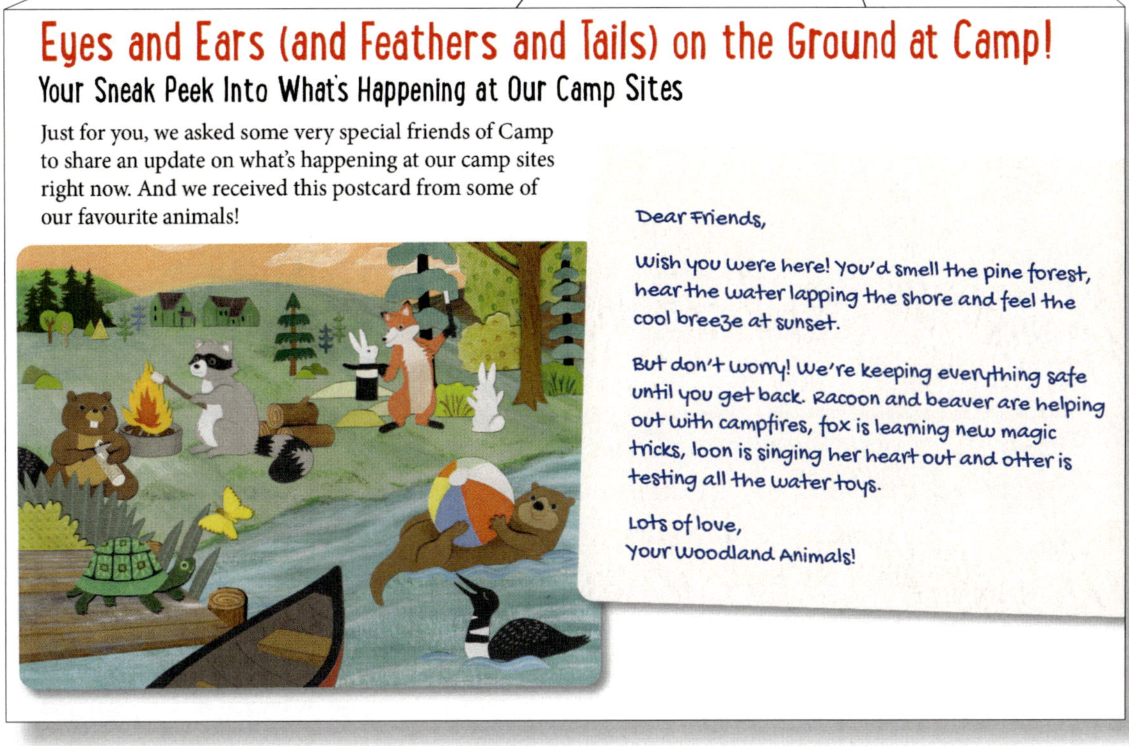

Fig. 10.5

there, excitedly waiting to greet all the wonderful kids and their families after a long 16 months apart.

We developed this piece (**Fig. 10.6**) for Camp Ooch's mid to high-level donors. A 5″ x 5″ storybook designed to give families a friendly tour around camp. It was a space where our woodland friends overlapped with real life. Where we could let everyone come back together.

We wanted to show donors the things they made possible.

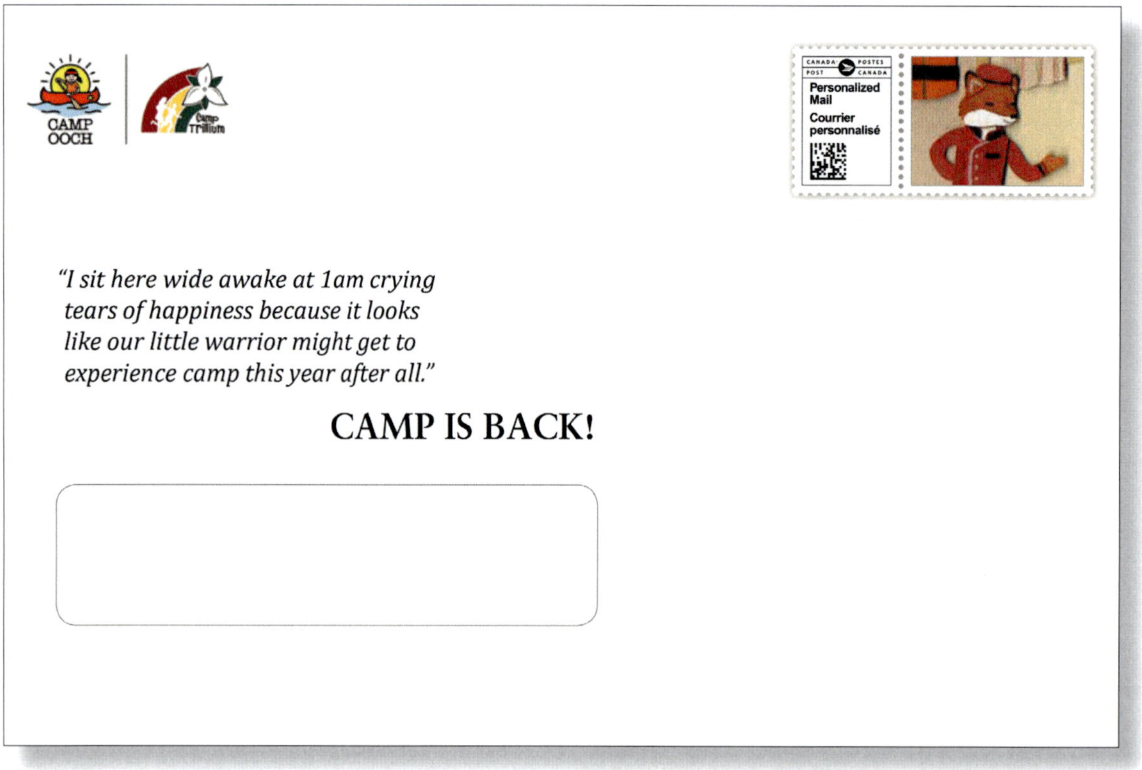

Fig. 10.6

By the time the donor flips to the final page of this lovingly-prepared insert, they fully understand how their support is needed, how appreciated it will be and how it will make such a difference to the returning families.

The point is this: sometimes in fundraising (just like in life), we are handed tough situations that make our work difficult. Look at it as an opportunity to get creative in keeping your donors connected with their giving.

Soaring overhead, Eagle can show you what's happening at archery and on the ropes course. For these beloved camp activities, two Camper families will be able to participate at once, while staying in their own bubbles.
Over on the ropes course, one family can scale the rock wall while another one braves the high ropes. Between families, staff will do a thorough cleaning of all the harnesses and equipment before welcoming the next family!
"And when Dad fires his arrow into the woods, he'll just have to go collect it himself!"

"Keep 6 ukuleles apart to maintain your safe distancing!"
Beaver is ready for improvised jazz jams and music of all kinds in our music programs! Campers will play their hearts out around the campfire on ukuleles and percussion, with lots of clapping and foot stomping instead of loud singing.
"Step right up!"
Turtle and bunny are here at the arts and crafts window. A little planning won't dampen our creativity! Campers just hop up to the window to request paint supplies, slime kits, bling materials or whatever their heart desires, and we'll offer fresh, clean supplies for each family every single time.

"Safety first—but fun right after that!"
Racoon is here to remind you: he's been rocking the mask since long before COVID. In addition to masks, there will be hand washing and hygiene stations everywhere on our camp sites. Each Camper will have their own PPE Kit too.

"Welcome!"
Fabulous Mr. Fox is like a fancy hotel concierge, showing you our updated cabins! Every Camper family has their own cabin and washroom, and this is their safe family space. Parents can have their morning coffee right here, and some of our meals will be picnic style so families can eat them here or just outside.
Each cabin will have a Wilderness Kit for when Campers just gotta go chase a butterfly. Oh, and when Campers arrive, everyone gets their own lifejacket, to be kept at their cabin when not on the water.

Otter says:
"Grab your lifejackets and join the waterfront adventures!"
A group of teens is heading off on a week-long canoe trip of a lifetime. And meanwhile, kids and families can take turns with various water sports. Keep two pool noodles apart on the dock and you're good to go!

"Day is done, gone the sun,
from the lakes, from the hills,
from the sky, all is well,
safely rest, camp is nigh."
As the sun sets on our story today, remember that your kindness and generosity today will mean more camp adventures for kids and their families impacted by childhood cancer. Thank you!

STONE SOUP

I'll say it again. The hard work is yours. Your job is to find stories that creatively engage donors in their giving. Far too often I hear, "we don't have any stories to share" or "we don't have any stories that highlight what we are asking donors for." The worst are those organizations that barely even try to inject even the tiniest bit of creativity into their asking.

And then there are organizations that are willing to take a big creative leap.

The following example is an early-in-the-year appeal we created for Food Banks Canada.

The objectives were to:

- Educate and engage supporters by maintaining focus on donor impact and telling inspiring, meaningful stories
- Create highly-personalized version(s) for intermediate, leadership, and special supporters
- Connect with supporters on multiple channels: e-blasts, integrated messaging
- Reactivate lapsed, lapsing supporters

Agents of Good pitched four ideas for the appeal:

CONCEPT 1: SHORTFALL

Earnest. Urgent. Honest. You express to your donors that you are not where you want to be as you approach your year-end. "We're simply not where we wanted to be and we are looking at a shortfall of $25,000 from our community of supporters like you." Acknowledge the reasons — increased transportation costs, delivery of special programs and projects, expansion of programs, spike in need for help from local food bank partners.

Test Considerations:

- The right "Shortfall" pack is simple, direct, and a bit breathless. Rather than test creative, we would recommend using funds available for testing to use real stamps, closed-face envelopes, high-touch personalization (even if it's done at the mail house) for an expanded group of donors and prospects to see how it lifts response.

- Consider a follow-up pack (or testing a follow-up pack).

CONCEPT 2: KIDS

Focus on children and youth as a growing segment of food bank recipients. Rally around the shared belief that no child should go hungry. Share a story about a child, or create a profile to paint a picture for your donors. Use "kid art" as part of the creative to stand out in the mailbox and echo across channels.

Test Considerations:

- High-end premium like a notepad/shopping list.
- Pass-along piece to share with a friend to help feed a hungry kid right now (adapted from the "symbolic" offers we had in the fall prospect pack).

CONCEPT 3: STONE SOUP

Use the fable of Stone Soup as a way to talk about Food Banks Canada: we all add what we can and together we create nourishing, delicious meals for hungry families.

Test Considerations:

- High-end premium like a Recipe Card(s), Cookbook bookmark(s).

CONCEPT 4: LOVE

Send a little love to hungry families. Core offer is to share Valentines. Pack comes with one (or 2?) Valentine hearts that donors can send back with their gift to share with food bank partners, or share with a friend and spread the word about Food Banks Canada. A short story or testimonial would be great—perhaps even the same one we could use for kids.

Considerations:

- TIMING: Absolutely needs to go out on or ahead of schedule. And it's tight!
- Likely keep any testing simple to accommodate tight timeline, likely no opportunity for premium.

We decided to move ahead with the old fable of "Stone Soup." Do you know it?

A few days before the appeal was dropped into the mail system, we sent out this email teaser to all donors that we had addresses for. It linked back to the Food Banks website and was simple in design. An email teaser can help boost response rate to a mailing, even without a link back to the site.

A few days later, this envelope showed up in the mailboxes of donors across the country.

It was oversized and engaging.

The letter inside looked personal: 13 point type, large margins and it had the donors name and address at the top.

The full-size, 8.5″ x 11″ reply form offered a tailored gift array, based on the donor's previous giving. It had plenty of white space with zero tiny boxes for donors to write their credit card information in to. (I know, you've heard this before!)

Then, we created a lift piece **(Fig 10.7)** to bring the story of Stone Soup to life.

The finished (or folded size) was 5″ x 3.5″.

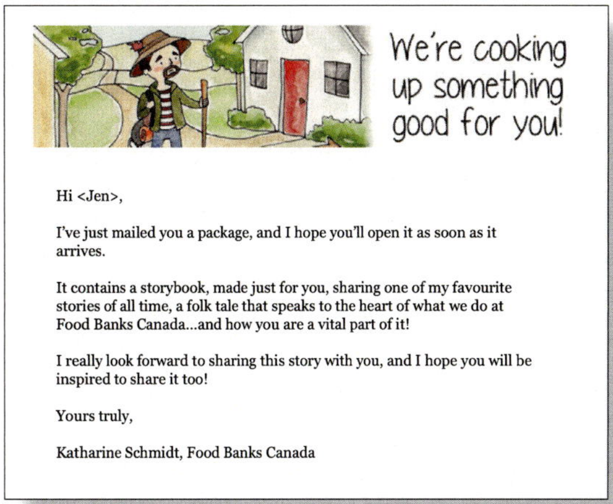
We're cooking up something good for you!

Hi <Jen>,

I've just mailed you a package, and I hope you'll open it as soon as it arrives.

It contains a storybook, made just for you, sharing one of my favourite stories of all time, a folk tale that speaks to the heart of what we do at Food Banks Canada...and how you are a vital part of it!

I really look forward to sharing this story with you, and I hope you will be inspired to share it too!

Yours truly,

Katharine Schmidt, Food Banks Canada

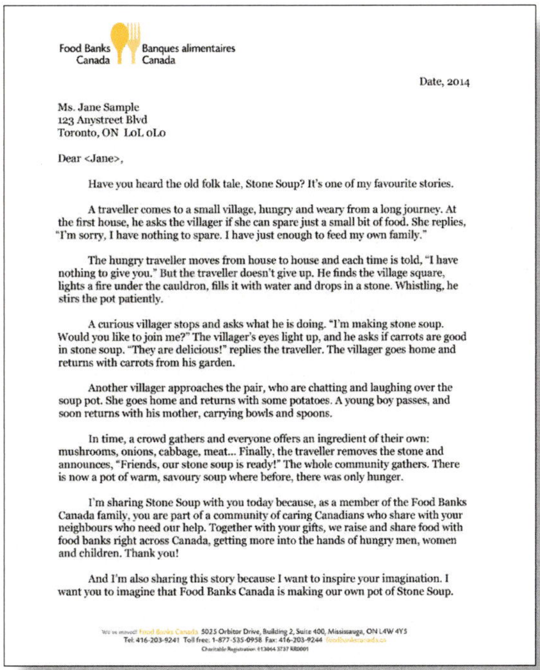
Food Banks Canada | Banques alimentaires Canada

Date, 2014

Ms. Jane Sample
123 Anystreet Blvd
Toronto, ON LoL oLo

Dear <Jane>,

Have you heard the old folk tale, Stone Soup? It's one of my favourite stories.

A traveller comes to a small village, hungry and weary from a long journey. At the first house, he asks the villager if she can spare just a small bit of food. She replies, "I'm sorry, I have nothing to spare. I have just enough to feed my own family."

The hungry traveller moves from house to house and each time is told, "I have nothing to give you." But the traveller doesn't give up. He finds the village square, lights a fire under the cauldron, fills it with water and drops in a stone. Whistling, he stirs the pot patiently.

A curious villager stops and asks what he is doing. "I'm making stone soup. Would you like to join me?" The villager's eyes light up, and he asks if carrots are good in stone soup. "They are delicious!" replies the traveller. The villager goes home and returns with carrots from his garden.

Another villager approaches the pair, who are chatting and laughing over the soup pot. She goes home and returns with some potatoes. A young boy passes, and soon returns with his mother, carrying bowls and spoons.

In time, a crowd gathers and everyone offers an ingredient of their own: mushrooms, onions, cabbage, meat... Finally, the traveller removes the stone and announces, "Friends, our stone soup is ready!" The whole community gathers. There is now a pot of warm, savoury soup where before, there was only hunger.

I'm sharing Stone Soup with you today because, as a member of the Food Banks Canada family, you are part of a community of caring Canadians who share with your neighbours who need our help. Together with your gifts, we raise and share food with food banks right across Canada, getting more into the hands of hungry men, women and children. Thank you!

And I'm also sharing this story because I want to inspire your imagination. I want you to imagine that Food Banks Canada is making our own pot of Stone Soup.

5025 Orbitor Drive, Building 2, Suite 400, Mississauga, ON L4W 4Y5
Tel: 416-203-9241 Toll free: 1-877-535-0958 Fax: 416-203-9244

Food Banks Canada | Banques alimentaires Canada

Yes, Katharine! I'll help contribute to our Stone Soup!

Here is my gift of:

❍ $50 ❍ $100

❍ $200 ❍ I prefer to give $______

❍ I have enclosed my cheque, payable to **Food Banks Canada.**

OR

❍ I prefer to use my credit card. Please charge my ❍ **VISA** ❍ **Mastercard** ❍ **AMEX**

Card Number: ______ Expiry: ______

Signature: ______ Date: ______

Thank you for your gift today!

Information update:

My phone number is: ______

My email address is: ______

Please write in any changes to your mailing address as it appears below.

Your privacy is very important to us. The information you provide will be used to keep you informed of our activities or to contact you regarding your donation. You can read our full privacy policy at foodbankscanada.ca

Ms. Jane Sample
123 Anystreet Blvd
Toronto, ON LoL oLo

5025 Orbitor Drive, Building 2, Suite 400, Mississauga, ON L4W 4Y5
Tel: 416-203-9241 Toll free: 1-877-535-0958 Fax: 416-203-9244

Fig. 10.7

It was a simple story, creatively told, that engaged donors by showing them the impact of their giving — in a fun way!

We created a banner **(Fig. 10.8)** for the Food Banks Canada website home page. It linked to a page **(Fig. 10.9)** that retold the stone soup story — and of course offered the chance to make a gift.

We also incorporated the story into Food Bank Canada's Twitter feed **(Fig. 10.10)** and Facebook page **(Fig. 10.11)**.

And, even the website donation page.

So, what's the point?

Food Banks Canada cherishes every single gift we receive.

Just like the villagers in this story who bring carrots or potatoes, when you give what you are able to share, and give from your heart, each and every gift is equally and vitally important. People like **you** help Food Banks Canada make our own Stone Soup. And it's a perfect and delicious recipe, made with love to help warm the bellies and hearts of our neighbours. **Thank you!**

Food Banks Canada | Banques alimentaires Canada
foodbankscanada.ca

Well, a couple things.

- Food Banks Canada donors had never seen anything like this before. It was obvious that stock illustrations were not used. The images were intentionally created just for them. In fact, Food Banks Canada received many requests for extra copies of the Stone Soup storybook.
- Sprinkling bits of this story across all of the channels that donors were using allowed them to interact in whatever channel they wanted. The organization wasn't mixing messages and visuals.

Fig. 10.8 homepage banner , 10.9 internal web page, 10.10 twitter feed, 10.11 Facebook header

As I like to remind our Agents of Good clients, if you are doing this work properly, then every time you send an appeal, you should measure the response across ***all*** of your channels, not just one or the other in isolation.

FIELD WORK

Here is one last example of how you can creatively tell stories even when there might not be a lot of stories to tell.

COVID-19 forced us to rethink how we tell stories. The following two-page letter from Caroline, the Executive Director at Ontario Nature, really nailed that idea.

Conservation and field work had been scaled back in 2020. Obviously not because of the rain or wind, but because of a global pandemic. Nevertheless, important work was still happening at Ontario Nature, and this letter shares how and what was happening.

The package included a simple reply form as well as this lovingly-crafted "field notes" lift piece (Fig. 10.12) from some of the amazing conservation staff.

The words came from Nature Ontario staff, and then the talented Veronica Davies, did the simple illustrations to bring their words to life.

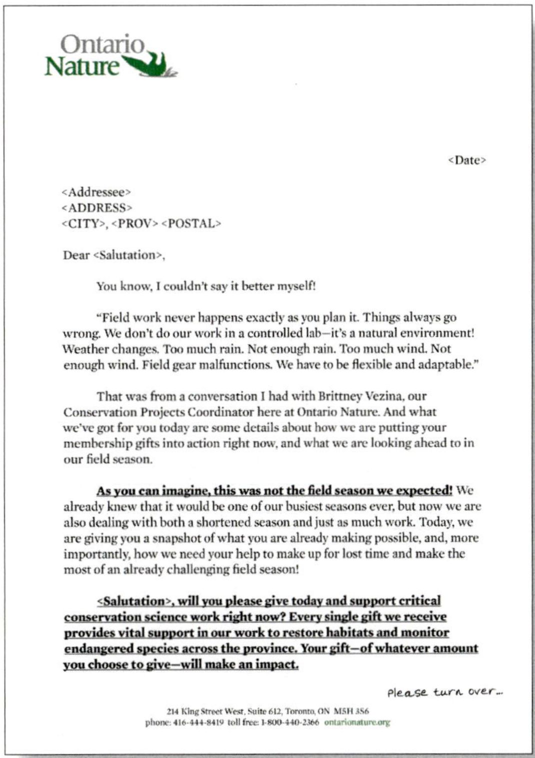

Ontario Nature

<Date>

<Addressee>
<ADDRESS>
<CITY>, <PROV> <POSTAL>

Dear <Salutation>,

You know, I couldn't say it better myself!

"Field work never happens exactly as you plan it. Things always go wrong. We don't do our work in a controlled lab—it's a natural environment! Weather changes. Too much rain. Not enough rain. Too much wind. Not enough wind. Field gear malfunctions. We have to be flexible and adaptable."

That was from a conversation I had with Brittney Vezina, our Conservation Projects Coordinator here at Ontario Nature. And what we've got for you today are some details about how we are putting your membership gifts into action right now, and what we are looking ahead to in our field season.

As you can imagine, this was not the field season we expected! We already knew that it would be one of our busiest seasons ever, but now we are also dealing with both a shortened season and just as much work. Today, we are giving you a snapshot of what you are already making possible, and, more importantly, how we need your help to make up for lost time and make the most of an already challenging field season!

<Salutation>, will you please give today and support critical conservation science work right now? Every single gift we receive provides vital support in our work to restore habitats and monitor endangered species across the province. Your gift—of whatever amount you choose to give—will make an impact.

Please turn over...

214 King Street West, Suite 612, Toronto, ON M5H 3S6
phone: 416-444-8419 toll free: 1-800-440-2366 ontarionature.org

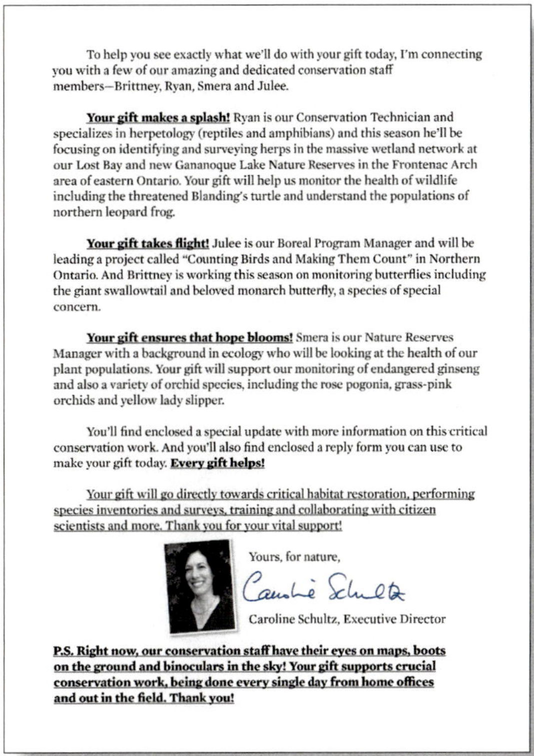

To help you see exactly what we'll do with your gift today, I'm connecting you with a few of our amazing and dedicated conservation staff members—Brittney, Ryan, Smera and Julee.

Your gift makes a splash! Ryan is our Conservation Technician and specializes in herpetology (reptiles and amphibians) and this season he'll be focusing on identifying and surveying herps in the massive wetland network at our Lost Bay and new Gananoque Lake Nature Reserves in the Frontenac Arch area of eastern Ontario. Your gift will help us monitor the health of wildlife including the threatened Blanding's turtle and understand the populations of northern leopard frog.

Your gift takes flight! Julee is our Boreal Program Manager and will be leading a project called "Counting Birds and Making Them Count" in Northern Ontario. And Brittney is working this season on monitoring butterflies including the giant swallowtail and beloved monarch butterfly, a species of special concern.

Your gift ensures that hope blooms! Smera is our Nature Reserves Manager with a background in ecology who will be looking at the health of our plant populations. Your gift will support our monitoring of endangered ginseng and also a variety of orchid species, including the rose pogonia, grass-pink orchids and yellow lady slipper.

You'll find enclosed a special update with more information on this critical conservation work. And you'll also find enclosed a reply form you can use to make your gift today. **Every gift helps!**

Your gift will go directly towards critical habitat restoration, performing species inventories and surveys, training and collaborating with citizen scientists and more. Thank you for your vital support!

Yours, for nature,

Caroline Schultz

Caroline Schultz, Executive Director

P.S. Right now, our conservation staff have their eyes on maps, boots on the ground and binoculars in the sky! Your gift supports crucial conservation work, being done every single day from home offices and out in the field. Thank you!

Fig. 10.12 — The field notes insert

Could we have used photographs? **Yes.**

Could we have used no images or illustrations? **Yes.**

However, this piece instantly becomes much more engaging by using the distinct voices and compelling "sketches" from Ontario Nature's staff.

As a result, lovely things happened.

Donors noticed.

Just like in real life, people appreciated the effort.

Never take your donors or their generosity for granted.

The time it takes to creatively tell stories, to show donors the importance of their giving and to sincerely thank them — that's our hard work.

The donor has done their work by considering making a gift.

Sometimes, you need to go further afield and wander off the well-trodden trail in order to imagine how to tell your stories. If you do the hard work, however, you'll keep your donors connected to their giving and to the causes they care very much about. Often, the more creative you can be, the more engaged they will become.

> Recently, I made a small donation to your organization in response to an appeal letter, dated May 28, 2020, from Caroline Schultz. Although I am a big fan of Ontario Nature and its mission and activities, I am not usually in the habit of making such donations. Instead, I have chosen to support your organization financially through a bequest in my will... It wasn't so much the letter that hooked me (although Caroline's writings are always good; I especially like her introductory columns in the ON Nature magazine). No, it was something else that convinced me to give: It was the lovely artwork! The wildlife sketches struck a chord in me. I would give my left arm [don't worry, I'm right-handed!] to be able to draw or paint like that.

Deviation Discoveries

There are many talented creatives out there who can help tell your stories in new ways. Using custom illustrations or photography doesn't have to be expensive, and it will entice your donors to engage with your appeals more fulsomely, since they are looking at something they have never seen before.

1. A picture is worth 1,000 words. But, sometimes, getting a photograph is impossible. Using an illustration can bring life to a person or situation that goes well beyond what words can describe.
2. Use images or illustrations to tell a different part of your story. Avoid head shots or people up against a wall. (Or — gasp! — people in suits holding cheques.)
3. Do what you can to bring donors closer to the impact of their giving. What can you feature in an image, video or illustration that shows donors how their gifts are making a difference?

Deviation 11 — Gratitude

This deviation looks at ways you can thrill your donors and help them feel more connected to their giving and to your organization. This includes gratitude reports, newsletters and other pieces you can use to show impact in creative ways (as well as a good old-fashioned thank you letter). Imagine!

It shouldn't come as surprise that one of the largest chapters or deviations in this book focuses on the topic of gratitude.

Some organizations believe that all you need to say thanks to your donors is a basic thank you letter that starts off with "On behalf of… "

Um… No.

GRATITUDE REPORTS

You might like to think that your beloved donor is sitting near the front entrance of her home, waiting to hear the footsteps of the letter carrier approaching the door. After hearing the metal clunk of the mailbox lid, she will throw open the door, remove your wonderful annual report and exclaim, "*It's HERE!*"

Unfortunately, that's not even close.

The reality is that your beloved donor doesn't know when she is supposed to get your annual report (or newsletter, or mail pack) and she very likely isn't sitting by the door waiting for it.

Your donor is busy. She has friends to meet, grandkids to shuttle to hockey games and doctor appointments to remember.

The last thing she's doing is wondering when you are going to send her that booklet that has nothing to do with her — and everything to do with you.

Isn't that what most "Annual Reports" are? Annual Report: two words that send eyeballs rolling, directors scurrying and donors yawning.

I've talked to fundraisers who would rather [insert any mundane or painful task that comes to mind] than work on the annual report for their charity.

I don't blame them.

Most of them are boring. Soul-crushingly so.

But they don't have to be.

I'd like you to forget about pulling together a 48-page annual report that will adhere to your overly commercial graphic standards, that will be filled with abstract images, organization-centric copy, and page after page of names typeset in teeny tiny 8-point font.

Those are not communications that inspire donors. In any way, shape or form.

A great annual report should really be an inspirational report full of gratitude and love for your donor.

At Agents of Good, we prefer to call annual reports "Gratitude Reports" because it helps us and our amazing clients focus on creating something that a donor will read and cherish.

Agent Jen says, "*As they turn the last of the pages of the gratitude report, your donor should remove their glasses, take another sip of their tea (or sherry), and nod their head in appreciation, knowing that their gift to your cause was absolutely the right decision.*"

Our goal is always to craft something that your donor wants to read while sitting in her favourite chair, with the dog nestled by her feet and a cup of tea steaming on the end table.

A great gratitude report:

- Tells a great story from a new perspective
- Gushes love and gratitude for the donor
- Is mostly externally focused and acknowledges the efforts of others

The objective remains painfully simplistic: *tell a great story that illustrates donor impact from a unique perspective, in a way that is surprising to the donor.*

As with all things, there is more than one way to do this.

We have created reports that feature **staff members** who share the ways donors have impacted their work.

We have shared **donor** stories, using their own words to explain why they care so deeply for the organization they support.

We have created reports that show how a **beneficiary's** life has been dramatically changed, thanks to donor support.

Different gratitude reports do different things, but ultimately they can all be boiled down to one thing—they celebrate donors.

Not you, the charity. Not them, those guys in suits holding large cheques.

They celebrate donors.

Some straightforward goals of your gratitude report should be:

- To tell a story, ideally from a unique perspective.
- To remind all your donors, regardless of the size of their donation, that their giving is valued.
- To celebrate your donors and show them how they helped the organization's beneficiaries "win."

CASE STUDY #1: THE REDWOOD – ANA'S STORY

Sometimes the perfect story lands on your desk and when it does, what a gift it is to you and your donors!

For this gratitude report, we wanted to share the personal story of a woman who was helped by The Redwood, a small but mighty women's shelter located in Toronto, Canada.

We thought that the right story could show the donor the journey of just one woman who had a place to turn to in a time of desperate need. It would highlight the ways that the organization helps so many women just like her. It would show the impact of the donor's support in a personal way they may have never seen or felt before.

When I got Ana's story, I read it through line by line, moment by moment, through my tears. When I reached the end of her story, I put it down and wondered how I could honour her and the many women like her. How could I share this story with donors in a way that would allow them to feel the full weight of the profound effect they had on Ana's life?

It starts:

"I don't have a clue how to start so I will write it down the way that comes out of my memory.

My name is Ana..."

Those first two lines were so strong, we decided to begin the 2014 Gratitude Report with them. Just these simple words from Ana's hand and heart.

I'll admit, it's a brave organization that approves something that looks like this.

Fig. 11.1 — Cover of the 2014 Redwood Gratitude Report

A black cover **(Fig. 11.1)**. No logo. No design. Only some powerful, authentic words.

How could you look away from this?

It's a story that starts in a place of darkness, so we began the report the same way.

I wanted the images to tell as much of the story as Ana's words did. Not competing, but complementing. We only had a few images from Ana to work with, but the ones we received were incredibly strong **(Fig. 11.2)**.

(One really good image is always better than three poor ones, so be selective.)

Ana's story talked of isolation. The agonizing moments before—and frantic seconds after—calling for help **(Fig. 11.3)**.

I worked with photographer Dan Banko, during a photoshoot to capture the other photos we needed.

We needed images that would honour Ana while at the same time telling a story on their own.

This is often the hardest part.

Fig. 11.2

Fig. 11.3

Fig. 11.4

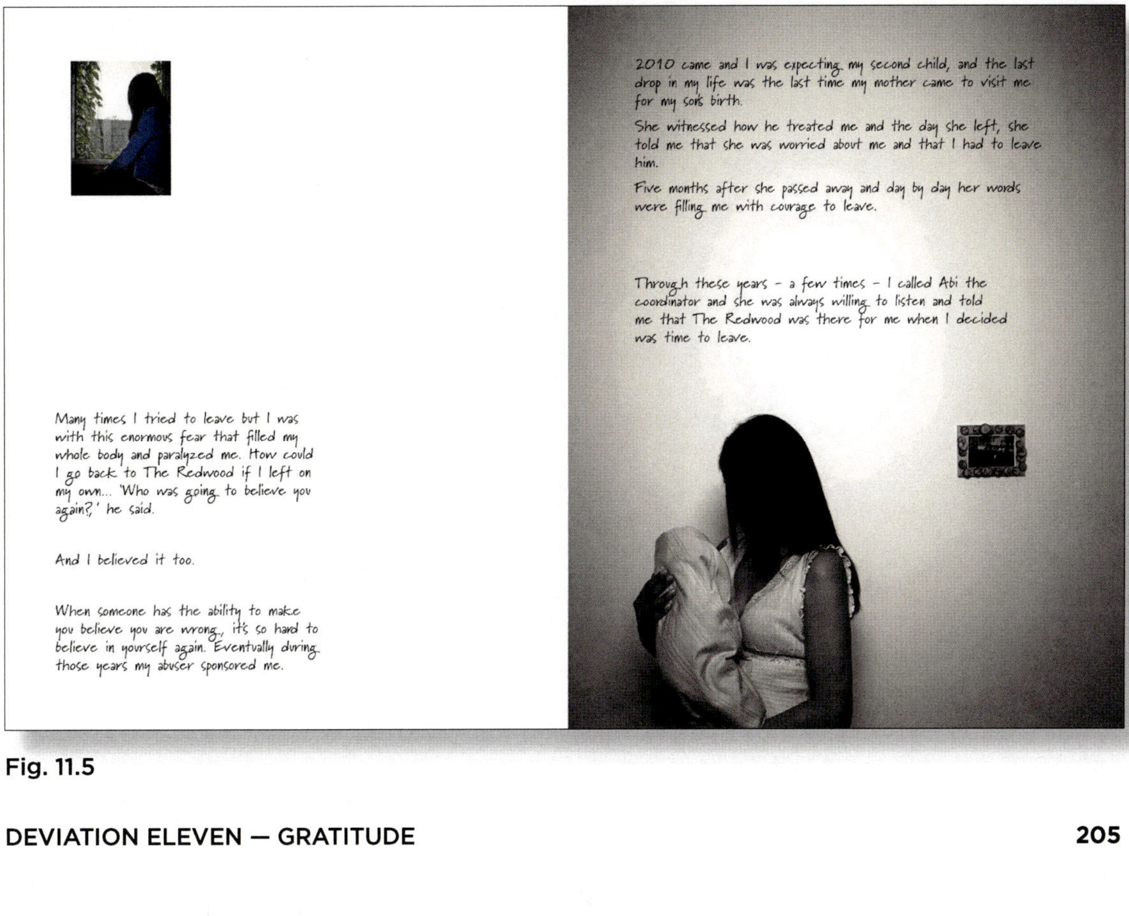

Fig. 11.5

I didn't want the photos to look like stock images (which we generally avoid anyway). I never want a donor reading an emotive appeal or gratitude report and see the same image used to sell accident insurance on a highway billboard.

These pages give the donor a glimpse into Ana's reality **(Fig. 11.4)**. They recount the incredibly difficult decision she made to return to her abuser, a place of normalcy for herself and her children. It was not the place to attempt to gloss over Ana's story or to try to make it more palatable.

This report wasn't about slapping a shiny image on the page followed by a monotonous, bulleted list of all the daily tasks the program staff had to do.

It also wasn't about overwhelming the donor with the facts and figures behind the constantly opening and closing front door of the shelter.

It's not that those things aren't important. They absolutely are, but they're not effective ways to share what your donor has made possible.

Ana's story is, and she led the way, guiding us through it all **(Fig. 11.5)**.

Though the word "you" only appears 14 times in this report, the donor is an intimate witness to Ana's whole story.

It is a story that, like all good fundraising and communications, features a unique

Fig. 11.6

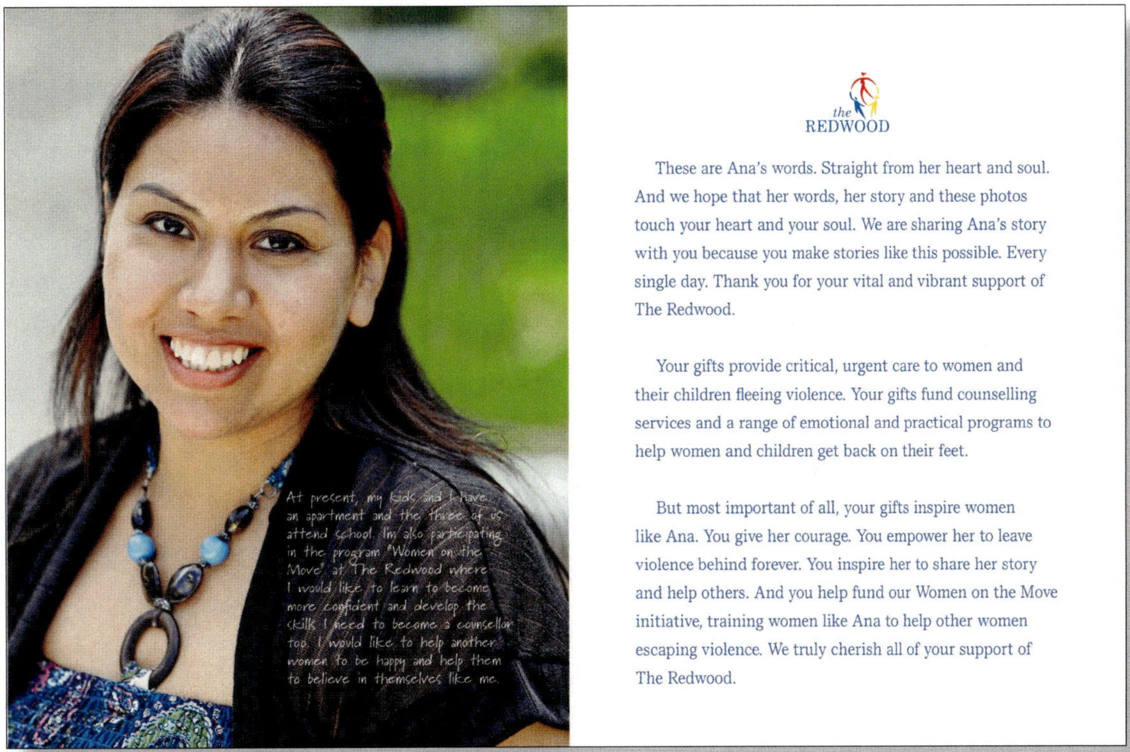

Fig. 11.7

voice from a unique perspective. It tells a story filled with emotion and values.

Unlike a fundraising appeal, it doesn't leave the story unfinished.

(By the way, that's my daughter's favourite stuffie, "Bunny" in the photo. **(Fig. 11.6)**)

Our hero, Ana **(Fig. 11.7)**.

On the day of the shoot, she told us that for years, she never wanted her photograph taken. She believed she wasn't worthy of someone capturing her image on film.

Even without her words, a donor can see her impact.

In the right column, for the first time in the entire report, we hear the voice of the organization. Rather than use this as an opportunity to take on a more formal tone, we douse the donor in love and appreciation for allowing women like Ana to have a safe place to go, for supporting their courage to get the help they need, and providing them with the chance to get back on their feet.

A gratitude report still can, and should, share the details of the organization's financial picture **(Fig. 11.8)**. But these facts and figures aren't the focus of the report. Ana's story is.

Donors are moved by stories, not statistics.

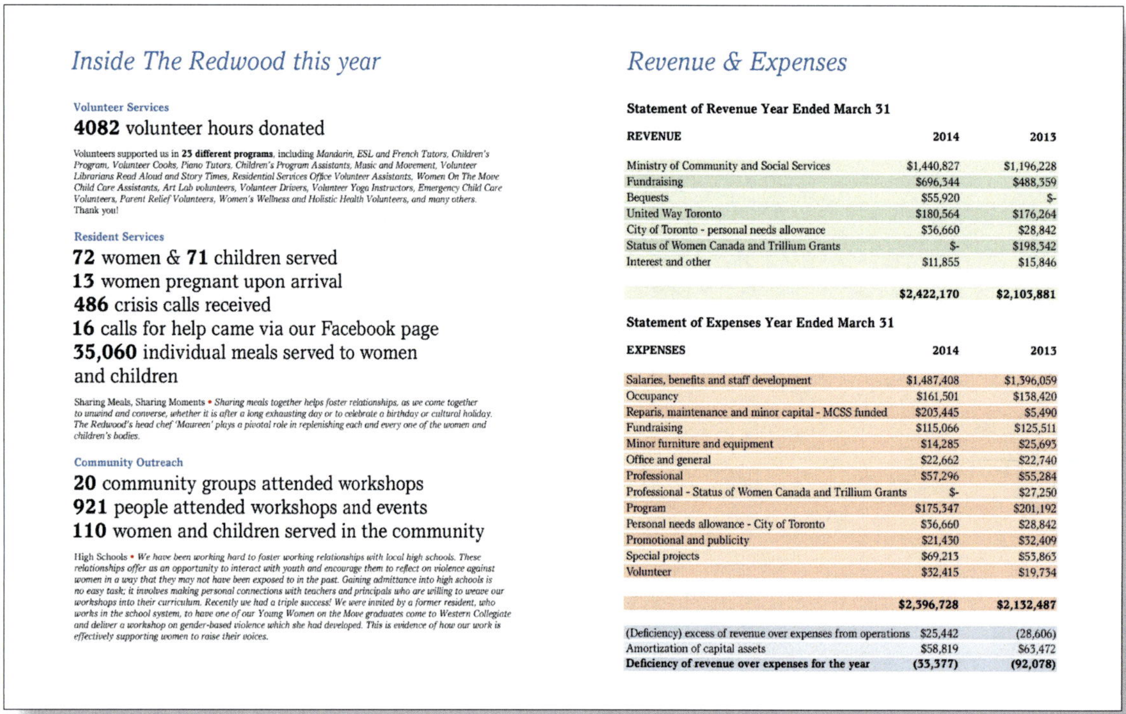

Inside The Redwood this year

Volunteer Services

4082 volunteer hours donated

Volunteers supported us in **23 different programs**, including *Mandarin, ESL and French Tutors, Children's Program, Volunteer Cooks, Piano Tutors, Children's Program Assistants, Music and Movement, Volunteer Librarians Read Aloud and Story Times, Residential Services Office Volunteer Assistants, Women On The Move Child Care Assistants, Art Lab volunteers, Volunteer Drivers, Volunteer Yoga Instructors, Emergency Child Care Volunteers, Parent Relief Volunteers, Women's Wellness and Holistic Health Volunteers, and many others.* Thank you!

Resident Services

72 women & **71** children served
13 women pregnant upon arrival
486 crisis calls received
16 calls for help came via our Facebook page
35,060 individual meals served to women and children

Sharing Meals, Sharing Moments • *Sharing meals together helps foster relationships, as we come together to unwind and converse, whether it is after a long exhausting day or to celebrate a birthday or cultural holiday. The Redwood's head chef 'Maureen' plays a pivotal role in replenishing each and every one of the women and children's bodies.*

Community Outreach

20 community groups attended workshops
921 people attended workshops and events
110 women and children served in the community

High Schools • *We have been working hard to foster working relationships with local high schools. These relationships offer us an opportunity to interact with youth and encourage them to reflect on violence against women in a way that they may not have been exposed to in the past. Gaining admittance into high schools is no easy task; it involves making personal connections with teachers and principals who are willing to weave our workshops into their curriculum. Recently we had a triple success! We were invited by a former resident, who works in the school system, to have one of our Young Women on the Move graduates come to Western Collegiate and deliver a workshop on gender-based violence which she had developed. This is evidence of how our work is effectively supporting women to raise their voices.*

Revenue & Expenses

Statement of Revenue Year Ended March 31

REVENUE	2014	2013
Ministry of Community and Social Services	$1,440,827	$1,196,228
Fundraising	$696,344	$488,359
Bequests	$55,920	$-
United Way Toronto	$180,564	$176,264
City of Toronto - personal needs allowance	$36,660	$28,842
Status of Women Canada and Trillium Grants	$-	$198,342
Interest and other	$11,855	$15,846
	$2,422,170	**$2,103,881**

Statement of Expenses Year Ended March 31

EXPENSES	2014	2013
Salaries, benefits and staff development	$1,487,408	$1,396,059
Occupancy	$161,501	$138,420
Reparis, maintenance and minor capital - MCSS funded	$203,445	$5,490
Fundraising	$115,066	$125,511
Minor furniture and equipment	$14,285	$25,693
Office and general	$22,662	$22,740
Professional	$57,296	$55,284
Professional - Status of Women Canada and Trillium Grants	$-	$27,250
Program	$175,347	$201,192
Personal needs allowance - City of Toronto	$36,660	$28,842
Promotional and publicity	$21,430	$32,409
Special projects	$69,213	$53,863
Volunteer	$32,415	$19,734
	$2,396,728	**$2,132,487**
(Deficiency) excess of revenue over expenses from operations	$25,442	(28,606)
Amortization of capital assets	$58,819	$63,472
Deficiency of revenue over expenses for the year	**(33,377)**	**(92,078)**

Fig. 11.8

Fig. 11.9

Every donor looking at this back cover is hugging Ana (**Fig. 11.9**).

This is a gratitude report—a celebration of your donors, and the stories they make possible.

Some take-aways:

- **Stories not stats.** Donors want to read about the things they make possible through their giving. They want to hear unique stories, using unique voices, from unique perspectives. This isn't about dusting off last year's underwhelming report and just updating the numbers.
- **Get creative.** There are so many ways you can visually bring your donors closer to the stories they

make possible. How can you visually tell the story?

- **It's about (YOU) the donor, not (WE) the organization**. This isn't a vehicle for your branding and communications gang. This isn't the time for abstract images or ideas. Find a story that highlights the importance of a donor's gift and make sure they feel the organizational love and appreciation for being an important supporter to your cause. Make them feel connected to the things they make possible.
- **When talking with beneficiaries, ask the right, emotional questions** to get emotional answers and stories. For example:
  - *Tell me about your connection to our organization. What was happening with you before you connected with us?*
  - *Tell me about a particular person you remember helping you and how that made you feel.*
  - *How is your life different today?*
  - *What would you say to supporters of our cause?*

CASE STUDY #2: OREGON ZOO FOUNDATION

When we start these projects, objectives are often simple and straightforward:

- Craft a gratitude report filled with donor love thanking donors for their incredible support.
- Share a story that demonstrates donor impact (or in this case, how donors make the Oregon Zoo's world-class conservation, animal exhibits, and educational programs possible).
- Help donors feel inspired by the crucial role the zoo plays in the community, and illustrate how donors are at the heart of their zoo!

A question that we get asked all the time is, "*How can I get a report like this approved by people who are more comfortable with traditional approaches, strategies and execution?*"

More often than not, it boils down to three things (see *Deviation 8* for the seven other things):

- Trust
- Expectations
- Conversations

OREGON ZOO FOUNDATION
OUR GRATITUDE REPORT
TO YOU, OUR CARING DONORS
Hairy body
Bigger ears
Longer tail
Approximate height= 6.6 to 9.8 feet
SCIENTIFIC NAME:
Elephas maximus borneensis
This is Chendra.
She's an endangered Borneo Pygmy Elephant...

We spent a lot of time with the amazing team at Oregon Zoo Foundation, led by Charu Uppal and Julie Fitzgerald, talking about #donorlove, the role of a gratitude report vs. a typical annual report, and why donors deserved a report that told a commonplace story in a unique way.

In the end, the Zoo's donors deserved it! As do your donors. They are tired of seeing and hearing the same old boring things from you.

Our concept was to curate a scrapbook about Asian elephant conservation.

We focused on showing donors a side of the Zoo they had never heard or seen before.

Working with our designer and illustrator Veronica Davies, we used beautiful, "from the field" illustrations. Combined with copywriting by Rachel Zant, we told the story of Chendra, an endangered Borneo Pygmy Elephant, as it might be documented by a conservationist.

See how the donor is right there, in the first few words? (And emphasized with the swoop of a highlighter!)

"Our gratitude report to YOU, our caring donors" — with "YOU" in the big type.

Even if we had nothing else on the cover, the donor would be flipping the page, wanting to read more. We made it clear from the very first line that this would be a celebration of their efforts.

The cover is warm and approachable. (The coffee stains, as I talked about in *Deviation 4*, are there on purpose! They say to donors in a visual, almost subconscious way that someone read this and passed it along to them, thinking they'd want to read it too.)

The report goes on to introduce our hero, Chendra, to the donor (**Fig. 11.10**).

These simple sketches do much more than any photography would have done. They allow us to tell the story in ways a camera could never capture. The emphasis on certain words allows even the people who skim the pages of the report, rather than devour every word, to still experience the heart of the story.

- *Chendra doesn't know where her mom is.*
- *She has no idea how to find food or water.*
- *Some friendly people come to help Chendra.*
- *But Chendra seems sad and lonely.*

HERE'S WHERE YOU COME IN!

Who me? Yes YOU! The donor (**Fig. 11.11**)!

Fig. 11.10

Fig. 11.11

High feeder baskets located throughout Elephant Lands encourage Chendra and the other elephants to get up on their hind legs and exercise those muscles.

Kneeling to search hollowed out logs.

Or, they might bend down to look in strategically placed hollow logs for something to munch on.

Keepers use the water cannon to create a more enriching (and fun!) environment for the elephants. Chendra and Lily love to roll in the mud!

Sam and Chendra play in the pool.

How do you safely introduce a 10,000 lb elephant to the herd? Slowly! Our new "Howdy" system helps the animals to safely interact with each other without conflict.

Now, almost 20 years later, "Auntie Chendra" is a thriving and active member of the herd. She dotes on the little ones, playing in the pool with young Samudra and taking mud baths with little Lily.

And, because of everything we've learned about Chendra and her herd, we can help create a brighter future for other Malaysian palm oil plantation orphans like her.

Thanks to donors like you.

Fig. 11.12

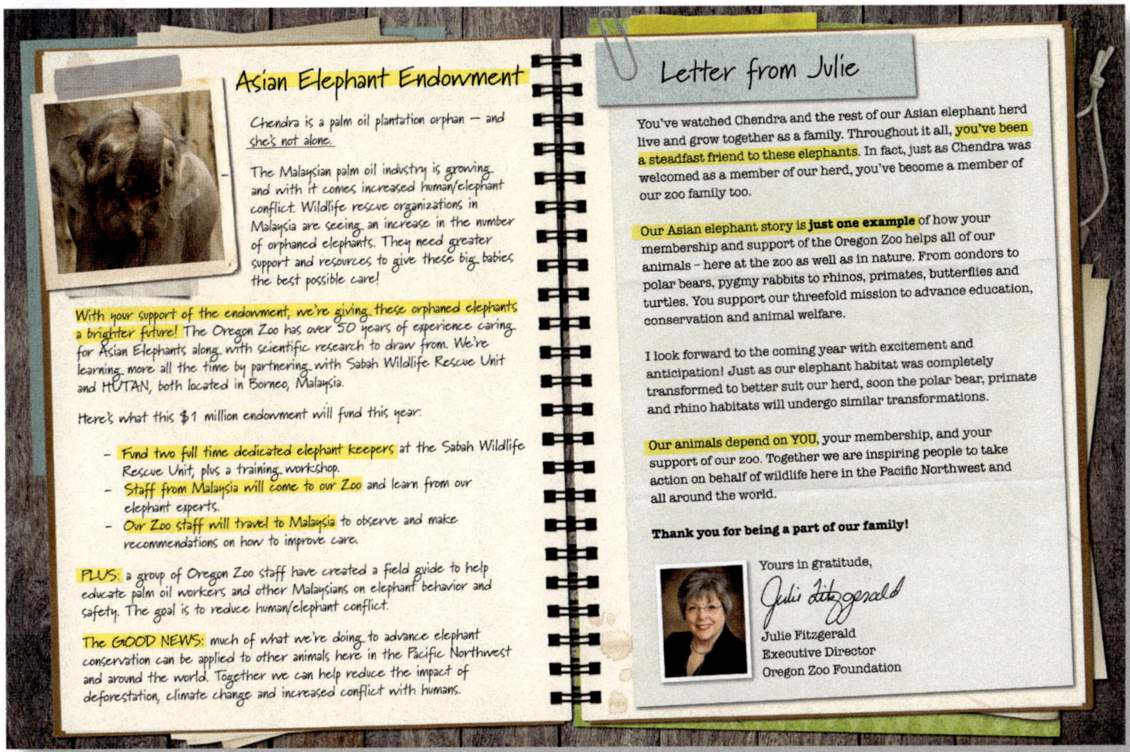

Asian Elephant Endowment

Chendra is a palm oil plantation orphan — and she's not alone.

The Malaysian palm oil industry is growing and with it comes increased human/elephant conflict. Wildlife rescue organizations in Malaysia are seeing an increase in the number of orphaned elephants. They need greater support and resources to give these big babies the best possible care!

With your support of the endowment, we're giving these orphaned elephants a brighter future! The Oregon Zoo has over 50 years of experience caring for Asian Elephants along with scientific research to draw from. We're learning more all the time by partnering with Sabah Wildlife Rescue Unit and HUTAN, both located in Borneo, Malaysia.

Here's what this $1 million endowment will fund this year:

- Fund two full time dedicated elephant keepers at the Sabah Wildlife Rescue Unit, plus a training workshop.
- Staff from Malaysia will come to our Zoo and learn from our elephant experts.
- Our Zoo staff will travel to Malaysia to observe and make recommendations on how to improve care.

PLUS: a group of Oregon Zoo staff have created a field guide to help educate palm oil workers and other Malaysians on elephant behavior and safety. The goal is to reduce human/elephant conflict.

The GOOD NEWS: much of what we're doing to advance elephant conservation can be applied to other animals here in the Pacific Northwest and around the world. Together we can help reduce the impact of deforestation, climate change and increased conflict with humans.

Letter from Julie

You've watched Chendra and the rest of our Asian elephant herd live and grow together as a family. Throughout it all, you've been a steadfast friend to these elephants. In fact, just as Chendra was welcomed as a member of our herd, you've become a member of our zoo family too.

Our Asian elephant story is **just one example** of how your membership and support of the Oregon Zoo helps all of our animals - here at the zoo as well as in nature. From condors to polar bears, pygmy rabbits to rhinos, primates, butterflies and turtles. You support our threefold mission to advance education, conservation and animal welfare.

I look forward to the coming year with excitement and anticipation! Just as our elephant habitat was completely transformed to better suit our herd, soon the polar bear, primate and rhino habitats will undergo similar transformations.

Our animals depend on YOU, your membership, and your support of our zoo. Together we are inspiring people to take action on behalf of wildlife here in the Pacific Northwest and all around the world.

Thank you for being a part of our family!

Yours in gratitude,

Julie Fitzgerald

Julie Fitzgerald
Executive Director
Oregon Zoo Foundation

Fig. 11.13

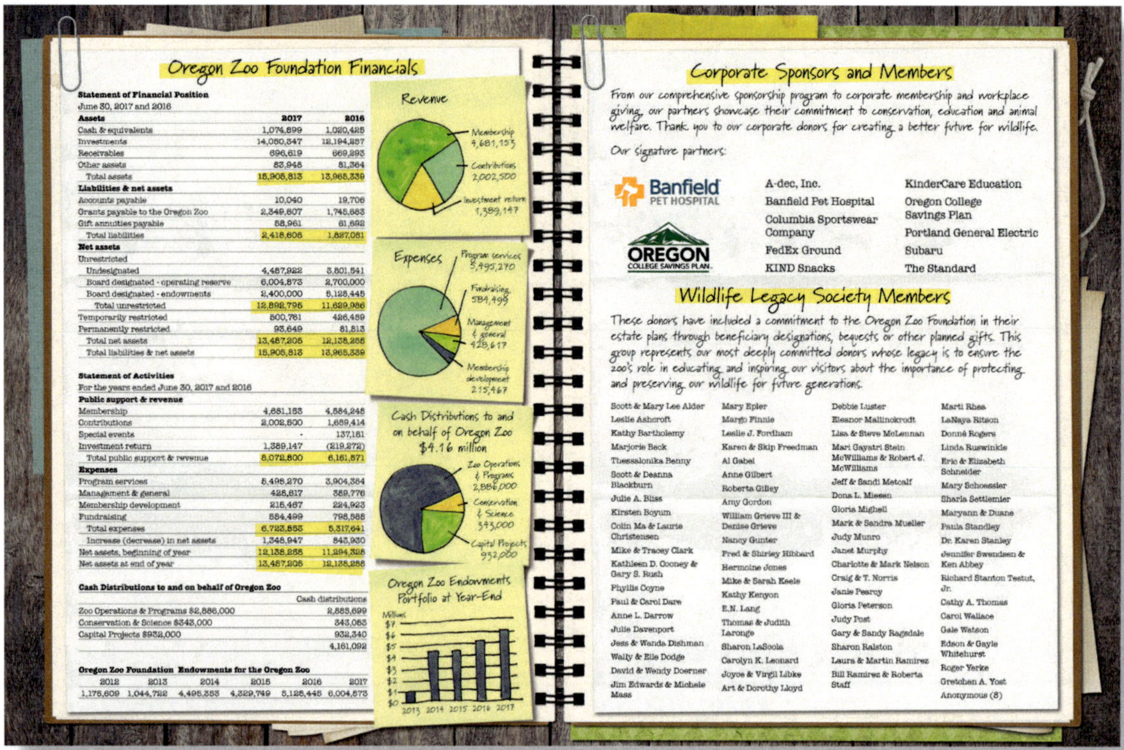

Fig. 11.14

Fig. 11.15

This whole piece feels lovingly crafted (and it was!) The handwritten passages and playful illustrations were right for the story and for the donor. No style guides required.

It's factual. It's emotional **(Fig. 11.12)**. It tells a moving story and gives donors an insider, up close look at their giving. And like the last line says, this is all…

THANKS TO DONORS LIKE YOU.

We always want to balance "all the feels" with other information that adds to and supports the case **(Fig. 11.13 & 11.14)**.

The best fundraising appeals do the same thing. They use stories, facts, images and creativity to pull a donor in and keep them engaged with what they are being asked to do, and why they are being asked to do it right now.

In the context of gratitude reports, the donor's job is done. Now it's time for her to flip through to the last page, rest her hands on the arms of the chair, and take a final sip of tea before she moves on with her day.

But before you let her go…

Always leave your donor smiling (Fig. 11.15).

Some take-aways:

- **What's the heart of the story?** Often the hardest part is deciding where to start and stop the story. Get to the part where the donor steps in to help as soon as possible.
- **Get your donor in the big type**! Even skimmers should be able to see where their impact is felt.
- **Make it feel personal**! It's the little touches that make a piece like this feel hand-curated for the reader. It's not overly designed; it looks like a hand drawn scrapbook with smudges, smears, paper clips and taped-in images. The less the design elements are obvious, the more personal it will feel.
- **How do you interview your boss**? It might be hard to interview your own colleagues, or your boss, in a way that pulls out the best, most emotionally compelling stories to tell your donors. We interview program staff and CEOs frequently. Here are a few key questions to help you get to the emotional juiciness and pull out the stories that **donors want to hear** from your program staff or leadership.
  - *Tell me why donations are key to the program you're offering—or to this organization. How do gifts directly help you do your important work each day?*
  - *How do donors directly impact the people (animals, environment, etc.) that our organization helps?*
  - *What's one of the best stories you can think of that illustrates the impact of a donation in action? How does that make you feel?*
  - *You get into an elevator with a person who hands you a cheque for your program. What do you say to them? How do you express your gratitude, and just how important their gift is?*

Most of the time we already have an idea or a creative framework in mind for a gratitude report, so we steer the interviews to help pull out specific details and relevant stories that will fit within that creative theme.

INTERVAL HOUSE
Celebrating You
2011 GRATITUDE REPORT

CASE STUDY #3: INTERVAL HOUSE

This gratitude report is a literal celebration of donors.

We wanted to craft a warm, inviting, straightforward report that celebrated donors—without overdoing it.

Creatively, we didn't want it to look too designed or too professional, so we decided to shoot all of the photos using an iPhone with the help of photographer, Daniel Banko. We added warmth to the images with the use of a few basic filters.

The report starts with a note from the organization (lovingly-crafted by Agent Jen Love), that is anything but organization-focused. Again, YOU is highlighted in the emphasized type. From there, we share the stories – the WHY – of just a few of their donors. Each story starts with the word "celebrating."

We also shared information about Interval House's programs (made possible by donors!), using lots of white space and large type.

We made an early decision to **not** send a copy of the report to every supporter and donor.

Instead, we sent out a simple postcard and note to donors letting them know the report was available. This helped to keep costs low on something the organization thought donors might not want.

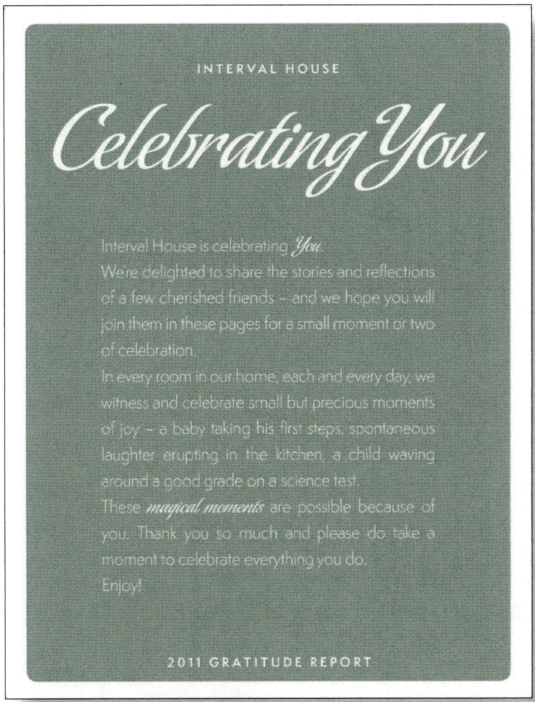

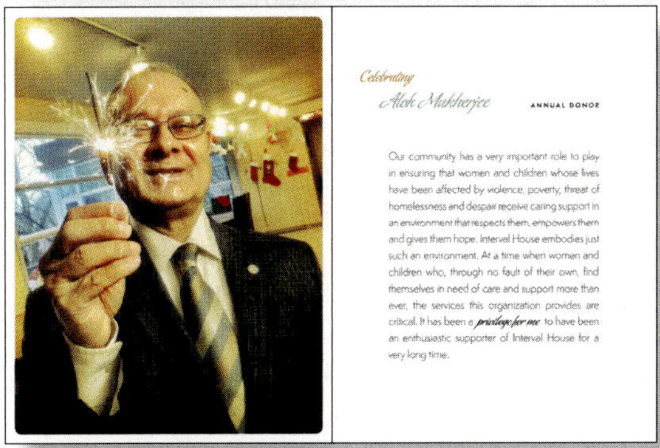

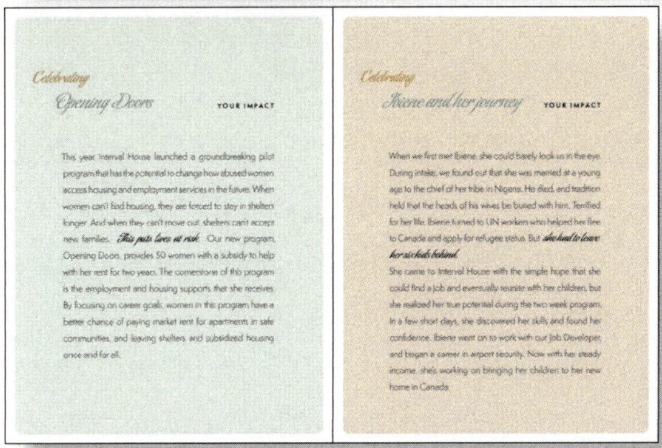

Some take-aways:

- **Be externally focused.** Who helps to make your mission possible? Recognizing and sharing the "WHY" of the many individuals who make your mission possible is a good starting point for a gratitude report.
- **It doesn't have to look like it cost a million dollars.** Cheap and cheerful is more effective anyway! Large type and white space make a piece readable and approachable. The message is more important than the medium.
- **Sharing donor stories is like holding a mirror up to the donor** reading the report. They will see and feel echoes of their own values and emotions in the words of others. That's a powerful connector and motivator.
- **You will get the best stories for your gratitude reports** (or any of your fundraising materials for that matter) by being strategic and thoughtful about how you conduct interviews. Your goal is to create an environment where your subject will speak naturally and from the heart. Here is our framework for an ideal donor interview:
  - *What inspired you to give to our organization in the first place?*
  - *What matters most to you about the work we do?*
  - *Why is this so important and urgent right now?*
  - *What makes you feel good about supporting our work?*
  - *What would you say to others about giving to us?*

NEWSLETTERS

Does your organization send a newsletter(s) to your donor throughout the year?

I really hope so. A fantastic, donor-loving newsletter pack can help raise a lot of money for your organization. When I say, fantastic and donor loving, I tend not to think of those bloated, overly branded 24-page monstrosities crafted by your marketing team that brag about how amazing your organization is.

I am talking about a good old-fashioned printed newsletter. I know your boss eagerly wants to "shift to digital" to save money and because "no one reads newsletters anymore" but I am here to tell you that you are potentially making a critical mistake.

A great, donor-loving newsletter should do four things:

- Report back on the impact of donor gifts.
- Show a ton of gratitude for those gifts.

- Make a case for future need and continued support.
- Tell and share amazing and inspiring stories.

Doing these four things can help you raise a lot of money.

Here are a few examples of how you can create something inviting for your donors.

STAR WARS

A few years ago, in a galaxy far, far away, I sat down with my pal and fundraiser Rory Green.

Rory is an exceptional fundraiser who has "donor love" pumping through her veins and heart. She comes by it naturally, as her dad Fraser is also a well-known Canadian fundraiser.

Rory emailed me to ask if I knew of a "Direct Mail 101" guide that people could follow along with; check some boxes and hopefully come out the other side with a half decent pack that could perform pretty well. She had been stewing on this idea for a while and when she asked about this — I knew it was something I wanted to be a part of!

We wrote and designed a newsletter pack, using a story that we assumed most people would know, and crafted it into an effective direct mail piece. Generally, we are all familiar and "plugged in" to the story of our own organizations and causes, but often come up short or aren't quite sure how to express the good work

If you like fundraising AND Star Wars, then we have some posts you might like on the agentsofgood.org blog!

that is made possible because of our loyal, passionate and caring donors. We hoped this series would serve as a guide for other fundraisers in the development of their own fundraising program.

The piece was vetted by a number of colleagues to ensure that anything we were suggesting was following best practices, based on testing and real life examples.

They (donor newsletters) should never be considered a money waster if done properly, yet more and more we are hearing and seeing charities that are deep sixing them and only doing e-newsletters.

So, let's have a look, shall we?

The outer envelope. We used an oversized 9.5″ x 5.875″ white envelope with a first class stamp. Its size, the use of visuals and donor-focused tagline were all chosen to help this envelope get opened. You could also consider using no image or tagline. The weight of the pack, because of the enclosed newsletter, may be intriguing enough to get it opened. It could be worth testing the two approaches.

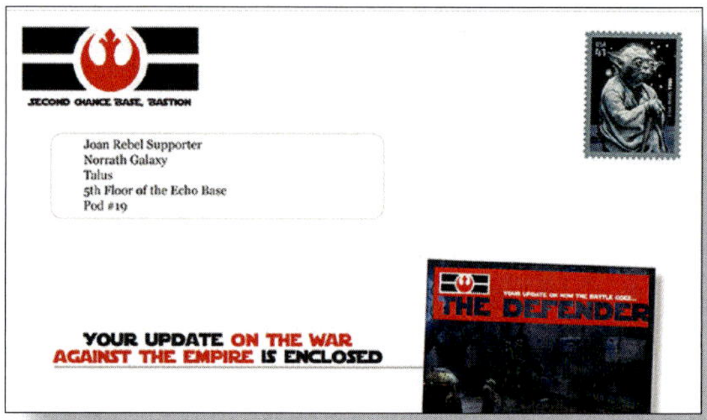

The letter. In this case, we felt short and sweet was the way to go. The copy answers the question "why am I getting this?" (To show you the impact of your gift.) Belief/value statements create mental nods for your reader. This letter reminds the reader about their own beliefs/values. Amazingly, "Leia" took the time to add some handwriting, underlining and a personal note! Any/all of these things will dramatically help your letter get read and increase the likelihood of a gift. Also, this is all possible to do electronically without your ED having to reach for her pen!

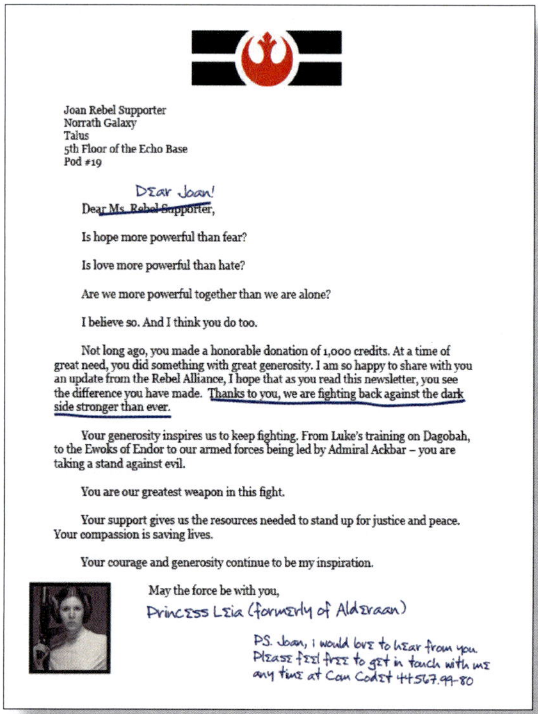

Joan Rebel Supporter
Norrath Galaxy
Talus
5th Floor of the Echo Base
Pod #19

Dear Joan!

~~Dear Ms. Rebel Supporter,~~

Is hope more powerful than fear?

Is love more powerful than hate?

Are we more powerful together than we are alone?

I believe so. And I think you do too.

Not long ago, you made a honorable donation of 1,000 credits. At a time of great need, you did something with great generosity. I am so happy to share with you an update from the Rebel Alliance, I hope that as you read this newsletter, you see the difference you have made. Thanks to you, we are fighting back against the dark side stronger than ever.

Your generosity inspires us to keep fighting. From Luke's training on Dagobah, to the Ewoks of Endor to our armed forces being led by Admiral Ackbar – you are taking a stand against evil.

You are our greatest weapon in this fight.

Your support gives us the resources needed to stand up for justice and peace. Your compassion is saving lives.

Your courage and generosity continue to be my inspiration.

May the force be with you,

Princess Leia (formerly of Alderaan)

P.S. Joan, I would love to hear from you. Please feel free to get in touch with me any time at Com Codet 44567.99-80

The Newsletter. Four pages is the magic length. Rory's Star Wars-obsessed husband described this newsletter as "delightfully corny" — which it is. Corny is good.

Here are some things you should and should not do in your donor newsletter:
Should do:

- Repeatedly show your donor the impact of their gifts
- Use simple easy-to-read language
- Make it conversational
- Trigger emotions
- Tell stories
- Have a call to action. A good story should inspire a donor to do more, and give them a specific action to take. Every single story has a specific call to action and gift amount, which is referenced on the donor reply form. For the love of goodness — do NOT bury these asks. Bold them. Make them stand out
- Keep the words small, your font big, and the language simple. A word count is helpful to the writer and editor as it tells them how much copy they can fit on one page. I usually work with a 50/50 ratio. No more than half the page should be filled with copy. The other half is reserved for images, pull quotes and white space. I used 12 point Adobe Caslon with a leading of 14.4 pt. Each article should ideally have a reading ease somewhere in the region of 80% and a reading level between grade 4–6.
- Use words like "you," "your" and phrases like "because of you."
- Make sure it is skimable. Pay attention to your headlines, photo captions and bolded words. Ask yourself, what would happen if this was ALL the donor read? Do they follow newsletter best practices?

Should NOT do:

- Brag about your organization
- Talk about how old you are
- Use endless lists of statistics
- Use jargon
- Take all the credit for your mission work
- Use words like "us," "we," "The Rebel Alliance" and phrases like "Strategic plan," "operational roll out," "enhanced care," "a special message from our CEO"

Your Gifts At Work In Dagobah: Notice the headline on the cover is "*Your Gift at Work In Dagobah*" NOT "*A Special Message From Luke Skywalker*" **(Fig. 11.16)**

The purpose of this story is to show Joan what her last gift did. It is a message right from Luke thanking Joan and emphasizing HER role in his training. It doesn't brag about how great Luke is — because Joan is the hero of this story.

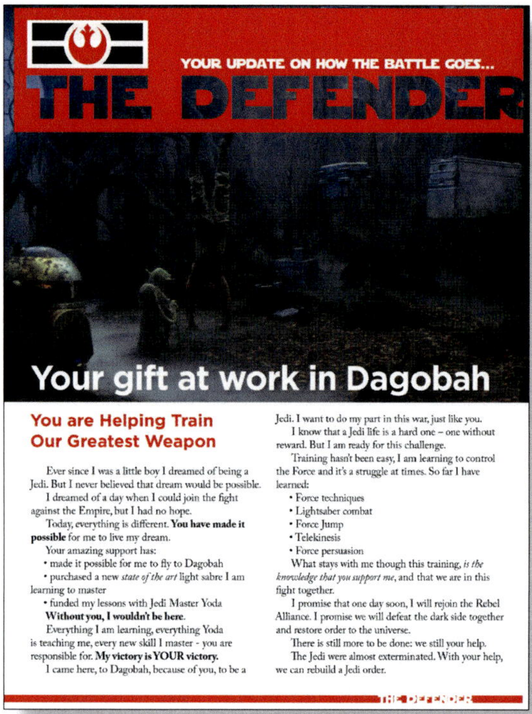

YOUR UPDATE ON HOW THE BATTLE GOES...

THE DEFENDER

Your gift at work in Dagobah

You are Helping Train Our Greatest Weapon

Ever since I was a little boy I dreamed of being a Jedi. But I never believed that dream would be possible.

I dreamed of a day when I could join the fight against the Empire, but I had no hope.

Today, everything is different. **You have made it possible** for me to live my dream.

Your amazing support has:

• made it possible for me to fly to Dagobah

• purchased a new *state of the art* light sabre I am learning to master

• funded my lessons with Jedi Master Yoda

Without you, I wouldn't be here.

Everything I am learning, everything Yoda is teaching me, every new skill I master - you are responsible for. **My victory is YOUR victory.**

I came here, to Dagobah, because of you, to be a Jedi. I want to do my part in this war, just like you.

I know that a Jedi life is a hard one – one without reward. But I am ready for this challenge.

Training hasn't been easy, I am learning to control the Force and it's a struggle at times. So far I have learned:

• Force techniques

• Lightsaber combat

• Force Jump

• Telekinesis

• Force persuasion

What stays with me though this training, *is the knowledge that you support me*, and that we are in this fight together.

I promise that one day soon, I will rejoin the Rebel Alliance. I promise we will defeat the dark side together and restore order to the universe.

There is still more to be done: we still your help.

The Jedi were almost exterminated. With your help, we can rebuild a Jedi order.

THE DEFENDER

Fig. 11.16

continued from front page...

Right now, there are younglings across the galaxy in need of Jedi training.

It was almost too late for me to be trained as a Jedi. Please help make sure that never happens again. We need to invest in our children now before it is too late.

A gift of just $500 Alliance Credits will go towards training the next generation of Jedi.

The time to act is now. You can make a better tomorrow with your gift today.

May the force be with you.

- Luke Skywalker

Master Yoda (left) gives young Luke (right) some extra tips during a well deserved break from training in the humid heat of Dagobah.

Save the Ewoks for Endor from the Empire

My first memory of Endor was the smell of the forest, the rich dark soil the cedar trees. I remember running through the forest with my brothers and sisters as a child. I remember the sun streaming through the tall trees, warm against my fur.

I love this planet Endor. It is my home.

But it is in danger. The danger that faces my planet is the same danger that threatens you: *the Empire.*

Without you, my home could be destroyed.

The empire does not care about things like beauty, nature, family. The empire's battle droids cannot smell the forest, or feel the soil beneath their feet.

The Ewoks are a peaceful people. We spend our time taking care of nature, and do not have droids or weapons to defend ourselves. We are in huge danger of extinction.

The Empire has made a base on Endor, cutting down the forest to build military bases. Droids patrol the planet, killing anything in their way. My people live in constant fear.

I am afraid for my planet, and my family. I could lose everything I love. The only thing standing between the Empire and my home – **is you.**

You are helping to build defenses against the Empire. Every day, you help the Ewoks of Endor build walls and force fields that will keep our home safe. I know you have stepped up supported fight - but we still need help.

Your generous gift of $1,000 credits will fortify an entire Ewok village against the Empire.

I know the risks that face us should The Alliance give up: we must, now more than ever, come together and continue to fight.

I hope my children can one day be able to run through the forest, free and unafraid. Without you, I would be hopeless. Please consider a donation today to help the Ewoks of Endor.

- Wicket Wystri Warrick

The Ewoks of Endor need heroes like you!

You helped Nysteria rebuild her home and her life

Do you know what's like to worry where your kids will sleep tonight? Where their next meal will come from? Where they will live and grow and play?

Nysteria does.

When her planet Alderaan was destroyed, Nysteria lost her family, her friends and her home.

"*You never think this could happen to you,*" Nysteria said. "*It is something from my worst nightmare.*"

They were on vacation in Coruscant when Nysteria heard the news. "*I had to tell my daughters their home had been destroyed. They cried all night in my arms. The sound of their sobs will stay with me for the rest of my life. It broke my heart.*"

Alone and stranded on a strange planet, Nysteria worried what would happen to her family. "*As a mother, all I want is for my children to be loved, to be happy, to be taken care of. I was so scared. I didn't know where we would go, or where we would live.*"

Nysteria turned to the Rebel Alliance for help, and soon found herself relocated to a safe location. Today, her and her two children have a home, and are building new lives.

You have helped Nysteria, and Alderaan refugees like her, rebuild their lives – and funded refugee communities for families like Nysteria's. Thanks to your help, Nyiestra and her family have a new home.

"*I now have a home. My children have beds to sleep in and food to eat. Instead of tears, I hear their laughter and giggles. It is the most beautiful sound in the world. Thank you, from the bottom of my heart.*"

Although the Death Star has been destroyed, the innocent families of this universe are not safe from the Empire.

"*The empire destroyed my home. It happened to me and it could happen to you.*" Nysteria warns, "*We need to make sure this never happens again.*"

You are enabling the Rebel Alliance to fight the terror and evil of the Empire. You continued support takes us one step closer to a day where no mother needs to fear losing her home at the hands of the Empire.

Nysteria is a success story – but there are still many Refugee families who need your help.

A gift today of $1,500 credits will provide food and shelter for an Alderaan Refugee for one week.

"*I have been helped so much,*" Nysteria says "*I now want to give back – because there are so many people who need help. Even a small donation goes a long way for a family in need.*"

Secrets of the Rebel Alliance Revealed: Admiral Akbar finds New Weapon in War Against Empire

Did you know, the Empire's weapon of choice is droids? Droids that have no compassion or empathy. Our rebel alliance is an army of living beings who can think critically, make decisions and treasure life.

The men and women of the rebel alliance are our secret weapon. We know *what the empire doesn't* - that hope, empathy and love are the most powerful weapons of all.

These men and women of the tireless alliance rely on you. **I rely on you.**

Your donations fund protective gear, ship repairs and food for the men and women risking their lives in this war. You are making it possible to keep them safe and alive. Your gifts provide:

• new defensive helmets designed to deflect stormtrooper laser blasts

• shield technology to keep ships out of sight of the Empire

• radar devises that help us locate enemy ships

The Alliance is growing. Every

...continued on back page...

THE DEFENDER

THE DEFENDER

Fig. 11.17

"You" helped Nysteria rebuild her home and her life (Fig. 11.17): There are hundreds of Alderan refugees — but the story of ONE is more compelling than any number, statistic or graph I could show you.

Nysteria is one person, with a relatable experience.

Appealing to the senses: the sound of her children sobbing, the sound of their giggles. Stories become more powerful when one of the five senses plays a role.

Hope/Fear and Happiness/Sadness are most powerful when paired together. This story pairs the happy story of Nysteria with the reminder that people just like her still need help — and that "It happened to me and it could happen to you."

A specific call to action (give) with a tangible outcome of a gift: *"A gift today of $1,500 credits will provide food and shelter for an Alderaan Refugee for one week."*

Secrets of the Rebel Alliance Revealed: Admiral Akbar finds New Weapon in War Against Empire. Words like "secret" make the information new and exciting to your readers.

Using bullet lists breaks up the copy and shows impact of gift.

Obi-Wan Kenobi's Legacy (Fig. 11.18): Includes a story of a boomer (Obi-Wan Kenobi) — your prime target for legacy giving.

Introduces two important and essential concepts in legacy giving: 1) He's taken care of his family but also wants to give to this cause, 2) Anyone can do this. You don't have to be rich.

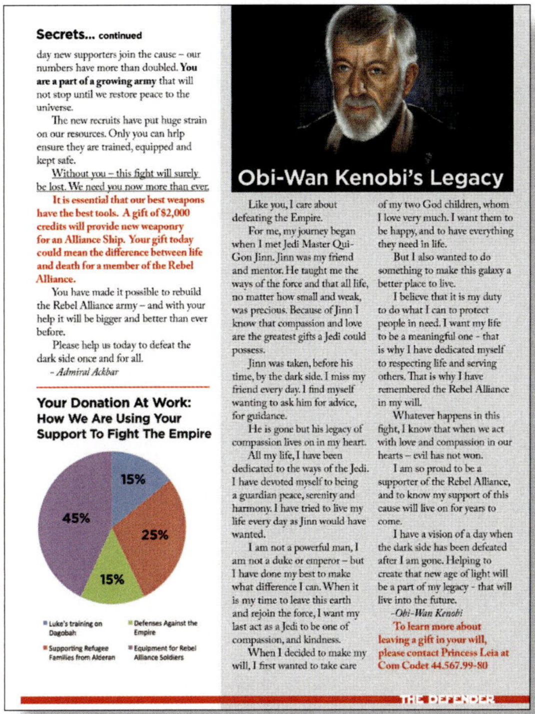

Secrets... continued

day new supporters join the cause – our numbers have more than doubled. **You are a part of a growing army** that will not stop until we restore peace to the universe.

The new recruits have put huge strain on our resources. Only you can hrlp ensure they are trained, equipped and kept safe.

Without you – this fight will surely be lost. We need you now more than ever.

It is essential that our best weapons have the best tools. A gift of $2,000 credits will provide new weaponry for an Alliance Ship. Your gift today could mean the difference between life and death for a member of the Rebel Alliance.

You have made it possible to rebuild the Rebel Alliance army – and with your help it will be bigger and better than ever before.

Please help us today to defeat the dark side once and for all.

– Admiral Ackbar

Your Donation At Work: How We Are Using Your Support To Fight The Empire

Obi-Wan Kenobi's Legacy

Like you, I care about defeating the Empire.

For me, my journey began when I met Jedi Master Qui-Gon Jinn. Jinn was my friend and mentor. He taught me the ways of the force and that all life, no matter how small and weak, was precious. Because of Jinn I know that compassion and love are the greatest gifts a Jedi could possess.

Jinn was taken, before his time, by the dark side. I miss my friend every day. I find myself wanting to ask him for advice, for guidance.

He is gone but his legacy of compassion lives on in my heart.

All my life, I have been dedicated to the ways of the Jedi. I have devoted myself to being a guardian peace, serenity and harmony. I have tried to live my life every day as Jinn would have wanted.

I am not a powerful man, I am not a duke or emperor – but I have done my best to make what difference I can. When it is my time to leave this earth and rejoin the force, I want my last act as a Jedi to be one of compassion, and kindness.

When I decided to make my will, I first wanted to take care of my two God children, whom I love very much. I want them to be happy, and to have everything they need in life.

But I also wanted to do something to make this galaxy a better place to live.

I believe that it is my duty to do what I can to protect people in need. I want my life to be a meaningful one - that is why I have dedicated myself to respecting life and serving others. That is why I have remembered the Rebel Alliance in my will.

Whatever happens in this fight, I know that when we act with love and compassion in our hearts – evil has not won.

I am so proud to be a supporter of the Rebel Alliance, and to know my support of this cause will live on for years to come.

I have a vision of a day when the dark side has been defeated after I am gone. Helping to create that new age of light will be a part of my legacy - that will live into the future.

-Obi-Wan Kenobi

To learn more about leaving a gift in your will, please contact Princess Leia at Com Codet 44.567.99-80

THE DEFENDER

Fig. 11.18

A few other nerdy design notes:

I usually begin the design process by setting up my grid, which helps to ensure that any element I have on the page will line up with any other element.

In the case of "The Defender," I went with a five column grid. I tend to use an uneven number because although using an even number will always allow me to

keep things balanced, an uneven number means a little more design work to balance off elements, but the result is a visually interesting piece. Notice how everything plays off the grid.

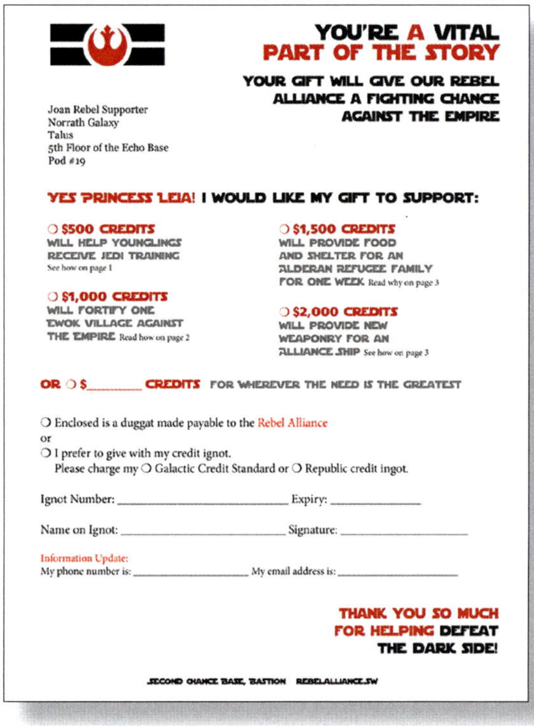

YOU'RE A VITAL PART OF THE STORY

YOUR GIFT WILL GIVE OUR REBEL ALLIANCE A FIGHTING CHANCE AGAINST THE EMPIRE

Joan Rebel Supporter
Norrath Galaxy
Talus
5th Floor of the Echo Base
Pod #19

YES PRINCESS LEIA! I WOULD LIKE MY GIFT TO SUPPORT:

❍ $500 CREDITS
WILL HELP YOUNGLINGS RECEIVE JEDI TRAINING See how on page 1

❍ $1,500 CREDITS
WILL PROVIDE FOOD AND SHELTER FOR AN ALDERAAN REFUGEE FAMILY FOR ONE WEEK Read why on page 3

❍ $1,000 CREDITS
WILL FORTIFY ONE EWOK VILLAGE AGAINST THE EMPIRE Read how on page 2

❍ $2,000 CREDITS
WILL PROVIDE NEW WEAPONRY FOR AN ALLIANCE SHIP See how on page 3

OR ❍ $________ CREDITS FOR WHEREVER THE NEED IS THE GREATEST

❍ Enclosed is a duggat made payable to the Rebel Alliance
or
❍ I prefer to give with my credit ignot.
Please charge my ❍ Galactic Credit Standard or ❍ Republic credit ingot.

Ignot Number: ______________________ Expiry: ____________

Name on Ignot: ______________________ Signature: ____________

Information Update:
My phone number is: ______________ My email address is: ______________

THANK YOU SO MUCH FOR HELPING DEFEAT THE DARK SIDE!

SECOND CHANCE BASE, BASTION REBELALLIANCE.SW

The reply device. Full size, large type, personalized, specific asks that all link back to the stories your donor just read. Make it easy to fill out and give a massive reminder to your donor of their value in meeting the needs of the cause they care so much about.

The Business Reply Envelope. Finally, please, please, please include a business

reply envelope (BRE) so your donor can easily return their response form and "duggat" (gift) while their heart and mind still swell with good feelings, knowing they have helped the empire to fight another day.

We are constantly asked what are the best types of articles to fill a newsletter? Some of our go-to recommendations are:

- updates on previous appeals (impact, goal and story),
- feature a donor and their reason for giving,
- share donor words (or responses to a previous appeal),
- a teaser for an upcoming appeal.

THANK YOU LETTERS

I have so many feelings about thank you letters and thanking in general. So much of what crosses my desk feels automated and like an afterthought.

CHECK! We sent out a thank you! Now back to asking for more money!

Thanking is such an important function in the context of fundraising.

The ideal cycle of donor communications… asking, thanking and reporting back on what you did with the gift.

Also, thank you letters provide a great opportunity for you to unlock more giving from your donors.

Think about it for a second.

Your donor has just written a cheque and put it in the business reply envelope. She has a smile on her face and a warm glow in her heart. When she heads out later, she stops by the post office and puts it in the mailbox feeling good about herself. She is a good human who is helping make a difference.

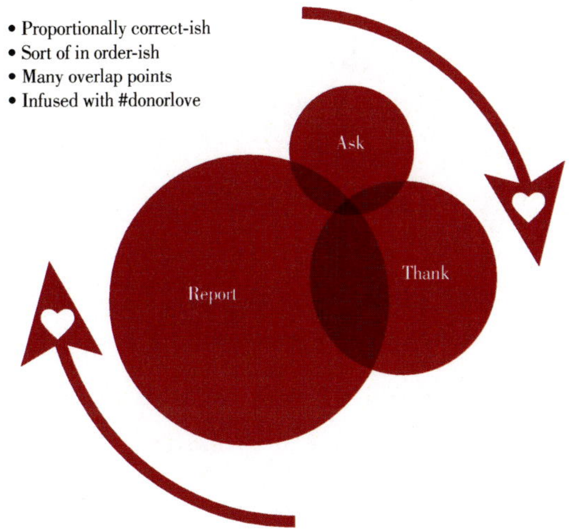

Then… silence.

Finally, the day comes where the donor heads to her mailbox, pulls out a stack of #10 envelopes, one of which is yours with your logo on it and a strapline that says "*Tax receipt enclosed.*"

She pulls out the letter and begins to read, "*On behalf of…*"

I weep.

Thoughtfully thanking your donor is akin to looking at them, eyeball to eyeball and saying, "I SEE YOU!" "You're important to me!" "You are good and I value you!" and "Thank you!"

I remember having my mother-in-law over for dinner a few years ago. She is your donor. She's everyone's donor. I asked her, "When was the last time an organization you care about did something for you that made you feel treasured, valued and seen?"

She stopped, fork hovering in midair… a clump of steaming, buttery mashed potatoes resting on top of it.

She looked at me and said, "*I can't think of a one.*"

Once again, I weep.

This is a donor who gives to about 30 organizations throughout the year, a monthly donor to a number of them. She gets between 30–40 appeals a week during the busy fundraising seasons, and she can't think of one instance where an organization went above and beyond to make her feel thanked.

The bar is so low.

The Redwood from Toronto, Ontario is one organization I love a lot. I first became aware of the work they were doing when our friend and colleague, Emma Lewzey reached out and asked if we could help them with their annual report. This was years before the "Ana" Gratitude Report that was featured earlier in this deviation.

We have never helped The Redwood with thanking donors. This is an organization that "gets" gratitude.

I am a donor to The Redwood and this is only a small fraction of the thank

you letters I have gotten through the years. Some have come with special appeals, impact reports and/or just after having made a gift.

The Redwood knows it's not just the Executive Director's job to thank donors. Everyone has a hand in gratitude.

Every summer, The Redwood runs a fundraiser called "Summer Fun" that ensures that the kids of Redwood can do fun "kid" things like a pizza party in the park, or a movie night with popcorn and treats, maybe even an outing to an amusement park.

Even though I'm a monthly donor, I always support this fundraiser since every kid should enjoy delicious pizza in the park. I made a gift to the appeal a few years ago. It was the Friday of a long weekend leading into summer. I came home to a message on my phone. You can imagine my surprise when it was from Anthea Windsor, president of The Redwood board. Her call, which I share in presentations, was delightfully unscripted, enthusiastic about my gift and so heartfelt. It was approximately 30 seconds long but made me feel so treasured that this VIP took time from her holiday weekend to call me and say thanks. So simple.

Through the years, The Redwood has found all sorts of creative ways for me to feel loved and cherished.

Sometimes the piece has been handmade, or printed fresh off their laser printer. Sometimes the gratitude has been a bit random, or was sent around a holiday and it is always cheesy! But so heartfelt.

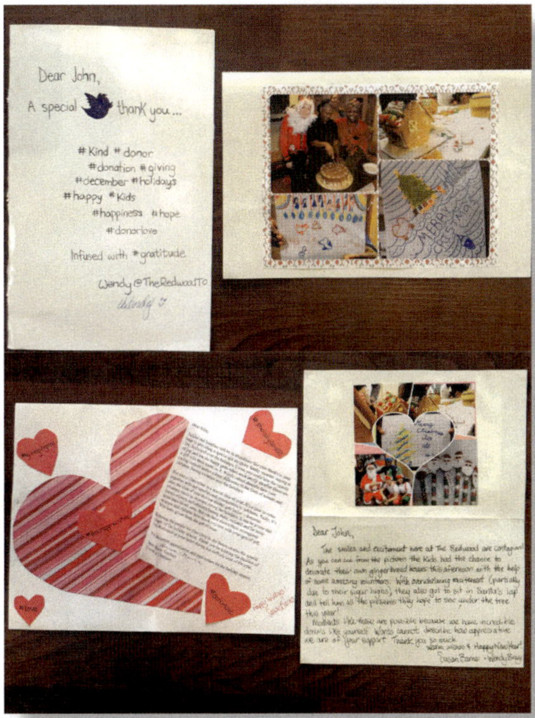

These are simple things you can do for your donors that have massive impact, the sort of impact you can't measure. I remember meeting a fundraiser who told us the only stuff that she doesn't have to get her bosses approval on was sending gratitude to donors, and guess what? She poured her whole heart into it. I bet no one drew the line to this work when the donors continued to give more and more often.

The Redwood treats me just as we all

treat the people in our lives that mean the most. This is what loving your donor can look like. This piece made me tear up when I received it. It was a 17″ x 11″ house and all of the windows and doors had messages to me from the amazing folks across The Redwood telling me how amazing I was and valued as a supporter and donor. I still get choked up looking at it.

Can you do this for all of your donors? Of course not. But you can likely identify those special people that care so much about you and your work and then you can make them feel seen and special.

When I speak about lost opportunity,

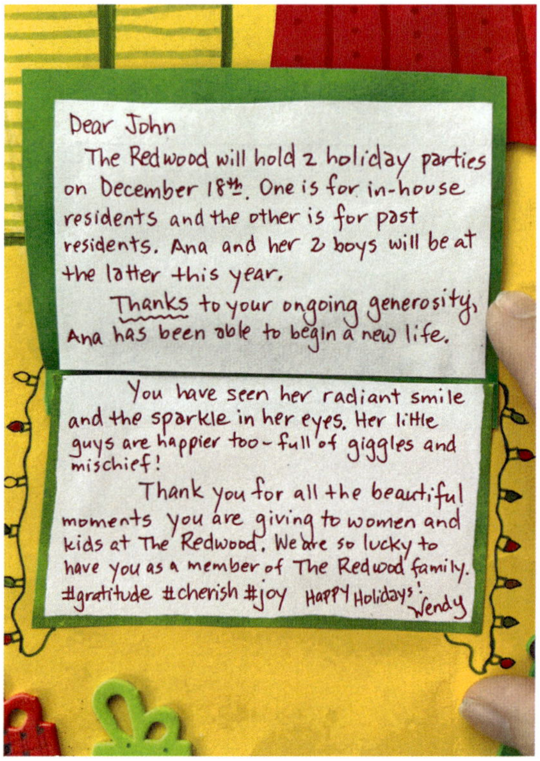

there is something else you need to understand.

When your donor gets out her pen, checks a gift amount on your reply form and carefully writes your organization name on a cheque before putting it in the reply envelope, she is feeling something wonderful that goes beyond the transaction of giving a gift to you.

I'm not a neuroscientist, but the nutshell is this: giving releases good feeling chemicals like dopamine, serotonin and oxytocin. I've heard it called "the happiness trifecta."

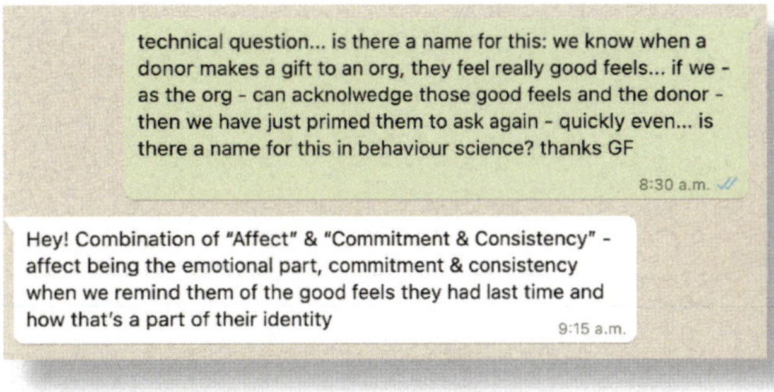

Whatsapp convo with Dana Segal

Just like when we were little kids doing things that caused us joy, we want to feel that way again as soon as possible.

Here is your opportunity.

Saying thank you as soon as possible is a powerful act that allows you to ask again as soon as possible. Because your donor loves to feel good about herself and her giving.

Saying "thank you" says "I see you. You are important to me. You are good and you are valued."

That's why thanking is such an important part of your fundraising.

Over the years, I've had many fundraisers bring up concerns about asking too much, or too often. First off, you aren't and it is testable. Second, if you are asking thoughtfully every time, and you actually need a donor's help with a problem, then taking the time to lovingly thank that donor for their help while showing them the impact their gift had on your problem leaves them primed to be asked for help again as soon as possible.

People who are concerned about asking too much likely aren't willing to do the hard work to make sure that they are doing the other parts too. As a sector we are sort of "ok" at the asking part — we are absolutely rubbish at the other parts. We can do better.

Here's a check-list look at how to write a perfect thank you letter. This example comes the way of my colleague Cathy Barrick who is the Chief Thank YOU Officer at the Alzheimer Society of Toronto.

This was an automated thank you, but likely puts the hard copy version that you keep in your bottom drawer to shame. What makes it so good?

- It is personalized. It doesn't start with "Dear Friend" or "On behalf of..."
- It has more "YOU" than "WE." Seriously, count them. This one has 15 out of the 110 words.
- It has a Flesch Reading ease score of 88.4. (Anything higher than 80 is excellent.) It is written at a grade level of 2.9. (We are looking between grade 4–6 level — so this is even better!)
- Cathy's letter speaks to what the gift was for. Be as specific as possible.
- Remind your donor of your shared victories. In her letter, Cathy reminds me that Sylvia and Larry are fighting this disease with my help and they are so appreciative of that.
- It invites personal contact. Cathy is a real person and she would love to hear from me anytime!
- It is honest and heartfelt. I love the line "Your care for other people inspires us."
- You sign off with something memorable. Cathy's doesn't but it could have said something like, "Yours, for helping those with dementia, forever!"
- It is hand signed.
- It is filled with lots of good, human feelings. Your donor is left with the lasting impression that when they gave their gift to you, it was completely the right decision.

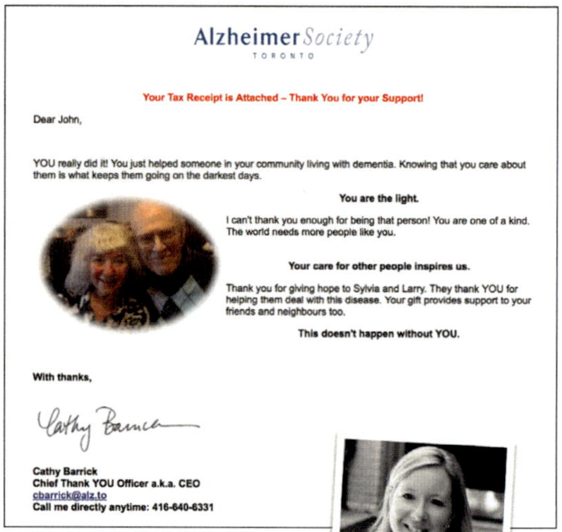

Alzheimer Society
TORONTO

Your Tax Receipt is Attached – Thank You for your Support!

Dear John,

YOU really did it! You just helped someone in your community living with dementia. Knowing that you care about them is what keeps them going on the darkest days.

You are the light.

I can't thank you enough for being that person! You are one of a kind. The world needs more people like you.

Your care for other people inspires us.

Thank you for giving hope to Sylvia and Larry. They thank YOU for helping them deal with this disease. Your gift provides support to your friends and neighbours too.

This doesn't happen without YOU.

With thanks,

Cathy Barrick
Chief Thank YOU Officer a.k.a. CEO
cbarrick@alz.to
Call me directly anytime: 416-640-6331

Cathy Barrick
Chief Thank YOU Officer
Alzheimer Society Toronto

Flesch Reading Ease	88.4
Flesch-Kincaid Grade Level	2.9
Passive Sentences	7.6%

Bonus Tips

Dr. Jen Shang from the Institute of Fundraising UK has shared the nine moral adjectives that can move people to give more and more often. They are: *caring, compassionate, fair, friendly, generous, helpful, honest, hardworking* and *kind.*

These adjectives describe a core sense of who we actually are and a core sense of who we ideally want to be.

Deviation Discoveries

We were taught, almost from the moment we could speak, to say thank you. It is such a simple gesture that so many organizations ignore it or think a form letter will convey. Saying thank you to donors can be done in many small and large ways, but always ensure it is heartfelt and real.

1. Ditch this year's Annual Report that no one, aside from your boss or board, will look at. Focus on crafting a gratitude report that tells a great story of how you are able to meet the needs of your mission thanks to wonderful supporters.
2. A newsletter is a simple way to say thank you for your support. It acknowledges the impact of donor gifts and can highlight an ongoing need for funding. Every fundraising program should send out at least one a year (or at least one for every two mailings).
3. Your soul-destroying and transactional gift receipt is not a thank you. It doesn't count. If you can't find time to send your donor a simple note of thanks, then you probably shouldn't be asking them for help in the first place.

Deviation Twelve — Knock 'em dead

This deviation talks about that tree you should have planted 20 years ago. We are at the beginning stages of one of the biggest transfers of wealth in history. It's time to discuss the special types of conversations you should be having with your donors, and some unique ways to approach the subject.

Up until now, most of the focus of this book has been on the design of your annual fundraising communications. Almost everything I've shared with you has been a version of best practice that has been "in practice" for a long time.

However, now I'd like to talk to you about *legacy fundraising*. In terms of legacy fundraising, we're still in a bit of a Wild West when it comes to tracking how the work will perform. The best folks are trying things, collecting data and trying to analyze a somewhat incomplete picture.

But, as the Godfather of Good, David Love says, a legacy gift is one gift we will not be able to close. It will be up to our donors.

This section isn't meant to be definitive. It's a guide. Consider it a gentle support and reminder that you can always do *something* to advance your legacy program.

Some markets, like the UK, have been having legacy conversations with its donors for some time. In Canada or the US, the bulk of organizations haven't even started this meaningful exchange.

The majority of your legacy gifts will come from the pool of donors that tend to get ignored the most. These donors are loyal. But probably not rich.

In many organizations, the same person who is running the legacy program is also responsible for major gifts. Sadly, this usually means the program that "may" bring in gifts tomorrow sits closer to the corner of the desk than the program where the big gifts come today.

"THAT" DONOR PYRAMID

Most of your legacy gifts will come from "minor" donors.

The competition should be fierce for these donors, but most organizations are barely talking about legacy gifts. The bar drops even lower when you consider the terrible job we do at stewarding our annual donors.

That means... when you start treating your donor like a caring, loving, emotional donor you'll be at a serious competitive advantage when it comes to legacy gifts. What a concept! It's right up there with stamps affixed on an angle or the addition of paperclips. But here we are.

The average bequest size differs market to market and organization to organization. North America tracks a bit lower than donors in the UK or Australia, which likely has more to do with the way we are having (or not having) legacy conversations with our donors.

The math is constantly evolving in terms of the number of donors that can be expected to actually put your organization in their Will and keep you there. So much depends on how your relationship with that donor plays out over the course of a multiple-year timeline.

In 2022, we are seeing some consistent trends. These might shift or be different for you but can give you the ability to make a case to invest in this type of fundraising.

Let's assume yours is a small charity with **5,000 active donors** (have given a gift in the past 16 months).

Let's also assume that today you've started to invest in a strategic, ongoing, donor-loving legacy program.

I will show you some examples soon, but first, let's start with some math.

If you take the time to send your amazing and active donors a well-timed, thoughtful legacy appeal, you can expect that 2% of those donors will actually become legacy donors. They will leave you a gift in their Will.

2% x 5,000 = 100 donors.

You can further expect that 5% will become legacy prospects (donors who are thinking about it or intend on becoming legacy donors).

5% of 5000 = 250 donors.

About 10% of those prospects will actually become donors.

10% x 250 = 25 donors.

100 donors + 25 prospects converted to donors = **125 legacy donors.**

Also, for every donor who tells you they have left a gift in their Will, there are 4 more who will not tell you ahead of time. (125 x 4 = 500 donors who you will not know about and will likely have never heard of.)

125 legacy donors + 500 unknown donors = 625 legacy donors

Currently in Canada, the average bequest gift size (quite conservatively) is about $33,000 CDN.

625 x $33,000 = $20,625,000.

That money will start flowing pretty fast and keep flowing until the year 2040, as this generation of donors passes on to whatever lies beyond this beautiful world of ours.

Legacy gifts = connecting to the core values of your donors

I know how much our sector loves crunching numbers, but let's not forget, our work still comes back to the stories we get to share with our beloved donors acknowledging the role they play in making our world a better place.

Your donors are humans that have their own story to tell. They can be moved by the smallest of gestures at times.

Your charity is a vehicle for your donor to do something that they care deeply and passionately about. They care about your cause and want to take action for something they believe in. They want to help. They want to fix something. They want to make an impact and they want to feel good about it.

Simple.

Down to earth with Monte Hummel: https://www.youtube.com/watch?v=iK9r8Hq2DXM)

Our job is to connect to our donor's values and emotions in every conversation. Not just the legacy conversation. (We talked a bit about this in *Deviation 3* about how using values and emotions in appeals make for effective fundraising.)

The donor in this image is clearly expressing his values and emotions about an issue he cares about.

One of the greatest lessons you can learn is that money follows value.

24 hours before every organization was founded, a bunch of restless people got together and insisted on action. They knew they had to do more for something they believed in: human rights, social justice, saving the environment, the health of loved ones.

These are not transactions. These are things that define us as individual humans. These are things that speak to our core values that we are emotionally connected to.

Tell stories that connect to the shared values of your donors. Demonstrate how their gifts allow you to put those values into action.

LEGACY SEEDS

Legacy seeds are tiny seeds planted in your donor's heart that, if tended properly, will grow into something beautiful.

An effective annual program should be constantly planting these seeds. I'm talking about something beyond that basic legacy check box on the bottom right corner on the back of your tiny reply form. Seriously… that's not how you run a legacy program.

Here are a few examples.

For St.Thomas Elgin General Hospital, we created this simple buckslip that went into every tax receipt pack.

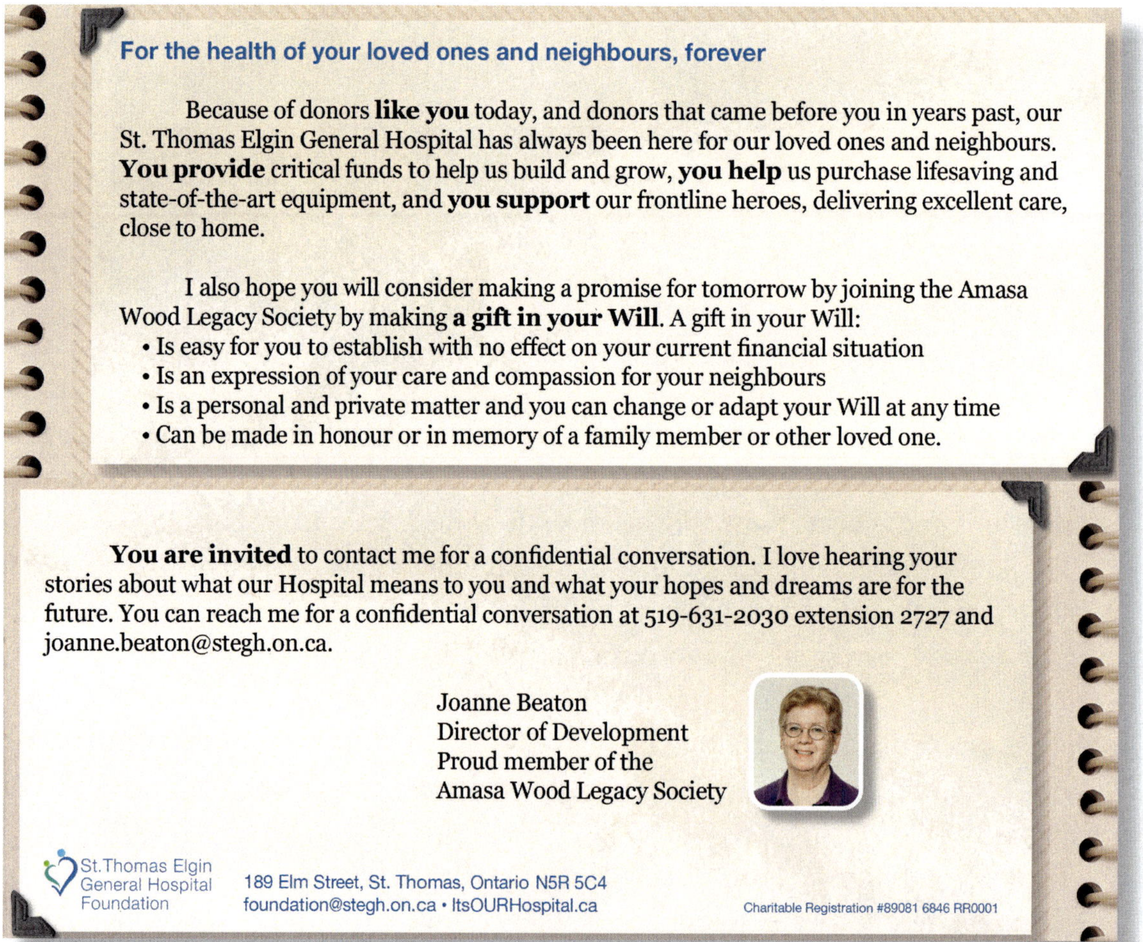

For the health of your loved ones and neighbours, forever

Because of donors **like you** today, and donors that came before you in years past, our St. Thomas Elgin General Hospital has always been here for our loved ones and neighbours. **You provide** critical funds to help us build and grow, **you help** us purchase lifesaving and state-of-the-art equipment, and **you support** our frontline heroes, delivering excellent care, close to home.

I also hope you will consider making a promise for tomorrow by joining the Amasa Wood Legacy Society by making **a gift in your Will**. A gift in your Will:

- Is easy for you to establish with no effect on your current financial situation
- Is an expression of your care and compassion for your neighbours
- Is a personal and private matter and you can change or adapt your Will at any time
- Can be made in honour or in memory of a family member or other loved one.

You are invited to contact me for a confidential conversation. I love hearing your stories about what our Hospital means to you and what your hopes and dreams are for the future. You can reach me for a confidential conversation at 519-631-2030 extension 2727 and joanne.beaton@stegh.on.ca.

Joanne Beaton
Director of Development
Proud member of the
Amasa Wood Legacy Society

St.Thomas Elgin General Hospital Foundation

189 Elm Street, St. Thomas, Ontario N5R 5C4
foundation@stegh.on.ca • ItsOURHospital.ca

Charitable Registration #89081 6846 RR0001

Meant to look like something out of a photo album, the message points out the importance of a legacy gift, what a legacy gift will help do and invites personal contact

AN UPDATE ABOUT THE IMPACT OF YOUR GIVING

Aspen Grove Society:

Legacy Giving In Support Of Humber

Dear To Our Heart: Remembering Audrey

"I will always remember my Granny for how cheerful she was," says Mark. "She was always in a good mood. She loved to laugh." Mark's grandmother Audrey was born January 30th, 1913 in Kingston, and passed away peacefully last August at 106 years old.

At eighteen, she attended Shaw Business College and went on to work for the Bank of Montreal. In the early 1930's she met the love of her life, Steve, who was in the Royal Regiment of Canada. Together they had a daughter, Christine. Audrey's great joys in life were family, friends, and travel. She volunteered at Humber River Hospital's Keele Legacy Site (Northwestern Hospital). She loved to throw parties and had a passion for music, singing, and dancing.

"My Granny was very tough. She lived alone for thirty years taking care of herself after my grandfather died." When Audrey was 105, she came down with pneumonia and was admitted at Humber River Hospital's new Wilson site. Mark was out West at the time and rushed home.

"We all thought it was goodbye," he remembers. "But when I arrived at 4:00AM she was in a great mood. She loved the new Hospital, especially that it was spacious enough for her family to visit. We are all happily surprised when she recovered and was discharged."

After a fall where she broke her hip, Audrey spent the last few months of her life at a nursing home. The two organizations that Audrey honoured in her Will were Humber River Hospital and the Royal Regiment of Canada.

"They were the two things most dear to her heart," says Mark. "She loved to help people. She would love to know that she is helping people heal and enjoy life, because that's what she was all about. That makes me happy."

aspen grove society

I want to thank Audrey and her family for sharing this story with us. If you would like to know more about our **Aspen Grove Society**, a group of donors like Audrey who support our Foundation with a gift in their Will, I would be happy to connect with you for a confidential conversation. I love hearing from our donors about what matters to you most about our Hospital. You can reach me at 647-232-6064, or cmagisano@hrh.ca. Thank you! **– Caterina Magisano, Director of Development**

to a real human named Joanne. The donor can even see what she looks like!

This is a pretty big "seed" to a donor who just made a $50 gift to the holiday appeal, but it is very intentional.

Another place to plant a legacy seed is in your donor newsletter, which already gushes love and appreciation for the hard work of your donors.

This is a recent version of a newsletter Agents of Good worked on with Humber River Hospital Foundation. We often place articles about volunteers, monthly donors, annual donors and legacy donors on the back of page 4 where the reader is least likely to miss it.

You donor gets to read a lovely story that shares the "why" of this donor deciding to leave a gift in her Will to Humber. Other Humber donors will be nodding along to Audrey's story, recognizing bits of themselves in her words and her shared values. Once again, space was provided to invite personal feedback.

Another opportunity in your print materials would be your annual report (or gratitude report as I hope you are now considering it!).

As mentioned in *Deviation 11* — one example of a good gratitude report is a collection of donor voices. Undoubtedly, they will represent just a sampling of the completely normal and utterly amazing humans who support your organization!

Lastly is another example from Ontario Nature (Fig 12.1). If you print your own membership magazine, you can hopefully find space to do some advertising for your legacy program.

The Ontario Nature ad is simple and straight forward. The donor is invited to connect with Kirsten, who is happy to chat anytime.

Obviously, you can plant legacy seeds in your emails and in your social platforms. Try using video testimonials and voices of donors both past and the present.

Fig 12.1

LEAD GENERATION

Let's assume you've done a fantastic job planting seeds and you are hopefully starting to see that hard work pay off in the form of interested phone calls and emails.

Now it's time to be intentional.

The following examples are not "new" ideas. Versions of these types of mail packs have been circulating since well before my career, but I want to share a couple of examples of appeals that Agents of Good has created to help organizations find new legacy donors within their current pool of donors.

To start there are a few things you need to think about:

- Who is the mailing going to?
- When should it go out?
- What will these donors receive from you when, and if, they respond?
- Then what?

First off, you likely won't want to send your legacy mailing(s) to every human you have in your database. AOG recommends clients start by sending it to active donors, loyal donors, lapsed donors, donors who RSVP'd no to events, and monthly donors.

When should you be mailing the package out? AOG have historically tried to send legacy mailings in the spring time, seen as a time of new birth and renewal. Don't get tied up trying to avoid a conflict with your annual program, since this is a completely different conversation and will likely look and feel different than your spring appeal. We also suggest you make it a "rolling mailing," something that you mail out 100 or 200 at a time.

Ideally, you will be signing, stamping and sealing as many of these mail packs in-house as you can with your own blood, sweat and tears. Doing a massive mailing of 5,000 is unrealistic, but doing them in chunks of 100 or 200 makes it a) possible and b) possible for you to manage your engagement with donors who respond. Sending out a 5,000-piece mailing and getting 100 or 200 donors who want to have long conversations with you will be quite difficult to manage. So, let's not do that.

Ontario Nature

Your legacy mail pack should look very different from the other appeals your donor tends to get from you. This appeal is something to be considered. Something to be dwelled upon over a cup of tea.

This mailing is invitation-sized, sent in a 7″ x 5″ closed-face outer envelope. We created a special logo for the legacy appeal and its program, which is seen on the outside of the envelope. Some of these envelopes were lasered with the donor's name

Ontario Nature

Date, 2017

Ms. Jane Sample
123 Anystreet Blvd
Toronto, ON
1A1 A1A

Dear Ms. Sample,

When was the last time nature took your breath away?

For me, it was this past spring when I was walking amongst a stunning patch of Virginia Bluebells at the Sydenham River Nature Reserve, Ontario Nature's newest nature reserve.

Nature lovers like you and me experience these moments frequently. Whether it's on a walk or just looking out the window, you and I both know nature can take your breath away—as long as you're connected to it. And when we have these stunning moments, they become some of our most cherished memories.

As a long-time supporter of Ontario Nature (and The Federation of Ontario Naturalists before that), you make these moments and memories

- 2 -

possible. Thank you for your gifts that allow us to act to save nature in Ontario.

Taking action for our shared values is at the heart of what we do. Every single day, we act on our values: **Protect. Connect. Advocate. Educate.** With your kind and caring support over the past 86 years, we have enjoyed remarkable success.

But as Shakespeare reminds us, "the past is prologue." What about the future?

What kind of an Ontario do we want to leave behind? With growing endangered species lists, the ecological toll of climate change and unbridled development in parts of our province, it seems Ontario is under siege.

This letter is only going to a special group of supporters at Ontario Nature. I know that you are concerned about the plight of nature today. I hope you will also support Ontario Nature tomorrow.

What kind of future can Ontario Nature create? How about a future where the endangered species list stops getting longer? A future of protection.

How about a future where more people in Ontario create on-the-ground nature conservation groups? A future of connection.

How about a future where lawyers and

- 3 -

judges act for nature in the courtroom? A future of advocacy.

How about a future where more children experience the magic of nature? A future of education.

Protect. Connect. Advocate. Educate. These values will remain at the core of what Ontario Nature does. In 10, 20 even 50 years, we will still act for nature. Here today. Here tomorrow.

Ontario Nature has a number of generous individuals who have remembered nature in Ontario with a gift in their Will. These compassionate donors are in our exclusive **For Nature Forever Circle**. They still make regular gifts to our work. But they went the extra step and put Ontario Nature in their Will. I'm asking you to join us.

Making a legacy gift is a personal decision. Of course, you will want to look after your family first. But, as a growing number of our members have discovered, you can also leave a gift to nature.

Your legacy for nature is surprisingly easy to establish and can have no effect on your current financial situation.

With this letter, you will find your special reply form. The first part, the Confidential Reply, asks you to consider leaving a gift in your Will to Ontario Nature.

- 4 -

The second part, the Confidential Survey, asks a few questions about your interest in nature so that we can get to know you a bit better.

If you have any questions, please contact Kirsten Dahl at 416-444-8419 X 235 or email kirstend@ontarionature.org. She would be delighted to have a confidential conversation with you.

Thank you for considering my special invitation.

For nature, forever,

Caroline Schultz

Caroline Schultz
Executive Director

P.S. When was the last time nature took your breath away? As you reflect on that moment, I hope you'll also reflect on joining me as a member of our **For Nature Forever Circle** by leaving a gift in your Will to Ontario Nature. You'll make sure these moments are available forever. Thank you for your confidence and trust.

Ontario Nature

CONFIDENTIAL REPLY

Ms. Jane Sample
123 Anystreet Blvd
Toronto, ON 1A1 A1A

Dear Ms. Sample,

❍ I have already left a gift in my Will to Ontario Nature

❍ I will consider leaving a gift in my Will to Ontario Nature

❍ Please call me for a confidential discussion.
My phone number is
❍ Home (______) ________________
❍ Business (______) ________________

❍ I would like more information about leaving a gift in my Will to Ontario Nature.

❍ I am not interested at this time.

PLEASE TAKE A FEW MINUTES TO FILL OUT THE CONFIDENTIAL SURVEY ON THE BACK OF THIS FORM.

PLEASE RETURN IN THE ENVELOPE PROVIDED TO:
214 King Street West, Suite 612, Toronto, ON M5H 3S6
phone: 416-444-8419 toll free: 1-800-440-2366 ontarionature.org

Ontario Nature

CONFIDENTIAL SURVEY

In order to learn what matters to you, and help us meet your expectations, we would like to know more about you and your interests. Your reply will be treated confidentially.

1. My interests include (please tick all that apply):
❍ Hiking ❍ Nature walks
❍ Gardening ❍ Birding
❍ Natural history ❍ Canoeing/kayaking
❍ Cross-country skiing/snowshoeing
❍ Photography
❍ Other ________________

2. We invite you to tell us about the last time nature took your breath away, or any other reflections you have about Ontario Nature.

____

____

____

____

PLEASE RETURN IN THE ENVELOPE PROVIDED TO:
214 King Street West, Suite 612, Toronto, ON M5H 3S6
phone: 416-444-8419 toll free: 1-800-440-2366 ontarionature.org

and address, while some were handwritten. First class postage was used. The stock was slightly higher end, nothing too crazy, but the paper had texture and softness and it felt a bit heavier than normal. These are all things that get the donor dwelling, and considering.

The letter was typeset on invitation-sized paper and was four pages long, using very large, serif type. You'll note the nice short lines from left to right and plenty of white space. It opens by asking the donor to think about the last time nature took their breath away.

Caroline's letter is filled with the values of the organization and the importance of having an organization like Ontario Nature in the province, protecting the wild spaces and wild species we love the most.

We included a two-page reply form, marked as confidential.

It was also personalized.

Donors who return this form are signaling their intent as a legacy donor, a legacy intender or a legacy prospect.

The back of the reply form allowed the donor to share bits of personal information

Our Life Story

Together with members like you, we take action to protect wild species and wild spaces in your back yard, our boreal forest and beyond. Every single day, we act on our shared values: **protect, connect, advocate, educate**.

This timeline highlights proud victories for nature—made possible because of caring members like you! And we also share some dreams for nature in our province—dreams you can make real by leaving a gift in your Will to protect nature in our province forever.

1931 28 members from 7 clubs form the Federation of Ontario Naturalists (now Ontario Nature)

1934 Our work results in the first wilderness areas in Algonquin Park designated as off-limits to logging, and a nature reserve created at Point Pelee

1956 We champion protecting Lake Erie's shore, leading to Long Point, Turkey Point, and Hawk Cliff provincial parks

1962 We buy our first nature reserve at orchid-rich Dorcas Bay on the Bruce Peninsula

1971 Ontario's first Endangered Species Act is passed

1983 155 new parks created, including 5 new wilderness parks

1987 First Atlas of the Breeding Birds of Ontario is published

Our natural heritage campaign results in establishing Bruce Peninsula National Park and Fathom Five National Marine Park

1994 Wabakimi Wilderness Park expansion campaign results in the park growing sixfold to 892,000 hectares, protecting vital woodland caribou habitat

1999 Partnership for Public Lands campaign results in 2.4 million hectares protected in 378 new parks and conservation reserves in northern and central Ontario

2001 Oak Ridges Moraine Conservation Act passed

2003 Our Boreal Conservation office opens in Thunder Bay, keeping our members and the northern conservation community connected to our work to protect Ontario's boreal forest, which plays a vital role in climate change mitigation by removing carbon dioxide from the atmosphere and locking it away in trees and peatlands

2005 Greenbelt Act is passed to conserve green space and contain urban sprawl in the Greater Golden Horseshoe

2006 In collaboration with First Nations, bird checklists are developed in English and Ojibway, allowing collection of species data in remote areas of Northern Ontario—providing the first detailed maps tracking the health of boreal birds

2007 New Endangered Species Act is passed

2010 Forest and Freshwater Foods project increases understanding of importance of boreal foods to our economy, health and the environment

2013 Lawsuit challenges exemptions granted to industry under the Endangered Species Act

2015 Our Youth Council plays an instrumental role in convincing the provincial government to restrict use of neonicotinoid pesticides

2016 Our reserve network expands as our 25th property, the Sydenham River Nature Reserve, is established, now protecting more than 7,000 acres of land forever

Federal lawsuit filed challenging the unlawful registration of neonic pesticides

7th Annual Youth Summit for Biodiversity and Environmental Leadership is our largest ever, with over 100 participants from 60 diverse communities

2017 Hunting of at-risk snapping turtles is outlawed

Protected Areas campaign launched to increase the amount of land and freshwater protected in Ontario from 10% to at least 17%

After 8 years, the Ontario Reptile and Amphibian Atlas reaches 420,000 records

TODAY

2020 5 new forests in Northwestern Ontario are certified by the Forest Stewardship Council (meaning any logging meets requirements to ensure species and habitats are protected)

2025 Ontario Nature leads campaign that results in permanent protection of more than 17% of Ontario

2027 Our Greenway program drives the conservation of habitat core and corridors—the cornerstone for climate change adaptation—through the identification of regional natural heritage systems across Ontario

2030 Ontario is a world leader in the ecologically sustainable use of natural resources

Former members of our Youth Council are among our political, business, academic and civil society leaders

2035 Populations of woodland caribou and other species at risk are recovering

2067 Our nature reserves network has expanded to 200 properties protecting over 50,000 acres of critical habitat for rare and endangered plants and animals

Your Life Story

As you look at our life story, how does this connect with your story? With members like you, we've achieved a lifetime of conservation victories, and you can now help keep these stories alive forever.

about themselves that can be utilized in many ways with donors who want to have a conversation with you.

The final piece in the pack, aside from a stamped return envelope, was a donor-focused timeline, sharing the joint victories this organization had as a result of its donors and their support. It also talks about the vision Ontario Nature has for the future.

As she reads through the letter and the timeline, your blessed donor should hopefully be reflecting on the story of her own life and how much nature has been a part of it. She should also feel happy that she has been a big part of ensuring that the important work of the organization can continue. Yesterday, today… forever! You hope this donor will connect the events in the timeline to the anchors and milestones in her own life.

Of course you also hope she'll be inspired to reach out and ask for more information about leaving a gift in her Will, or to let you know that she has already done so.

Humber River Hospital Foundation

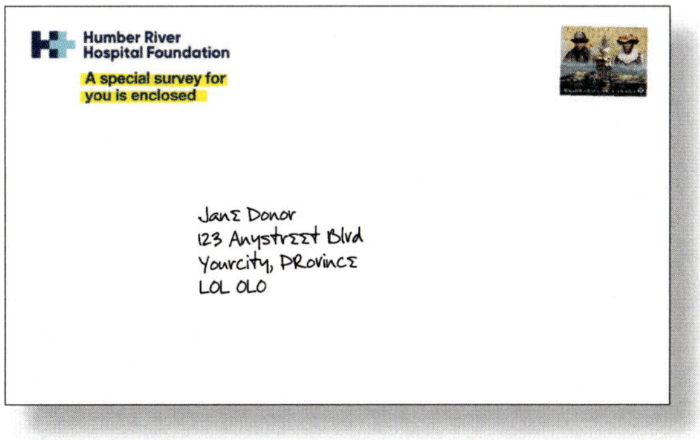

Here is another example of a legacy pack that you can consider for your organization.

For Humber River, this legacy lead generation piece went out in a large, 9.5″ x 5.875″ envelope that was closed-faced, hand-addressed and had a first class stamp on it. We will often use an even larger 9″ x 12″ envelope as well.

The pack included a simple one-page letter from Caterina Magisano about how the donor reading the letter could help be a part of the future.

The main component of this pack was a four-page survey.

Legacy gifts from your donors come from the autobiographical part of their brain, which is why surveys are a great tool to use when prospecting for these amazing donors. They allow the donor to think about their relationship to your organization and more importantly, your cause and mission. Surveys also put the donor in control of a very important conversation around how they want to be remembered. It makes donors feel in control and listened to.

The first page was personalized with a note from Caterina and the first question of the survey.

The survey isn't jam-packed with 1,000 deep questions. It uses simple questions, with straight-forward, potential answers.

The first few questions connect to the personal values of the donor.

Other questions are designed to get the donor thinking about their relationship with the charity and the cause they care about. The survey closes with some demographic questions.

Research tells us why donors leave a legacy gift. In a nutshell, a legacy gift comes when a donor thinks deeply about what really matters to her or him. This is why a survey-type pack can be a great legacy lead generation piece for donors.

Humber River Hospital Foundation

Confidential Survey for:

Ms. Caring Donor
123 Lover's Lane
Suite <3
Toronto, ON XoX oXo

Dear Caring,

As a dedicated supporter of Humber River Hospital Foundation, your ideas and opinions are important to us and help us better serve you and all our kind and caring donors.

Please take a few minutes to complete this short survey. Your answers will inform our plan for the future and ensure our work continues to champion excellent healthcare in the Greater Toronto Area.

Your privacy is important to us. Your answers will remain strictly confidential.

Caterina Magisano, CFRE,
Director, Legacy Giving
416-242-1000 Ext. 81516,
cmagisano@hrh.ca

YOUR VOICE FOR HEALTHCARE AT HUMBER RIVER HOSPITAL

About You and Humber River Hospital

1. Why do you support Humber River Hospital? *(check as many as you like)*
❍ Humber is a vital community Hospital.
❍ I have a personal connection to Humber.
❍ Supporting healthcare matters to me.
❍ It feels good to help others when they need the Hospital.
❍ Other: ____________________

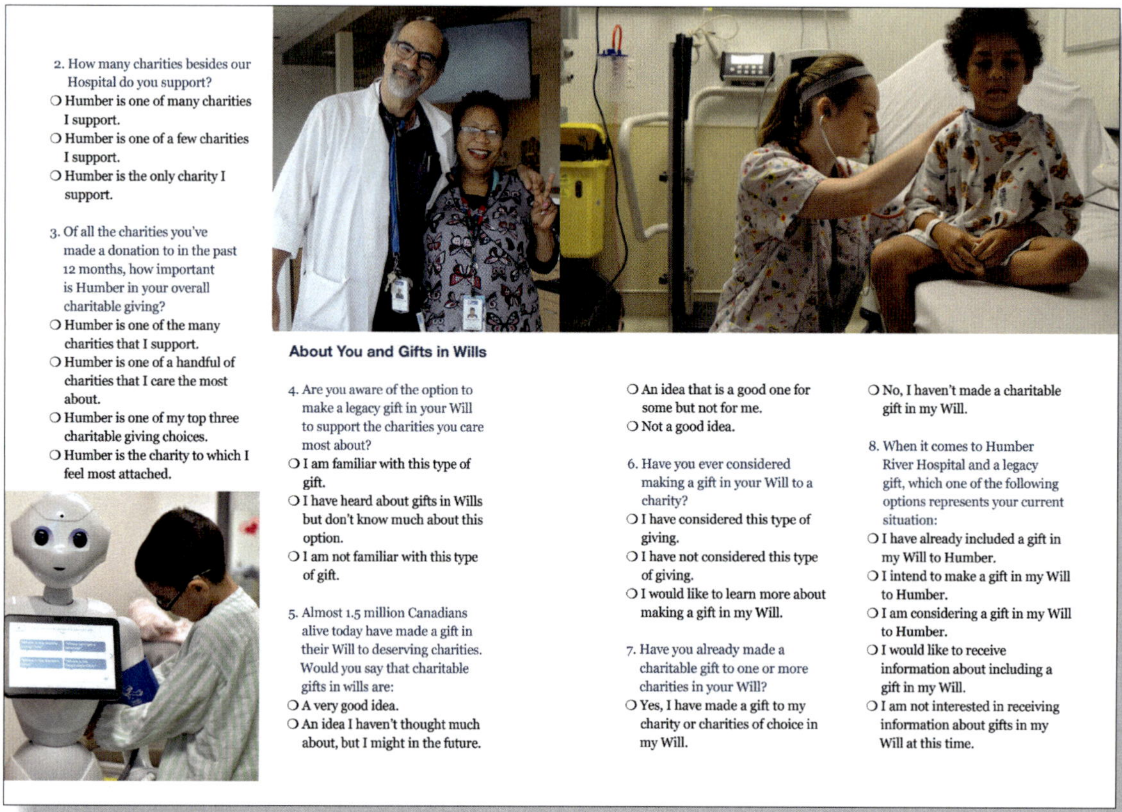

2. How many charities besides our Hospital do you support?
❍ Humber is one of many charities I support.
❍ Humber is one of a few charities I support.
❍ Humber is the only charity I support.

3. Of all the charities you've made a donation to in the past 12 months, how important is Humber in your overall charitable giving?
❍ Humber is one of the many charities that I support.
❍ Humber is one of a handful of charities that I care the most about.
❍ Humber is one of my top three charitable giving choices.
❍ Humber is the charity to which I feel most attached.

About You and Gifts in Wills

4. Are you aware of the option to make a legacy gift in your Will to support the charities you care most about?
❍ I am familiar with this type of gift.
❍ I have heard about gifts in Wills but don't know much about this option.
❍ I am not familiar with this type of gift.

5. Almost 1.5 million Canadians alive today have made a gift in their Will to deserving charities. Would you say that charitable gifts in wills are:
❍ A very good idea.
❍ An idea I haven't thought much about, but I might in the future.
❍ An idea that is a good one for some but not for me.
❍ Not a good idea.

6. Have you ever considered making a gift in your Will to a charity?
❍ I have considered this type of giving.
❍ I have not considered this type of giving.
❍ I would like to learn more about making a gift in my Will.

7. Have you already made a charitable gift to one or more charities in your Will?
❍ Yes, I have made a gift to my charity or charities of choice in my Will.
❍ No, I haven't made a charitable gift in my Will.

8. When it comes to Humber River Hospital and a legacy gift, which one of the following options represents your current situation:
❍ I have already included a gift in my Will to Humber.
❍ I intend to make a gift in my Will to Humber.
❍ I am considering a gift in my Will to Humber.
❍ I would like to receive information about including a gift in my Will.
❍ I am not interested in receiving information about gifts in my Will at this time.

A "WHY" BROCHURE & "HOW" BROCHURE

So then what? You've sent an invitation-type pack or maybe a survey.

Obviously if someone signals that they have left a gift to you in their Will or are thinking of it, you will be picking up that phone immediately to thank them profusely and to talk to them more about their decision.

For those who are looking for more information, we will craft two additional pieces. A lot of donors know how to add a charity to their Will, but for some reason, we spend a lot of time talking about the technicalities of how to do it.

What tends to be missing is the "why" component.

It's the "why" in fundraising that often compels us to join in, to take action. Yet, it's so easily overlooked or pushed aside.

The "why" brochure answers the question — Why leave a legacy gift to us?

This is what the "legacy-interested" donor would have received from Ontario Nature. It was a full size, 8.5″ x 11″ booklet designed to look like something quite familiar to a lot of environmentalists: a field guide. It's the sort you keep in your top pocket to make note of or sketch your most recent field find, fake leather skin and all.

This piece shares the amazing and inspiring stories of donors who have left a gift to Ontario Nature. Some still living, some who have passed.

This isn't some sort of 8.5″ x 3.5″ tri-fold bequest brochure with photos of sunsets and daisies.

We filled it with sketches, clippings, typed notes and the personal stories of many beautiful people.

These were snapshots of people's lives. Their stories. Their dreams. Their wishes.

We included a promise to donors about what being a part of the legacy society meant and about the care they would receive as a member of that group.

The "why" piece closed with a letter from Caroline Schultz, the Executive

She loved puzzles, cards, walking, cycling, cross-country skiing, sewing and reading. Her most beloved activity was gardening--she had a real passion for orchids. And she enjoyed fine Scotch whisky. Vida sounds like my kind of lady.

I never met Vida Bain, but I feel like I know her. It's been my pleasure and my honour to work with her husband, Colin, to use the gift Vida left to Ontario Nature in her Will in ways that would delight her. Because of Vida, we have been able to fund vital stewardship work on our Nature Reserves and also employ several interns and staff just starting their careers in conservation--energetic and dedicated young scientists who may not otherwise have had this opportunity.

For me, a highlight was taking a group of members on an orchid hike in June on our Petrel Point Nature Reserve--a place close to Vida's heart where we invested some of her legacy gift. We saw white bog orchids, grass pink orchids, yellow lady's-slippers, showy lady's-slippers and more. During the hike, we took a moment to honour Vida, letting the group know that her kindness and generosity had made this work possible. It was a beautiful moment on a beautiful day--a memory I will most certainly never forget.

I'm inspired every single day by your stories and memories, and I love hearing what matters to you and your dreams for nature in Ontario. I'm proud to help caring members and their families take action to protect nature forever. You are welcome to contact me anytime for a confidential discussion about how you can protect nature forever with a gift in your Will. Thank you!

Kirsten Dahl, Ontario Nature
416-444-8419, extension 235
kirstend@ontarionature.org

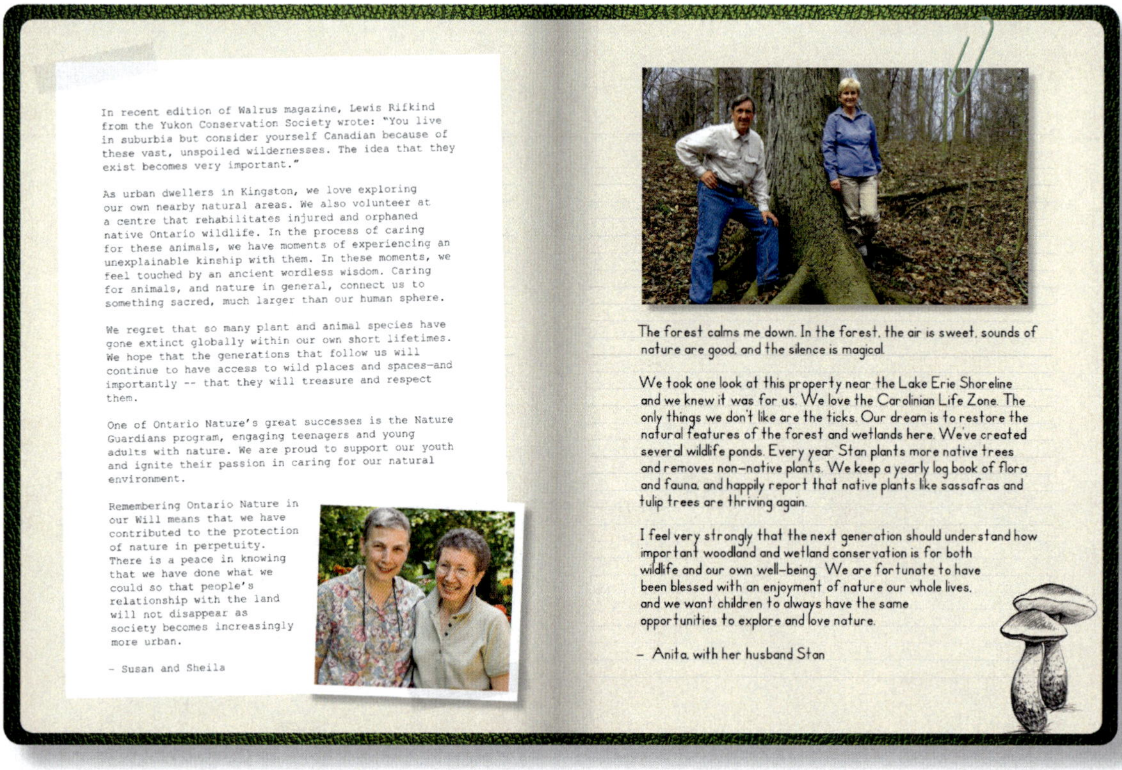

In recent edition of Walrus magazine, Lewis Rifkind from the Yukon Conservation Society wrote: "You live in suburbia but consider yourself Canadian because of these vast, unspoiled wildernesses. The idea that they exist becomes very important."

As urban dwellers in Kingston, we love exploring our own nearby natural areas. We also volunteer at a centre that rehabilitates injured and orphaned native Ontario wildlife. In the process of caring for these animals, we have moments of experiencing an unexplainable kinship with them. In these moments, we feel touched by an ancient wordless wisdom. Caring for animals, and nature in general, connect us to something sacred, much larger than our human sphere.

We regret that so many plant and animal species have gone extinct globally within our own short lifetimes. We hope that the generations that follow us will continue to have access to wild places and spaces-and importantly -- that they will treasure and respect them.

One of Ontario Nature's great successes is the Nature Guardians program, engaging teenagers and young adults with nature. We are proud to support our youth and ignite their passion in caring for our natural environment.

Remembering Ontario Nature in our Will means that we have contributed to the protection of nature in perpetuity. There is a peace in knowing that we have done what we could so that people's relationship with the land will not disappear as society becomes increasingly more urban.

- Susan and Sheila

The forest calms me down. In the forest, the air is sweet, sounds of nature are good, and the silence is magical.

We took one look at this property near the Lake Erie Shoreline and we knew it was for us. We love the Carolinian Life Zone. The only things we don't like are the ticks. Our dream is to restore the natural features of the forest and wetlands here. We've created several wildlife ponds. Every year Stan plants more native trees and removes non-native plants. We keep a yearly log book of flora and fauna, and happily report that native plants like sassafras and tulip trees are thriving again.

I feel very strongly that the next generation should understand how important woodland and wetland conservation is for both wildlife and our own well-being. We are fortunate to have been blessed with an enjoyment of nature our whole lives, and we want children to always have the same opportunities to explore and love nature.

- Anita, with her husband Stan

Director, who shared the legacy and future vision for the organization.

There were no boring checklists and no bullet points listing the transactional aspects of leaving a gift in your Will.

Our job is to hold a mirror up to our donors, showing them how normal people like them have done transformative things for the organization. We also need to make it easy for them to get involved and do the same.

The donor will read the stories and hear echoes of them in her heart.

Finally, we also created a simple "how" piece that is sent out alongside the "why" brochure as a follow up to the wonderful folks who have taken the time to check a few boxes.

The "how" piece focuses on some of the nuts and bolts of leaving a legacy gift to your organization. It's not meant to be overly inspirational, just "the facts" about how to go about this important step as it relates specifically to your organization.

Here's an example **(Fig 12.2)** we created for our friends at St. Thomas Elgin General Hospital Foundation.

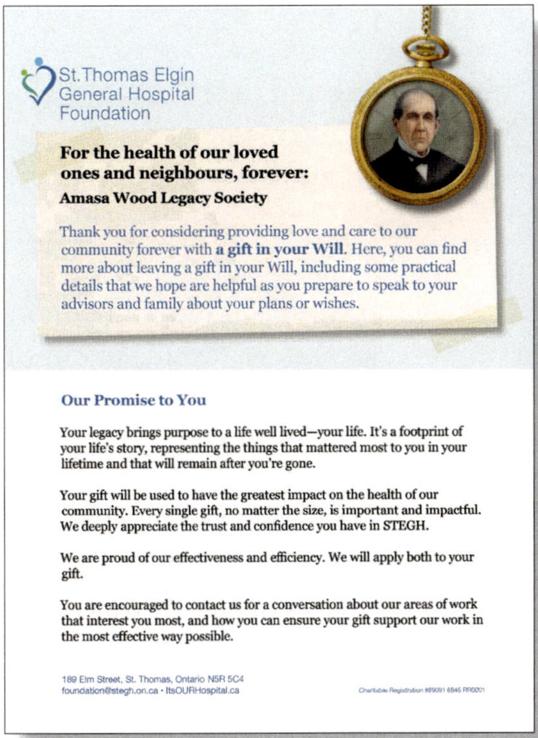

St.Thomas Elgin General Hospital Foundation

For the health of our loved ones and neighbours, forever:
Amasa Wood Legacy Society

Thank you for considering providing love and care to our community forever with **a gift in your Will**. Here, you can find more about leaving a gift in your Will, including some practical details that we hope are helpful as you prepare to speak to your advisors and family about your plans or wishes.

Our Promise to You

Your legacy brings purpose to a life well lived—your life. It's a footprint of your life's story, representing the things that mattered most to you in your lifetime and that will remain after you're gone.

Your gift will be used to have the greatest impact on the health of our community. Every single gift, no matter the size, is important and impactful. We deeply appreciate the trust and confidence you have in STEGH.

We are proud of our effectiveness and efficiency. We will apply both to your gift.

You are encouraged to contact us for a conversation about our areas of work that interest you most, and how you can ensure your gift support our work in the most effective way possible.

189 Elm Street, St. Thomas, Ontario N5R 5C4
foundation@stegh.on.ca • ItsOURHospital.ca

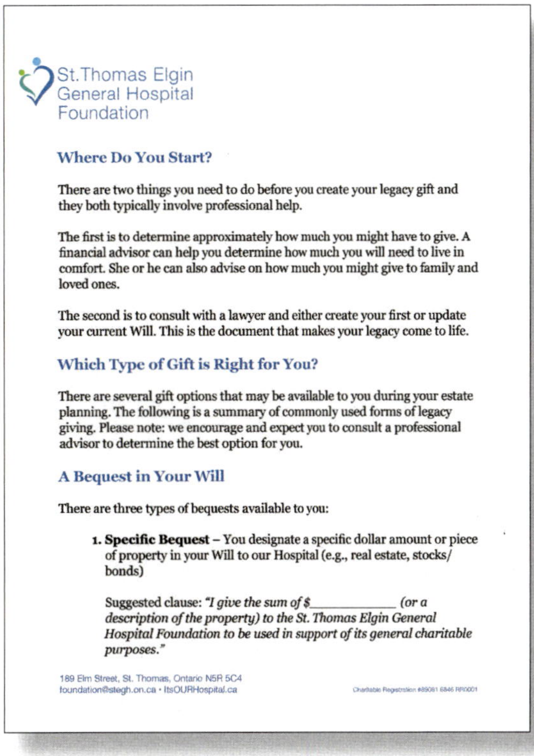

St.Thomas Elgin General Hospital Foundation

Where Do You Start?

There are two things you need to do before you create your legacy gift and they both typically involve professional help.

The first is to determine approximately how much you might have to give. A financial advisor can help you determine how much you will need to live in comfort. She or he can also advise on how much you might give to family and loved ones.

The second is to consult with a lawyer and either create your first or update your current Will. This is the document that makes your legacy come to life.

Which Type of Gift is Right for You?

There are several gift options that may be available to you during your estate planning. The following is a summary of commonly used forms of legacy giving. Please note: we encourage and expect you to consult a professional advisor to determine the best option for you.

A Bequest in Your Will

There are three types of bequests available to you:

1. **Specific Bequest** – You designate a specific dollar amount or piece of property in your Will to our Hospital (e.g., real estate, stocks/bonds)

   Suggested clause: *"I give the sum of $____________ (or a description of the property) to the St. Thomas Elgin General Hospital Foundation to be used in support of its general charitable purposes."*

189 Elm Street, St. Thomas, Ontario N5R 5C4
foundation@stegh.on.ca • ItsOURHospital.ca

Fig 12.2

WHAT'S THE LOVE STORY?

You've sent out your lead generation mail piece to some of your best donors. Some donors answered that they are leaving a gift in their Will to you. A few say they are thinking about it. There are others who want more information. Some donors have said nothing at all.

Now what?

Well for those donors who have, might be or are thinking about leaving a gift in their Will to you, a lot of hard work starts.

Imagine your donor is 65 years old, has put you in their Will and now goes on to live until she's 93. Bless her.

Some donors will tell you they have left a gift in their Will to you but after they pass, you find out that they didn't. It happens. We don't know why.

A donor might change their mind. You might have offended them. Their life circumstances might have changed. We don't know.

Like everything else in our work, let's not focus on what the donor might or might not do. Let's focus on the hard work that will hopefully ensure that they *will* take the action we want them to take.

Our job is to help donors stay connected to their giving and the issues they care deeply about.

Having a "love story" will help you to consider this emotional conversation over the months and years to come.

A "love story" can be developed for all your donors.

The Love Story Grid maps out all of the touch points between you and your donors (or your community) and it's anchored around the feelings that we want your donor to have. Sometimes you are asking them for support in an appeal, sometimes you are thanking them and/or reporting back on their impact, and sometimes it is all three.

LOVE STORY GRID

	Week 1	Week 1-2	Week 4	2nd month	3rd month	4th month	5th month	6th month	7th month	8th month	9th month	10th month	11th month	12th month
objective	welcome!	thank you & receipt	getting to know each other	surprise and delight	ask, highly variable	action	surprise and delight	demonstrate impact	action	surprise and delight	how are we doing?	action	surprise and delight	demonstrate impact
what is it?														
feeling	sincere, happy, friendly	transparent, accountable	this is a dialogue, a relationship	wow! Amazing!	I can see how my gift will make a difference	this is great! I can do more than just give	wow! Amazing!	proud to be part of this	this is great! I can do more than just give	wow! Amazing!	they care about what I think	this is great! I can do more than just give	wow! Amazing!	proud to be part of this
metrics														

We also develop these for legacy donors.

You can see how a legacy love story overlays the love story for annual donors but adds in a number of different touch points for these most special of donors.

Having a Love Story Grid allows you to keep having meaningful and special conversations with these most important donors year over year. Consider crafting one for your organization.

FUNDRAISING PLAN: YOUR DONOR LOVE STORY!

	Nov	Dec	Jan	Feb	March	Apr	May	June	July	Aug	Sep	Oct	Nov
objective	raise funds	#donorlove	inform and engage, demonstrate donor care	raise funds	raise funds	new monthly donors	inform and engage	raise funds	inform and engage		inform and engage	#donorlove	raise fu
what is it?	Year End Appeal	Giving Tuesday	magazine, nudge about receipts	Renewal	Renewal Reminder	Reg giving Conversion	magazine, reader survey	Spring Appeal	magazine		magazine	Thanksgiving	Year En
feeling	I'm inspired to give and know what my gift does.	I'm happy to be part of this community	I'm informed, I've got what I need and I feel satisfied	I see my values echoed and I know that I'm needed.	I see my values echoed and I know that I'm needed.	I'm part of something bigger, I see my shared values in action	I'm informed and they want to hear what I think	I'm helping fix a problem that I care about.	I'm informed and connected to what other ppl like me are doing		I'm informed	I feel appreciated and valued.	I'm insp give and what my does.
channels	print appeal, echoed online and in social media	online	print, online, phone	print appeal, echoed online and in social media	print appeal, echoed online and in social media	print and phone	print, online, phone	print appeal, echoed online and in social media	print		print	print (to your best donors), email and social media	print ap echoed in social
metrics	response rate, average gift, gross and net revenue	engagement metrics, anecdotal	gifts, anecdotal	response rate, average gift, gross and net revenue	response rate, average gift, gross and net revenue	new monthly conversions, anecdotal	gifts, survey responses, anecdotal	response rate, average gift, gross and net revenue	gifts, anecdotal		gifts, anecdotal	anecdotal	respons average and net

FINDING MORE LEGACY PROSPECTS

You have all communication working smoothly and chugging along. But now you want to reach further, beyond your current donor pool. Can we find some new potential legacy donors for your organization?

Yes, we can.

There isn't a shortage of places where your donors are and where you can plant some seeds for this type of gift.

Small community newspapers, regional television, magazine inserts and a big one: social media platforms.

Facebook

Digital and social media are a constant-evolving thing. With changes in privacy, the way data is managed and as the platforms evolve, what is working right now might not even be possible in the future (i.e., When you are reading this. Sigh.).

The data on who is using social to find legacy prospects changes year over year, but there are a few things to consider. As your donors age:

- some have moved from their homes (which might be the mailing address you have for them on file),

- some may have their mail vetted for them on an ongoing basis, and
- maybe some stopped giving to you because they were operating off a pension.

A lot of these same donors are quite active on social media. They watch cat videos and zoom their grandkids just like the rest of us.

Some may be especially active on Facebook as a way to keep up with old friends and neighbours.

Facebook advertising can be extremely targeted and therefore quite effective. You can also turn it on and off, budgeting how much you want to spend. Most importantly, unlike mail, you can find out pretty quickly if it is "working" or not.

A few more things to consider.

- You still need to be thoughtful about creative.
- You still need a good offer.
- The experience still needs to be frictionless. And,
- You still have to care and tend for these folks very thoughtfully.

Back to Nature Canada.

We wanted to test four different visual ideas using a beneficiary (a baby animal), a beneficiary (a piece of nature), a future vision (of kids playing on the dock) and a donor (we used a couple).

Although the kids did better in testing than the couple, it didn't mean that kids were better. It could mean we needed a different couple or maybe just a single donor. Another thing we found was that if an image of the fawn, for example, was testing well, it would often do better the more you zoomed in on it.

You can also test a small carousel of images or short video. The only way to know is to make the investment and start trying different options.

As discussed in *Deviation 3*, you still need a great offer. Every channel, every time.

The best idea is to pick an offer when you test your image. Then, when you have a winning image you can start to test your offer.

For these specific ads, we found that the fawn or the donors did the best in testing, depending on the audience, etc.

We also found that protecting nature for future generations worked better than "forever."

headline:

You can protect Nature for generations with a Gift in your Will.

OR

You can protect Nature forever with a Gift in Your Will.

OR

Leave Something Beautiful Behind.

From the ad, donors could click through to a page on the Nature Canada website that would allow them to request more information.

Every step in this process is testable and you're only limited by the experience of your team or degree of desire to get ultra nerdy about it.

Ideally, your donor will give you their email (don't ask them for 1,000 details since you will likely lose them if you do), and you should get a notification in your inbox from the email being submitted. Don't let those emails go to some generic inbox that is looked at once a month!

The generous people who took the time to respond should get a reply email pretty quickly with a "hello" and some sort of hybrid document of a WHY and HOW piece.

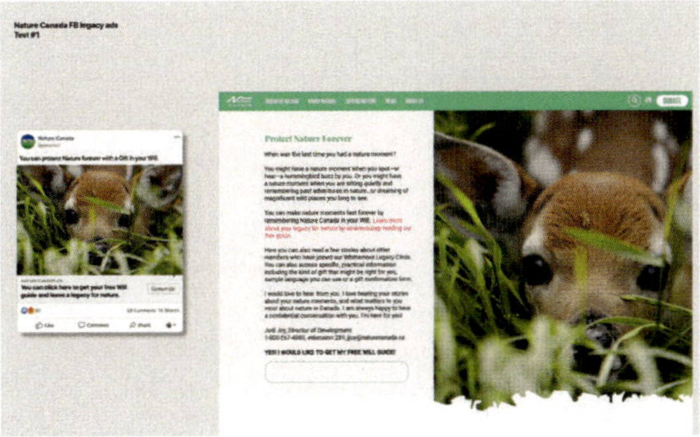

You can create your own "Love Story" for these prospects. It's a different challenge than maintaining contact with your current donors.

A follow-up email in a few weeks, creating some open space for questions or contact might be all that you can get.

PLEASE **do not** put them into your regular marketing and communications e-blast schedule (unless of course they have asked you to do that).

You can consider crafting a very light, personal, welcome series as it is all testable. It again will depend on your capacity to maintain a personal level of contact with these folks.

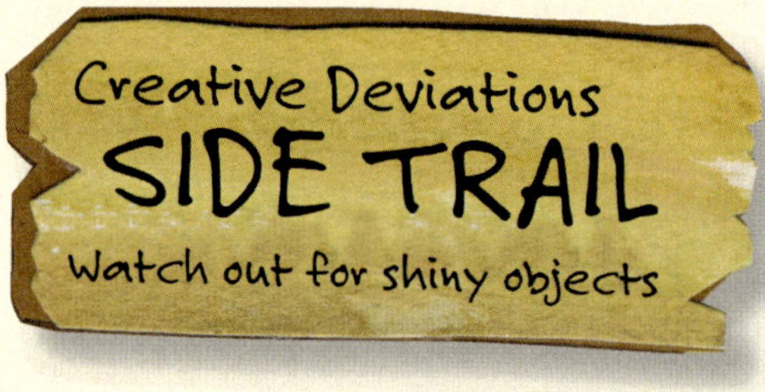

THREE DEATHS

A story Agent Jen and I often share in AOG presentations is about the three deaths.

Have you heard of this?

It comes from the book, "*Sum: Forty Tales from the Afterlives*," by David Eagleman.

The nutshell of the story is that we all die three deaths.

The *first time* we die is when the air leaves our lungs for the final time and our physical body stops functioning.

The *second time* we die is when our family buries our body or celebrates/mourns our passing.

We die a *third and final time* when our name is last spoken for all of eternity.

I share this with you because, in the context of legacy giving, we have the beautiful privilege of ensuring that our donors' names and lives will never be forgotten.

(*If that doesn't make you want to have a quick ugly cry before you get back to work then…*)

DEVIATION DISCOVERIES

The idea that fundraising is a long game is never more accurate than when discussing legacy giving. You can potentially get a donor telling you that they are interested, or plan on leaving you a gift in their Will, up to 20 years before you find out if they actually did or did not carry through.

1. Listen! Every day our colleagues around the world are trying and learning new things about legacy giving. Ask questions, look at the research and data, listen to what fundraisers are learning about their donors and then apply it to your program.
2. Your donors, all donors, want their lives to have meaning after they are gone. You can provide that opportunity by focusing on the intention in their heart and not the bulge in their wallet.
3. In North America we are in the early stages of the greatest transfer of wealth that has ever been seen. The time to start your donor-loving legacy program was yesterday. However, if you didn't start it yesterday, then now will work too.

Bonus Deviation: The Story of Humbert

In 2014, AOG were asked to meet with Stephanie Highfield and Helga Schnider at Humber River Hospital Foundation about their individual giving program. They were in the middle of a capital campaign and trying to raising significant funds for a new hospital, the most technologically advanced of its kind. We sat down and had a great chat about the program and walked out of the meeting ready to help the foundation reconnect with its individual donors.

Sometimes, when an organization is running a capital campaign, the day-to-day donors, (the ones we tend to forget about since they aren't the ones we are looking for during a capital campaign) just stop giving. This is because all the hoopla is over big gifts, oversized cheques and people that resemble nothing like "me."

It's not intentional. It just happens.

I've often used the analogy of the "idiot driver."

How often have you been cruising down the highway, seeing a sign for your destination that is 40 kms away. In a few blinks of your eyes, BOOM — now it is only 5 kms!

Highway hypnosis. It's a thing.

We've all experienced that moment where we look in the rearview mirror and see a car approaching from behind, weaving in and out... speeding up to us... the idiot driver.

It forces us to pay attention. We can't help it. If we were experiencing any sort of highway hypnosis, it stops with that glance in the mirror.

Donors, like all of us humans, have a tendency to move through our day in a hypnotic kind of way. It gives us comfort.

So — I jokingly suggest that charities must become that idiot driver. What can we do to wake our drowsy and bored donors and get them to pay attention to us?

Often, my suggestion is that we do something that the donor wouldn't have expected us to do, ever.

We want to send something that makes them take notice and then reward them when they do.

We can use a bit of surprise and delight. We can give them a donor-sized problem that they can help solve. We can acknowledge that we know who they are, that we need their help and show appreciation for them in the process. We can make it easy for them to know what we want and for them to give.

With all that in mind, we gathered to plan our first appeal for Humber River Hospital Foundation (H+).

We needed to find a way to point out all of the small ways that donors would have impact in this new BAZILLION* (not factually correct) dollar hospital. This message should be delivered by someone different than whoever had been signing the other appeals.

We had a story of a patient named Bernice. An 85-year-old woman who was active, independent and healthy. She was rushed to the hospital with an irregular heartbeat and while her treatment initially was a bit touch and go, she received a life-saving pacemaker. Her son, Gordon shared how appreciative they were of Bernice's treatment and care.

"Everyone, from Dr. Bauer, to the nursing staff to the people who brought in meals, treated us like family, not like patients. My mum has many more fulfilling years ahead of her, and I felt like the team treated her like she was their own mother — with respect and care. I couldn't be more thankful or appreciative to Humber River."

Good stuff.

The ask focused on the small things that would make a difference to families like Bernice and Gordon's during difficult times.

The two things that we kept coming back to was this idea that the donors **AND** the doctors, nurses and support staff combined are the true heart of any healthy hospital so we needed to use a someone that would be (or could be) witness to all of these small things and the moments that can be easily overshadowed by all the big tech and equipment.

As a creative team, Jen Love and I kept talking back and forth as the new campaign went from a brief into storytelling.

We talked about the interview, if there was one, what we were asking the donor to do, what sorts of pieces or creative would help make the story and ask shine.

We knew we wanted to have a lift note and decided pretty early on that we wanted a map. Jen loves maps and they make amazing lift notes.

We wanted a map that connected the new, razzle-dazzle hospital with feelings, represented by hearts.

The last note we had in our draft said, "Last one could be putting the donor in the middle of the hospital... You're the true heart of a healthy hospital. Thank you for your support!"

We had all the pieces to make for a pretty solid appeal but to come back to the analogy, we wanted to be that idiot driver (in a good way) and how could we do that?

Like most of the best ideas, how we got to what we presented is a little lost in the sands of time.

But we came up with our pal, Humbert.

Like many great ideas, it's not really that much of a stretch. The logo was a "H+".

Every hospital has this big blue H on the side of it. If anything was going to be witness to all of the drama, happiness and sadness, moments big and small, it was going to be that "H"...

Humber-t. Get it?

I know... Razzle dazzle.

Jessica Rae Gordon and I worked on a couple prototypes for our new friend and settled on this.

MAILING #1: SPRING

I wanted to use our new friend straight away on the outer envelope.

It might be our first and only shot to get the donor's attention.

So, alongside the first draft of the copy, we also presented this to the client:

It was a larger size, 9.5″ x 5.875″ envelope with this remarkable character on it. I had also decided to not use the logo or the name of the organization on it since I didn't know if that was getting in the way of a donor opening it. Yes — your organization name and/or logo may be hurting your results.

Tagline: "*Nice to meetcha!*"

We presented Humbert as the custodian of donor love and care. He might be attached to the side of the building, high up in the air, but he could see and hear all of the heartfelt moments that would make donors swoon and feel connected in a totally new way to their giving.

This was a tough sell. No matter how we positioned it.

We had a number of discussions about how great fundraising needs to be creative, heartfelt, vulnerable, emotional and has to create or leave space for donors to be an active and acknowledged participant in making things happen!

We had laid some of the ground work to present an idea like this. Still, how do you get buy in from the boss? The boss' boss? The marketing folks? Branding police?

Buy in wasn't easy. Lots of calls and emails ensued.

We had to change Humbert. It was too similar to their logo. It was decided that if we could morph him away from the logo, he could stay.

We added the construction hat instead of the fedora (I don't even know why he originally had a fedora — it was a little hipster in retrospect) since the new hospital was still a hole in the ground with lots of cranes and construction crews about.

And then we moved into drafting the first version of this spring pack.

The revised OE had a new tagline. I considered making Humbert a bit of a poet by having him rhyme everything he said — which turned in to a bit of a nightmare from a copy-writing point of view.

We broke a few "rules" with this pack. It didn't use the organizational logo. It was oversized. A departure from the standard #10 envelopes they had tended to use.

And it featured Humbert. When have you ever seen an envelope like this in your mail box?

We also mocked up the insert since that was the other important piece in this pack.

And with approvals, we moved on to a final draft.

The insert was 8.5″ x 11″, folded in half and focused on the many small ways donors and their gifts would have an impact around the new hospital.

Humbert was there to show them all of the small ways they were having impact! He had a voice unlike everyone else. He wasn't a doctor or a nurse or an administrator of any kind. He was the custodian of donor love and care, an important voice during a time of large, cheque signings and architectural drawings.

Humbert could share human emotions, the stories and the people that made this hospital great. He reminded donors that digital technology and zipping about robots are great, but this is a patient-first hospital. Donors make that part possible.

This is why Humbert was so effective. He was as far away from all the things that didn't really matter to "normal" donors as you could possibly get. The irony.

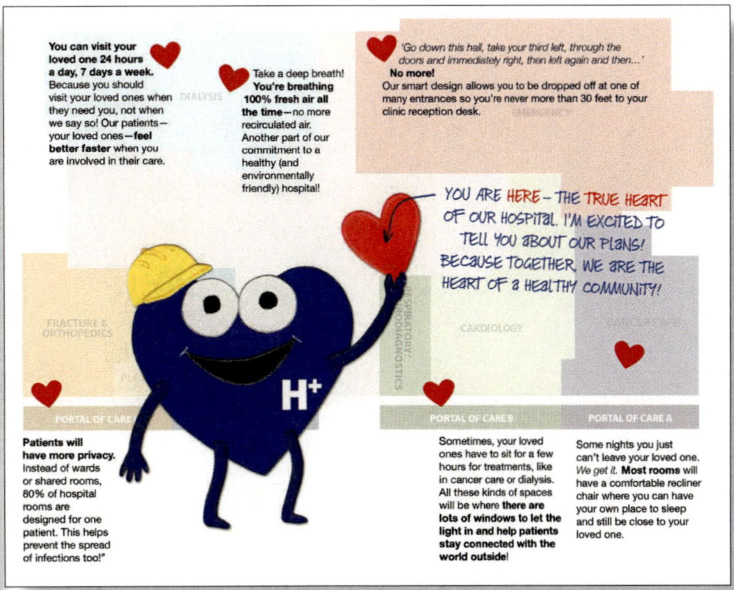

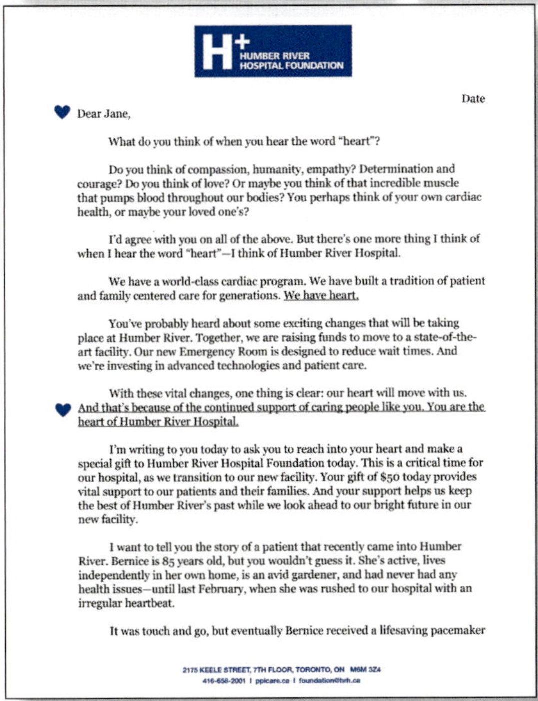

HUMBER RIVER HOSPITAL FOUNDATION

Date

Dear Jane,

What do you think of when you hear the word "heart"?

Do you think of compassion, humanity, empathy? Determination and courage? Do you think of love? Or maybe you think of that incredible muscle that pumps blood throughout our bodies? You perhaps think of your own cardiac health, or maybe your loved one's?

I'd agree with you on all of the above. But there's one more thing I think of when I hear the word "heart"—I think of Humber River Hospital.

We have a world-class cardiac program. We have built a tradition of patient and family centered care for generations. We have heart.

You've probably heard about some exciting changes that will be taking place at Humber River. Together, we are raising funds to move to a state-of-the-art facility. Our new Emergency Room is designed to reduce wait times. And we're investing in advanced technologies and patient care.

With these vital changes, one thing is clear: our heart will move with us. And that's because of the continued support of caring people like you. You are the heart of Humber River Hospital.

I'm writing to you today to ask you to reach into your heart and make a special gift to Humber River Hospital Foundation today. This is a critical time for our hospital, as we transition to our new facility. Your gift of $50 today provides vital support to our patients and their families. And your support helps us keep the best of Humber River's past while we look ahead to our bright future in our new facility.

I want to tell you the story of a patient that recently came into Humber River. Bernice is 85 years old, but you wouldn't guess it. She's active, lives independently in her own home, is an avid gardener, and had never had any health issues—until last February, when she was rushed to our hospital with an irregular heartbeat.

It was touch and go, but eventually Bernice received a lifesaving pacemaker

2175 KEELE STREET, 7TH FLOOR, TORONTO, ON M6M 3Z4
416-658-2001 | ppicare.ca | foundation@hrh.ca

by our heart specialist Dr. Robert Bauer. Bernice's son Gordon was right by her side throughout her stay. He took part in every conversation with members of our medical team, squishing his 6'5" frame into an uncomfortable chair while his mother rested.

Gordon says that his experience at Humber River was unlike any other he'd ever had in a hospital setting. "Everyone, from Dr. Bauer to the nursing staff to the people who brought in meals, treated us like family, not like patients. My mom has many more fulfilling years ahead of her, and I felt like the team treated her like she was their own mother—with respect and care. I couldn't be more thankful or appreciative to Humber River."

And as for Bernice, she said, "I'm forever grateful, and I know I wouldn't be here if it wasn't for Dr. Bauer and Humber River Hospital".

I love hearing stories like Bernice and Gordon's. I'm very proud of the work we do at Humber River, but I'm also mindful of the need to constantly improve patient care and experiences.

That's why—among many other enhancements—our new facility will include more space than ever before for family members in patient rooms, while still maintaining patient privacy. There will even be pullout recliner chairs for sleeping, so your loved ones will not have to squish into an office chair in the corner, like Gordon did! The companionship and involvement of loved ones are a vital part of the treatment and healing process, and we have designed our new hospital to make this shared belief a reality.

You will find enclosed some more information about the exciting improvements we have planned for our new facility. We are bringing the best of the past and the best of the future of hospital care together. We want you to be a part of it with your special gift today! You are the heart of our hospital. And together, we are the heart of a healthy community.

Yours for bringing the heart of our past to our exciting future,

Heather Hurst
President & CEO

P.S. Your gift brings together the best of Humber River's past with future advances in patient care. Will you please support the heart of a healthy community with your gift to Humber River Hospital Foundation today?

The letter was personalized and we added hearts in the margin to add extra emphasis to the things we wanted the skimmers to read.

It passed the classic red pen test. Go through your letter and circle all of the "you" and "your" words. If you've done a good job it should look like your letter has the measles.

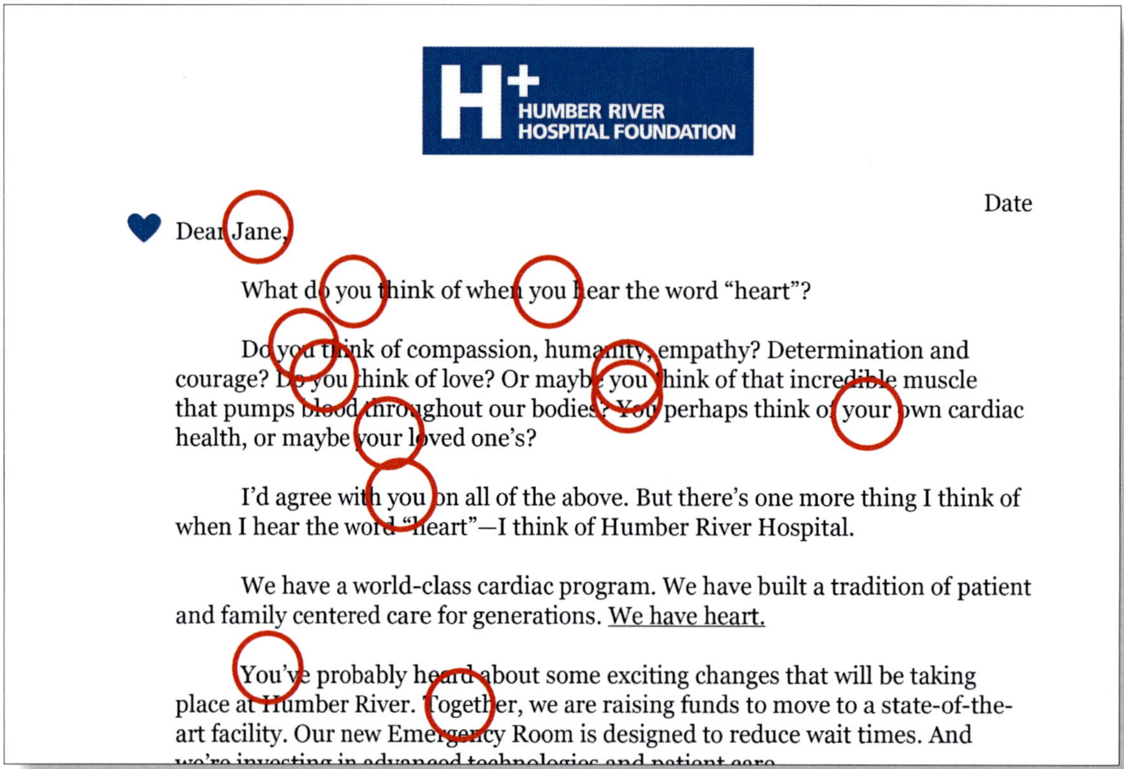
HUMBER RIVER HOSPITAL FOUNDATION

Date

Dear Jane,

What do you think of when you hear the word "heart"?

Do you think of compassion, humanity, empathy? Determination and courage? Do you think of love? Or maybe you think of that incredible muscle that pumps blood throughout our bodies? You perhaps think of your own cardiac health, or maybe your loved one's?

I'd agree with you on all of the above. But there's one more thing I think of when I hear the word "heart"—I think of Humber River Hospital.

We have a world-class cardiac program. We have built a tradition of patient and family centered care for generations. We have heart.

You've probably heard about some exciting changes that will be taking place at Humber River. Together, we are raising funds to move to a state-of-the-art facility. Our new Emergency Room is designed to reduce wait times. And

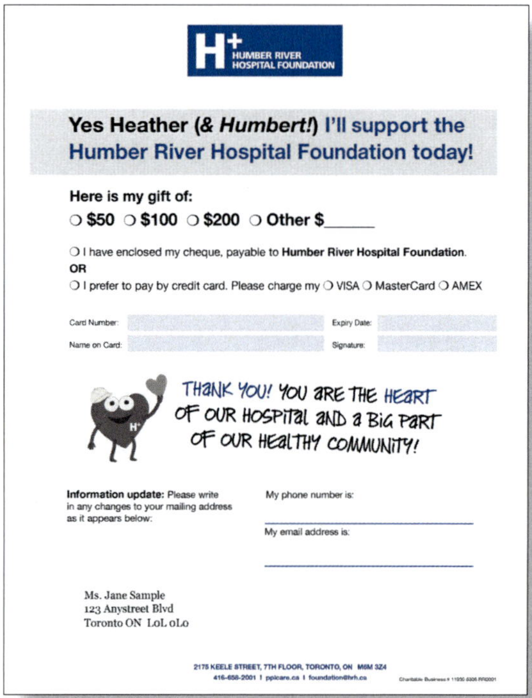
HUMBER RIVER HOSPITAL FOUNDATION

Yes Heather (& *Humbert!*) I'll support the Humber River Hospital Foundation today!

Here is my gift of:

❍ **$50** ❍ **$100** ❍ **$200** ❍ **Other $______**

❍ I have enclosed my cheque, payable to **Humber River Hospital Foundation**.

OR

❍ I prefer to pay by credit card. Please charge my ❍ VISA ❍ MasterCard ❍ AMEX

Card Number: Expiry Date:

Name on Card: Signature:

Information update: Please write in any changes to your mailing address as it appears below:

My phone number is:

My email address is:

Ms. Jane Sample
123 Anystreet Blvd
Toronto ON L0L 0L0

2175 KEELE STREET, 7TH FLOOR, TORONTO, ON M6M 3Z4
416-658-2001 | ppicare.ca | foundation@hrh.ca

The letter made the connection between Humber River Hospital having a heart for its patients and the hearts of its donors. Nothing is possible without them. They are needed now and in to the future.

Donors certainly hadn't heard from the foundation like this before.

The reply was full-sized and segmented to be appropriate to previous giving. Humbert returned to say "Thank you!"

We included a business reply envelope and the team at Humber River created an in-house, high touch version of this pack for the top 20% of their donors (see *Deviation 9* for more information on that).

So — how did Humbert do?

In a nutshell, donors seemed to love Humbert.

The appeal did well enough that we gained the confidence to be a little different in our approach.

We get scared of new ideas for many reasons. But there is always room in your program to try something new. A new approach, a fresh voice, something outside of the status quo — whatever that might be for you.

You're not going to break it — "it" being your program or your donors.

Your donors stop giving to you because they are either bored with your self-centered appeals or because all you ever do is ask them for money.

They don't stop giving because of appeals like this.

We were asked what Humbert was going to do or say next in the year ahead. Just like real life, we didn't know at the moment but we knew we would know when we got there. He would be present and vocal when the donors needed to be reminded how much they mattered.

If you work in individual giving and part of your job is to send donor appeals throughout the year, you need to think of your work like a symphony made up of a lot of notes and noises.

Every mailing, every email, every touch point is a "note" that we must try to make as true and pitch-perfect as possible in all of the thousand ways — in the story it tells, in its acknowledgement of the donor and who they are, in the space it creates for the donor to be a part of our story.

Pitch-perfect. Every "note."

When you step back and look at each note, especially as they relate to the one before it and after it, you and your donors should feel a part of a beautiful movement.

Emotional, thoughtful and connected.

Further to the point, it's why you can't look at a single appeal (or note) and decide to remove it if it doesn't do as well as you had hoped. You have to measure the bottom line of ALL your "notes." Is it beautiful noise or a bunch of clanging gongs?

But I digress.

MAILING #2: EARLY FALL

The subject was digital technology. Da Vinci robots, x-ray units, infant isolation units. Doesn't exactly give you the warm and fuzzies does it?

This is a great example of what something (someone) like Humbert can do for your appeals.

He can add feelings, levity and visual interest to something that could come across as cold and mechanical.

We originally considered making our digital technology come to life alongside Humbert but someone drew the line there.

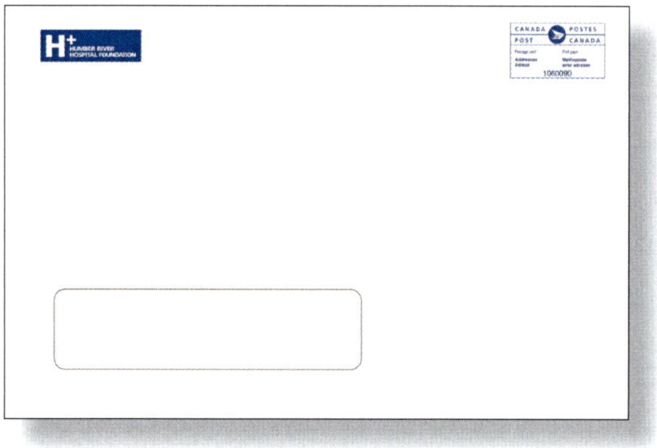

We used a full-size, simple envelope. On the back, Humbert announces "I'm back and I want you to meet a few of my pals!"

Even if you were a newly acquired donor or recalled the pack from the spring — this is an effective outer.

What sort of pals would Humbert have? Donors would want to know.

The two-page letter came from Heather Hurst.

We used a little bit of handwriting on the "...please turn over ..." and PS to add some human elements to the letter. (If my colleague Sonya is reading this, she will recognize her handwriting immediately as I had it made into a font many years ago!)

Humbert shows up on the bottom of the letter, asking readers to follow along with him to the insert!

The insert was a simple 8.5″ x 11″ folded into three panels with Humbert doing

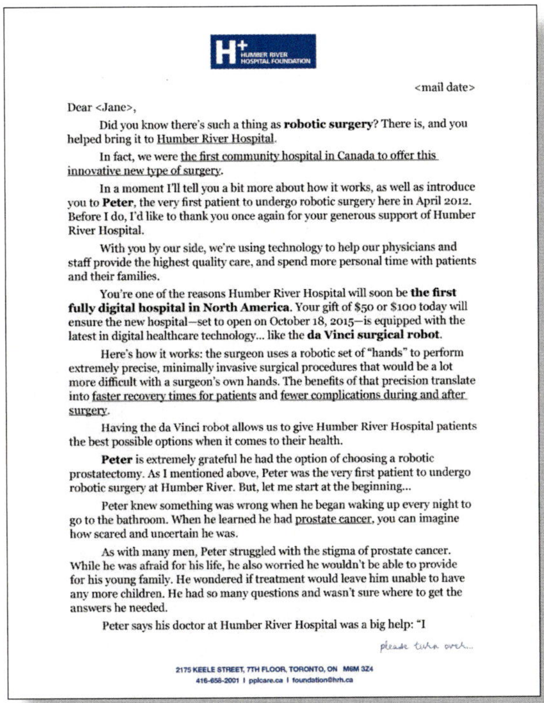

HUMBER RIVER HOSPITAL FOUNDATION

<mail date>

Dear <Jane>,

Did you know there's such a thing as **robotic surgery**? There is, and you helped bring it to Humber River Hospital.

In fact, we were the first community hospital in Canada to offer this innovative new type of surgery.

In a moment I'll tell you a bit more about how it works, as well as introduce you to **Peter**, the very first patient to undergo robotic surgery here in April 2012. Before I do, I'd like to thank you once again for your generous support of Humber River Hospital.

With you by our side, we're using technology to help our physicians and staff provide the highest quality care, and spend more personal time with patients and their families.

You're one of the reasons Humber River Hospital will soon be **the first fully digital hospital in North America.** Your gift of $50 or $100 today will ensure the new hospital—set to open on October 18, 2015—is equipped with the latest in digital healthcare technology... like the **da Vinci surgical robot**.

Here's how it works: the surgeon uses a robotic set of "hands" to perform extremely precise, minimally invasive surgical procedures that would be a lot more difficult with a surgeon's own hands. The benefits of that precision translate into faster recovery times for patients and fewer complications during and after surgery.

Having the da Vinci robot allows us to give Humber River Hospital patients the best possible options when it comes to their health.

Peter is extremely grateful he had the option of choosing a robotic prostatectomy. As I mentioned above, Peter was the very first patient to undergo robotic surgery at Humber River. But, let me start at the beginning...

Peter knew something was wrong when he began waking up every night to go to the bathroom. When he learned he had prostate cancer, you can imagine how scared and uncertain he was.

As with many men, Peter struggled with the stigma of prostate cancer. While he was afraid for his life, he also worried he wouldn't be able to provide for his young family. He wondered if treatment would leave him unable to have any more children. He had so many questions and wasn't sure where to get the answers he needed.

Peter says his doctor at Humber River Hospital was a big help: "I

please turn over...

2175 KEELE STREET, 7TH FLOOR, TORONTO, ON M6M 3Z4
416-658-2001 | pplcare.ca | foundation@hrh.ca

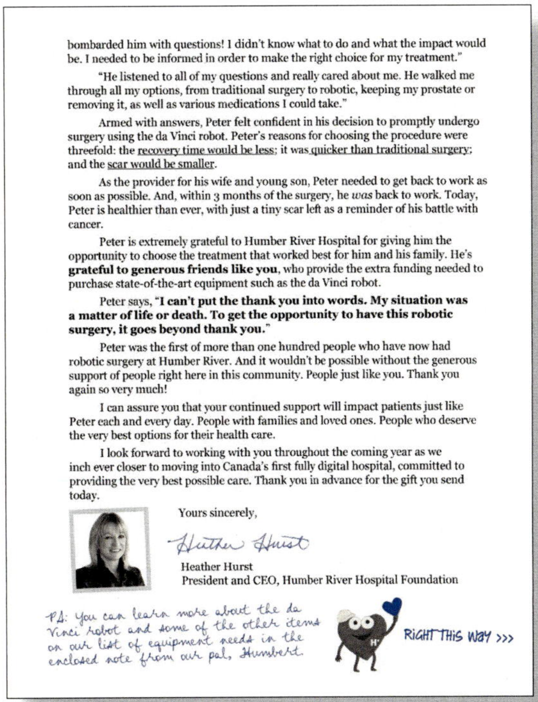

bombarded him with questions! I didn't know what to do and what the impact would be. I needed to be informed in order to make the right choice for my treatment."

"He listened to all of my questions and really cared about me. He walked me through all my options, from traditional surgery to robotic, keeping my prostate or removing it, as well as various medications I could take."

Armed with answers, Peter felt confident in his decision to promptly undergo surgery using the da Vinci robot. Peter's reasons for choosing the procedure were threefold: the recovery time would be less; it was quicker than traditional surgery; and the scar would be smaller.

As the provider for his wife and young son, Peter needed to get back to work as soon as possible. And, within 3 months of the surgery, he *was* back to work. Today, Peter is healthier than ever, with just a tiny scar left as a reminder of his battle with cancer.

Peter is extremely grateful to Humber River Hospital for giving him the opportunity to choose the treatment that worked best for him and his family. He's **grateful to generous friends like you**, who provide the extra funding needed to purchase state-of-the-art equipment such as the da Vinci robot.

Peter says, **"I can't put the thank you into words. My situation was a matter of life or death. To get the opportunity to have this robotic surgery, it goes beyond thank you."**

Peter was the first of more than one hundred people who have now had robotic surgery at Humber River. And it wouldn't be possible without the generous support of people right here in this community. People just like you. Thank you again so very much!

I can assure you that your continued support will impact patients just like Peter each and every day. People with families and loved ones. People who deserve the very best options for their health care.

I look forward to working with you throughout the coming year as we inch ever closer to moving into Canada's first fully digital hospital, committed to providing the very best possible care. Thank you in advance for the gift you send today.

Yours sincerely,

Heather Hurst

Heather Hurst
President and CEO, Humber River Hospital Foundation

PS: You can learn more about the da Vinci robot and some of the other items on our list of equipment needs in the enclosed note from our pal, Humbert.

RIGHT THIS WAY >>>

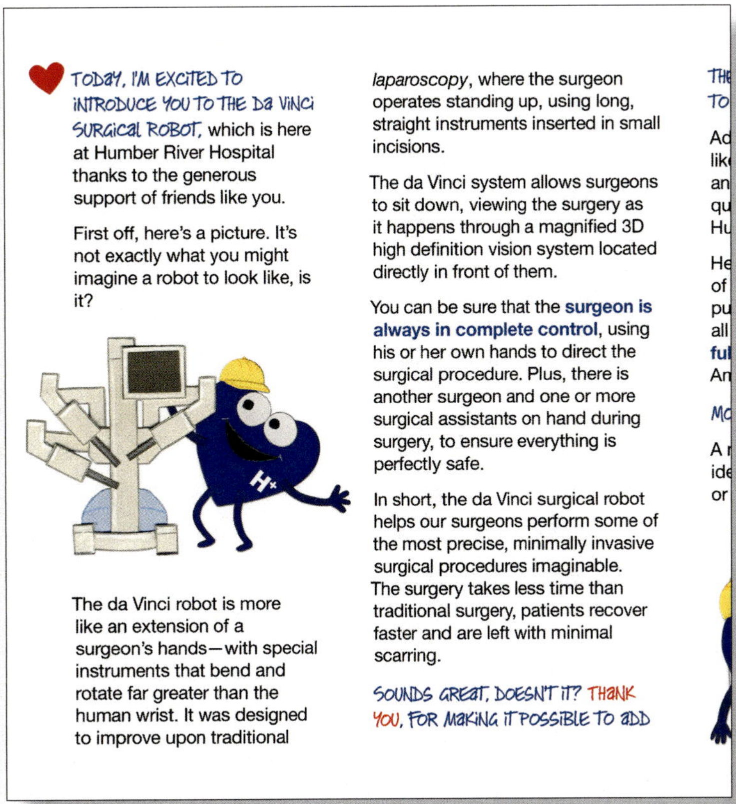

what he did best; reminding donors of all the ways they are connected to their community hospital — digital technology or not.

This pack also out-performed the previous year.

Humbert could speak and share stories in a way that (sadly) a lot of professions feel uncomfortable with and he made the act of giving — FUN! Imagine that.

MAILING #3: THE HOLIDAY PACK.

We wanted to do a visually bolder envelope, so we used a reverse window envelope where the donor's name and address show through a window on the back side and this was the front.

This would very much stand out in the sea of white #10 envelopes the donor would be getting at this time of year.

The personalization at the top of the letter immediately pulls the donor in.

The letter looks like a personal letter and is filled with emotion, vulnerability, and inclusion, and hinges around the idea of sending back your heart.

The reply was full-size and very plain. It had lots of white space and focused on asking for a single cash gift.

We included this very simple heart ornament.

Donors want to talk to you. They want to share their story and feel connected to the act of giving. Simple pieces like this heart do that.

As you will notice, we deviated from Humbert for this pack since the story and messaging were strong on their own. We didn't need to bring him into the mix to add lightness or some emotion.

Within the first six days of this pack hitting mailboxes, it started crushing the campaign goal. Donors sent in their stories and hearts at a remarkable pace.

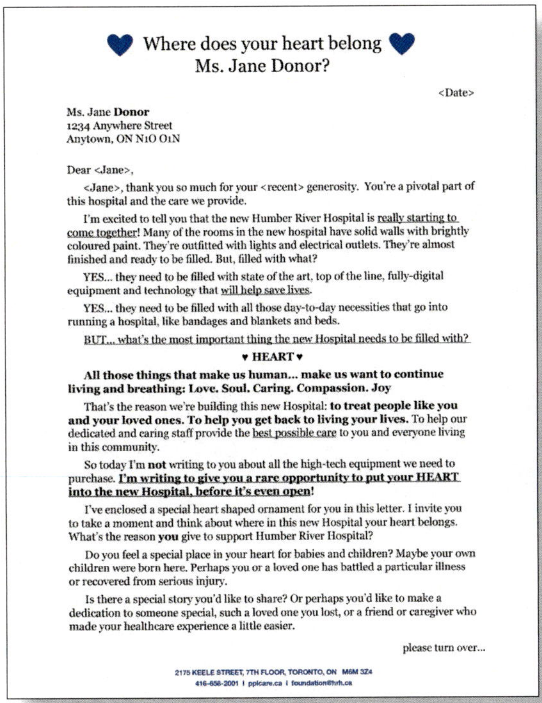

♥ Where does your heart belong ♥
Ms. Jane Donor?

<Date>

Ms. Jane **Donor**
1234 Anywhere Street
Anytown, ON N1O O1N

Dear <Jane>,

<Jane>, thank you so much for your <recent> generosity. You're a pivotal part of this hospital and the care we provide.

I'm excited to tell you that the new Humber River Hospital is really starting to come together! Many of the rooms in the new hospital have solid walls with brightly coloured paint. They're outfitted with lights and electrical outlets. They're almost finished and ready to be filled. But, filled with what?

YES... they need to be filled with state of the art, top of the line, fully-digital equipment and technology that will help save lives.

YES... they need to be filled with all those day-to-day necessities that go into running a hospital, like bandages and blankets and beds.

BUT... what's the most important thing the new Hospital needs to be filled with?

♥ HEART ♥

All those things that make us human... make us want to continue living and breathing: Love. Soul. Caring. Compassion. Joy

That's the reason we're building this new Hospital: **to treat people like you and your loved ones. To help you get back to living your lives.** To help our dedicated and caring staff provide the best possible care to you and everyone living in this community.

So today I'm **not** writing to you about all the high-tech equipment we need to purchase. **I'm writing to give you a rare opportunity to put your HEART into the new Hospital, before it's even open!**

I've enclosed a special heart shaped ornament for you in this letter. I invite you to take a moment and think about where in this new Hospital your heart belongs. What's the reason **you** give to support Humber River Hospital?

Do you feel a special place in your heart for babies and children? Maybe your own children were born here. Perhaps you or a loved one has battled a particular illness or recovered from serious injury.

Is there a special story you'd like to share? Or perhaps you'd like to make a dedication to someone special, such a loved one you lost, or a friend or caregiver who made your healthcare experience a little easier.

please turn over...

2175 KEELE STREET, 7TH FLOOR, TORONTO, ON M6M 3Z4
416-658-2001 I pplcare.ca I foundation@hrh.ca

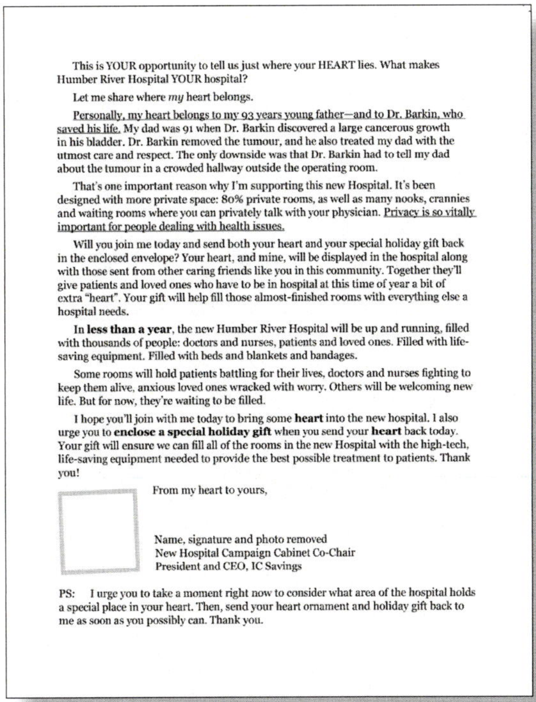

This is YOUR opportunity to tell us just where your HEART lies. What makes Humber River Hospital YOUR hospital?

Let me share where *my* heart belongs.

Personally, my heart belongs to my 93 years young father—and to Dr. Barkin, who saved his life. My dad was 91 when Dr. Barkin discovered a large cancerous growth in his bladder. Dr. Barkin removed the tumour, and he also treated my dad with the utmost care and respect. The only downside was that Dr. Barkin had to tell my dad about the tumour in a crowded hallway outside the operating room.

That's one important reason why I'm supporting this new Hospital. It's been designed with more private space: 80% private rooms, as well as many nooks, crannies and waiting rooms where you can privately talk with your physician. Privacy is so vitally important for people dealing with health issues.

Will you join me today and send both your heart and your special holiday gift back in the enclosed envelope? Your heart, and mine, will be displayed in the hospital along with those sent from other caring friends like you in this community. Together they'll give patients and loved ones who have to be in hospital at this time of year a bit of extra "heart". Your gift will help fill those almost-finished rooms with everything else a hospital needs.

In **less than a year**, the new Humber River Hospital will be up and running, filled with thousands of people: doctors and nurses, patients and loved ones. Filled with life-saving equipment. Filled with beds and blankets and bandages.

Some rooms will hold patients battling for their lives, doctors and nurses fighting to keep them alive, anxious loved ones wracked with worry. Others will be welcoming new life. But for now, they're waiting to be filled.

I hope you'll join with me today to bring some **heart** into the new hospital. I also urge you to **enclose a special holiday gift** when you send your **heart** back today. Your gift will ensure we can fill all of the rooms in the new Hospital with the high-tech, life-saving equipment needed to provide the best possible treatment to patients. Thank you!

From my heart to yours,

Name, signature and photo removed
New Hospital Campaign Cabinet Co-Chair
President and CEO, IC Savings

PS: I urge you to take a moment right now to consider what area of the hospital holds a special place in your heart. Then, send your heart ornament and holiday gift back to me as soon as you possibly can. Thank you.

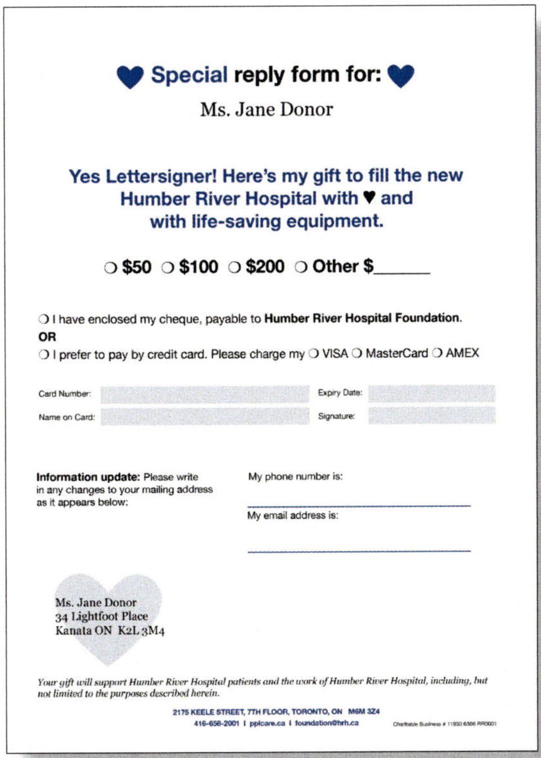

♥ Special reply form for: ♥
Ms. Jane Donor

Yes Lettersigner! Here's my gift to fill the new Humber River Hospital with ♥ and with life-saving equipment.

❍ **$50** ❍ **$100** ❍ **$200** ❍ **Other $______**

❍ I have enclosed my cheque, payable to **Humber River Hospital Foundation.**
OR
❍ I prefer to pay by credit card. Please charge my ❍ VISA ❍ MasterCard ❍ AMEX

Card Number: Expiry Date:
Name on Card: Signature:

Information update: Please write in any changes to your mailing address as it appears below:

My phone number is:

My email address is:

Ms. Jane Donor
34 Lightfoot Place
Kanata ON K2L 3M4

Your gift will support Humber River Hospital patients and the work of Humber River Hospital, including, but not limited to the purposes described herein.

2175 KEELE STREET, 7TH FLOOR, TORONTO, ON M6M 3Z4
416-658-2001 I pplcare.ca I foundation@hrh.ca

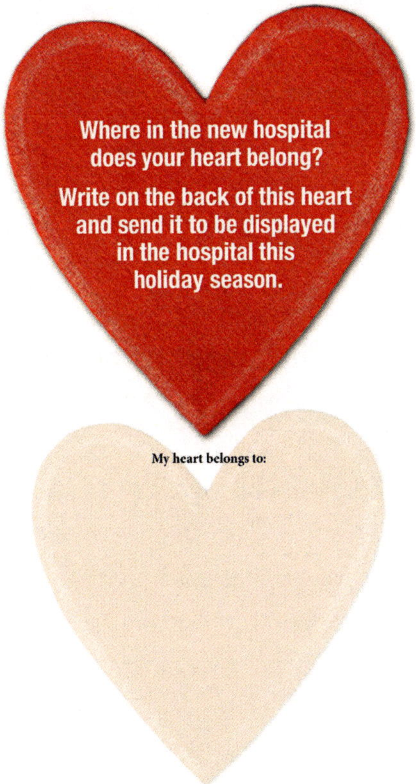

MAILING #4: THE HOLIDAY REMINDER PACK.

We decided to send out a holiday reminder pack (Mailing #4)– a first for H+.

But we hit a snag with this reminder. A bit of an "oops," if you will.

Every donor received this appeal with someone else's name on it. Right address. Wrong name.

After we all took a few deep breaths, we sent out a letter with an apology in a closed face envelope with first class postage.

Donors are wonderful. Many wrote back or called in to express their empathy.

Messing up can be a good thing. It reminds your donors that you are human and it also gives you an extra opportunity talk with them — which is never a bad thing.

MAILING #5: FEBRUARY

We always want to ensure that there is at least one appeal each year that has a solid acknowledgement of donor support and shares the organizational vision for the year ahead.

This is a very nuts and bolts appeal, but considering where we had come

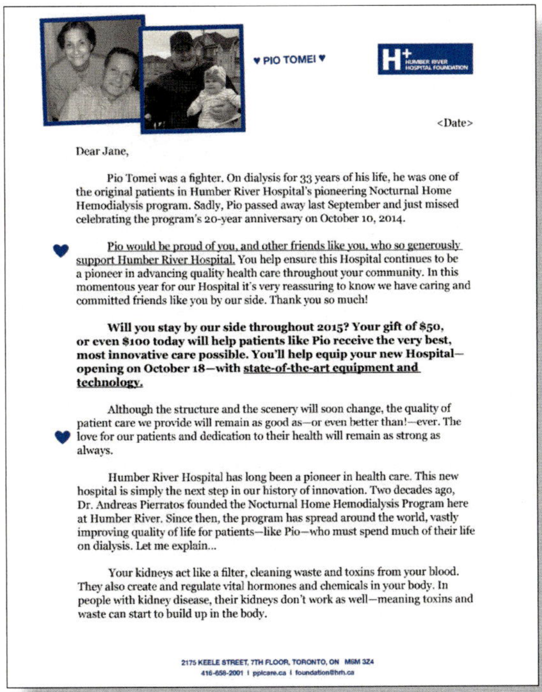

♥ PIO TOMEI ♥

HUMBER RIVER HOSPITAL FOUNDATION

<Date>

Dear Jane,

Pio Tomei was a fighter. On dialysis for 33 years of his life, he was one of the original patients in Humber River Hospital's pioneering Nocturnal Home Hemodialysis program. Sadly, Pio passed away last September and just missed celebrating the program's 20-year anniversary on October 10, 2014.

Pio would be proud of you, and other friends like you, who so generously support Humber River Hospital. You help ensure this Hospital continues to be a pioneer in advancing quality health care throughout your community. In this momentous year for our Hospital it's very reassuring to know we have caring and committed friends like you by our side. Thank you so much!

Will you stay by our side throughout 2015? Your gift of $50, or even $100 today will help patients like Pio receive the very best, most innovative care possible. You'll help equip your new Hospital—opening on October 18—with state-of-the-art equipment and technology.

Although the structure and the scenery will soon change, the quality of patient care we provide will remain as good as—or even better than!—ever. The love for our patients and dedication to their health will remain as strong as always.

Humber River Hospital has long been a pioneer in health care. This new hospital is simply the next step in our history of innovation. Two decades ago, Dr. Andreas Pierratos founded the Nocturnal Home Hemodialysis Program here at Humber River. Since then, the program has spread around the world, vastly improving quality of life for patients—like Pio—who must spend much of their life on dialysis. Let me explain...

Your kidneys act like a filter, cleaning waste and toxins from your blood. They also create and regulate vital hormones and chemicals in your body. In people with kidney disease, their kidneys don't work as well—meaning toxins and waste can start to build up in the body.

2175 KEELE STREET, 7TH FLOOR, TORONTO, ON M9M 3Z4
416-658-2001 | ppicare.ca | foundation@hrh.ca

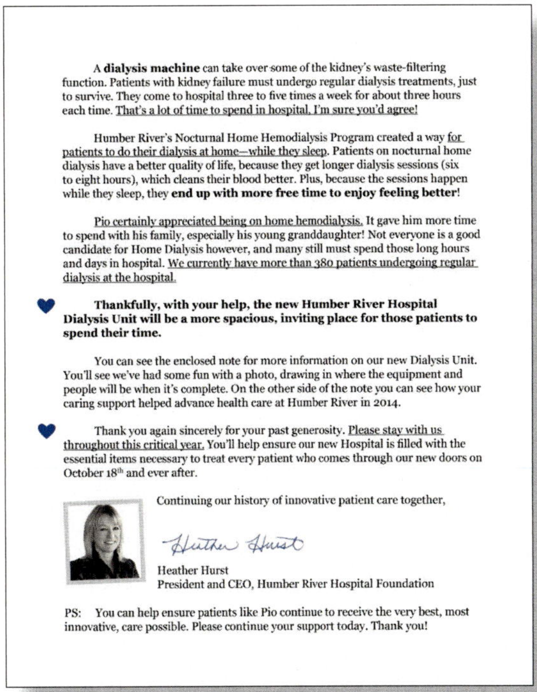

A **dialysis machine** can take over some of the kidney's waste-filtering function. Patients with kidney failure must undergo regular dialysis treatments, just to survive. They come to hospital three to five times a week for about three hours each time. That's a lot of time to spend in hospital. I'm sure you'd agree!

Humber River's Nocturnal Home Hemodialysis Program created a way for patients to do their dialysis at home—while they sleep. Patients on nocturnal home dialysis have a better quality of life, because they get longer dialysis sessions (six to eight hours), which cleans their blood better. Plus, because the sessions happen while they sleep, they **end up with more free time to enjoy feeling better**!

Pio certainly appreciated being on home hemodialysis. It gave him more time to spend with his family, especially his young granddaughter! Not everyone is a good candidate for Home Dialysis however, and many still must spend those long hours and days in hospital. We currently have more than 380 patients undergoing regular dialysis at the hospital.

Thankfully, with your help, the new Humber River Hospital Dialysis Unit will be a more spacious, inviting place for those patients to spend their time.

You can see the enclosed note for more information on our new Dialysis Unit. You'll see we've had some fun with a photo, drawing in where the equipment and people will be when it's complete. On the other side of the note you can see how your caring support helped advance health care at Humber River in 2014.

Thank you again sincerely for your past generosity. Please stay with us throughout this critical year. You'll help ensure our new Hospital is filled with the essential items necessary to treat every patient who comes through our new doors on October 18th and ever after.

Continuing our history of innovative patient care together,

Heather Hurst

Heather Hurst
President and CEO, Humber River Hospital Foundation

PS: You can help ensure patients like Pio continue to receive the very best, most innovative, care possible. Please continue your support today. Thank you!

from since the previous Fall, this "note" makes perfect sense.

Humbert reappears on the back side of the insert — right where he should be — sharing love and appreciation to the amazing people we call donors.

This very simple, plain appeal smashed the previous year's results. Remarkable!

Each appeal was about something specific and connected donors to their community hospital and their giving. Humbert was a large part of that.

THANKS TO YOU! 2014 IN REVIEW

"MY HEART BELONGS TO YOU! THANKS SO MUCH FOR SENDING YOUR HEARTS—AND YOUR LOVE—BACK TO HUMBER RIVER HOSPITAL OVER THE HOLIDAYS. OUR WALL OF HEARTS SHONE BRIGHT, GIVING HOPE AND LOVE TO OUR PATIENTS AND THEIR FAMILIES."

The new Hospital is almost complete!
It's really coming together—thanks to your ongoing support! The green roof has been installed and many departments are fully finished, waiting for the equipment to be delivered. These include: cancer care, dialysis, cardiology, as well as the medical and surgical inpatient floors.

Remember Vince?
The advanced surgical OR is near completion, waiting for the da Vinci surgical robot to be installed!

The first piece of equipment delivered!
In October 2014 the magnets for two new Magnetic Resonance Imaging (MRI) machines were installed! To be used in the new Hospital's Medical Imaging Unit, MRI offers the most comprehensive information and is the cornerstone of a medical imaging department. The MRI plays an integral role in ensuring the highest level of quality patient care, diagnosis and treatment.

THANK YOU AGAIN SO MUCH FOR YOUR PAST SUPPORT. PLEASE STAY WITH US THROUGHOUT 2015 AND HELP GIVE THE BEST POSSIBLE TREATMENT TO EVERY PATIENT WHO WALKS THROUGH YOUR NEW HOSPITAL'S DOORS ON OCTOBER 18TH!

MAILING #6: SPRING

The hospital was due to open in the Fall so the Spring pack focused on healing gardens and green areas around the grounds and the importance of nature to healing and mental health. Again, this would seem a pretty typical appeal. How could we make it interesting and engaging for donors?

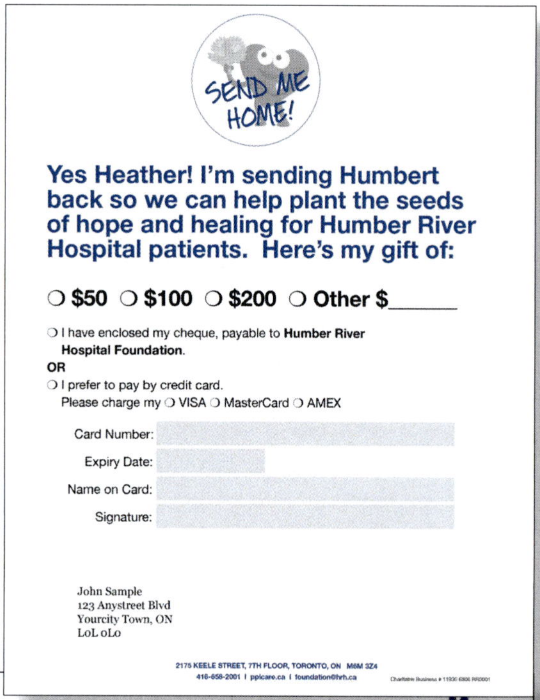
SEND ME HOME!

Yes Heather! I'm sending Humbert back so we can help plant the seeds of hope and healing for Humber River Hospital patients. Here's my gift of:

❍ **$50** ❍ **$100** ❍ **$200** ❍ **Other $______**

❍ I have enclosed my cheque, payable to **Humber River Hospital Foundation**.
OR
❍ I prefer to pay by credit card.
Please charge my ❍ VISA ❍ MasterCard ❍ AMEX

Card Number:
Expiry Date:
Name on Card:
Signature:

John Sample
123 Anystreet Blvd
Yourcity Town, ON
LoL oLo

2175 KEELE STREET, 7TH FLOOR, TORONTO, ON M6M 3Z4
416-658-2001 | ppicare.ca | foundation@hrh.ca

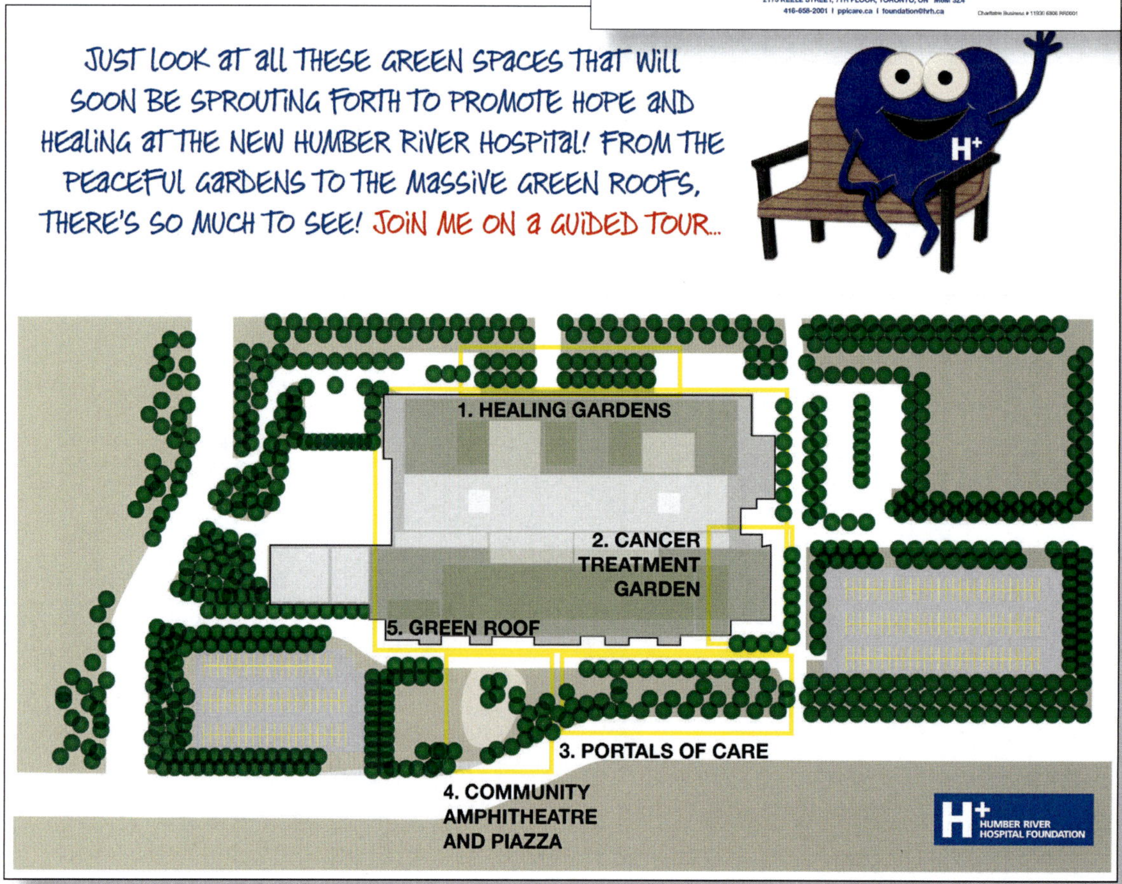

1. HEALING GARDENS	These will have beautiful walking paths with multi-coloured bricks to inspire patients and loved ones as they walk amongst the native plants and flowers. Trees will provide a shaded canopy, offering protection from the elements. Numerous benches located throughout the garden will provide a peaceful space to sit and breathe fresh, healing air.
2. CANCER TREATMENT GARDEN	This will give outpatients going through cancer treatment a natural and uplifting view. Plus it will provide visual privacy from the sidewalk.
3. PORTALS OF CARE	This area has been painstakingly designed to simplify hospital access for outpatients. There will be clear and separate areas for each clinic, with different landscaping and seating areas for each, along with highly visible passenger drop off areas. Identifiable landmarks will make it easier for returning patients and visitors.
4. COMMUNITY AMPHITHEATRE AND PIAZZA	This vibrant area will be the social hub of the hospital, featuring many seating areas, such as picnic tables and benches, for staff, patients and community members to sit and have lunch or simply enjoy the fresh air. The outdoor Ampitheatre will provide a beautiful outdoor space for both hospital and community formal events.
5. GREEN ROOF	The new Hospital has the second largest green roof ever installed in Canada. It covers more than half of the new hospital's roof. Green roofs provide multiple benefits, including reduced impact on the environment, reduced energy costs, and increased oxygen in the air. They also provide a much nicer view for patients than the traditional black tar roof!

Our full-size reply form had space to put Humbert into action. We created a simple sticker for donors to peel off and put on the coupon. It offered a simple moment of physical engagement with their giving. Simple and effective.

We used (another) map for the insert to let donors visualize the green spaces around the grounds and let Humbert explain why these areas were needed. An insert like this is a simple way to add to your case in the letter. Even without Humbert, it's an easy extra piece to add to the pack.

MAILING #7: FALL

This was it.

After a year of re-engaging with donors, the moment the foundation had been talking about for years was here. The hospital was ready to open its doors and help serve the Humber community.

We decided that more than in any other pack, Humbert needed to be there for the donor. This was a big moment for all of them.

This was the outer envelope. It was from Humbert.

HUMBERT
CUSTODIAN OF DONOR LOVE AND CARE
C/O HUMBER RIVER HOSPITAL FOUNDATION
2175 KEELE STREET, 7TH FLOOR
TORONTO, ON M6M 3Z4

YOU HAVE NO IDEA HOW LONG I'VE BEEN WAITING TO WRITE THIS LETTER...

"You have no idea how long I've been waiting to write this letter..."

The pack either had a first-class stamp, if it was going out to mid to high value donors or an indica for the remainder.

The letter focused on two things: 1) That funds raised would still be used for all the small, but meaningful things that would be needed to provide comfort for patients and their families. 2) The opportunity for donors to share an encouraging word or thought to the first patients entering through the new doors.

With Humbert we didn't need to go over the top with the idea of a talking heart. But this "heart" could speak from his, and deeply and emotionally connect with the reader.

"I may be heart-shaped... but YOU are the true heart of Humber River Hospital!

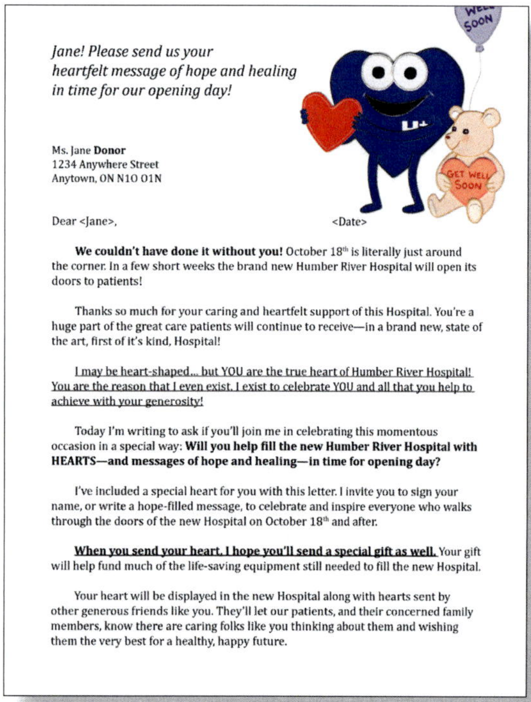

Jane! Please send us your heartfelt message of hope and healing in time for our opening day!

Ms. Jane **Donor**
1234 Anywhere Street
Anytown, ON N1O 01N

Dear <Jane>, <Date>

We couldn't have done it without you! October 18th is literally just around the corner. In a few short weeks the brand new Humber River Hospital will open its doors to patients!

Thanks so much for your caring and heartfelt support of this Hospital. You're a huge part of the great care patients will continue to receive—in a brand new, state of the art, first of it's kind, Hospital!

I may be heart-shaped... but YOU are the true heart of Humber River Hospital! You are the reason that I even exist. I exist to celebrate YOU and all that you help to achieve with your generosity!

Today I'm writing to ask if you'll join me in celebrating this momentous occasion in a special way: **Will you help fill the new Humber River Hospital with HEARTS—and messages of hope and healing—in time for opening day?**

I've included a special heart for you with this letter. I invite you to sign your name, or write a hope-filled message, to celebrate and inspire everyone who walks through the doors of the new Hospital on October 18th and after.

When you send your heart, I hope you'll send a special gift as well. Your gift will help fund much of the life-saving equipment still needed to fill the new Hospital.

Your heart will be displayed in the new Hospital along with hearts sent by other generous friends like you. They'll let our patients, and their concerned family members, know there are caring folks like you thinking about them and wishing them the very best for a healthy, happy future.

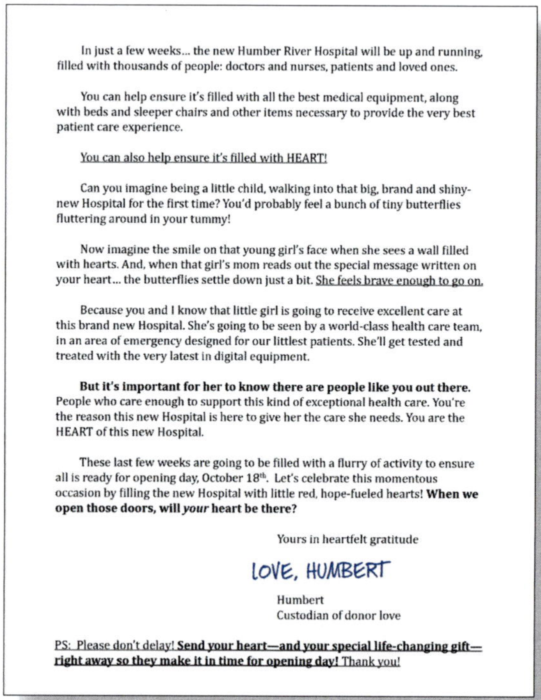
In just a few weeks... the new Humber River Hospital will be up and running, filled with thousands of people: doctors and nurses, patients and loved ones.

You can help ensure it's filled with all the best medical equipment, along with beds and sleeper chairs and other items necessary to provide the very best patient care experience.

You can also help ensure it's filled with HEART!

Can you imagine being a little child, walking into that big, brand and shiny-new Hospital for the first time? You'd probably feel a bunch of tiny butterflies fluttering around in your tummy!

Now imagine the smile on that young girl's face when she sees a wall filled with hearts. And, when that girl's mom reads out the special message written on your heart... the butterflies settle down just a bit. She feels brave enough to go on.

Because you and I know that little girl is going to receive excellent care at this brand new Hospital. She's going to be seen by a world-class health care team, in an area of emergency designed for our littlest patients. She'll get tested and treated with the very latest in digital equipment.

But it's important for her to know there are people like you out there. People who care enough to support this kind of exceptional health care. You're the reason this new Hospital is here to give her the care she needs. You are the HEART of this new Hospital.

These last few weeks are going to be filled with a flurry of activity to ensure all is ready for opening day, October 18th. Let's celebrate this momentous occasion by filling the new Hospital with little red, hope-fueled hearts! **When we open those doors, will *your* heart be there?**

Yours in heartfelt gratitude

LOVE, HUMBERT

Humbert
Custodian of donor love

PS: Please don't delay! **Send your heart—and your special life-changing gift—right away so they make it in time for opening day!** Thank you!

You are the reason that I even exist. I exist to celebrate YOU and all that you help to achieve with your generosity!"

I long to read such words from an Executive Director. So do your donors.

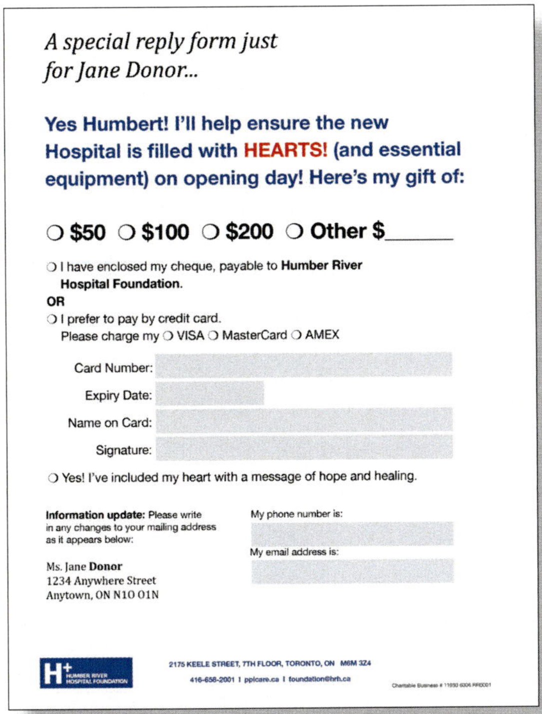
A special reply form just for Jane Donor...

Yes Humbert! I'll help ensure the new Hospital is filled with HEARTS! (and essential equipment) on opening day! Here's my gift of:

❍ $50 ❍ $100 ❍ $200 ❍ Other $______

❍ I have enclosed my cheque, payable to **Humber River Hospital Foundation.**

OR

❍ I prefer to pay by credit card.
Please charge my ❍ VISA ❍ MasterCard ❍ AMEX

Card Number:

Expiry Date:

Name on Card:

Signature:

❍ Yes! I've included my heart with a message of hope and healing.

Information update: Please write in any changes to your mailing address as it appears below:

Ms. Jane **Donor**
1234 Anywhere Street
Anytown, ON N10 01N

My phone number is:

My email address is:

HUMBER RIVER HOSPITAL FOUNDATION

2175 KEELE STREET, 7TH FLOOR, TORONTO, ON M6M 3Z4
416-658-2001 | pplcare.ca | foundation@hrh.ca

Charitable Business # 11930 6306 RR0001

It was a full-sized reply form. Very personal. Not crammed with 1,000 check boxes. The donor only had to make ten decisions to fill it out completely.

Ask and get out of the way.

We included this very simple heart as an insert.

5″ x 5″. Plain paper. Not a smidgen of razzle-dazzle.

This was it.

The future had arrived. A brand new, state-of-the-art, one-of-a-kind hospital was fully operational.

And Humbert had helped to reconnect donors, with all sizes of wallets, to their giving, to their community hospital and the impact of their gifts.

So, what happened?

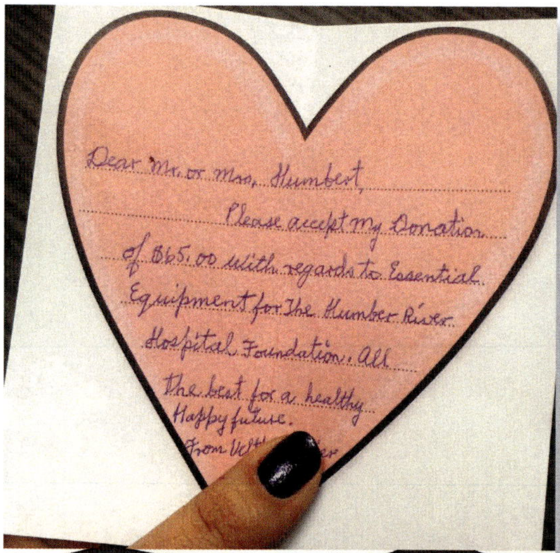

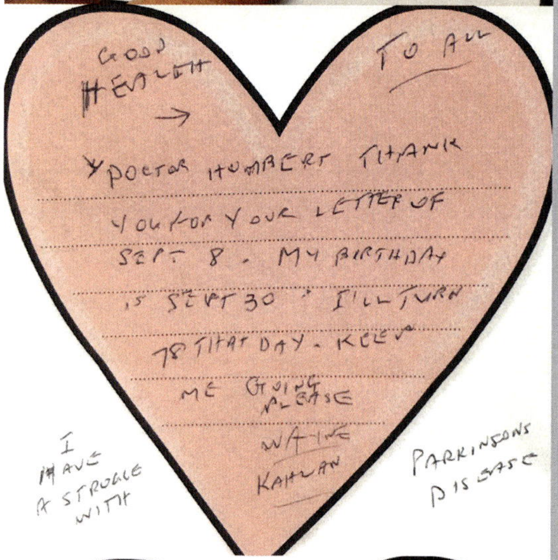

"Dear Mr or Mrs Humbert, Please accept my donation of $65 with regards to essential equipment for the Humber River Hospital Foundation. All the best for a healthy happy future..."

"Doctor Humbert! thank you for your letter of Sept 8. My birthday is Sept 30. I'll turn 78 that day. Keep me going please!"

This is how the appeal did. We had a number of these boards that lined the hallways for patients and their families to read.

These donors **are not** having a transactional exchange with a charity they give to. You can read that in their words.

This is an example of something you can't measure on an Excel sheet or easily explain to the board.

But this is what *fundraising for donors* looks like.

We continued to use Humbert after the hospital opened its doors. He popped up when we needed to reconnect donors in small, meaningful ways to their giving or just to provide some lightness.

Hope-fueled Hearts from
Donors in your Community!
THANK YOU!!

H+
I ♥ #DONORLOVE

We have one job, to keep playing pitch-perfect "notes" with and for our donors. It isn't always thrilling, but it can be rewarding when you remind yourself of this privilege we have of connecting one lovely human, with her gift and intention of helping someone else. Along the way her desire to be a good and valued person also gets fulfilled.

She is good and she is valued. And she is cherished. Regardless of "the gift."

If we continue to do our part and remain ever grateful and thoughtful about the needs of our donors, they will do their part as well.

The work we exhaustively do every day is emotional. It's sometimes messy and it is real.

We are having beautiful conversations with amazing humans.

Talk and listen to your donors. Ask with thoughtfulness. Thank with love and graciousness. Always remind them how much you need them and appreciate the amazing work they make possible. Share the stories that happen around you and measure what TRULY matters, which is, your beautiful donors.

Most importantly, please do your work with love.

Thank you for taking the time out of your busy life to read this book. I am so grateful.

John Lepp
March 2022

CAISTORVILLE

POPULATION: Maybe 100? On a holiday weekend?

Epilogue: Where the trail began

Sometimes when you are at the end of the trail, you need to remind yourself how you got there. A journey, with all of its challenges, blocks, and dead ends, informs our experiences. It is about the lessons we learn from the mistakes we make.

How did we get here? How did I come to write this book that you are reading?

It has a lot to do with storytelling.

Growing up in the country in southern Ontario, I worked with my dad around the house and on a few of my friends' farms. I had a lot of small jobs that were formative to who I am.

I worked at a feed mill, cut grass for our neighbours as well as at the local crappy golf course. I dug graves at the local church (I didn't last long there!), worked for a few summers at an all-night laundromat washing clothes for rich kids who were at camp, and spent many hours pumping gas and restocking the shelves at the village gas station.

I would hear all of the latest gossip, the local take on politics, concerns about the weather and plenty of swearing. Story after story.

I remember a time when a local farmer finished going off about something that was really bugging him. He was sharing his story with Roger, the owner of the gas station who was wiping down the counter by the cash register. I was standing near the door watching for anyone who needed a fill-up at the pump.

The farmer turned to me and said, "*Well John? What do you think? What do you have to say about this?*"

I said I had nothing of value to add to the conversation.

Roger shifted his weight towards me and said, "*Good John. You'll always learn more by listening than talking.*"

This is something I still believe in. It's something I share with AOG clients and it comes through in the work that we do each day.

We learn more by listening to our donors than just talking at them all the time.

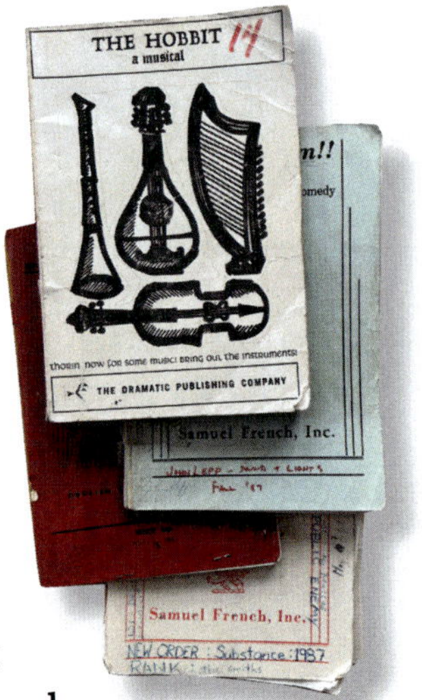

I left that small town to head to the "big city" to study creative writing. It was that, and journalism, I wanted to have a crack at.

I had been involved in theatre throughout high school, both behind and on stage but, I wasn't a very good actor or singer and had zero coordination for dancing. So, that was that. However, the lessons I learned about telling stories through drama or comedy, of standing on a stage, of taking space and of giving space — these things served me well when I started to do presentations and workshops.

I went to university for creative writing and partied like it was 1999 (except it was 1994!). I got kicked out. The sad part is, I didn't even get to attend any classes for writing. I did, however, write and publish three of my own books of stories and poems. On my own, I learned about my writing and creative process, how to observe and catalogue the stories that were happening around me.

My dad tried to drag me back to the country village. I knew that if I went back, I'd likely still be pumping gas at that small station, listening to farmers complain about the weather and the cost of feed. Dad said that was it. If I was staying in Toronto then they weren't supporting me anymore. I was 19.

I got a job at the local YMCA working the front desk and running the summer kids camp (I had no idea what I was doing but I knew how to play guitar, do crafts from my days at vacation bible school and corral kids from one activity to the next) and then working at the front desk.

I think everyone should work a job where they encounter the public every day, for all the good, bad and ugly of it. I did lots of listening, empathizing and problem solving. I also developed appreciation for the people I encountered who had jobs like me. These lessons helped me start my own business working with clients and their donors or customers.

I starved, saved and got a loan so I could go to Humber College for journalism. It was a two-year certification course. All of my classmates were university grads with English degrees and no real job opportunities.

One week into the school year, the Dean of the program sat me down to tell me they wanted to move me into the three-year program. They said my acceptance into the two-year track was a mistake, since my marks in high school were not very good. Mostly Cs and Bs. I had already been kicked out of university. What I *did have* was an impressive writing portfolio (of newspaper articles and books) that helped me get admitted.

Thankfully, I pled my case and was given one chance to stay in the program. If my grade point average slipped too low, I was going to get kicked out again. This activated a confidence in me (maybe a stubbornness too), that I knew, like KNEW, I could do this. I believed it.

I stayed and learned how to do hard news writing, radio reporting, (slicing and dicing tape!) television news, feature writing, photography and layout and design. (These were the early days of desktop publishing so sometimes it was Quark on a Mac Classic and some days it was paste up on full broad sheets using bits of cut up newspaper.)

I had a teacher who worked at the Globe and Mail who tired of my attempts at hard news writing, (I agreed. I hated it.) and told me I would have to find something else to do. Thank you Carey French. I sit here writing this book because of you.

I really enjoyed layout and design. I never sketched when I was younger, but I loved looking at typography and bringing balance to a page.

I was offered a job as an art director at a startup trade magazine for chiropractors and "jobbed out" of Humber a few months early. This was totally permitted and obviously the goal. Graduated with honors.

The job was a total nightmare.

I had no idea what I was doing. I knew nothing about the technicalities of printing and publishing. I barely knew how to design, but I listened and learned from the old guys at the publishing press. **Leaning on others to get across the line**. It was another lesson that serves me well to this day.

If you wait to be 100% ready to launch something or change something – you'll never be ready. Sometimes you just have to step forward and be ok with figuring it out as you go along. Sometimes, you have to lean into the things you don't know and be ok with being vulnerable. Ask for support or guidance. Surround yourself with smart people.

From there, I got a job at a small marketing agency as a designer and IT guy. I could troubleshoot computer problems. My brain was very good at using logic and removing variables to get to a solution.

I worked with Peter, an old creative director who had one big "win" from back in the day when he worked at Saatchi and Saatchi. He would rush into the studio every day about 15 seconds after I arrived to stand over my shoulder and art direct ad after ad for banks, trucks, and businesses… all while chewing on his toothpick.

"I want this truck to have a mountain in the back of it! A mountain with clouds and birds and trees on it!"

This was Adobe Photoshop 1.5 days.

I had to go through hundreds of stock photo books, finding the right birds, the right trees and mountains. Then I had to scan them. A single scan took ages on the flatbed scanner. Next came importing, cropping, and sizing the images. Something that would take 15 minutes today, took me days back then. Peter stormed around behind me while I worked, huffing and puffing. Throwing half eaten toothpicks on the ground.

I learned to work quickly. This skill served me later in fundraising when I was managing many different accounts and clients. I learned to shift mental gears job to job, not overthinking too much or striving for perfection.

I also worked with an English creative named Richard. Richard was an older, witty, chain smoker who taught me a lot. I loved hearing about the old advertising agency days and he obsessed — OBSESSED — over type. We would stand over a light table, with a bright light over our heads, smoke swirling around and he would force a loupe into my hand.

"Look at that 'A'. Look at its lines. Look at the relationship it has to the 'S' beside it. Is it angry? Sad? What does that 'A' tell you about itself?"

Seriously this would go on for hours. I learned to be obsessive over type. Over everything.

This obsession taught me that every element in design needs considering.

- Why is it here?

- What is it doing?
- What do I want it to say?

A designer has to deeply understand all the parts, to make sure it all works together.

I worked at a number of other agencies and continued to develop as a designer, learning about creativity, storytelling and marketing along the way.

I was hired to do some freelance design for an agency called Stephen Thomas and Associates (STA). Not long after, Steve offered me a job working with him on all of the accounts for his direct response agency. I knew nothing about fundraising. I didn't know a prospect pack from a bang tail to a BRE. No idea. But I certainly knew how to make it up as I went along. I knew how to benefit from the intelligence of those around me, and I knew how to listen.

I learned very early on that donors are forgiving. My creativity, or lack of it, wasn't going to stop them from giving. Donors used to, and still do, give — despite how crappy we treat them or talk at them. I love them for this.

I got to work with, meet and learn from some of the very best fundraisers of that time.

I did some freelance work with my AOG business partner, Jen Love, when she was working at STA as an account manager. As it turned out, she was leaving the agency just as I arrived.

Steve was one of the most unique creatives I had ever worked for. I mean that with a lot of respect. He would come up with out-of-the-box creative ideas that worked like gangbusters (i.e., raised a lot of money). He was an exceptional fundraising copywriter. He had learned from political fundraisers in the US and was well connected internationally.

When I left Stephen Thomas, I continued to develop my design business, called Idea Design, which I had begun in my freelance days. I reached out to other direct response agencies across Canada to see if they needed freelance help. Harvey McKinnon, FLA Group (now GoodWorks), Stratcom, and a number of others were a few of the partnerships that developed.

I learned strategic best practices from all of these agencies that shared their knowledge, strategy and data with me, simply because I asked.

There was a new agency in Toronto called Pareto, a satellite office for the main agency based in Australia. I reached out to Jonathon Grapsas and he said he could use someone like me to grow his business.

Each mailing that Pareto created for their clients asked for something specific and unique. This was different than the more typical "annual appeal" approach here in North America, where we asked donors to "renew your support of our organization."

Dedicating every appeal to its own topic, ask, and goal is the approach AOG tends to use in our work but truly, you don't have to pick one. You don't have to decide if an "annual appeal" approach is better than a "special" only one. Depending on your organization, your mission and your donors, one approach might work better than the other.

In any case, working with Pareto opened my brain up to a whole new way of thinking about storytelling.

It was around this time that Jen and I started to seriously talk about working together.

I was a creative (mostly known as a designer) and I knew I needed someone to balance me. I had a ton of strategic experience but couldn't seem to utilize that in my work as a freelancer for other agencies. So, in 2009 we quietly launched (as in, we didn't tell anyone) Agents of Good.

When we started operating as Agents of Good, we only had a handful of clients. This meant we could meet with or have calls together with every client.

We knew what appeal was coming up, what the objective was and what we were asking for at the same time.

We could brainstorm about the type of story we thought would work best (if at all) to really make the ask stand out and who (or what) might be the best voice for the appeal.

Jen would do an interview if needed, and would then call me sobbing to share the beautiful story she had just heard. I would be thinking about how to capture that in the most effective way to move donors to give.

She would draft the lead and first few paragraphs and share it with me, watching as I read. Watching my face change.

Smile. Or drop. Or squint. Or hitch.

I would read it trying to forget everything I knew about this appeal, with a fresh mind. Just like a donor would.

We'd discuss. Put it aside. Tweak. Go out for walks and just let it sit there for a bit.

We'd talk about the rest of the creative or would just let it percolate.

For the most part, we still follow this "process."

I wouldn't start design until I had the final approved copy in my hands. The exception being if we wanted to include some illustrations.

Once I receive the final copy, I don't do a thing until I read it from beginning to end.

- What are we asking donors for?
- Why should they care right now?
- Why should they do this thing we are asking them to do right now?

Then I start obsessing about the outer envelope.

What's the point of all this?

My point is that each of us has a journey. I want to honour my journey since it has made me who I am today as much as I want you to honour yours.

CHARITY SELF-HELP

I read an article about self-help advice as it relates to individuals. A life coach had curated what she believed to be the top 10 nuggets of happiness from over 500 books.

While reading her list, it struck me that many of the best nuggets also relate to ourselves and the organizations we work with every day.

1. **Be yourself**. The key to organizational happiness is to be yourself. Do you know who you are? I've never met a charity who said that the work they do is simple. Every organization is complicated: a mess of programs, personalities, missions, visions, silos. What is the unique reason a donor should support you? It will be a simple expression of why you exist. Simplify how you express what you are trying to fix, help, change. Be yourself for all of your ugly cries, weak moments and passion. We need more of those.

2. **You have nothing to prove**. This isn't exactly true. You do have to prove to your donors that your work is worthy of their support and that their support matters, realizing that pleasing all donors is impossible. You really are only going to be relevant to 20% of all donors (however you want to define "all"). Be positive in your interactions with them. You aren't begging for help. What you're doing at this moment is enough, but more can always be done with help and support.

3. **You can't control anyone**. You can't control your donors. I'm sorry. You can't make them give to your appeal. You can't make them give to you online. So stop trying. Take advantage of the channels and the technology to share the amazing work your donors make possible. Remind them why they are so

important to your cause. Have conversations with them. Be human. You do YOU. They will do the rest.

4. **Don't take yourself too seriously**. Everyone is so freakin' serious! So professional. So conservative. Lighten up! We are doing important work! How lucky are we? We are helping this world for ourselves and for our children. Be angry. Be happy. Be funny. Be frustrated. Celebrate. Cry. Sigh. Be serious. But not all the time. When you allow yourself to be not so serious, amazing (like truly transformative) things can happen.

5. **You're doing great**. When was the last time you took a moment to celebrate the little successes? If you are at your desk or out in the field and working hard, being thoughtful, going to conferences and reading blogs — you ARE trying and you ARE definitely getting better. More importantly, you're already doing more than many others. Keep going! Keep asking why! Thank you for the GREAT work that you do.

6. **The only time you have is now**. This is the moment. You can make a decision. You can do whatever you are doing in this moment more thoughtfully, or you can constantly worry about things that may (or may not) come. Need a break? Take one. Thinking of a donor? Call them. Need something different? Let's talk about it. Don't let this moment, or the next, just pass you by.

7. **Failure isn't final**. It might seem like it is, but trust me every time you fail, you become better. Failing teaches you something important and of value. It means you're trying. I know it sucks, especially when you send out your direct mail piece with the wrong donor name and the wrong address on every piece. Yes. It happened. But we figured it out, sent an apology letter to every donor and the mailing beat every projection. We were human and we made a mistake.

8. **99% of limitations are imagined**. Excuses, I've heard a few. Most of the excuses for success (happier donors, better retention, higher response rates and so on) come from internal limitations. Your own. Your boss. Your board. Most limitations stem from fear. Fear of failure. Fear of being judged. Fear of moving

away from the way things have always been done. All of these things stop growth and progress. Acknowledge the road blocks, then find ways to go around them (assuming you can't always go over them!).

9. **No one else knows what they are doing either**. This is the dirty secret of our sector, and life too. We are all making it up as we go along. Hopefully we are using our experiences, our brains, our hearts and our networks to help make smart decisions that will move us forward. Like the saying goes, we are all just doing our best with what we know. Be kind to others and yourself.

10. **Only love is real**. When you stop thinking of donors as data, when you write that letter with tears streaming down your face, when you lift the phone in joy knowing you will be sharing gratitude with another human for the things you — and they — make possible… you are living your life emotionally, lovingly and fully. Do your work with love. Everyday.

Ohm.

About the Author

John Lepp is a direct response, marketing and graphic design expert with almost 25 years of experience working with charities around the world to help them tell better stories and to inspire donors to give, both online and offline. He is a respected and coveted international speaker who has traveled the world helping fundraisers be more "human" and "vulnerable" to these other amazing humans we call donors.

Let him know what you think! You can reach him at john@agentsofgood.org or at Agents of Good, Box 82003, RPO Towne Plaza, Waterdown, Ontario, Canada, L0R 2M0

Made in United States
Orlando, FL
22 August 2023

36333425R00168